OLD WHITCHURCH

The Story of a Glamorgan Parish

OLD WHITCHURCH

The Story of a Glamorgan Parish

BY

EDGAR L. CHAPPELL

MERTON PRIORY PRESS

Published by Merton Priory Press Ltd
7 Nant Fawr Road, Cardiff CF2 6JQ

First published by The Priory Press Ltd, Cardiff, 1945
Second edition, with new Preface, 1994

ISBN 1 898937 02 8

© New Preface: E.M. Humphreys and P.J. Riden, 1994
 Original text and illustrations: The Estate of Edgar Leyshon Chappell Deceased, 1945, 1994

The publisher of this edition has made substantial efforts to trace the owners of the copyright of the original edition but without success. This reprint is therefore published without their permission. The publisher would be grateful for any information leading to the identification of the copyright owner.

The illustration on the dust-jacket and those on pages xix–xxx are reproduced from postcards in the collection of Stephen Rowson.

Printed by Hillman Printers (Frome) Ltd
Handlemaker Road
Marston Trading Estate
Frome
Somerset
BA11 4RW

Edgar Leyshon Chappell
(By courtesy of Dr A.G. Chappell)

PREFACE TO NEW EDITION

Edgar Leyshon Chappell was born in April 1879 at Ystalyfera in the upper Swansea Valley, the son of Alfred Chappell, a shoemaker and commercial traveller.[1] His mother Ellen was a daughter of Leyshon Watkins of Deri Cottage (now renamed Dolau Gae), Rhiwfawr. The 'Watkiniaid' and 'Leyshoniaid' had lived in the Gwrhyd and Rhiwfawr areas for centuries and claimed to trace their roots to Thomas ap Leyshon, the last abbot of Neath Abbey. Chappell was proud of his Welsh ancestry and tended to be known by his full name.

Educated at local schools, Chappell trained as a teacher at University College, Cardiff, in 1898–1900 and by 1910 was head of an elementary school at Rhiwfawr, his mother's birthplace. The following year he gave up teaching in favour of working full time as campaigner on housing and other social problems, initially by serving as a secretary and publicist for better known figures in the same field. He worked closely with H. Stanley Jevons, Professor of Economics at Cardiff, on the garden village movement in South Wales and both were among the first residents of the pioneer scheme at Rhiwbina, north of Cardiff.

During the First World War Chappell secured appointments as secretary to various government inquiries and in 1921, now settled in Cardiff, he was elected to represent Whitchurch on the newly reorganised Cardiff Rural District Council. From 1931 he also sat for a division which included Whitchurch on Glamorgan County Council, of which he was later an alderman. He remained interested in housing and town planning issues, and also education.

By now something of an elder statesman in the public life of South Wales, Chappell continued to write on a variety of topics during the reconstruction period towards the end of the Second World War, notably the need for local government reform and devolved administration for Wales.

From the early 1930s, if not before, Chappell was director of a number of property development companies, both in Cardiff and the London area. His

---

[1] Except where otherwise indicated, this account of Chappell's life and work summarises the main conclusions of E.M. Humphreys, 'Edgar Leyshon Chappell (1879–1949). A biography' (University of Wales College of Cardiff Local History Diploma Dissertation, 1993), where full references to sources are given. A copy of this work is available in Cardiff Central Library.

only son, Noel, qualified as a chartered surveyor and practised with his father in the firm of Chappell & Chappell, estate agents of Dumfries Place, Cardiff. It was probably mainly as a result of these interests that Chappell left the sizeable sum of £34,000 at his death in August 1949.

*

Edgar Leyshon Chappell is most widely remembered today for his publications on local history, particularly his *History of the Port of Cardiff* (1939), *Historic Melingriffith* (1940) and *Old Whitchurch* (1945), all of which have stood the test of time and remain valuable secondary sources. He was, however, one of those multi-talented, public spirited individuals who made a major contribution in many different fields, albeit often in the shadow of men who had the academic and professional qualifications or social standing which he lacked.

Chappell was an ardent Socialist from his early days, and was credited as one of the pioneers who made a Labour government possible. He was a gifted teacher and always retained an interest in the education system, promoting the development of new schools and serving as a governor. While still a teacher, he made himself an expert on housing problems, adopting a scientific approach in the collection and analysis of statistical data and presenting his arguments in a clear and logical way. This concern for housing and social reform led him to promote 'garden cities' and town planning schemes for urban areas. Working first with Jevons and then with various housing and planning pressure groups, Chappell was a major force in persuading Welsh local authorities to undertake house-building and improvement projects and to plan the future development of their areas.

His expertise in these fields was recognised by his appointment to government commissions in the 1920s relating to socio-economic and industrial development issues. He was always able to take a broad, regional view of problems and derided those who took a parochial or narrow view. In later years he was appointed to the Welsh National Industrial Development Council.

For over twenty-five years Chappell represented Whitchurch on Cardiff Rural District Council and Glamorgan County Council, where he was a conscientious and effective member. His particular achievements were in the establishment of modern schools for Whitchurch, new highways and housing and town planning schemes. Drawing on his extensive knowledge of local administration, both in Cardiff and throughout Wales, he also developed the case for the reform of local government, suggesting a great reduction in the number of councils in the hope of increasing efficiency.

As if this were not sufficiently radical, Chappell also campaigned for a federal government for Wales, together with devolved regional administration. In 1943 he published a pamphlet on *The Government of Wales*, discussing ideas developed further in *Local Government: its future in Wales*, which was published in translation as *Llywodraeth Leol: ei dyfodol yng Nghymru* (1946). 1943 also saw the publication of Chappell's better known essay, *Wake up Wales!*, described as a survey of home rule activities and containing his ideas for the restructuring of central government. The pamphlet is typical of Chappell's approach: well researched, a thorough analysis supported by examples and statistics, yet presented in a straightforward and readable way. Rejecting both complete independence and devolution for purely cultural reasons, he argued for a federal system with a Welsh Parliament and a Welsh Secretary on more pragmatic grounds, in that the growth of bureaucracy was leading to delay, inefficiency and the concentration of too much power in the hands of civil servants. The reorganisation of local government in 1974 and the establishment of the Welsh Office in 1965 incorporated many of his proposals, although the regional government he advocated has still to be achieved.

Throughout his career, Chappell wrote extensively for the local press: campaigning pieces on social and housing reform; local history articles and war-time information. As editor, he transformed the rather staid *Welsh Outlook*, and in later years developed the weekly *Cardiff and Suburban News*. His simple and direct style; his pragmatic approach, based on extensive experience, and his humorous yet sensitive slant, endeared him to his readers. It is possible, however, that his popular following prejudiced the Welsh 'Establishment' against giving him his due rewards. It was not until 1946 that the University of Wales awarded him an honorary degree, and then only that of M.A. Other honours and appointments were similarly made late in his life when he was already debilitated by illness, and some organisations, such as the Labour Party, apparently omitted to recognise the role which he had played in their establishment.

*

Chappell's interest in local history may be traced from his time as a teacher in the Swansea Valley, when he took his pupils out of the classroom to look at the remains of abandoned collieries and ironworks. Similarly, from an early period, his papers contain many drafts of unfinished historical essays. But it was after he was elected to represent Whitchurch on the rural district council in 1921 that his interest seems to have become more focused, as he came to believe that he should build up a better knowledge of the area, past as well as present: 'thus I added local historical research to my list of hobbies'. The interest stayed with him for the rest of his life: his last major work, *Old Whitchurch*, appeared only four years before his death in 1949. By this time he had written numerous historical articles for the local press and published the two other substantial monographs, one on Pentyrch Ironworks and Melingriffith Tinplate Works and the other on the port of Cardiff, on which his posthumous reputation rests.

Chappell's connection with the parish of Whitchurch, whose history he was later to study in so much detail, began just before the First World War, when he was working as 'Literary and Economics Assistant' to Stanley Jevons, a prime mover in the establishment of Rhiwbina Garden Village.[1] Both were among the first residents of the new community: Chappell and his wife Alice, whom he married in 1904, made their home at 18 Y Groes from 1914 until the mid-1920s. The village, whose development was retarded by both the financial difficulties of its original promoters and the outbreak of the First World War, was planned to occupy some 200 acres immediately to the north of the then recently opened Cardiff Railway, between Whitchurch Station and Rhiwbina Halt. It thus fell entirely within Whitchurch parish, which extended in all to 3,400 acres on the east bank of the Taff to the north and west of Cardiff, stretching from what was by the turn of the century the outer limit of the city's built-up area (around Whitchurch Road) as far as the wooded hills of the Wenallt and Rhiwbina. To the east lay the parish of Llanishen, the boundary separating the two following a line which ran between Caerphilly Road (most of which was in Llanishen) and Heol-y-deri, which was in Whitchurch.

As in all the parishes surrounding Cardiff, early settlement in Whitchurch was divided between a nucleus around the medieval church too small to be called a village and a large number of individual farms on both the lowland portion of the parish to the south and, to a lesser extent, in the hills further north. Towards the south-eastern corner of the parish a substantial area remained common waste until the beginning of the nineteenth century, when Cardiff Great Heath was finally enclosed. By this date, the future pattern of development in Whitchurch had been largely determined first by the building of a new main road up the Taff valley from Cardiff to Merthyr Tydfil in

---

[1] See generally W. Davies, *Rhiwbina Garden Village: a history of Cardiff's garden suburb* (Bridgend, [1985]).

1767, replacing the older roads over the Wenallt and Thornhill, and then by the construction of the Glamorganshire Canal, also linking Cardiff and Merthyr, which was completed in 1798. The first half of the nineteenth century saw a good deal of new building along the turnpike road through Whitchurch, as the outline of the modern 'village' gradually evolved. Similarly, there was some canal-side development at the southern end of the parish, which was continued on a much larger scale after the opening of the Taff Vale Railway between Merthyr and Cardiff in 1840–41, when a new community of 'Llandaff Yard' (the modern Llandaff North) grew up between the canal and the railway.

Meanwhile, there was a quite separate growth of population in the northwest corner of the parish, close to the boundary with Eglwysilan and Pentyrch, associated with the revival of iron-smelting based on the haematite deposits of the Taff Gorge. In the 1560s blast furnaces had been built on both the Pentyrch and Whitchurch–Eglwysilan banks of the river but both closed down in the seventeenth century — the furnace at Pentyrch in about 1616 and the other works probably in the 1680s.[1] In 1740 the Pentyrch site was restarted and about ten years later a corn-mill, Melin Griffith, on the Whitchurch bank of the Taff about a mile downstream, was converted into a tinplate works. The two operated in tandem and from the beginning of the nineteenth century were owned by the same company. Although Pentyrch was small by comparison with most South Wales ironworks and Melingriffith was isolated from the main groups of tinplate works in the Neath–Llanelli area and the Eastern Valley of Monmouthshire, the Booker family, who acquired control of the works in 1820, was easily the largest employer in Whitchurch during the first three-quarters of the nineteenth century.[2] There was no large-scale housing development associated with Melingriffith but further north the villages of Gwaelod-y-garth on the west bank of the Taff (in Pentyrch parish) and Tongwynlais on the east bank, which lay partly in Eglwysilan and partly in Whitchurch, both owe their origin mainly to the ironworks and associated mines.

The Bookers' enterprise failed in the slump of the late 1870s and the blast furnaces at Pentyrch closed for good. Melingriffith, however, passed into the hands of Richard Thomas and eventually became part of the tinplate combine

---

[1] P. Riden, 'Early ironworks in the lower Taff valley', *Morgannwg*, 36 (1992), 69–93.

[2] Chappell's own study, *Historic Melingriffith. An account of Pentyrch Iron Works and Melingriffith Tinplate Works* (Cardiff, 1940) remains the best account of the enterprise; for the parish generally in this period see E.J. May, 'The parish of Whitchurch, 1841–1851' (Cardiff Local History Diploma Dissertation, 1983).

bearing his name. Apart from these works, and some small foundries, patent fuel works and brickyards alongside the canal and railway at Llandaff North, Whitchurch remained principally a farming parish into the twentieth century, although its modern function as a residential suburb for the professional and business classes of Cardiff was also beginning to emerge.[1] Probably chiefly for this reason, Whitchurch was included in the large area to the north of the existing city boundary which Cardiff Corporation unsuccessfully sought to take over in 1911. Their application was renewed after the war and in 1922 much of Llandaff and Llanishen was incorporated into the city. They failed, however, to secure Lisvane and only two small areas of Whitchurch were transferred: Llandaff North, to the south of the Taff Vale line, and a strip of land at the southern end of Caerphilly Road.[2] As it turned out, the residents of both Whitchurch and Lisvane were able to resist later attempts to absorb their communities into the city until the major reorganisation of 1974.[3]

The boundary change of 1922 had consequences for Cardiff's rural hinterland as well as the city. Since 1872 the country parishes of Cardiff Poor Law Union had formed a rural sanitary authority, remodelled in 1894 as the Llandaff & Dinas Powis Rural District Council and renamed Cardiff RDC in 1922. More important than the change of name, however, was the way in which the transfers to the city greatly enhanced the importance of Whitchurch within the rural district, in which it was now by far the most populous parish and, partly because of the tinplate works as well as the growing residential suburbs, provided the lion's share of the authority's rate income. It is against this background that Chappell's decision to enter local politics through a seat on a rural district council, rather than the far more prestigious arena of either the county council or city council, should be viewed: to represent Whitchurch on Cardiff RDC was to occupy a position of much greater importance than is normally associated with local government at this level.

Chappell successfully contested elections for the Rhiwbina Ward of the RDC until he retired from public life in 1948, the year before his death. He and three colleagues initially stood on a non-party 'business' platform, arguing for greater efficiency and professionalism (but not necessarily 'economy') in local government. Interestingly, throughout his career, Chappell

---

[1] A.K. Hignell, 'Suburban development in north Cardiff, 1850–1919: a case study of the patterns and processes of growth in the parishes of Llanishen, Lisvane and Whitchurch' (Unpublished University of Wales [Cardiff] Ph.D. thesis, 1987) is a comprehensive survey.

[2] See the map of 'Modern Whitchurch' below.

[3] See P. Riden and K. Edwards, *Families and farms in Lisvane, 1850–1950* (Cardiff, 1993) for the later development of that parish.

campaigned quite openly, as part of his general belief in larger local authorities with rational boundaries, for the incorporation of Whitchurch into Cardiff, whereas traditionally RDCs on the edge of large towns fought against such transfers, so that their electors could continue to enjoy the benefit of most county borough services without the concomitant rate burden. This was no doubt the view of both Cardiff RDC and Whitchurch Parish Council, and it says much for Chappell's personal standing that he was able to retain his seat on the RDC while holding a distinctly unpopular view on such a crucial issue.

Chappell's leading position in local government in the area was recognised by his election as chairman of the rural district council in 1930–31 and his election to Glamorgan County Council in the latter year as an independent member for Kibbor Ward, which included part of Whitchurch. In 1938 he was appointed a county alderman, a particularly significant achievement in view of the firm control exercised over the authority by the Labour Party, with which by this date Chappell had long severed all links.

Throughout his local government career, Chappell was particularly interested in two main policy areas. One was housing and town planning, with which he had been concerned since his early campaigns in the Swansea Valley, and the other was education, which was also to be expected, given his years as a teacher and headmaster.

From 1924 Chappell chaired Cardiff RDC's Housing and Town Planning Committee, which was probably established at his suggestion in the first place. The mere existence of such a committee indicates a level of interest unusual among rural district councils in this period, although even Chappell, with his long involvement in housing and planning matters, especially through the Welsh Housing and Development Association, the main pressure group for reform in South Wales, was unable to achieve very much during the inter-war years. This was partly because of the economic difficulties of the period, although these affected Cardiff and its immediate environs far less than the South Wales coalfield, and partly an inevitable consequence of the shortcomings of town planning legislation prior to the comprehensive Act of 1947. But it may also have owed a good deal to the way in which even large and generally progressive authorities such as Cardiff and Glamorgan, much less the smaller bodies, failed to appreciate the need for 'planning' in the modern sense and still thought mainly in terms of building regulations, or the need for roads to be a certain width and sewers a certain diameter.

By contrast, Cardiff RDC enjoyed considerable powers under the Housing Acts and, perhaps largely at Chappell's insistence, made good use of them. As well as securing the demolition or reconditioning of substandard houses and building houses to rent, the authority had by 1937 advanced almost half a million pounds under the Small Dwellings Acquisition Acts, enabling over a thousand borrowers, nine-tenths of them residents of Whitchurch, to buy their own homes. The RDC thus made a significant contribution to the way in which Whitchurch expanded between the wars as a predominantly middle class outer suburb of Cardiff, not merely by controlling the layout of new building under the Public Health Acts but also by encouraging a particular type of development (the three-bedroomed semi-detached house costing about £600) through loans to owner-occupiers. It is for this reason that parts of Whitchurch are so similar in appearance to areas that were added to the city in 1922, where large amounts of land were subsequently released for housing and again the local authority made extensive mortgage advances between the wars.[1]

Although rural district councils ceased to be highway authorities in 1930, Chappell continued to advocate (and in some cases secure) improvements to the roads in Whitchurch, which were necessary in view of the very rapid development of the area during this period. In his election address of 1937 he claimed credit for the widening of Rhiwbina bridge and the rebuilding of Pantmawr Road and Wenallt Road. More important was the decision by the county council to go ahead with a new arterial road through the parish, Northern Avenue (Manor Way), by-passing Merthyr Road, which by this date was fully built-up and could not easily have been widened to accommodate the growing volume of motor traffic between Cardiff and the Taff valley.[2] The village centre was thus largely relieved of through traffic well before similar schemes were executed elsewhere, although conversely the decision to release land on either side of Manor Way for housing and other development seems strange to modern eyes.

Among the schemes devised for the land adjoining the arterial road was one especially close to Chappell's heart — new elementary and senior schools. Chappell's long-standing interest in education is obvious from the vast quantity of notes and drafts on both history and modern policy among his papers,[3] as well as numerous publications, and once elected to the county council in 1931, he clearly pressed for new schools in the area he represented. By this date, despite the rapid growth of population, the only

---

[1] Cf. *Cardiff 1889–1974. The story of the County Borough* (Cardiff, 1974), pp. 43–4.

[2] Cf. *The jubilee of county councils. 1889 to 1939. Fifty years of local government. Glamorgan* (1939), p. 93.

[3] Chiefly those of his papers which be bequeathed to Cardiff Central Library, whose contents are listed in Mrs Humphreys's dissertation, pp. 78–80.

additions made by the county council to the buildings inherited from Whitchurch School Board in 1903 (some of which had started life as National schools before the board was set up twenty years earlier) were new premises at Tongwynlais (1914), an infants' school at Glanynant (1916) and an infants' and mixed elementary school at Rhiwbina (1929). Nothing had been done to provide secondary schools locally, and children had to travel to either Penarth or Caerphilly, or attend Cardiff schools as fee-paying pupils.[1]

The first of Chappell's two major achievements was the building of a mixed grammar school for 320 pupils on a site near the parish church, which was opened in 1937 by Lord Portal (the industrialist Wyndham Portal, whose numerous South Wales interests included a directorship of the Great Western Railway and who in 1931 had undertaken a survey of the economic problems of South Wales for the government). Chappell was a governor of the school from its opening until his death. Two years later he himself performed the opening ceremony at a mixed senior school for 480 children on a site alongside Manor Way, of which Chappell became chairman of the governors. Plans to build a new elementary school on the rest of the land had to be postponed until after the Second World War, as did proposals to extend the secondary schools, but by the outbreak of war Whitchurch had at least acquired, probably largely thanks to Chappell's advocacy, its own selective school and one of the reorganised senior schools urged on local education authorities by the Hadow Report as the best means of catering for older pupils who did not secure grammar school places.

While Chappell's interest in the history of education in Whitchurch, as well as the need for better provision for the future, is obvious from the detailed chapter on the subject in *Old Whitchurch*, his research for the book ranged far more widely. It also clearly originated not in an antiquarian interest in the visible reminders of the past which were the mainspring of so much topographical writing of his day but in a concern to master the history of local institutions so as to understand the present and plan the future. Indeed, Chappell states quite clearly that his study of the history of Whitchurch began after he was elected to the RDC in 1921, when he felt he should learn more about the development of the community. As he discovered, little had previously been written about the area and much of that

---

[1] See Chappell's own very full account of the local educational history, below, Ch. XII, an essay which first appeared in the inaugural issue of the grammar school magazine published for the opening in 1937, although he avoids any mention of his own part in the story. See also C.W. Evans, 'The evolution of secondary and post-primary education in the Whitchurch area of Cardiff 1902–1951' (Unpublished University of Wales [Cardiff] M.Ed. thesis, 1983).

was unreliable, depending more on speculation and reminiscence than the study of records.

Chappell's own approach was very different, as he explains in the preface to *Old Whitchurch*. Quite remarkably for a local historian of his day, he systematically approached all the likely custodians of local records, both official and private, and asked to see what survived. Sometimes, seeking material from a period in which many public authorities engaged a solicitor in private practice to act as their clerk, who did not always pass documents on to his successor, he discovered he was too late; similarly, Chappell was soon to find how extensively the reliance on honorary officers by most congregations has led to the loss of nonconformist records. Occasionally, he was able to save material which would otherwise have been destroyed, notably papers from Melingriffith and Pentyrch, which had been put aside to be burnt, some of which he was able to retrieve from private hands and eventually place in the National Library of Wales. But the main point is that Chappell based all his work on a careful analysis of documentary sources, whether they were minute books, annual reports, business papers, the published texts of original documents in the Public Record Office, or articles in the proceedings of local societies. It is this approach which makes Chappell such an important figure in the development of local history in South Wales and gives his books a continuing value today. Indeed, Chappell stands somewhat apart from the antiquarian tradition which dominates the study of local history until recent times. In both his decision to investigate the past as an aid to understanding the present and his systematic methods of work, Chappell is if anything closer to the tradition of social enquiry developed to its fullest extent in his day by Sidney and Beatrice Webb, with whose monumental *History of Local Government* he would obviously have been familiar.

Whilst the bulk of Chappell's historical research was concerned with Whitchurch, his first major publication was a history of the port of Cardiff, published in 1939 as part of the celebrations to mark the centenary of the opening of the first modern dock, although these had to be curtailed because of the outbreak of war.[1] The following year, despite the war, Chappell published a history of the works at Pentyrch and Melingriffith, based partly on the documents he had rescued, which was the first case-study of any enterprise in the South Wales iron and steel industry to use archival evidence. Two years later came *Album Monasterium*, an account of the church at

---

[1] *Cardiff 1889–1973*, pp. 63–4.

Whitchurch, and then in 1945 Chappell finally published what was by far his most ambitious work, a full-length history of the parish which he had represented on two local authorities for nearly a quarter of a century.

Almost fifty years on, the original edition of *Old Whitchurch* may not seem as inviting as some more recent histories of towns and villages.[1] In part this is a legacy of the difficulties under which it must have been produced at the end of the war, printed on poor paper from worn type with narrow margins.[2] Nonetheless, the book was stoutly bound and contained over forty half-tone plates, many from photographs in Cardiff Central Library, others from pictures taken by Chappell's sister Hilda. There were also two maps and a good index, features sadly lacking in so many similar works. But above all, there was a lengthy account of both the general history of the parish and a wide variety of institutions, perhaps most notably (despite Chappell's complaints about the loss of records) the numerous nonconformist congregations established in Whitchurch since the early nineteenth century. The two topics on which he had written previously — the parish church and the ironworks — are dealt with only briefly, although the essay on education already mentioned was reprinted without revision from the school magazine of 1937. Throughout the book, Chappell's concern for statements based on evidence, preferably that of original sources, shines through. True, there are chapters (mostly near the end!) with titles like 'Ancient Local Folklore' or 'Miscellaneous Historical Notes' but in general the text, even the sections dealing with the middle ages, is far more solid, as well as far more extensive, than most parish histories of the period. Only a few references are given in footnotes, but every chapter has its 'Short List of Sources', which the keen student could follow up in the well-equipped surroundings of Cardiff Central Library, where Chappell himself spent so much time and to which he was to bequeath many of his papers.[3]

*

---

[1] For Whitchurch itself see H.M. Thomas, *Whitchurch: a brief history* (Cowbridge, 1982).

[2] It should be stressed that although this facsimile is on far superior paper than anything available in 1945, it is impossible to overcome the problems created by the use of worn type, unevenly set. This edition has, however, been printed on a slightly larger page than the original so that the margins appear less mean.

[3] In addition to the bequests to Cardiff Central Library and the National Library of Wales already mentioned, smaller gifts were made to Coleg Harlech and Whitchurch High School, while Chappell's fine collection of printed maps was given to the Glamorgan Record Office.

Apart from a short book on Cardiff's Civic Centre (1946), *Old Whitchurch* was Chappell's last separately published piece of local history. In 1943 he and his wife moved from 'Y Ddwy Onen', a substantial detached house at 36 Rhiwbina Hill, where they had lived since the mid-1920s, to 27 Beulah Road, a bungalow close to the chapel at which they worshipped. Shortly before his death they moved again to 159 Heol-y-deri. Chappell's final years were marred by ill-health and he died, at a nursing home in Penylan, in August 1949. His memory lives on, however, as a pioneer of housing reform and town planning in South Wales, as an advocate before his time of the reorganisation of central and local government in Wales, and, most widely, as a local historian whose books set new standards in their day and remain both readable and informative for a later generation. No further explanation is needed to justify the reissue of *Old Whitchurch* almost half a century after it was first published.

Cardiff Margaret Humphreys
September 1994 Philip Riden

A panoramic view of Cardiff from the Wenallt, with the reservoir in the foreground, Rhiwbina below and Whitchurch immediately beyond. East Moors Steelworks is visible on the horizon to the left of the picture.

Greenmeadow, Tongwynlais, the home of one of the branches of the Lewis family, who also lived at New House, Llanishen, and The Heath. Greenmeadow was sold after the First World War and demolished in the 1940s; a housing estate now occupies the site.

Wenallt Road, Rhiwbina, looking north, before the road was fully made up.

All Saints' Church, Llandaff North, shortly after it was erected in 1890–91 to the design of F.R. Kempson and C.B. Fowler. Extended in 1914, the church was badly damaged by bombing in 1941 and rebuilt on different lines after the war.

The Square (now Bridge Road), Llandaff Yard (now Llandaff North), looking north towards the Cow & Snuffers public house at the junction with Gabalfa Road.

The southern end of Merthyr Road, Whitchurch, looking north, with Tabernacle Presbyterian Church of Wales on the right.

A view from the garden in front of Whitchurch Library, where six roads meet, including, at this date, the main A470 from Cardiff to Merthyr Tydfil.

Milward's Terrace (87–111 Merthyr Road), a typical late nineteenth-century 'by-law housing' development, with Whitchurch Brook on the opposite side of the road.

The Parade, one of the streets near the Taff Vale station developed at the turn of the century to cater for the business and professional families who were moving to Whitchurch.

The second Ararat Baptist Chapel at Gwauntreoda, erected in 1851 and replaced by the present building in 1914–15.

Whitchurch Post Office, Fire Station and Parish Council Offices in Bishop's Road. The police station stood opposite, completing a miniature precinct of public buildings.

The northern end of Heol Don, looking through the fence to the large Cardiff Corporation Mental Hospital.

CONTENTS.

		Page
PREFACE		VII
CHAPTER I—THE PHYSICAL BACKGROUND		1
,, II—LOCAL CONDITIONS OF PRE-NORMAN DAYS		3
,, III—THE WELSH LORDSHIP OF SENGHENYDD		6
,, IV—THE MEDIEVAL MANOR		14
,, V—THE INSURRECTION OF LLYWELYN BREN		31
,, VI—THE PARISH CHURCH		40
,, VII—LOCAL ANTIQUITIES		43
,, VIII—THE LORDSHIP OF ROATH KEYNSHAM		53
,, IX—THE DESCENT OF OLIVER CROMWELL		58
,, X—THE STORY OF LOCAL GOVERNMENT		65
,, XI—DEVELOPMENT AND PUBLIC SERVICES		73
,, XII—THE STORY OF THE SCHOOLS		84
,, XIII—HISTORIC MELINGRIFFITH		102
,, XIV—THE GROWTH OF DISSENT		105
,, XV—EBENEZER AND TABERNACLE METHODIST CHURCHES		108
,, XVI—HERMON CALVINISTIC METHODIST, TONGWYNLAIS		118
,, XVII—WHITCHURCH METHODIST CHURCH		124
,, XVIII—AINON AND SALEM CHURCHES, TONGWYNLAIS		131
,, XIX—ARARAT BAPTIST CHURCH		143
,, XX—BETHEL BAPTIST CHURCH		149
,, XXI—BEULAH CONGREGATIONAL CHURCH		154
,, XXII—BETHESDA CONGREGATIONAL, TONGWYNLAIS		171
,, XXIII—RECENTLY FOUNDED CHURCHES		174
,, XXIV—RHIWBINA, ANCIENT AND MODERN		181
,, XXV—LOCAL ESTATES AND THEIR OWNERS		189
,, XXVI—LOCAL PLACE NAMES		196
,, XXVII—ANCIENT LOCAL FOLKLORE		213
,, XXVIII—TALES OF THE TWMPATH AND CASTELL COCH		222
,, XXIX—MISCELLANEOUS HISTORICAL NOTES		228
INDEX		243

LIST OF ILLUSTRATIONS.

Plate No.		Facing Page
1—FRONTISPIECE: ALDERMAN EDGAR L. CHAPPELL.		—
2—MAP OF MODERN WHITCHURCH.		—
3—MEDIEVAL LORDSHIPS OF CARDIFF.		Preface
4—YNIS HOUSE AND BRIDGE.		24
5—CASTELL COCH FROM CANAL BANK, TONGWYNLAIS.		24
6—CASTELL COCH.		25
7—TONGWYNLAIS FROM CASTELL COCH.		25
8—ST. MARY'S CHURCH, WHITCHURCH.		40
9—OLD PARISH CHURCH, 1902.		41
10—PORCH OF OLD PARISH CHURCH, 1902.		41
11—WENALLT CAMP SITE.		56
12—THE TWMPATH, RHIWBINA.		56
13—CASTELL COCH RUINS BEFORE RESTORATION.		57
14—CASTELL COCH, TONGWYNLAIS		57
15—DRAWING ROOM, CASTELL COCH, 1892.		72
16—THATCHED COTTAGES, NEAR MALTSTERS' ARMS, 1903.		72
17—THATCHED COTTAGES, MERTHYR ROAD, 1899.		73
18— ,, ,, OLD CHURCH ROAD, 1903.		73
19—VIEW EASTWARDS FROM CHURCH TOWER, 1903.		76
20—THATCHED COTTAGE, JUNCTION OF TYNYPWLL AND PENLLINE ROADS, 1904		76
21—LAST LOCAL COUNTRY CARRIER, 1904.		77
22—FORLAN FARM, WHITCHURCH.		77
23—WHITCHURCH GOLF CLUB HOUSE, FORMERLY PENTWYN FARM		84
24—WHITCHURCH GOLF COURSE. NORTHERN PORTION.		84
25—WHITCHURCH GOLF COURSE. SOUTHERN PORTION.		84
26—WHITCHURCH SECONDARY SCHOOL.		85
27—RHIWBINA COUNCIL SCHOOL.		88
28—THE "FOX" SCHOOLROOM.		88
29—TYNYPARC ROAD, 1911.		89
30—HEOLYFORLAN, 1911.		89
31—AERIAL VIEW OF MELINGRIFFITH WORKS.		104
32—HEOLYDERI, RHIWBINA, 1903.		105
33—HEOLYDERI, RHIWBINA.		105
34—COED Y WENALLT PARK.		120
35—WENALLT ROAD FROM THE DERI.		120
36—NANT CWM NOFYDD.		121
37—WHITCHURCH BROOK NEAR RHIWBINA HALT.		121
38—WHITCHURCH BROOK LEAVING CWM NOFYDD.		136
39—WENALLT RESERVOIR.		136
40—OLD BUTCHERS' ARMS BEFORE RECONSTRUCTION.		137
41—HEOLYFELIN, RHIWBINA.		137
42—RHIWBINA HILL FROM NEAR THE TWMPATH.		152
43—CWM NOFYDD AND GELLI QUARRY.		152
44—THATCHED COTTAGES AT THE PHILOG.		153
45—CYM Y MWYALCHEN COTTAGES, THE PHILOG		153

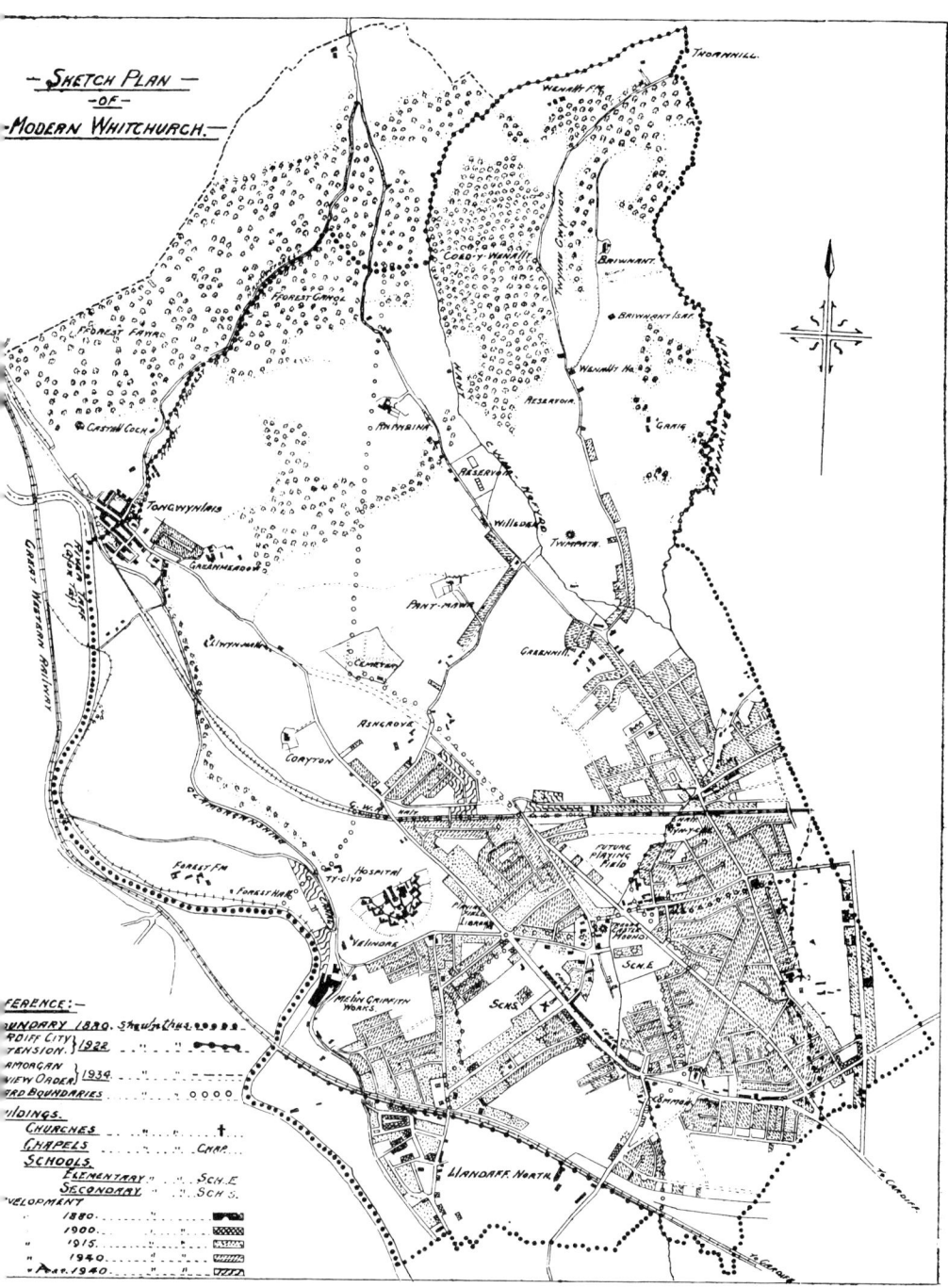

MAP OF MODERN WHITCHURCH   J. Parry Williams

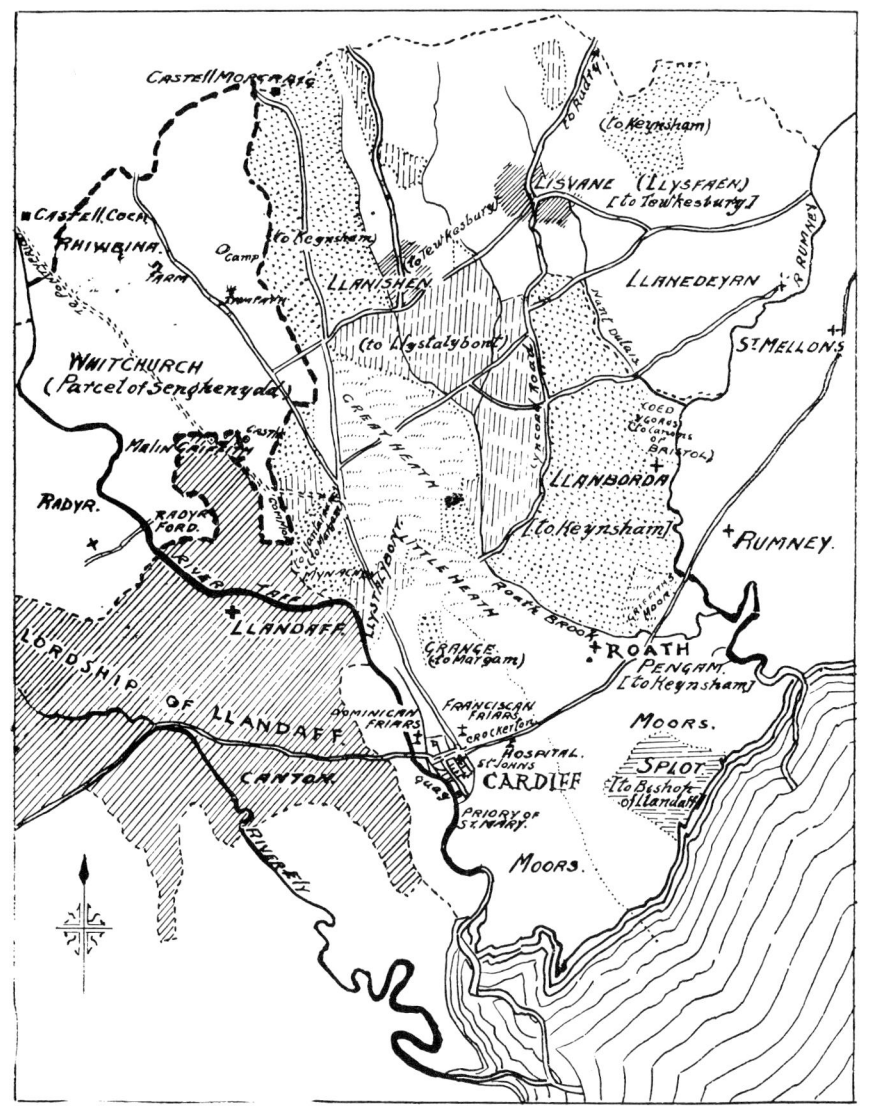

Medieval Lordships of Cardiff   Cardiff Development Committee

Preface

For more than forty years I have been associated with movements for the better planning and development of towns and the improvement of housing and general social conditions in South Wales. It was natural, therefore, when in 1921 I was elected a representative of Whitchurch on the Cardiff Rural District Council, that I should specialise in these branches of public administration. Soon I was appointed Chairman of its Housing and Town Planning Committees, and it became incumbent on me to acquire a sound knowledge not only of existing conditions and development tendencies but also of the past history of the parish.

There was little or no difficulty in getting information relating to the present, but when I sought knowledge of the past I could find little except odd facts in various publications; no historical account of Whitchurch had ever been written. Nor could I hear of any person who had ever worked on the subject; indeed, except for one or two persons, nobody seemed to have any interest in the matter. It was up to me, therefore to dig out and arrange the facts relating to the past for myself. Thus I added local historical research to my list of hobbies.

The getting of information has not been easy. Happily I found that some medieval manorial and other records had been reproduced in *Cartae Glam* and in the *Cardiff Records*, and this saved me the task of going through the various *Calendars* and inspecting documents at the Record Office, although doubtless much local unpublished material remains to be collected from that and other depositories.

When I sought for local records of more modern times I found that few were available. At the Parish Church, except for the Registers of Births, Marriages and Deaths, there were no old documents. The Tithe Map, the Churchwardens' Accounts and the Vestry Records were missing, nor were they in the custody of the Parish Council. Similarly the Old Valuation and Rating Lists, etc., of the Parish had disappeared.

When I turned to the Melingriffith Works, perhaps the oldest industrial undertaking in South Wales, I found that a few years previously there had existed a vast quantity of old Account Books and other papers and correspondence, but in order to make accommodation for other records most of these had been destroyed. Happily not all these documents were burnt, and I was able to find some salvaged material in the possession of local residents. Most of this I have since deposited at the National Library of Wales.

Then I turned to the schools. Most of the log-books were intact, but one or two of the very oldest had been taken away by a former schoolmaster and could not be traced. The minutes and other documents of the Whitchurch School Board, formed in 1883 and dissolved in 1900, I expected to find at the Glamorgan County Hall. But not so. They had been retained by the former solicitor-clerk and upon his death these documents passed with his practice to another solicitor by whom they were destroyed.

Similar disappointments faced me when I sought information regarding local churches. In most cases, the only documents (apart from those relating to property title, kept in safe custody at the churches or by the church officers) were current or fairly recent minute books and cash books. In few instances was there any official material available which dated back very far.

The practice seems to have been for a retiring secretary or treasurer to hand over to his successor the current books, and to retain older books, correspondence and the like in his possession. Most of this has probably been destroyed, but I was able to trace odd records in the possession of some former officers or of members of their families. Doubtless there are others in existence, and I hope the authorities of churches and other local organisations will take steps to recover and safely store any fugitive records which may throw some light on their past history.

However, from such few records as I have been able to examine, supplemented by information contained in a variety of publications and that obtained by personal inquiry of a large number of old residents, I have been able to assemble a fairly substantial body of material,—sufficient at any rate to enable me to prepare a fair account of the past history of the parish.

The story of our chief local industry has already been told in *Historic Melingriffith*; and in *Album Monasterium* I have recounted the salient facts connected with the history of the Parish Church. This is a more ambitious venture. It aims to deal not only with outstanding local events and personalities, but with the development into an important suburban community of a once sparsely populated agricultural parish, with environmental changes and with the evolution of social institutions.

The account is by no means complete, but I hope its publication will inspire more competent investigators with greater leisure and opportunity for research to expand the story more fully. I have refrained from detailed documentation, but I have indicated generally the chief sources from which I have drawn my facts.

It would be impossible to mention the names of the dozens of persons who have supplied me with items of information. To all who have assisted I tender thanks. I must, however, express my special thanks to Mr. A. J. Richard, M.A., of the Whitchurch Secondary School, for services rendered in many ways, and particularly for reading the proofs and relieving me of the drudgery of preparing the index. I also wish to thank Mr. Parry Williams for preparing two maps, and Mr. W. Morgan Davies and others for providing me with photographs for the illustrations of this work.   E.L.C.

CHAPTER I.
THE PHYSICAL BACKGROUND.

Whitchurch is a parish of about 3,376 acres, extending northward from three to six miles from the centre of Cardiff, of which it is a popular and rapidly developing suburb. Its greatest length from north to south is a little over three miles, whilst its greatest width is 2⅓ miles. It lies outside the city limits within the Cardiff Rural District and the Administrative County of Glamorgan.

The only industry of any magnitude is the Melingriffith Tinplate Works (converted for War-time purposes to other uses), and the overwhelming majority of the population are employed in Cardiff and elsewhere, a very large proportion in commercial and professional occupations. The locality is a very pleasant residential area. The elevated northern portions, which are well-wooded and undulating, are not only in themselves picturesque, but command extensive scenic views over the northern heights as far as the Breconshire Beacons and southward over the Coastal Plain and the Severn Sea.

The developed areas are for the most part flat and form part of the Coastal Plain, which was formerly deemed to be included within the limits of the lowland plateau known as the Vale of Glamorgan. This plain in the Cardiff area is divided from the Coalfield Plateau by a steep border ridge known in medieval times as Cefn or Craig* Cibwr (or Kibbor), which extends from Rhiwperra to the Lesser Garth and today bears several sectional names, viz., Craig Lisvane, Cefn Onn, Craig Llanishen, Caerphilly Common, Cefn Carnau, Twynaugwynion, Y Wenallt and Fforest Goch. The greater portion of the last four sub-ridges is situated within the Parish of Whitchurch, and their summits lie between 500 and 800 feet above sea-level. Coed-y-Wenallt was some years ago acquired as a natural park reserve by the Cardiff Corporation and is much patronised by hikers and holiday trippers.

North of the parish lies the Caerphilly Urban District, west the parish of Radyr, east the parish of Lisvane and part of Cardiff, whilst the Llandaff North portion of Cardiff adjoins its southern boundary. Whilst the coal measures outcrop in Cefn Cibwr, they do not fall within the Whitchurch limits. The upland areas of Whitchurch include the Millstone Grit and Carboniferous Limestone measures which underlie the coal seams, and for this reason are known to miners as the *Farewell Rocks*.

The upper slopes of the hills drop sharply to a height of about 200 feet, and then by an easier gradient to the flat, lower-lying portions of the parish. It may be of interest to point out that the 200 feet contour line passes through such well-known landmarks as The Deri, Whitchurch Golf Club House, Coryton House and the entrance gates of Castell Coch. From the Deri the land falls to 134 feet O.D. at Rhiwbina Halt and it is probable that the average height above sea-level of the built-up portions of Rhiwbina below the Deri does not exceed 145 feet O.D. There has, as yet, been very little building development within the

---
* A Plymouth Deal (N.L.W.M.S., 431) of April, 1443, refers to a grant of lands in Eglwys Ilan lying between *Kreic Kybor* and a river called *Nat yr Globylle* of Keven Onne and the royal way from Kerdyff to Kerfyly.

parish above 200 feet O.D., although building is possible in parts up to 300 feet O.D. Nearly all such buildings at these elevations are in Rhiwbina above the Deri.

The drainage system of the parish is fairly simple. Near Thornhill rise two streams, Nant Nofydd on the northern slope and Briwnant (formerly called Castan) on the southern slope. These streams follow courses in valleys on either side of Twynaugwynion, and unite near the Deri to form the Whitchurch Brook, which finally discharges its waters into the River Taff. Another stream arises near Blaengwynlais, flows through the deep and narrow valley between Fforest Goch and Fforest Ganol and joins the Taff at Tongwynlais.

The lower portions of Rhiwbina form part of an extensive plain covering practically the whole of the Whitchurch residential area at an average height of about 120 feet above sea level. Llandaff Station, the Parish Church, Glanynant Schools and portions of the Philog are near the 100 feet contour, Whitchurch Library at 116, the Mental Hospital Lodge at 127 and the Hollybush Inn at 135 feet. Tongwynlais forms a distinct little community lying between 110 and 175 feet O.D.

From the Whitchurch plain there is a considerable, and for the most part a sharp, drop to another flat area, an alluvial plain extending along the left bank of the River Taff. At Llandaff North the average elevation is about 67 feet O.D. Within the Whitchurch limits it extends from Melingriffith to Tongwynlais and is deemed unsuitable for residential development. It was formed first by glacial action during the Ice Age and was later extended by river action.

The soil of the river plain was formed of debris left by glaciers and of deposits of mud, sand and boulders brought down by the river. The soil is therefore alluvial boulder clay, and it possesses a fair degree of fertility. The remainder of Whitchurch lies on the Old Red Sandstone series, and its soil consists for the most part of marls and conglomerates. The soil of the upper slopes of the hills is derived mainly from Carboniferous Limestone and Millstone Grit. On account of its gravelly nature Whitchurch soil is generally fairly dry, easy of cultivation and fertile.

Formerly arable farming was extensively carried on, and the chief secondary activity was stock-rearing. During the past half century very little corn has been grown and although a few farmers still rear stock most of them now concentrate on milk production. A few areas of land are, however, used for market gardening and nursery purposes.

The climatic conditions of Whitchurch are fairly favourable. By reason of its situation in regard to the Atlantic and the direction of the prevailing winds the weather tends to be moderately mild and moist. Nearly 60 per cent. of local winds blow from a westerly direction, and whilst they often bring rain they are usually fairly warm. The number of wet days per annum averages about 151 as compared with 177 in the Swansea district.

The average annual rainfall in Whitchurch is about 45 inches compared with 40 inches in Cardiff and 35 inches at some points on the Glamorgan seaboard. This figure is not unduly high when contrasted with Treforest 55, Merthyr 60, Aberdare 70, Rhondda 75-80, and 90 inches at Craig-y-Llyn overlooking Rhigos at Hirwaun.

CHAPTER II.

LOCAL CONDITIONS OF PRE-NORMAN DAYS.

That South Wales was peopled thousands of years ago has been proved by an examination of ancient camps, barrows, hearths, weapons, pottery and other relics of the stone, bronze and iron periods, and it is inconceivable that throughout the ages the Whitchurch district was peopled by wild animals alone, even although the finds of ancient relics have not locally been very numerous. The existence in neighbouring localities of such remains, proving their occupation by different races of people of varying standards of civilisation, is in itself *prima facie* evidence of the occupation of the Whitchurch locality by similar people.

Archaeological "finds" covering the Stone, Bronze and Iron Ages have been made at several places within half a dozen miles of Whitchurch. Neolithic polished flint axes have been found at Cardiff, St. Fagans, Pentyrch and Llanfedw, and a few years ago a similar object was found at Waunfawr Road, Rhiwbina. Similar finds of Bronze Age palstaves, socketted axes, spear-heads and like objects have been recorded at Cardiff, Penarth, Gabalfa, Llandaff, St. Fagans, Creigiau, Llanfedw, Rumney and St. Mellons. In addition to finds of small objects of the Iron Age there exists proof around us within a short distance in the form of camps, residential settlements, burial places and the like dating from this and earlier periods. Thus we find tumuli at Tynant and on the Garth, an ancient cooking hearth near Radyr Railway Station, and a cave in the Lesser Garth, which have provided evidence of human existence in prehistoric times. Probably other "finds" will in due course be made.

Recent researches have also proved conclusively that the Romans had an important military station at Cardiff for several hundred years and that this station was connected in an easterly and westerly and northerly direction by road with other stations. The line of the northern road has not yet been defined, but there is a possibility at any rate that it passed through Rhiwbina. The discovery at various times of coins, pottery and other records at a quarry on Rhiwbina Hill seems to suggest that there was a minor military structure in that locality. According to tradition also, there existed formerly adjoining the site of the old churchyard at Whitchurch a military work of supposed Roman origin, and on early editions of the Ordnance Survey maps this tradition found expression in words denoting the existence of a Roman camp. On an 18th century estate map I have noted the field name *Cae Moat* (moat field) applied to an adjoining enclosure, and this would seem to indicate the former existence of some military work, although not necessarily one of Roman origin. The "Roman Camp" idea, however, may have arisen from confusion in regard to the near-by Norman motte.

In all probability the fertile lands in the Cardiff district were settled to some extent by a civilian population and it may be that some day traces will be found locally of the remains of Roman villas such as those which have been explored at Ely and Llantwit Major. Until such evidence is available we can only assume that our fertile lands were cultivated by the Romans, possibly with the aid of British slave labour.

In the Dark Ages that followed the Roman evacuation of Britain it seems certain that Glamorgan was a stronghold of the Christian faith. Not only were there large and important monasteries in the sixth and succeeding centuries at Llantwit Major and Llancarfan; there was also a similar institution at Llandough, and it is almost certain that the diocese which has its centre at Llandaff was a development of an important monastic institution established in that locality by Teilo, a disciple of St. Dyfrig. Llandaff is recognised as almost the oldest ecclesiastical See in the British Isles. In course of time the Church at Llandaff was enriched by gifts of land and other property, and before the advent of the Normans to the district it had become a wealthy and important land-owning institution.

Even after the Norman Conquest the Lordship of Llandaff continued wealthy and extensive and included a substantial area of the village of Whitchurch, the inhabitants of which were served in religious matters by the Cathedral itself. On account of its close proximity to the Mother Church, in all probability it was not necessary, as in districts farther afield, for Welsh monks to institute locally a subsidiary religious settlement or 'llan', such as Mordaf, Edeyrn, and Isan did in the neighbouring localities of Llanforda,* Llanedeyrn and Llanishen, although in very early days it is likely that some monks from Llandaff had a cell with an associated chapel on the banks of the River Taff at a point described in the Book of Llandaff as Stuntaf or Ystum-Taf, meaning the bend in the Taff, an appellation which seems to indicate a site near Melingriffith. It may perhaps be assumed that the application by the Normans of the names *Album Monasterium, Blancminster,* and *White Church* to the manor of Whitchurch is reminiscent of an earlier Welsh religious settlement at Ystum-Taf.

Dr. Paterson's valuable researches into place nomenclature in the Cardiff district have demonstrated that the Norsemen and Danes ravaged the coastal territory of Glamorgan—a fact established not only by historical record but also by existing native sagas of these hardy sea-rovers—and also that numbers of them possibly settled not only in Cardiff, but also in the neighbouring countryside. Dr. Paterson's deductions seem very conclusive in regard to some portions of the Vale, but his suggestion that local place names such as *Kibbor, Treoda,* and *Rhyd Walla* indicate Scandinavian influence at Whitchurch, is open to serious question.

The name Craig or Cefn Kibbor was in medieval times given to the ridge of hills extending from Rhiwperra to the Wenallt, and probably to

---

* *Llanforda* or *Llanbordan* stood on the west side of the road from Penylan to Llanedeyrn, a short distance south of Coed-y-Gores. A tenement called Chapel House occupies the site of the ancient church or chapel.

Castell Coch. On the Wenallt exists an ancient camp, probably of Iron Age period, and Dr. Paterson suggests that the ridge was given the name *Kibbor* by reason of the existence of this camp.* The name Kibbor he interprets as follows, viz. :—

> Low German *kip*, a jutting point or a pointed hill,
> Old Norse *borg*, a fortified height,
> or *bord*, a ridge.

The name, therefore, according to Paterson, means either the point of a ridge, or the fort on a pointed hill. The other names referred to are discussed in a later chapter.

In due course the Normans seized Glamorgan from the native Welsh, and Cardiff became the military and administrative headquarters of their government. They seem to have confined the Welsh mainly to the hill districts north of Craig Kibbor, the fertile plain being in the main settled by the Normans themselves. Whitchurch, on account of its proximity both to Cardiff Castle and to the Welsh territory, became a kind of buffer territory and was doubtless the scene of many a hard-fought struggle. For this reason, in addition to its close connection with the Church of Llandaff, it may be assumed that Whitchurch played an important part in ancient local history. The problem of the historian is to recover from the misty past facts on which an intelligent and reliable account can be based.

SHORT LIST OF SOURCES.

Baring Gould and Fisher. Lives of the British Saints.
W. F. Grimes. Guide to the Collection illustrating the Prehistory of Wales.
Sir J. E. Lloyd. History of Wales.
D. R. Paterson. Early Cardiff.
R. E. M. Wheeler. Prehistoric and Roman Wales.
A. H. Williams. An Introduction to the History of Wales, Vol. I.

---

* Early Cardiff, p. 46.

CHAPTER III.

THE WELSH LORDSHIP OF SENGHENYDD.

The traditional account of the Winning of Glamorgan by the Norman, Robert Fitzhamon, and his Twelve Knights has been shown to be largely fictitious, and it is now certain that the Welsh of Morgannwg were not conquered in one big battle some time around 1090-3. Considerable research has been made during the past half century into the circumstances connected with the Norman annexation of Glamorgan, and a good deal of fictitional matter has been torn away, leaving a basis of fact and some probable theory which still awaits positive proof.

The *Annals of Margam* has a record under the year 1081 that *edificata est villa Cardiviae sub Willelmo primo rege*—'Cardiff was built under King William I,' and it is supposed that this refers to the raising of the Castle Mound at the time of the Conqueror's march through South Wales to St. David's. A later record under 1086 refers to the confirmation by King William of the gift by Robert Fitzhamon of Llancarfan Church to St. Peter's Abbey, Gloucester. From these facts it is deduced that Norman settlements had taken place in the Vale at least ten years before the date generally attributed to the Conquest of Glamorgan.

In all probability, however, the Welsh natives of certain areas, and particularly those resident in the hill region, had not accepted foreign control, and Robert Fitzhamon and his followers, with the King's backing, probably took advantage of strife between rival Welsh kings to bring the whole of Glamorgan under their domination. In this they were in a measure successful, and in all probability Fitzhamon forced the Welsh to recognise him as their overlord.

This conquest, however, was political rather than economic. The Vale was doubtless fully Normanized by the introduction of manorial laws and methods. Perhaps, however, because he put little value on the hill districts, Fitzhamon was content with the nominal recognition of his suzerainty, and he made no attempt to occupy those areas, but allowed the native inhabitants to continue managing their affairs in accordance with ancient Welsh tribal customs. Nearly two centuries were to pass before the *Blaenau* or hill districts were conquered in an economic sense and brought within the manorial framework.

After securing general acknowledgment of his lordship over Glamorgan, Fitzhamon took steps to organise his new possession, and he developed Cardiff Castle and its ancillary borough as his military and administrative headquarters. He retained as his own private share of the plunder, in addition to his overlordship, Cardiff and the adjoining territory south of the Cefn Onn range, Llantwit Major, and the littoral between Ogmore and Afan, and possibly Llysworney. Most of the remaining land in *Y Fro* (*Bro*, Vale), however, was distributed either by him or his successors amongst their chief Norman followers, conditional on their rendering certain services or making certain payments in accordance with feudal custom. Some territories were also later given to monastic institutions.

The hill districts, however, were not thus allotted to Norman barons, possibly because they could not have held them except with very great difficulty. They seem to have been placed in the ownership and control of Welsh chiefs of the families which had ruled over them in the past. Six separate areas of hill territory—known as Nedd, Afan, Tir Iarll, Miscin, Glynrhondda, and Senghenydd—were separately organised as *Member Lordships*, each under a native ruler, and although these were nominally subject to Norman control, they were allowed to retain Welsh courts, laws and customs, and rendered no services or payments to the overlord except a heriot of a horse and arms at death.

The Member Lordship of Senghenydd was the largest and most important of the hill divisions. Being near Cardiff and peopled by a particularly bold and warlike race, it constituted a direct and constant menace to the Overlord, and was the last of the member lordships to come under full Norman control.

Senghenydd originally comprised the territory of a pre-Norman, Welsh *Cantref Breiniol* (meaning the 'privileged' cantref), which included all the land between the rivers Taff and Rhymney from Breconshire to the sea. It seems to have been divided into three divisions or *commotes*, known as

Uwch-Caiach (or Upper Senghenydd), the territory north of the Caiach* brook;

Is-Caiach (or Lower Senghenydd), the territory south of the Caiach brook as far as the Cefn Onn range;

Kibbor (Welsh, *Cibwr*), from the Cefn Onn ridge to the Severn Sea.

These commotes under the Welsh kings of Glamorgan were independent administrative divisions, and each had its own separate headquarters and courts for the purpose of adjusting disputes, trying criminals, and collecting taxes. The headquarters of Is-Caiach was probably at Caerphilly, and that of Kibbor possibly at Lisvane or at Roath.

Variations of commote boundaries may have taken place from time to time. Even before the Norman occupation Cardiff may have been excluded from Kibbor, and possibly also the land in the Whitchurch area belonging to Llandaff Cathedral. Kibbor was too rich and fertile a territory to be left entirely in Welsh hands, and Fitzhamon retained it as part of his share of the spoils of victory. In a portion of it at Lisvane and Llanedeyrn he seems to have settled a number of native Welsh—probably the more peaceable element—who were exempt from payments and services except the duty of attending his *comitatus* or court at Cardiff Castle once a month. The Welsh tribeland was known as the *Patria Wallensium* or *The Welshery*.

---

* The Caiach brook rises near Llancaiach and flows past Nelson through Cwm Mafon to join the river Taff a short distance below Quakers' Yard.

In later years Fitzhamon and his successors distributed other portions of Kibbor to religious bodies, such as Tewkesbury and Keynsham Abbeys, and at least one secular manor was also carved out in connection with Llystalybont. The remaining area, centred at Roath, continued as a private agricultural manor of the Overlord, from which supplies were obtained for the Castle of Cardiff.

That portion of Kibbor comprising northern Whitchurch seems to have been contested territory. The chief passes into the hill region from Cardiff were along the valleys of the Taff and Rhymney, but there were also two smaller but more difficult passes through Cwm Nofydd (Rhiwbina) and Cwm Gwynlais (Tongwynlais). No records of strife during the early days of the Norman re-constitution of Senghenydd are available, but it is not unlikely that the territory adjoining the mountain passes was the scene of many a hardfought fight between the Normans and Welsh hillsmen.

Whitchurch, perhaps, became a kind of 'no-man's land', sometimes in Norman and sometimes in Welsh possession. It may be that during this period was built by the Normans the *motte* castle, the mound of which, known as *The Twmpath* (Rhiwbina), still remains. Its purpose may have been to resist the attacks of Welsh enemies coming down the pass of Cwm Nofydd. A similar *motte* castle may also have been built at Whitchurch about the same time.

In the Kibbor territory taken over by Fitzhamon were certain possessions which were claimed by the Bishop of Llandaff. These included a considerable part of the modern village of Whitchurch. The dispute between the Normans and the Bishop over this area was settled at Woodstock in 1126 by the cession to the latter of the village of *Stuntaf*,* i.e., part of Whitchurch. The Normans, however, probably clung to the greater part of the Parish of Whitchurch, including Rhiwbina and Tongwynlais, and to this and other parts of Kibbor the Welsh hillsmen laid strong claim.

The hostility between Norman and Welshman was a persistent one. Three quarters of a century after the Norman occupation the men of Senghenydd continued their antagonism, and in 1158 Ifor ap Meurig, better known as Ifor Bach, the Welsh Lord of Senghenydd, in pursuance of his claim to lands in Kibbor, made his famous raid on Cardiff Castle, overcame its garrison, and carried off the Marcher Lord and his family as prisoners into one of his hill fastnesses.

This spectacular event was described by Giraldus Cambrensis† in 1188, only 30 years later, and its truth can therefore safely be assumed. The following is Giraldus' account translated from the Latin:

"An extraordinary circumstance occurred likewise at the Castle of Caerdyf: William, Earl of Gloucester, son of Earl Robert, who, besides the Castle, possessed by hereditary right all the province of Gwladvorgan, that is, the land of Morgan, had a dispute with one of his dependants, whose name was Ivor the Little, being a man of short stature, but of great courage.

---

* Rees, Liber Landavensis, p. 566.
† Colt Hoare, The Itinerary of Archbishop Baldwin through Wales, pp. 121-2

"This man was owner of a tract of mountainous and woody country, of the whole, or a part of which, the Earl endeavoured to deprive him. At that time the Castle of Caerdyf was surrounded with high walls, guarded by one hundred and twenty soldiers, a numerous body of archers, and a strong watch;

"The city also contained many stipendiary soldiers; yet, in defiance of all these precautions of security, Ivor, in the dead of night, secretly scaled the walls, and, seizing the Count and Countess, with their only son, carried them off into the woods, and did not release them until he had recovered everything that had been unjustly taken from him, and received a compensation of additional property."

It may reasonably be surmised that part, at any rate, of the lands of which Ifor had been deprived was the debatable territory in northern Whitchurch in the vicinity of the mountain passes above referred to. Ifor's success in imprisoning the Norman lord had forced the latter to make terms, and it is suggested that the Welsh claim to the retention of the greater part of Whitchurch in the Lordship of Senghenydd was now conceded.

Moreover, the compensation, in the form of additional lands mentioned by Giraldus, probably comprised two areas of moorland near the Rhymney River at Roath which, in later centuries, were known as Morfa Ifor (Ivor's moor) and Morfa Griffith (Griffith's Moor—Griffith being Ifor Bach's son).* In addition, the Earl of Gloucester is stated to have bestowed his base daughter in marriage on Gruffydd. It is the same Griffith, in all probability, whose name is commemorated in Melin Griffith.

This event seems to have settled the boundary question between Norman and Welsh, and it may be assumed that during the following century the greater part of the Parish of Whitchurch belonged to the Is-Caiach commote and owed allegiance to the Welsh Lord of Senghenydd. The remainder of the parish, however, was in three ownerships. A central portion of the village belonged to the Church of Llandaff; the Philog district, south-east of Whitchurch Common, may have formed part of the Manor of Llystalybont; and a district covered by the recently developed Homelands and Greenclose building estates with a part of Rhiwbina was in the ecclesiastical Manor of Roath Keynsham.

In due course Ifor Bach was succeeded as Lord of Senghenydd by his son Gruffydd ab Ifor (who died in 1211), then by his grandson, Rhys ap Gruffydd (who died in 1256), and lastly by his great-grandson, Gruffydd ap Rhys, who was dispossessed by the Normans in 1266. After the latter event the Is-Caiach section of Whitchurch was constituted a separate Manor of *Album Monasterium*, owing allegiance and rendering dues direct to the Overlord of Glamorgan himself. In order to soften the disgrace of lost independence it is quite likely that lords of Senghenydd or their important connections were appointed by the Overlord to serve as his stewards or bailiffs for the new manors carved out of the old Welsh lordship.

---

* See Rice Merrick, *Glamorgan Antiquities*, (1578).

The truce between William, Earl of Gloucester and his doughty little Welsh opponent, Ifor Bach, did not, however, end the hostility between Norman and Welshmen, and although the control exercised by Cardiff Castle over the hillsmen was little more than nominal, there can be no doubt that the latter cherished deep and lasting resentment against the rule of their foreign masters. The Normans were well aware of this, and realised that there was a strong disposition in their Welsh subjects to side with any movement or leader in conflict with their interests, and that therefore their hold on Glamorgan would be somewhat precarious until they had brought the Welsh under their complete domination.

The most menacing of the hill lordships were those nearest Cardiff, viz., Miscin, Glynrhondda, and especially Senghenydd. It was clear, therefore, that the power and influence of the Welshmen of these districts should be broken, and doubtless the Normans awaited suitable opportunities for dealing with them.

In 1230 the first Gilbert de Clare, Earl of Gloucester, and Lord of Glamorgan died, leaving an infant son as his heir. Henry III placed the young earl in the wardship of his uncle, Richard Marshall, third Earl of Pembroke, whilst charge of the Lordship of Glamorgan was given to Hubert de Burgh, Earl of Kent and Chief Justiciary of England.

About this time Llywelyn the Great was seeking to bring the whole of Wales under his rule. De Burgh set about the task of repressing Llywelyn, but his effort failed. Llywelyn proceeded to ravage the border counties. It is likely that he was supported by the fighting men of Senghenydd and the neighbouring hill commotes. During 1232 he made substantial progress in South Wales, and the interests of the Norman-English lordship of Glamorgan were threatened.

About this time Henry III became dissatisfied with Hubert de Burgh, and dismissed him from office. The king's ill-treatment of de Burgh, and his preference for foreign favourites, aroused the resentment of other barons, who joined de Burgh in a revolt against the king under the leadership of Richard, Earl of Pembroke, uncle and guardian of young Richard de Clare. Prince Llywelyn and the Welshmen of Glamorgan also supported the confederacy.

The confederate army marched into South Wales in 1233 and took Abergavenny and other castles and laid waste the countryside. Cardiff Castle was in the royal possession, and it is surmised that the confederate party, including the local Welsh hillsmen, at this time built *Castell Morgraig* (at Thornhill, now in ruins) in order to menace Cardiff and resist any advance of the Royalist army into Senghenydd.

The king assembled a large army of foreign mercenaries at Gloucester, and after considerable unsuccessful fighting in the Marches and in Monmouthshire, he crossed to Ireland and attacked the Earl of Pembroke's possessions there. The Earl hurried over seas to recover his lands, and was killed there in battle in 1234. On hearing this news the king made peace overtures to Prince Llywelyn, and eventually an agreement was reached favourable to the rebels. Possibly one of the terms of the treaty provided that the erection of Castell Morgraig should not be proceeded with.

Young Richard de Clare took over his Lordship of Glamorgan in 1240, when only 18 years old. Two years later Gilbert de Turbervill (Lord of Coity), Hywel ap Meredith (Lord of Miscin), and Rhys ap Griffith (Lord of Senghenydd) were engaged in a private war with one another. By direction of the young earl the Abbot of Tewkesbury and others conducted an enquiry into the dispute at a comitatus held at Cardiff Castle. Here they disciplined the quarrelsome lords, and took hostages to secure the good behaviour of the belligerents. One of these hostages was no less important a person than Gruffydd ap Rhys, son of the Lord of Senghenydd.

In 1245 Prince David had taken up the mantle of his father, Llywelyn the Great, and had sought to achieve the ambition of a united Wales. The Lords of Miscin and Senghenydd had lent him their support. Richard de Clare now saw an opportunity of strengthening his position in Glamorgan. Senghenydd was still too strong to be interfered with, but he succeeded in dispossessing Hywel ap Meredith of his lordship of Miscin, and a little later also got hold of the adjoining commote of Glynrhondda. To secure these lordships he built the Castle of Llantrisant, which he made the headquarters of his administration. Out of Miscin were carved several feudal manors, including those of Radyr and Pentyrch. The subjection of these two Welsh lordships prepared the way for the annexation twenty years later of Senghenydd.

Rhys ap Gruffydd was succeeded as Lord of Senghenydd by his son, Gruffydd ap Rhys, in 1256, and the *Extent of Glamorgan** records that he held two commotes in Senghenydd in 1262, owing no service to the Lord of Glamorgan except a heriot of a horse and arms at death.

From about 1260 Llywelyn ap Griffith, Prince of Wales (*Ein Llyw Olaf*, Our Last Prince), grandson of Llywelyn the Great, pursued his grandfather's ambition of driving the Norman-English invaders from Wales, and uniting the country under a Welsh king. His influence spread rapidly over the greater part of Wales, and he became, next to the King of Scotland, the most powerful rival of the English Crown. In 1265 Glamorgan was practically the only part of Wales which had not come under his rule, and he was seeking the support of the Welsh hillsmen for the conquest of that territory.

Earl Richard de Clare, Lord of Glamorgan, leader of the Barons and a supporter of Simon de Montfort in his struggle against Henry III, died and was succeeded in 1263 by his son, Gilbert 'the Red', Earl of Gloucester. This young man and also Prince Llywelyn supported de Montfort and the Barons against the Crown. In 1265, however, Earl Gilbert quarrelled with de Montfort and changed over to the King's party, which won a decisive victory over the Barons' Reform Party at Evesham later in the year.

---

* In the Public Record Office, cited by J. S. Corbett in *Glamorgan Papers*, p. 37.

Prince Llywelyn's interests were not much affected by the defeat. He retained his lands in Wales, and again sought to capture Glamorgan. Earl Gilbert, alarmed by Llywelyn's growing power in the hill territory, set about the task of bringing Senghenydd under closer control. No details of his military operations are available, but it is recorded that in 1266 he dispossessed Gruffydd ap Rhys of his lordship, imprisoned him first in Cardiff Castle, and later sent him to Kilkenny for greater security.

The Welsh lordship of Senghenydd now ended. Steps were taken to administer the territory on feudal lines, and to protect the Earl of Gloucester's interests against possible rebels. About this time, in all probability the portion of Is-Caiach south of the Gwynlais brook was converted into a separate manor of Whitchurch, and other manors were also possibly created elsewhere in Is-Caiach. Arrangements were made for administering Whitchurch through a bailiff with headquarters in a small castle built about this time in Whitchurch village, possibly on the site of an earlier motte.

The menace to the de Clare lordship, however, was not yet removed. Prince Llywelyn seems to have invaded Senghenydd in 1267 in support of the cause of Gruffydd ap Rhys, and by September, 1268, he was in control of Uwch-Caiach. The Barons' War was now ended, and the Treaty of Montgomery had confirmed Llywelyn in his possession of the extensive territories in the Marches from Chester to Abergavenny, and also his overlordship of the native princes. Under the latter provision he claimed that he had rights over the Glamorgan hill lordships and that Gilbert de Clare should relinquish his hold over them.

Against the establishment of this claim the Earl took defensive measures. He occupied Is-Caiach and proceeded with plans for the erection of castles at Tongwynlais and Caerphilly and the strengthening of Cardiff Castle. *Castell Coch* was probably intended to guard the approaches to the coastal plain through the Taff and Gwynlais valleys, and *Caerphilly Castle* to dominate the northern and eastern lines of approach towards Cardiff.

The erection of these castles was a direct challenge to Prince Llywelyn. Castell Coch was probably completed or approaching completion, and work was well advanced on Caerphilly Castle, when in October, 1270, Llywelyn marched on Caerphilly and destroyed the new structure. The king, fearing a renewal of national trouble, intervened, and efforts at bringing about a solution by arbitration were made, but without avail.

In June, 1271, de Clare commenced a new and much more imposing castle at Caerphilly, and in the following October Llywelyn again attacked. Again the king intervened, and peace was temporarily restored, de Clare handing over the castle to the King's custody and Llywelyn withdrawing his troops north of the brook Caiach, pending settlement of the dispute.

Three months or so later—the quarrel still not having been settled—in February, 1272, de Clare secured re-possession of the castle by means of a trick, and pushed forward with building operations.

Llywelyn's cause was now weakening. Other Marcher lords were taking up arms against him, and he deemed it wise to withdraw his forces from Senghenydd to Brecon. De Clare was able, therefore, to complete his task at Caerphilly, and also to build another castle at *Morlais*, north of Merthyr Tydfil.

In October, 1272, Edward I came to the throne, and immediately embarked on a campaign which ended in the defeat and death of Llywelyn and the conquest of Wales. The government of Senghenydd by independent Welsh lords was now definitely at an end.

SHORT LIST OF SOURCES.

G. T. Clark. The Land of Morgan.
J. S. Corbett. Glamorgan Papers.
J. A. Hobson. Cardiff Records
J. E. Lloyd. History of Wales.
J. E. Lloyd. Llewelyn ap Griffith and the Lordship of Glamorgan (Arch. Camb. 1913).
J. E. Morris. The Welsh Wars of Edward I.
William Rees. Caerphilly Castle.
William Rees. Map of South Wales and the Border (14th Century).

CHAPTER IV.

THE MEDIEVAL MANOR.

As has already been indicated the territory of modern Whitchurch was comprised within four medieval manors, two portions being in the ecclesiastical manors of Llandaff and Roath Keynsham respectively, the Philog area was in the Manor of Llystalybont, whilst the remainder was carved out of the Lordship of Is-Caiach or Lower Senghenydd after the deposition of Gruffydd ap Rhys in 1266. From this time forward there existed a separate Manor of Whitchurch, which seems, however, to have been regarded as a member of Lower Senghenydd (sometimes referred to as Caerphilly Castle), and was merged into the larger lordship some centuries later. Manorial records are not numerous. The records of the Chancellory centred at Cardiff Castle have been destroyed or lost, and we have to depend for our knowledge of most local medieval manors on returns made to the Crown after the death of a Marcher Lord or at periods when the Lordship was in Royal hands, as during the infancy of its holder.

A fairly full series of records exists for Whitchurch manor, dating from 1295—sufficient at any rate to give us a fairly clear picture of conditions during the 13th and 14th centuries. Before proceeding to deal with these records, it is perhaps necessary to describe the boundaries of the territory which is surmised to have been included within the ancient manor. The boundary on the north extended along the course of Nant Gwynlais from the Taff to a point above Cefn Garw Quarries and then crossed Rhiwbina Hill to Cwm Nofydd. It then followed Nant Nofydd as far as Castell Briwydd near Thornhill. From this point the eastern boundary struck over the hill to the Briwnant brook, west of New House, and followed that brook to a point a little east of the Wenallt Nurseries. It then proceeded southward in almost a straight line to the Tywern Farm in Tywern Road. The line from this point is irregular. It followed Tywern Road to the Tynyparc Cross Roads and thence in a south easterly direction to Whitchurch Common and then onward to the Taff Vale Railway.

The western boundary was the River Taff from the point where it is joined by the Gwynlais Brook to a point slightly north of Hailey Park (Llandaff North). The southern boundary cannot be accurately described without the aid of a map. Roughly it ran almost directly from the last point mentioned to the eastern boundary near the Taff Vale Railway, but with a substantial gap at a point where a tongue of land belonging to the Manor of Llandaff extended northward, occupying a considerable area of modern Whitchurch. The boundaries of this tongue were roughly from near the Fram Works to Llandaff Station, then along Heoldon, Velindre and Tynypwll Roads to the Whitchurch Brook, and then along the course of the brook to a point where that brook is crossed by the Taff Vale Railway.

From the foregoing description it will be gathered that the Merthyr Road area was mainly in Llandaff, part of Whitchurch east was in Roath Keynsham and the remainder in Llystalybont, whilst Northern Whitchurch and Rhiwbina, as well as the Llandaff North and Melingriffith sections, were in the Manor of Whitchurch. There was also an outlying portion of Whitchurch Manor lying between the Rhymney River and the Roath Power Station, Cardiff. This is referred to in the records as Griffithsmoor, and was probably the land granted by the Duke of Gloucester to Ifor Bach after his raid on Cardiff Castle in 1158. In this chapter it is proposed to deal with the records relating to the Manor of Whitchurch proper (or Album Monasterium), which was administered by a bailiff for the Lord of Glamorgan and Cardiff.

Before reciting these records a few preliminary explanations are necessary for their proper understanding. From the information available it appears that a substantial area of the manor of Whitchurch comprised *demesne* land, that is, land which originally was retained by and cultivated for and on behalf of the lord. Such land was usually in the vicinity of the lord's castle or manor house. A small castellet comprising a single large tower was built by the Norman lord, soon after he dispossessed Gruffydd ap Rhys of Senghenydd and carved out the Manor of Whitchurch, on a site adjoining the Whitchurch Brook (then possibly called Nant Castan), which is now occupied by a house called Treoda in Old Church Road.

This structure was probably built as the administrative headquarters of the manor, and it may safely be concluded that there was demesne land in the locality. Demesne land included park land and pasture as well as arable, and there were probably a farmhouse and buildings near by. It may be surmised that the ancient farm name, *Tynyparc* (the park homestead), was derived from its association with the lord's demesne. As the years rolled by it became usual to farm out portions of the demesne to tenants, and by 1316 the entire area of demesne seems to have been demised outright.

Any uncultivated land not let to tenants or in demesne was termed 'the lord's waste' and was also deemed to be the manorial lord's private property.

The remainder of the land of the manor was farmed out to tenants on a variety of tenures. The records show that much of the land was in the hands of *free* tenants on *socage* tenure, that is subject to special services including suit at the lord's court or *soke*. Military service, however, was not expected. Free tenants had liberty to sell or transfer their lands which, however, were subject to an annual payment called **rent** *of assize* to the lord of the manor.

A good deal of land at Whitchurch was let to *bound* tenants, who were practically territorial serfs, and held these lands at the will of the lord. Such land was usually allotted in consideration of service rendered by the tenants in cultivating the lord's demesne. Such tenants were known as *customary* tenants or *customars*. They were obliged to attend annually at a manorial court, and here took place a ceremony of transmitting a rod between the steward of the manor and the customar, which was the symbol of the dependence of the customar on the lord's will.

Customary tenants could not leave the manor without the lord's consent, and in return for their privilege of holding land from the lord and for his protection they were under obligation to render certain customary services on the lord's demesne. These services were in later times, when the demesne was farmed out, commuted for money payments. Not only were the lands of bound tenants held by custom; they were also grouped for cultivation near the demesne, and were probably worked in conjunction with the lord's lands. We shall find in the records numerous references to customary works.

Another class of feudal tenants were *cottars*—peasants who had squatted on the lord's waste, with or without the lord's permission, and were allowed to occupy a messuage and curtilage or small croft there as long as the lord was prepared to accept their labour. Some of them were doubtless fugitives from justice or Welsh *natives* who had forsaken their tribeland. The lord doubtless encouraged this class of landless men, who, in addition to increasing the lord's income by the payment of rents for their tenements, were available for employment as hired workers.

The lord of the manor also had other properties which he leased or farmed out to tenants in return for money or service. In the Manor of Whitchurch we find that revenue was derived from the letting of fishing rights in the Taff and from the lease of certain mills. Monies were also received in respect of various feudal aids and privileges, tolls and fines, and other perquisites of court, but in respect of these he maintained various officers who discharged police and other functions.

It is now proposed to give extracts from medieval records relating to Whitchurch with the object of establishing the continuity of the manor from its inception in the 13th century until its disappearance as an independent unit some time in the 16th century.

The first record is a post-mortem inquisition (circa 1295-6) after the death of Gilbert de Clare, the 'Red' Earl of Gloucester, and Lord of Glamorgan. A post-mortem inquisition was a return made to the Crown, usually by a local jury, on the death of a manorial lord, as to the extent and value of the deceased's landed possessions. In this case, Earl Gilbert, being a Marcher Lord, the inquisition covered a large number of manors and lordships, but we are concerned only with the Whitchurch section:

"Also the aforesaid Jurors say that there are at Album Monasterium 150 acres of arable land which are worth by the year 37s. 6d., price of an acre 3d.

Also 150 acres of arable land which are worth by the year 26s., price of an acre, 2d.

Also 60 acres of arable land at Rempny which are worth by the year 60s. Also 3 acres of meadow, price of an acre 12d. Sum 3s. Also 14 acres of meadow at Rempny which are worth 28s., price of an acre 2s.

Also there are of the rents of customars and cottars 13s. 4d. by the year. And of the customs of the same persons 4s.

And there is one mill which was wont to render 14s. 4d. And it renders nothing because it is burnt. Also the perquisites there are worth 13s. 4d.

Sum £9 4 2.

Also say the aforesaid Jurors that the aforesaid Gilbert, and Joan his wife, the daughter of our lord Edward, King of England, jointly held the aforesaid land and tenements of our lord the King in chief, by what service they know not. And they say that Gilbert de Clare, son of the aforesaid Gilbert, is his next heir and of the age of four years and upwards. In witness whereof the aforesaid Jurors to this Extent have set their seals.''

The land at Rempni referred to in the above documents was on the banks of the Rhymney River adjacent to Griffithsmoor. Rice Merrick writing in 1578 refers to areas of lands called *Morfa Yvor* (Ivor's Moor) and *Morfa Ryffidd* (Griffith's Moor) 'near Romney' given by William, Earl of Gloucester, to Ifor Bach after the raid on Cardiff in 1158. It may be that the land at 'Rempni' additional to Griffithsmoor was that described by Merrick as Morfa Yvor.

The mill referred to was undoubtedly Melin Griffith, so called after Ifor Bach's son. It seems at both these dates to have been out of use through destruction by war and fire. The destruction of mills was a regular feature of medieval wars, and manorial records teem with references to the damage done to these 'objects of military importance.' I am unable to mention the particular war which put Melin Griffith out of action in 1295, but I presume it was rebuilt after that date, and later again destroyed.

The burning recorded in the foregoing document may have taken place during a somewhat alarming insurrection which occurred in Glamorgan in 1294. In that year Edward I had set himself the task of winning back Gascony for the English Crown. He looked to Wales to provide him with men and supplies for achieving this object and introduced measures of compulsory enlistment. A general rising took place throughout Wales against the Crown. The King suspended or limited temporarily his foreign operations, and armies were sent to Wales to suppress the Rebellion and also at the same time to limit still further the power of the Barons.

In the previous Welsh wars of his reign Glamorgan had been involved only to a small extent, and its Lord, Gilbert de Clare, Earl of Gloucester, wielded such great power and influence that the King had found great difficulty in bringing him under his domination.

At the outbreak of the Welsh rising the Welshmen of Glamorgan do not seem to have been involved, probably because, owing to the powerful position of the Earl of Gloucester in that lordship, the King had not dared to apply such a severe levy as in the other Welsh territories. The Earl's prestige, however, had sustained considerable damage during four or five years preceding the Revolt, and simultaneously with the rising against Edward I in North and Mid Wales, Glamorgan Welshmen under Morgan (or Rhys ab Morgan), of Afan rebelled against their Lord, the Earl of Gloucester. He was joined by the men of Senghenydd, Miskin, Glynrhondda and Tir Iarll. It was during this rebellion, it is said, that the famous Welsh song "*Rhyfelgyrch Cadben Morgan*" (Captain Morgan's March) was composed, and sung by the rebels whilst advancing against their foes.

The fight was between the Welshmen and the Earl's men,—the Royal forces were not involved. The Welshmen swept through Norman Glamorgan, defeated the Earl's armies, and destroyed much property and crops. Senghenydd seems to have suffered badly. At Caerphilly mills were destroyed, many houses were burnt and the Castle was attacked, although without success. Attacks were probably also made on the strongholds of Castell Coch and possibly Whitchurch, and it is likely that during this onslaught Melin Griffith was destroyed.

Morgan's army " is said to have completely driven the Earl out of his lands, and to have occupied the castle of Morlais itself. " The King saw in the defeat of the powerful Earl an opportunity of restricting the power of the De Clares. In June, 1295, he led an army into South Wales and came to Merthyr Tydfil. He took the whole of the Lordship of Glamorgan into his own hands, accepted the submission of the insurgents against the wishes of the Earl, and appointed Walter Hackelute as royal custodian of the lordship. In the autumn of the same year, however, the King restored to Earl Gilbert and his wife Joan (the King's daughter) the lands of which they had been so bereft.

The manor of Whitchurch is referred to in several records in the early part of the 14th century. A Post Mortem Inquisition of 1307 relating to the possessions of Earl Gilbert and his wife Joan mentions Album Monasterium and Mor Griff (60 acres of land and 16 acres of meadow) as separate entities, but also refers to Album Monasterium as a member of the Castle and Town of Caerphilly. Other places mentioned as members of Caerphilly are Llanfedw, Castell Coch, Hendredenny, Cefncarnau, Rudry, Merthyr and Gelligaer and the entire tribeland of Senghenydd.

In passing we may also note a reference to a "pasture by Watford" (Caerphilly), which shows that name to be considerably older than is generally thought. An unusually early reference to the staple mineral of South Wales also occurs in the following extract relating to Cefn Carnau (Caerphilly Mountain): "and there is at Kevencarn one pit wherein sea-coals are dug, and the profit is worth by the year 20s.

The detailed return of 1307 relating to Album Monasterium reads as follows:—

"Also they say that there are 345 acres and a half of arable land in demesne; which are worth by the year 43s. $2\frac{1}{4}$d., price of an acre $1\frac{1}{2}$d.

And there are 44 acres of arable land which Kenewrek ap Howel holds at farm; and they are worth by the year $5/10\frac{1}{2}$, price of an acre $1\frac{1}{2}$d. And the said Kenewrec holds likewise there three acres of meadow which are worth by the year 18d., price of an acre 6d.

And there are in demesne 2 acres of meadow which are worth by the year 12d., price of an acre 6d.

And there is one water mill which Lewelin ap Griffith holds to farm by lease of the aforesaid Ralph (*sic*) and Joan, and it is worth by the year £4.

And there are certain freeholders who render by the year 4/-, namely, at the feasts of Saint Hilary, the Apostles Philip and James, and Saint Michael, equally.

And there is of rent of assize of certain customars 8/11 on the feast of Saint Michael only. And of the aforesaid customars there are 3 customars who owe by the year 240 manual works from the feast of St. Michael until the gules of August. And those works are worth 10/-, price of a work a halfpenny; namely, in each month 24 works. And they owe each month, from the gules day of August until the feast of St. Michael, 24 autumn works; and those works are worth 13/-, price of a work $2\frac{1}{4}$d. Also of the aforesaid customars there are 11 who owe 11 autumn works; and those works are worth $13\frac{3}{4}$d., price of a work $1\frac{3}{4}$d."

Sum £8 8 $7\frac{1}{2}$.

"*Griffithsmoor.*

"Also they say that there are 60 acres of land in demesne which are worth by the year 20/-, price of an acre 4d. And there are 16 acres of meadow which are worth by the year 10/-, price of an acre 8d."

"Sum 30/8."

The water mill referred to—Melin Griffith—was at this time held by a Welshman of Senghenydd who had married Lleuci, a female of the line of Ifor Bach, and was therefore a man of great influence in the Welsh districts. Llywelyn ap Gruffydd (sometimes also spoken of as Llywelyn ap Rhys) was popularly known as Llywelyn Bren, and it was he who headed the great insurrection of 1316 of which we shall hear later.

It will be observed that the services to be rendered by customars are spread over the year, their value being $\frac{1}{2}$d. per duty during ten months and $1\frac{1}{4}$d. and $2\frac{1}{4}$d. for autumn tasks.

At this period the demesne was apparently being worked for the lord, and customarial duties were rather heavy. Three men were required to devote 88 days each to the lord's service. Eleven others each rendered one day's work on demesne land during the harvest period. An interesting point is that rents of assize payable usually only by freeholders are chargeable also on some of the customars.

In the manors of Rumney, Roath, Leckwith and others in the Cardiff district the records deal with customary works in greater detail, showing that the tasks relate to ploughing, sowing, harrowing, hoeing, mowing, reaping, winnowing, hauling and thatching. In the return relating to the Manor of Radyr a reference is made to "8 customars who owe 8 works at ploughing for wheat-seed or oat-seed, for the will of the lord . . . also the aforesaid customars owe 8 works at gathering seed . . . . 16 works at reaping, on the lord's food."

Another important post-mortem inquisition was prepared in September, 1314, by Bartholomew de Badelesmere, Custodian of the Clare castles, manors and lands in Glamorgan, with the aid of a jury, after the death of the last Gilbert. This also contains much detail in regard to various local manors. The following is the section relating to Whitchurch:

"Also they say that at Album Monasterium is a certain castle which is nothing worth beyond reprise, which was burnt in the war.

And there are in demesne of arable land and pasture 327 acres by ancient measurement, which are worth by the year 54/6, price of an acre 2d. And there are 3 acres of pasture of meadow, which are worth by the year . . . .

Also there at Gruffismor 60 acres of arable land, which are worth by the year 30/-, price of an acre 6d. And there are beyond the water of Rempny 5 acres and a half of arable land, which are worth by the year 2/9. And there is a certain pasture which is worth by the year 6/8.

Also there are at Album Monasterium 18 acres of meadow; which are worth by the year 30/-, price of an acre 20d.

Also there are certain tenants who hold 19 acres of land at the will of the lord, and render by the year at the feast of Blessed Michael 12/-. And they owe 17 autumnal works, on the lord's food, and they are worth 16d.

And there is a certain water mill by the Taf, which is worth by the year 100/-.

And there is a certain fishery which is worth by the year 13/4. Pleas & perquisites are worth by the year 2/-.

to wit, sum £12 15 7."

In this inquisition occurs the first known reference to Whitchurch Castle. It was apparently at this date little better than a ruin. I am unable to assign a date to its destruction. The war referred to may have been the Welsh Revolt of 1294 above mentioned or the damage may have been more recently done by persons disaffected with Bartholomew de Badelesmere's administration. Badelesmere's record for Cardiff also mentions Cardiff Castle as being 'worth nothing beyond reprise.'*

The mill by the Taff is obviously Melingriffith, and the fishery referred to in this as in earlier and later documents was also in the Taff River between Tongwynlais and Llandaff Bridge. It should be noted in passing that in the Middle Ages the farming or leasing of fishing rights yielded a substantial revenue to the manorial lords. The records of the lordships of Cardiff, Leckwith, Roath and Rumney over centuries contain references to these rights.

The mill weirs were frequently let separately from the river stretches, and between Llandaff and the sea there were four or five separate lettings in the River Taff. Fishing rights in the Rumney were apparently held both by the Manors of Roath and Rumney. The Ely River also yielded good revenues to the Manor of Leckwith, and lamprey fishing is mentioned in several of the records of this interesting manor.

Badelesmere also in 1314 prepared a Minister's Account for the Glamorgan properties, covering a period of 14 weeks only, the Whitchurch portion of which reads as follows:

---

* By *reprise* is meant the oxpenses or other allowances deducted from rent.

"*Rents of Assize.* *

He answers for 12/- rents of assize to Michaelmas.

Farms.

"He answers for 18/10 for the letting of divers pastures here and there, for the aforesaid time. For perquisites of court he answers not, because none was holden for the aforesaid time. And for 25/- received for the herbage of 10 acres of meadow sold at 2/6 an acre. And 11 acres sold and mown in the Earl's lifetime. And for 16d. from 16 autumn works at 1d. each.

Sum of the whole receipts £4 2 2.

Stipend.

"In the stipend of one sergeant having custody of the manor, collecting and levying the rents and other issues for the aforesaid time 2/-.

Sum of all expenses 2/-."

Conditions in Glamorgan at this time became very difficult owing to political changes and the introduction of sterner methods of administration. After the death of the last Earl Gilbert de Clare at the Battle of Bannockburn in June, 1314, there was no male heir to the Glamorgan Lordship, and control passed for the time being to the Crown, who appointed Bartholomew de Badelesmere as Custodian. De Clare left three sisters, each of whom was married to a powerful English baron, who plotted and intrigued to secure the succession to the lordship.

Economic conditions also were unsatisfactory. Edward II's war with the Scots, in which he was supported by young De Clare, had been very costly and had involved heavy taxation on Glamorgan. In addition four exceptionally rainy summers from 1313 to 1316 had resulted in poor harvests with consequent distress.

De Badelesmere's task, therefore, was not a light one, and to make matters worse, instead of following a policy of conciliation with the Welsh leaders in the hill lordships, he did all he could to irritate them. His neglect of the Welsh hostages imprisoned at Cardiff Castle, and his general hostility to Welsh customs gave great offence, particularly to the Welshmen of Senghenydd, amongst whom Llywelyn ap Gruffydd (or Rhys), better known as Llywelyn Bren, was the popular leader.

During the year ended Michaelmas 1315 he seems to have farmed out as units the Manor of Album Monasterium for £12 15 7 and the Manor of Radyr for £14. Throughout this year the hostility to De Badelesmere grew and representations were made to the King, who replaced him as Custodian by a Welsh baron, Payn de Turbervill, Lord of Coity. This proved a change for the worse. Turbervill deprived Llywelyn Bren and other chiefs of their offices, and, as appeals to the King for the redress of their grievances failed, the Welshmen, headed by Llywelyn Bren, towards the end of 1315, broke into revolt. A detailed account of this insurrection will be given later. Here it is only necessary to state that Norman castles were attacked, and the Vale manors devastated, and their flocks and herds driven into the hill country.

---

* *Rents of Assize* were fixed payments made to the lord in lieu of customary services on the lord's land.

The King sent large forces into Glamorgan to suppress the rebellion. Llywelyn and many of his friends were captured and imprisoned and the revolt suppressed. Payn de Turbervill in turn was dismissed as Custodian, the appointment being placed in the hands of John Giffard de Brymmesfeld.

For the year ended Michaelmas, 1316, there are two Ministers' Accounts, one by Welthian, widow of Sir Payn Turbervill, from October to April and the other by John Giffard from April to September. Lady Turbervill's account covers the period of the revolt and is of a very scanty character, and no entry is made in respect of the Manor of Whitchurch. Both her report and the later one of John Giffard contain numerous references to the damage and loss resulting from the Revolt. The following is the Whitchurch section of the Giffard account:—

"*Rents of Assize.*

The same answers for 12/- received from rents of assize in the manor of Album Monasterium to the term of Saint Michael. Sum 12/-.

Issues of the Manor.

The same answers for 56s. received for 327 acres of land and pasture sold at the same place for the same time. And for 3s. received for the herbage of 3 acres of meadow sold at the same place.

And for 31s. received for the pasture of 60 acres of arable land in cultivation this year at Griffithesmoor. And for 3s. received for the pasture of $5\frac{1}{2}$ acres in cultivation beyond the water of Rempni. And for 6/- received for the pasture of a certain 'hame' there.

And for 26s. 8d. received for 18 acres of pasture sold at the same place.

And for 16d. received from 16 autumnal works issuing from the customars of the same place.

Sum £6 - 8 - 0.

Mills.

From the mills at the same place nothing because burnt and destroyed by war.

Issues of the Fisheries:

And for 6s. received from the issues of the fishery at the same place for the same time. Sum 6s.

Pleas and Perquisites: And for 13d. received from pleas and perquisites of the Court of Album Monasterium for the same time and not more because of the war. Sum, 13d.

Sum of all receipts, £7 - 7 - 1.

Expenses.

Prevost's Outgoings.—The same accounts in the wages of one Prevost of Album Monasterium from the 20th day of April until the morrow of Michaelmas for 163 days, taking $1\frac{1}{2}$d. per day, 20s. $4\frac{1}{2}$d., who used to take a quarter of corn per 10 weeks.

Sum of Expenses: 20s. $4\frac{1}{2}$d.

In the same year, as the Bailiff of Glamorgan, John Giffard in his account has the following Whitchurch item:

"Autumn Works.

The same answers for 16 autumn works received from customars of Album Monasterium for the same time, price of each work, 1d.

Sum 16 sold as above and nothing remains."

The *Calendar of Patent Rolls* of this period mentions numerous documents embodying instructions by the King for the repair of buildings and other works throughout the Vale of Glamorgan damaged during Llywelyn Bren's Rebellion. In September, 1316, John Giffard was ordered to repair the various mills and to lease these and the demesne lands in his custody, and to meet the cost of restitution out of the rents received. It is almost certain that Melin Griffith was rebuilt in accordance with the King's instructions.

At this time the weak and vacillating King, Edward II, was as wax in the hands of his favourite, the younger Earl Despenser. Despenser's wife was Eleanor, one of the Clare co-heiresses. A settlement of the inheritance problem was overdue. Despenser prevailed on the King in 1317 to allot to him the Lordship of Glamorgan and the associated manors (including the Manor of Whitchurch), the remaining territories around Newport and Tintern being respectively allotted to his two brothers-in-law. This division of the De Clare possessions, however, did not satisfy him for long, and soon he appropriated Newport. He next induced the King in 1319 to alienate from Roger Mortimer, husband of the heiress of William de Breos, his Lordship of Gower.

Despenser's greed and growing power alarmed the leading Marcher Lords, who now banded themselves together to attack Despenser. Glamorgan was invaded. The confederate barons attacked the castles of Newport, Cardiff, Caerphilly, Llantrisant, Kenfig and Neath, and ravaged the manors of Glamorgan. Included in the list of wrecked manors contained in the *Rolls* are Cardiff, Roath, Leckwith, Radyr and the 'manor of Blankmoster' (Whitchurch). The barons also attacked and destroyed Despenser properties in 69 townships in 18 different counties of England. As a result of this rising Parliament in 1319-20 ordered the Despensers, both father and son, to be banished from the country.

The King in the following year (1321-2) took up arms against the barons, and the Despensers were recalled. A battle was fought at Boroughbridge, and the King and the Despensers vanquished their enemies.

Next year trouble arose in the King's lands in Gascony and Queen Isabella was sent out to make peace. She declined to return to court, and commenced plotting with Roger Mortimer against the King and Despenser. In 1326 the Queen, accompanied by Mortimer and Edward, Prince of Wales, landed in Suffolk with an army of French mercenaries and pursued Edward and Despenser westwards.

The latter endeavoured to escape by sea from Chepstow, but bad weather forced them to land at Cardiff. After three days' stay at Cardiff Castle the King and Despenser went to Caerphilly and later to Neath Castle. Mortimer and other leading barons pursued them relentlessly, and ultimately they were captured near Llantrisant. Despenser was sent to the Queen at Hereford, where he was hanged. The King was imprisoned and afterwards murdered at Berkeley Castle.

For a time after Despenser's execution the Glamorgan Lordship was in the hands of the new king, Edward III, and later of his Queen, Philippa. In 1337 the lordship was again restored to the Despenser family in the person of a second Hugh le Despenser, who held it until his death in 1349, following which a post-mortem inquisition of his possessions was made by Simon Bassett, the King's Escheator, acting with a jury. The section relating to Whitchurch reads as follows:

"Also the aforesaid jurors say by their oath that the said Hugh le Despenser held of our lord the King in chief, in his demesne as of fee, on the day whereon he died, the Castle and Manor of Album Monasterium, with the appurtenances, by what services is not known. Which said castle, with the ditch around it, and the barton annexed, is worth by the year 3/4.

"Also they say that there are in demesne 409 acres of land; whereof each acre of 50 acres is worth by the year 6d., and each acre of 359 acres is worth by the year 3d. . . . . . .

"Also there are in one parcel called Griffithsmore by itself one messuage which is worth by the year 12d. ; and there are 56 acres of land . . . . . And so the sum of the value of Griffithesmore in the whole is 62/4.

"Also they say that there are in the said manor of Album Monasterium 14 customars of the petty tenure, who hold divers petty tenements in bondage . . . .

"Also there is a certain mill which is worth by the year £6 13 4. Also there is a certain fishery in the water of Taaf, which is worth by the year 10/-. Also pleas and perquisites of the Court there, with 'leirwyt' and heriots, are worth by the year 6/8.

"Sum of the whole extent of the manor, with Griffithesmore, £19 5 10."

The reference seems to indicate that the castle of Whitchurch was intact. I have already explained that this was a small stone structure, the mound of which still exists, but much reduced in height, in the garden of a house called Treoda in the Tynyparc locality. In olden times the Whitchurch Brook may have encircled the mound, so forming the ditch referred to in the record.

By the barton is probably meant the home farm and demesne with the central farm buildings, and this reference supports the suggestion made above that the Tynyparc farm lands, now largely built over, were the major demesne lands of the Whitchurch manor.* The term 'leyrwyt' or 'letherwyt' was a fine paid to the lord by persons found guilty of adultery or incontinence. The term also sometimes denoted the payment by a tenant to his lord for a licence for his daughter to marry. A 'heriot' was the payment made to the lord of a sum of money or the best animal or other goods of a tenant at death.

---

* In 1761 there was a tenement called Tir Parc near the left bank of the river Taff, a short distance below Melingriffith.

YNIS HOUSE AND BRIDGE, TONGWYNLAIS, WITH
CASTELL COCH IN BACKGROUND

Cardiff Development Committee

CASTELL COCH FROM CANAL BANK,
TONGWYNLAIS

*Cardiff Development
Committee*

CASTELL COCH — *Cardiff Library*

TONGWYNLAIS FROM CASTELL COCH — *Cardiff Library*

I have already shown how closely Glamorgan was associated with national affairs and national personalities during the reign of the weak king, Edward II. After the fall of Despenser the power of the barons was greatly weakened and the Marcher Lords came more and more under the domination of the Crown. Edward III and his son, the Black Prince, engaged in numerous wars in Scotland, France and elsewhere, in which they enlisted the aid of their chief barons. The antagonism between the barons and the Welsh gradually died down, and the King also became popular with the Welsh people. We find that in the French wars the Black Prince was strongly supported by archers and spearmen from the Welsh hill districts of Glamorgan. Many of these doubtless came from the Senghenydd lordship.

During the 14th century there were economic forces at work which weakened the force of the feudal arrangements. As the result of several visitations of the terrible bubonic plague, known as the Black Death,— there is evidence to show that Glamorgan did not escape its ravages— a large proportion of the population of the country was wiped out. In addition large numbers of the strongest men had gone away to serve in the French wars where they received wages of 3d. per day or nearly three times as much as was paid to land workers in the manors around Cardiff.

This depletion of man power resulted in an excess of demand over supply of labour, and farmers were faced with demands from their men for higher rates of pay. Attempts to stabilize labour conditions and wages by legislative action met with but little success. The foregoing events led to a rapid break-up of the old system of agricultural economy. The manorial lords were forced to farm out more of their land for money payments, and the tenant farmer class came into existence. The shortage of labour led to the substitution of sheep-farming for arable cultivation, and this in return produced a movement for the enclosure of common lands.

At the beginning of the 15th century there was great discontent throughout Wales as a result of the economic strain and agrarian exploitation caused by the Black Death and heavy taxation, and this condition had no doubt much to do with bringing about the rebellion under Owain Glyndwr. His appeal to Welsh feeling found a ready response, and when, in 1402, he made his famous descent on Glamorgan he was warmly supported by a large section of the Welsh population against the English of the Vale.

This is not the place to relate the history of that disastrous raid, and I need only point out that, for nearly a hundred years following, the records of Glamorgan bear witness to the devastation caused by him. During this revolt Cardiff Castle, Caerphilly Castle and other strongholds including, possibly, Castell Coch and Whitchurch Castle, were destroyed. The ruins of certain ecclesiastical buildings at Llandaff also constitute a memorial to his ruthless activities. The whole of the countryside of Glamorgan and Monmouthshire was devastated. As late as 1492 the records of Cardiff refer to loss of revenue due to the fact that 'all the aforesaid houses were destroyed and burnt in the time of the Rebellion in Wales in byegone years.'

Local manorial records for this era are few and the entries scant. A *Minister's Account* for 1376 rendered by Thomas Brown, Receiver, reported of Whitchurch and neighbouring areas as follows:
"And he doth not answer for certain issues of the Manor of Whitchurche, of the Castle of Keryfilly, of the lands or tenements of Senghenith-supra-Caugh [Caiach] and Senghenith-subtus-Caugh, Enysvaiglon, and Rothery [Rudry] .... for that, long before his reception of the aforesaid office, they were delivered unto Elizabeth, who was the wife of the aforesaid Edward (i.e., le Despenser) by the name of her dower."

He also accounts "for 63/8 in respect of a certain pasture called Griffithes-more."

The territory known as Enysvaiglon (possibly *Ynis Faelgwn*, Maelgwn's meadow) has not been definitely identified, but was believed by the late J. S. Corbett to be the property known as the Ynys at the foot of Castell Coch.

Next comes a post-mortem inquisition of the reign of Henry VI after the death of Isabella, Countess of Warwick in 1440. This lady seems to have held the Lordship of Glamorgan in her own right in 1422-3, and afterwards in conjunction with her husband, Richard Beauchamp, Earl of Warwick, until her death in 1439. In the Inquisition she is declared *inter alia* to be Lord of 'the tribeland of Kibour'—the Welshery, comprising the greater part of the parishes of Lisvane and Llanedarne—and of the Manor of Radyr, Senghenydd Forest, Senghenydd-subtus-Caeach, Griffithsmore and 'The Castle and Manor of Album Monasterium, also called the Castle and Manor of Whitchurche with its appurtenances in the Marches of Wales.'"

Unfortunately manorial details are not given and there is no evidence to show whether the castle had been rebuilt. In all probability, however, as it was only a small structure and the castle was the manorial headquarters, it was in being at this time.

We now come to an interesting record of 1492 in the reign of Henry VII extracted from the *Records of the Duchy of Lancaster.* Jasper, Duke of Bedford, was Lord of Glamorgan and so Lord of the Manor of Whitchurch from 1486 to 1495. The 'Prevost of Whytchurche' at this time was Mathew Deio, and the following return by him is interesting on account of the large number of local placenames mentioned which have since disappeared from use. I have interpolated within brackets the modern renderings or short notes regarding some of these names.

"*Rents of Assize.* But he answers for 16/- rents of assize as well of freeholders as of bondmen and customars there, paid at the feast of Saint Michael, by the year. And for 7/- rent of David ap Llewelyn, smith, to have a watercourse, by the year . . . .

. . . . And for 2d. increased rent of Ieuan Prest, by the year . . .

. . . . And for 12d. increased rent of Ieuan ap Ivor ap Ieuan, for one acre and a half of demesne land in Lyttelham, by the year.

And for 12d. increased rent of Llewelyn ap Ieuan Ithell, for 3 acres of land late in the hands of David Voya, to him demised for the term of his life, beyond 18d. old rent previously charged in that title above.

Old Whitchurch

For 2d. rent of Walter ap David, to have license to turn a certain footpath beyond the 5 acres of demesne land called Tirecroft (Croft lands), he doth not answer here, because the aforesaid land lies in the lord's hands.

Nor does he answer for 2d. new rent of the said William for one plot taken from the lord's waste on the north side of the church there, because it lies vacant.

Sum 22/10.''

Other parcels named under the lordship of Whitchurch, but without further details of importance, are:
  Orchardland, 3 acres.
  Farm of the Mill called Res Mill.
  Farm of the fulling mill, with a parcel of land called Tristype.
  Fishing of the river Taff.
  Netherfurlonge, 23 acres.

Demesne.
  20 acres of land near the ford of Radure [Adjoining Old Radyr Road, Llandaff North].
  Tirebailly, 12 acres. [Tir y beili, the steward's land].
  Tir Clanamit, 19 acres. [Tir Calan-Mai, May-day land].
  Tireberthelane, 3 acres.
    [Tir y berllan, land enclosed by a hedge, orchard land. Possibly the same land as the first item mentioned above].
  Lands at Water Lane.
  Tireconynger, 41 acres [Tir y cwningod, coney land, rabbit warren].
  Tireveyne, 3 acres [This may mean 'stoney land,' 'a small piece of land' or 'infertile land'].
  Garden called Carthcreke.
  Caireparke, 21 acres. [Possibly the Park Fields. This was perhaps a part of the modern Tynyparc Farm].

The Account also mentions pasture land at Griffithsmore farmed out to Morgan ap John Gwyn.

The 'Res Mill' was probably Melingriffith with a temporarily changed name. I have already indicated that this mill was held during the early part of the 14th century by the famous Llywelyn Bren, who is referred to in historical records both as Llywelyn ap Gruffydd and Llywelyn ap Rhys.

The next record, a Minister's Account of 1515 by Mathew Cradock, gives summarised returns of local prevosts or bailiffs. Morgan ap John David, Prevost of Whitchurche, accounted for £6 12 3 received of Whitchurch Manor. The 'Farmer of Gruffithmore,' Lewis ap John Gwyn, paid 66/8 for his holding. A similar return was made in 1519 by Thomas ap Ieuan ap Llewelyn, Prevost of Whitchurche.

In the reign of Edward VI (1547) Lewis ap Guilim, 'Prevost of Whitchurche', returned as follows;

"*Rents of Free and Bound Tenants.* But he answers for 35/9½ rents of free and bond tenants there, to be paid at the term of 'Hokedaye' and of St. Michael Archangel equally . . . . .

Farm of the Demesne Lands. And for £10 5 6½ of the farm of all the demesne lands there, so demised unto divers tenants there.

Commorth. For 4/1 arising from a certain custom unto our lord the King among the tenants of this lordship falling in every other year, namely, this year he doth not answer; for that in the last preceding year it was charged, and ought to be charged again next year as (being) the second year."

'Commorth Calanmai' was a tribute of cattle paid by Welsh tenants to the lord about May 1, usually in alternate years.

In the 1547 Account separate renders appear for Senghenydd (Upper and Lower) and it would appear that the Manor of Whitchurch had not yet been merged in Senghenydd. At this time the Lordship of Glamorgan was vested in the King.

We now come in 1550-1 to an event which takes us away from medieval times and relates our narrative with the family which today still discharges the now more or less nominal functions of local manorial lordships. Edward VI had a high regard for a nobleman, Sir William Herbert, whom he created Earl of Pembroke and on whom he conferred the old Lordship of Glamorgan which had been in the hands of the Crown since the death of Jasper Tudor without heir in 1495. With the Lordship went Cardiff Castle and the several manors belonging thereto.

From William Herbert, first Earl of Pembroke, was descended Lady Charlotte Herbert, who married Thomas, Viscount Windsor. A grand-daughter of this couple was Charlotte Jane Windsor, and by her marriage to John, the first Marquis of Bute, in 1766, the Glamorgan estates of the Herberts, with the various lordships, became vested in the Bute family.

The grants of Edward VI to Sir William Herbert are on record in the *Calendar of Patent Rolls.* The following extracts relate only to the local properties which were included in this munificent royal gift made about 1550-1551.

"Higher Senghenith, Lower Senghenith, Whitchurche, Rudre, Rothe, Liqueth, ... Radure, Cardiff .... and all our castles of Cardiff, Avon, Kenfegge and Kaerfellye ... And all those our forests and lands and hereditaments called and known by the names of Tallavan forest, Senghenith forest, Mavon Ely forest [Taff Valley] and the Redde fforest [above Castell Coch] ...... as also all our messuages, lands, tenements, burgages and hereditaments whatsoever in Kaerfillye .... and also all that Our land and pasture and Our hereditament called Griffithsmore, now or late in the tenure of John Gwyn, lying and being in Kybor."

This John Gwyn returned 66/8 for his land at Griffithsmore. This possession of 'Griffithsmore in Kybor' was described as consisting of 8 acres in Enermore" amongst the lands of the Lord herbart, and the rest is near the 'causey' leading from Romney to Cardiff; containing by estimation 53 acres." Another entry in the same document relating to Whitchurch reads:

'Rents arising from a certain custom called 'Commorth' at 4/1 falling to our lord the King every other year, to be paid by the tenants of the lordship aforesaid; namely in the value of such Commorth in ordinary years here valued, etc., 2/-."

The passing of the manor of Whitchurch to Sir William Herbert, Earl of Pembroke, probably led to its discontinuance as a separate manor and to its merge in the manor or lordship of Lower Senghenydd, from which it was carved above 250 years earlier. We cannot be certain of the date or the circumstances surrounding the merge. An *Inquisition* of 1559 after the death of Sir George Mathew of Radyr, however, seems to indicate that by this date its absorption in Lower Senghenydd had been brought about.

"And further the Jurors say that the said George Mathews was seized of certain lands and tenements in Whitchurch in the county aforesaid, in his demesne as of fee, and held the same of William, Earl Penbroch as of his Manor or Lordship of Saighenith Subtus in, socage."

This, however, is not conclusive for in the *Margam Abbey Muniments* there is an inquisition of 1567 taken by a jury of the possessions of the Earl of Pembroke in Glamorgan, which mentions

'Lower Sengehenythe lordship and manor extending and consisting between the parishes of Llanvabon, Egloussilan and Ruddry, and also extending to the Parish of Whitchurch and to parts of the parishes of Michelston Wenllock, Maghen and Bedwes.

'Whitchurche lordship and manor.

Karfillie manor lying and extending in the parish of Egloussilan.

Griffithesmore being a certain parcel of land lying in the parish of Rothe.

Lystallabont Manor.

Keyboo (Kibbor) lordship."

In the foregoing record the mention as separate manors of Whitchurch and Caerphilly may not necessarily mean that they are distinct from the Lordship of Lower Senghenydd. They may have been regarded as sub-manors or members of the larger territorial unit, or they may have been mentioned separately in order to make it clear beyond doubt that these old historical divisions were the property of the Earl.

Another interesting document of this period—a *Post Mortem Inquisition* in the year 1595 of the possessions of Thomas Lewis of Van— seems to confirm the fact of the merge. Thus

"And moreover the jurors say . . . . . . (Thomas Lewis) was seized on the day of his death, of and in three hundred messuages, cottages and tenements lying in the several parishes of Whitchurch, Lanyssen, Lanedern (etc.) . . . . . ; and that all and singular the premises in . . . . Whitchurch are holden of the aforesaid Earl of Penbroke as of his manor or lordship of Seinhenith in free socage."

Another *Post Mortem Inquisition* after the death of Henry, Earl of Pembroke, in 1601 (Queen Elizabeth's reign) gives a list similar to that in the Inquisition of 1567 mentioned above, with Whitchurch Manor referred to separately from Lower Senghenydd. Gryffythes Moore', is also separately mentioned.

I will now give a few extracts from two 16th century writers who wrote of Whitchurch within a comparatively short period after the manor passed into the possession of Sir William Herbert. Rice Merrick, in *A Book of Glamorgan Antiquities* (1578) wrote:—
"It is said that to it belonged a customary Mannor in Whitchurch but now, by what means I could not learn the certainty, reputed a parcell of Semgenyth Suptus, and annexed to it."
This quaint old writer was a well-known county gentleman who owned and lived at Cottrell (St. Nicholas) and his authority on local manorial questions of that time should carry great weight. It is clear from the above extract that by 1578 the Manor of Whitchurch had definitely been merged in Senghenydd and it has ever since been administered as a parcel of that lordship.

In 1596 was written the *Breviat and Notes of Rice Lewis,** which deals with the lineage of the Earl of Pembroke and describes his possessions in Glamorgan. The following extract relates to Whitchurch:—
"Whitchurch wherein standeth the redde castle butteth to thest p'te of Pentirghe, and hath free tenants and leases, and hath Cardif theire m'kett and is distant thence right north ii miles.
'St. Heineth subtus' or lowe St. Heinith wherein standeth the redd castle, the chiefe house and dwelling of Yvor petites (Ivor Bach) and his p'decessors lo (lord): of the said L'ip of Kybur both before fitzhamon's tyme and longe after."

Here it is not directly stated, but it may be implied that Whitchurch was included in the manor of Senghenydd Subtus or Lower Senghenydd.

Another document relating to the *Great Baronies of Wales* (1630) has a reference to the Manor of Whitchurch, but in the *Survey of the Manor of Roath Keynsham* (1650 & 1702) areas of land known to have been in the Manor of Whitchurch are described as being in the Lordship of Lower Senghenydd.

A Memorandum on the Manors of the Marquis of Bute in Glamorgan was prepared by the late J. Stuart Corbett for the *Royal Commission on Land in Wales and Monmouthshire* and is reproduced in the Appendix to the Land Commission Report. According to Mr. Corbett, whose authority on this subject cannot be questioned, the old Manor of Whitchurch, as well as those of Rudry and Llanfedw, are regarded as "members of the Manor or Lordship of Senghenith Supra et Subtus," and not as independent manors.

On the whole, therefore, it seems safe to conclude that Whitchurch Manor ceased to exist as a separate entity soon after it passed to the Herbert family in 1550 and has since then been merged in the Lordship of Senghenydd.

SHORT LIST OF SOURCES.

G. T. Clark. Cartae et alia munimenta . . . . de Glamorgan,
G. T. Clark. Manorial Particulars of Glamorgan.
J. S. Corbett. Glamorgan Papers.
J. Griffiths. Edward II in Wales.
J. H. Matthews. Records of the County Borough of Cardiff.
Rice Merrick. A Book of Glamorgan Antiquities.
William Rees. South Wales and the March.

---

* This is a manuscript deposited at Cardiff Public Library, A part of it is printed in Cardiff Records, Vol. IV, pp. 130-7.

CHAPTER V.

THE INSURRECTION OF LLYWELYN BREN.

In a previous chapter the story has been told of the events which led to the Welsh Lordship of Senghenydd being brought under the direct domination of Cardiff Castle by Gilbert de Clare, Earl of Gloucester and Lord of Glamorgan. Senghenydd was then organised on feudal lines, a number of manors being created, each in charge of a bailiff who collected taxes and administered laws on behalf of the Lord of Glamorgan.

Earl Gilbert was a very astute man, and there is good reason to believe that once the menace of Prince Llywelyn had been removed he adopted a conciliatory attitude towards his Welsh subjects, and tried to reconcile them to foreign control by continuing many of the privileges and customs which they had enjoyed under native rule and also by appointing their Welsh leaders as bailiffs of the new manors which he created. It is not unlikely that when Gruffydd ab Rhys was deprived of his Lordship in 1266 he was after a time appointed Bailiff of the several manorial units, and that after his death his heir succeeded him in those offices.

The 'Red Earl' died in 1295, and left an infant son, Gilbert, as his heir. Until he attained the age of 16 (in 1307) the Lordship of Glamorgan was administered by his mother Joan and her second husband, Ralph de Monthermer. During the next seven years until his death at the Battle of Bannockburn in 1314 the young Earl Gilbert continued his father's policy of conciliation.

After his death without issue, the Lordship of Glamorgan reverted for a time to the custody of the weak and incapable King Edward II. Gilbert had three sisters, all of whom were married to powerful nobles who had ambitions to succeed to the extensive De Clare estates, and particularly to the Lordship of Glamorgan, for the possession of this lordship conferred great power on its holder who, as a Marcher Lord, was to a large extent independent of the Crown.

One of the claimants was the King's favourite, Hugh le Despenser, who had married Gilbert's sister Eleanor in 1306. This wily baron worked on the weaknesses of the feeble monarch, and was in effect, before he obtained legal possession, practically in control of the Lordship. On his advice the De Clare policy of conciliating the Welsh hillmen seems to have been abandoned.

The bailiewicks of the several manors in Senghenydd at this time appear to have been in the hands of an influential native gentleman, described in some accounts as Llywelyn ap Rhys and in others as Llywelyn ap Griffith, but known in all records as Llywelyn Bren. If, as seems likely, the correct name was the latter, then Llywelyn Bren was possibly a son of Gruffydd ap Rhys (of the line of Ifor Bach) the last Welsh Lord of Senghenydd. The title *Bren* is possibly a contracted form of *brenin* (a king) or, used adjectively, of *brenhinol* (royal), and means 'chieftain.'

The personal particulars regarding Llywelyn Bren are somewhat scanty. It is known that he was a man of considerable possessions and refinement. In addition to land he owned much livestock, clothing, jewellery, and books in the Welsh and French languages. He probably owned more than one residence, but there is little evidence to show where these were located. Rice Merrick, writing in 1578, in a note on the Parish of Eglwysilan, states

"Within this Parish, neare the River Taf, standeth yet the house of Lln Brenn."

If Merrick is correct the location of this house was probably between Nantgarw and Tongwynlais, and the most likely position was at or near the place called The Ynis, at the foot of Castell Coch, a house which is believed to have been long associated with the line of Ifor Bach. Up to a century ago this house was known as *Ynis y Llewod Duon* (The Black Lions Meadow), and it is worthy of note that the black lion was a prominent feature in the coat-of-arms of Gwaethfoed, from whom the Welsh Lords of Senghenydd descended.

Through Despenser's influence, the warden appointed by the King to administer Glamorgan, pending a settlement of the inheritance question, was an officer named Bartholomew de Badelesmere, who proved himself to be strongly anti-Welsh in sentiment and action, and he soon caused great offence to the hill Welshmen, and particularly to those of Senghenydd, by withdrawing the privileges which had been permitted to them by the late lords of Glamorgan.

The records commencing March, 1315, inscribed in the *Calendar of Close Rolls*, prove conclusively that De Badelesmere had pursued a policy of harassing the Welsh hill folk, and that his actions had to some extent alarmed the King and caused him to issue instructions for a reversal of Badelesmere's decisions. It is doubtful, however, whether the King's orders were carried into effect. There is evidence that Badelesmere's attitude had aroused the indignation of Welshmen all over Glamorgan, and this general quarrel gave added force to the personal quarrel which developed between Llywelyn Bren and the Royal official.

The general quarrel was due to a series of oppressive actions which affected the dignity as well as the material interests of the Welsh. In the first place demands were made on Welsh freemen which had been confined in the past only to villeins or serfs. Secondly, the few Welsh bailiffs had been deprived of their offices and a much larger number of English officials appointed in their stead who levied fines and imposed other feudal obligations in a most harsh and unjust manner.

Thirdly, the Welsh hostages imprisoned in Cardiff Castle had been disallowed the scale of maintenance from the revenues of the Glamorgan Lordship which had been permitted to them under the De Clare régime. These and similar factors caused disaffection in all the Welsh districts, and the discontented Welsh only awaited a leader to break into revolt.

We now come to the ground of Llywelyn's personal quarrel. A post-mortem inquisition after the death of Gilbert de Clare (the 'Red') in 1307 records the fact that in the Manor of Whitchurch—
"there is one water mill which Lewelyn ap Griffith holds to farm by lease of the aforesaid Ralph and Joan and it is worth by the year £4."

This was the manorial mill known as Melin Griffith to which all the Lord's tenants sent their corn to be ground, in return for the payment of a toll in money or in kind. This mill was a profitable source of revenue to Llywelyn. He also probably held similar mills in Senghenydd.

De Badelesmere had apparently deprived Llywelyn of these mills, and placed them in charge of officers who probably levied more onerous tolls on the Lord's tenants, and also of certain lands to which he was entitled by gift from De Clare. He had also turned him out of his offices as bailiff of certain manors, and had ejected him from the head-quarters of the bailiewick of Whitchurch (*i.e.* Whitchurch Castle).

Against these indignities and disabilities Llywelyn had apparently appealed to the King, who on March 14, 1315, issued a series of orders (still available in the *Close Rolls*) cancelling or modifying some of De Badelesmere's actions relating not only to Llywelyn but also to the general body of Welsh hillmen. Thus:

1. "Order to deliver to Lewelyn ap Griffith the site of a fort (fortelettum) in that land, called Blaunk Moustier, which has been newly built (*in novo edificatum*), to be held by him during the King's will, saving to the king the mill and other profits pertaining to the same, Lewelin having petitioned the king for the same and for the mill and profits."

2. "Order to cause one of the bailiewicks that Lewelin ap Griffith held in the time of Gilbert de Clare, late earl of Gloucester and Hereford, in those parfs, to be delivered to one of his sons when opportunity permits, if he find any one of his sons fit for the office, Lewelin having petitioned the King to this effect."

3. "Order to permit the said Lewelin to hold in peace land of the yearly value of 2 marks in a place called 'Egloswladys,' if he find that he was enfeoffed thereof by the aforesaid earl Gilbert in part satisfaction of 10 marks of land yearly, as he has shewn by his petition that the said keeper and his ministers of those parts distrain him to pay 2 marks yearly for the same; because they find the land in question extended to 2 marks yearly in the extents of the lands of those parts."

These instructions did not fully remedy Llywelyn's grievances, even if De Badelesmere had acted on them, which he seems not to have done except in part.

In regard to the petitions of the 'Welshmen of Morgannok' on the same date King Edward issued the following orders:—

1. "Order to cause the Welsh hostages in his custody to have reasonable maintenance out of the issues of that land, as they have been wont to have, the Welshmen of Morgannok having petitioned

the King and his council that the hostages and such as may hereafter be taken may have their maintenance as the hostages had in the times of Gilbert de Clare, late earl of Gloucester, and his ancestors, formerly lords of that land."

2. "Order to requit the men of Neeth of 200 marks of the ransom imposed upon them by the King's ministers of those parts for their insurrection after the death of the aforesaid Earl Gilbert, the King having pardoned them that amount in answer to their petition."

3. "Order to maintain the men of the parts of Glamorgan in the laws and customs that they used in the time of the aforesaid earl and his ancestors, as they complain that they are adjudged according to the said laws and customs,"

4. "Order to certify the King of the cause of the sale by the aforesaid Earl Gilbert, shortly before his death, of the dead wood in his wood of Seyghenyth, forbidding the said Bartholomew to sell the same without special order from the King, as the men of Seyghenyth have shown to the king that they had a profit called 'husebote' and 'keybote' of the dead wood in the said wood, and that, on account of the above sale, they cannot have the same unless it be taken from the vert."

These orders apparently conceded most of the claims both of Llywelyn ap Gruffydd in regard to his personal grievances and also those of the Welsh population generally, but it is probable that in practice they were not fully adjusted. De Badelesmere's hostility still continued, and his anti-Welsh officials still remained in office and administered in an oppressive manner.

Throughout the summer and autumn of 1315 there was general discontent throughout Glamorgan, and numerous disturbances took place. The position became so bad that in September Bartholomew de Badelesmere was recalled, and his office was filled by Payn de Turbervill, Lord of Coity Castle. This man, like Badelesmere, was probably a minion of the scheming Despenser, who was now trying to influence the King to hand over Glamorgan to himself and his wife.

Turbervill proved just as hostile to the Welsh hillmen as his predecessor, and it is probable that as a result of his attitude discontent waxed greater, and there was an increase in the number and seriousness of acts of resentment committed by the long-suffering Welshmen. Llywelyn's protests fell on deaf ears. Turbervill was given authority to remove bailiffs and appoint others, but it is probable that these, if appointed, were no more tactful and sympathetic than their predecessors.

Turbervill denounced Llywelyn and his wife to the King as inciters of disturbance, and there is a contemporary record that the King accused Llywelyn, whom he dubbed the 'Son of Death,'

"that he perpetrates and desists not from perpetrating many murders, depredations, burnings and other felonies by himself and his accomplices, in contempt of us and to our no little cost, and to the manifest terror of the people of these parts and against our peace."

Llywelyn attended the King's court in person to present his grievances and those of his compatriots, but was treated with discourtesy and contempt. He was summoned to appear before a Parliament to be held at Lincoln on January 27, 1316.

In despair of securing redress he returned to Glamorgan, and put himself at the head of a large body of hillmen, by whom he was held in the greatest esteem, and who were only awaiting his decision to break into open and concerted rebellion against the English rule. In making his decision he was fortified by the support of his doughty wife Lucy and six stalwart sons.

Llywelyn raised his standard possibly at Whitchurch or near Castell Coch, the last named stronghold at that time being in the King's hands, and from this gathering point his army, recruited from Welshmen throughout Glamorgan, marched to attack the almost impregnable Castle of Caerphilly, the constable of which at this time was Lord William de Berkeroles, Sheriff of Glamorgan.

At the time of the attack the constable was holding his court outside the walls of the castle. He was captured, and the rebels succeeded in burning and destroying the outer works, but failed to get access into the stronghold. The *Chronicles of Mathew Paris*, referring to this attack, indicts Llywelyn Bren that:

"with his accomplices, he there killed full twelve other Englishmen, who were there on behalf of our Lord, the King of England. And they imprisoned the said Sheriff and the Governor. And so began the war between the Englishmen and Welshmen in these parts."

The attack on Caerphilly was accepted as the signal for the rising of disaffected Welshmen all over Glamorgan. Llywelyn's forces increased until at one time, it is recorded, that he had no fewer than 10,000 behind him.

The rebellion extended throughout the whole of the De Clare territory from Neath to the Wye. The hillmen soon had the Vale of Glamorgan almost completely under their control. Attacks were made on most of the manorial castles, including St. George's, Sully, Barry, St. Athan, Kenfig, etc., and only the most powerful, such as Coity, De Turbervill's stronghold, remained uncaptured. According to a record contained in *Iolo MSS.* Llywelyn

"killed such numbers of English and Normans that no Englishman could be found who would as much as entertain for a moment the idea of remaining in Glamorgan."

The local English forces were helpless and for about nine weeks in the early part of 1316, the rebels held sway over Glamorgan. Great damage was done to property and crops, and an enormous amount of booty, particularly flocks and herds, was removed into the Welsh hill fastnesses.

The rebels seem to have directed particular attention to the destruction of mills, and the records show that such structures were destroyed at Whitchurch, Pentyrch, Llanfedw, Glynrhondda (5), Talyfan, Neath, Merthyr, Gelligaer and elsewhere. This feature of the rebellion is an indication of the hostility felt against that characteristic manorial incident known as 'suit of mill,' i.e., the compulsory grinding of corn at a Lord's mill, with the accompanying toll.

The destruction, however, was not confined to castles and mills. In some instances almost entire villages—in those days the building material most used was timber—were burnt, e.g., 90 burgages at Llantrisant, 23 at Caerphilly, 80 at Neath, particularly at villages adjoining the more powerful castles.

The effects of the rebellion on the economic life of Glamorgan were felt over a long period. Reference to the damage caused occurs in records many years after the date of the rebellion. The destruction of crops, and the dread of a recurrence of further attacks paralysed development for nearly half a century.

The rebels were not, however, to be allowed for long to exercise mastery over the Lordship of Glamorgan. The King took immediate steps to suppress the revolt. He appointed Humphrey de Bohun, Earl of Hereford and Essex, as commander of a large body of troops to be sent to the relief of Turbervill. De Bohun was assisted by Lord Mortimer of Wigmore and other leading nobles and also by Rhys ab Gruffydd, a West Wales chieftain.

In February orders were sent by Edward II to the Sheriffs of Hereford, Gloucester, Salop, Warwick, Cheshire, Worcester, Somerset, Dorset and other counties to furnish immediately horsemen and footmen and money and victuals for their maintenance to help Bohun to suppress the insurrection. A large and well-equipped army was soon assembled at Cardiff ready to march northwards, and a similar force at Brecon was preparing to come south.

The Cardiff contingent, comprising about 2,000 footmen and 150 men at arms, moved towards Caerphilly, but finding itself opposed on Thornhill, possibly at Castell Morgraig, by a large body of Llywelyn's men, they were obliged to alter their course, probably past Castell Coch. The siege of Caerphilly Castle, where Lady de Clare was confined, was raised, the rebels being driven off with great loss.

A collapse of the insurrection was inevitable in face of the powerful and superior equipped English Army. Simultaneously the King made various concessions with a view to winning over the less ardent supporters of Llywelyn's cause. Llywelyn himself, with the main body of his men, retreated northwards towards Ystradfellte. He realised that success was now impossible, and in spite of the protests of his followers, he decided to make terms rather than sacrifice their lives. A message was therefore sent to Bohun by Llywelyn offering to surrender if the lives of himself and his followers were spared.

De Bohun, however, would accept nothing but unconditional surrender, and on March 26, 1316, Llywelyn gave himself up to his baronial conquerors, by whom he was treated with the greatest respect and civility. It is probable indeed, that after his surrender De Bohun and Mortimer promised full forgiveness, not for love of Llywelyn, but because they feared lest his death would ensure to their crafty foe, Hugh Despenser, ultimate domination over Glamorgan.

The *Close Rolls* records of March, 1316, contain a document ordering "Llewelin Bren and his wife and children and others who lately rose against the King in Wales and then surrendered themselves to him, to be taken into safe custody at the King's expense to the Tower." On the same day Payn de Turbervill was ordered "not to take fines or ransomes for any of the chief promoters of the insurrection but to cause the bodies of such promoters to be taken under safe custody to the Tower."

During their stay in the Tower "Llewelyn Pren and Leukina his wife" were allowed 3d. each per day for their maintenance while their sons and other prisoners were each allowed 2d. Llywelyn was kept in the Tower until June, 1317, when he was released, his wife and sons being detained as hostages for his good behaviour.

The clemency shown to Llywelyn Bren was probably exercised on the advice of De Bohun, and it was probably on the representation of the same noble that Edward II dismissed Payn de Turbervill as Custos of Glamorgan, and appointed John Giffard de Brymmesfeld in his stead. To this officer was given authority to forgive those Welshmen who were still in revolt. In November, 1316, a general amnesty was declared upon payment of fines and ransoms. Many who could not pay were outlawed. Giffard was also instructed to lease mills and farms and to use the revenues for the reconditioning of damaged property.

During the period of Llywelyn's imprisonment in the Tower the power of Hugh le Despenser steadily increased. Soon after his release Despenser succeeded in his ambition of becoming Lord of Glamorgan in succession to Gilbert de Clare. This preferment gave him in Glamorgan what was equivalent almost to royal power over his subjects, and made him to a large extent independent of the King.

As he was to a large extent an absentee lord, the government of Glamorgan was left largely in the hands of his creature, Sir William Fleming, whom he made sheriff. Despenser now set about the task of consolidating his position not by winning the friendship of the Welsh, but by crushing them.

One of his first acts was to despoil Llywelyn and his friends of their lands and other possessions. He also ordered Llywelyn—in spite of the fact that he had received the King's forgiveness—to be seized and imprisoned in Cardiff Castle. Shortly afterwards he had him tried by Fleming, who sentenced him to death. The following extract from the *Chronicles of Mathew Paris* is a brief but illuminating record of the event:

"This year Leulin Bren was condemned at Kerdif, as he deserved; and afterwards he was drawn by horses as a traitor, then hanged, his entrails burnt and scattered, his limbs cut off and sent through the whole of Glamorgan to strike terror into the traitors."

Afterwards his remains, or such as were left, were interred in the Greyfriars Chapel at Cardiff, some relics of which still exist.

A just retribution for this judicial murder overtook Sir William Fleming, who some years later was tried and executed for his action against Llywelyn Bren. Rice Merrick (writing in 1578) in his "*Morganiae Archaiographia* has the following note on Fleming:

"When the fortune of Spencers' altered, his misfortune approached; for hee was executed at Cardiff, for that as it was supposed, hee had wrongfully adjudged Llewellen Brenn of Senighenith, to death, and, as it is said, caused a Jebet (gibbet) to be raysed by the Black Towre (Tower) within a little Wall that enclosed about the Prison, then called Stavell and oged (the harrow chamber), and there caused him to be hanged; for which cause (as some affirmeth) hee was attaynted by the Statute of Rutland . . . . This Sir William Fflemynge was buried in the White (*sic*, Grey) ffryars without the North gate of the Towne of Cardiff, whose Tombe in a faire Stone, at the Suppression thereof, together with Llen Brenn his Tombe, made of wood, was defaced."

The murder of Llywelyn Bren was also an important factor in the downfall of Hugh Despenser and the deposition and murder of the ill-fated Edward II. South Wales had been well-disposed toward the king; the treatment of Llywelyn Bren alienated its affections, and some years later when he fled to South Wales for refuge and help, he was unable to find succour. The murder of Llywelyn and the continued dispossession of his widow and sons of their land and other property by Despenser had turned the Welshmen's affection and respect for the King to bitter hate.

Moreover, the friendship of De Bohun and Mortimer for the Senghenydd chieftain won over the Welsh to support the cause of the Barons against the King and his greedy and unscrupulous favourite. In 1321 the Barons submitted to Parliament an indictment of Hugh Despenser, in which the most damaging clause had relation to his treatment of Llywelyn Bren.

The following extract from the *Close Rolls* gives the relevant clause:—

"Also whereas the Earl of Hereford and the Lord of Wygemor were assigned by the King's order to go to war against Thlewelyn Bren, who had risen against the Lord of Glamorgan, whilst the lands were in the King's hands by the death of the Earl of Gloucester, the said Thlewelyn rendered himself to the said lords at the king's will, and the said lords promised him grace and received him under such condition and delivered him to the king, and the king received him in such form, and afterwards, whilst the said lords were out of the land, the said Hugh and Hugh who had accroached royal power as is aforesaid, took the said Thlewelyn and sent him to Kaerdif, after Sir Hugh, the son, was seised of his purparty there, and seizing jurisdiction, by their conspiracy where in this case they could have no jurisdiction according to reason, feloniously caused him to be there drawn, hanged, beheaded and quartered, for a thing done in the King's time, and so seizing royal power and jurisdiction that pertaineth to the Crown, in disinheritance of the Crown, and dishonour of the King, and of the said lords of Hereford and Mortimer."

After this indictment Despenser was forced to leave the country only to return later to share the doom of the ill-starred King. With this story, however, we are not here concerned.

It is necessary, however, to record that after the deposition of the King and Despenser in 1327 an order was issued restoring to Llywelyn's sons the lands and other possessions of their father 'of which they had been fraudulently dispossessed by the younger Hugh le Despenser.' It may be surmised that some of these lands continued for hundreds of years in the possession of their descendants, who in more recent times were known as the Lewises of Van, Llanishen, Greenmeadow, etc., and include at the present day the Earl of Plymouth.

SHORT LIST OF SOURCES.

Rev. Banks. King Edward II in South Wales (*Arch. Camb.*, 1887).
G. T. Clark. The Land of Morgan.
J. S. Corbett. Glamorgan Papers.
J. C. Davies. The Despenser War in Glamorgan (*R. H. S. Trans.*, 1914).
John Griffiths. Edward II in Wales.
H. H. Knight. Insurrection of Llewelyn Bren (*Arch. Camb.*, 1851).
J. Hobson Matthews (Ed.). Cardiff Records.
Rice Merrick. Morganiae Archaiographia (Glamorgan Antiquities).
William Rees. Caerphilly Castle.
J. F. Tout. Llywelyn ap Rhys (Llywelyn Bren) (*Dict of National Biography*).

CHAPTER VI.

THE PARISH CHURCH.*

The present Parish Church of St. Mary, Whitchurch, was opened in 1885, and superseded a much older church (demolished in 1904), which stood in the now disused burial ground in Old Church Road. The latter church was itself probably a 17th century reconstruction of a much older structure on the same site.

The earliest reference to a religious institution at Whitchurch occurs in a 12th century record entitled the Concord of Woodstock in the *Book of Llandav.* This document recounts the terms of settlement in 1126 of a dispute which had arisen between Urban, Bishop of Llandaff, and Robert, Duke of Gloucester and Lord of Glamorgan, regarding the rightful ownership of certain 'lands and other properties.

One of the items of the agreement vested in the Bishop the Chapelry of Stuntaf and the tithes of that township and all the land which the Earl allotted for the maintenance of a priest to serve the chapelry. The residents of Stuntaf were secured the right of burial at Llandaff, and were to attend the Mother Church at Christmas, Easter and Pentecost. *Stuntaf* (or *Ystum Taf,* the bend in the Taff) is generally identified as that portion of Whitchurch adjacent to the great curve in the river, viz., Melingriffith, and it is possible that there was an ecclesiastical institution, perhaps a monastic settlement (connected with Llandaff), in that locality in pre-Norman days. It seems clear from this record that there was at any rate a chapelry, with a place of worship at Whitchurch in the 12th century if not earlier, and in all probability between that period and the present day the church has had a continuous existence.

The only piece of definite evidence establishing this fact, however, prior to the last years of the 15th century, is to be found in the medieval name for Whitchurch. The name appears in various records in the Latin form *Album Monasterium* and in the Norman-French form *Blancminster,* names which denote "white minster or church." It was applied to the Manor of Whitchurch formed about 1266, and the first record of the name I know of occurs in a manorial document of 1295-6.

The headquarters of this manor were established in a small castle erected at a spot near the disused burial ground in Old Church Road, and I surmise that the first church was built near the castle about the time of the creation of Whitchurch Manor, or, alternatively and more probably, that the site of the castle was selected on account of its proximity to the church. The name of the church and local village

---

* This chapter is a very brief summary of the history of St. Mary's, which I have recorded in greater detail in my book *Album Monasterium.*

St. Mary's Church, Whitchurch

Old Parish Church, 1902 *W. Morgan Davies*

Porch of Old Parish Church, 1902 *W. Morgan Davies*

probably existed before the creation of the manor. The first reference within my knowledge to the existence of a church at the Old Church Road occurs incidentally in a document of 1492.

Whitchurch continued to be a chapelry of Llandaff until 1845, and services were conducted at the local church by the Vicars Choral of Llandaff. Until the early part of the 17th century it was a chapel of ease and "hath neyther christenyng nor buryall." In 1616, however, its status was advanced by the grant to it of a licence for the celebration of christenings, marriages and burials.

In the 16th century if not earlier the chapel seems to have been reconstructed on the same site. It may be from the fact of this new structure that Whitchurch derived its Welsh name *Eglwysnewydd* (New Church). This name was used by Leland in 1536 and was probably in existence much earlier, although no evidence is available. It may indeed have been applied to the church and locality, where, as I have already supposed, a new church was built on the site after the creation of the manor.

Whitchurch was a sparsely populated agricultural area comprising 50-60 small farms and cottages accommodating about 250 people up to the advent of the Melingriffith Works. By 1801 its population had increased to 696, and as before that year there were no dissenting churches in the locality the need for increased accommodation had arisen. This was met about 1784-5 by the erection of an internal gallery.

In 1845 Whitchurch was created an independent ecclesiastical parish with a perpetual curacy and endowed patronage vested in the Bishop. The first vicar was Rev. E. P. Thomas. During his incumbency, Tongwynlais was made a chapel of ease to St. Mary's. Temporary buildings were used for purposes of worship until 1876-7, when St. Michael's Church was built.

Mr. Thomas retired in 1867 and was succeeded in July, 1869, by Rev. D. T. Davies, M.A. The latter died in September, 1875. Next came Rev. J. T. Clarke, M.A., who served the parish for 28 years. Through his efforts the present St. Mary's Church was built and consecrated in 1885. The old church was now not much used and fell into a bad state of repair; ultimately in 1904 it was demolished.

Mr. Clarke died in June, 1903, and a few months later was succeeded by Rev. Llewelyn Lloyd Davies. During his incumbency in 1911 the subsidiary mission Church of St. Thomas was built in Pantbach Road to serve the Birchgrove district. As a result of his activities a commodious Church Hall was also built at Whitchurch in 1908.

Rev. Henry Williams, of Pentyrch, was inducted in succession to Mr. Davies, who died in March, 1914, and during his incumbency extensions and improvements were effected to St. Mary's in 1920. Mr. Williams died in December, 1924, and in the following April the present vicar, Rev. Emrys Rees, B.A., was preferred to the incumbency. By this year a great building boom had developed in Whitchurch and the considerable increase of population during succeeding years called for increased accommodation. In 1926 a movement was set afoot for the provision of a branch church at Rhiwbina. Funds were accumulated over a series of years, and in September, 1931, All Saints' Church was completed and consecrated for public worship. Two years later the building was extended.

Since the constitution of the parish in 1845 there have been two adjustments of ecclesiastical parish boundaries. In August, 1902, after the completion of All Saints' Church, Llandaff, the Llandaff North portion of Whitchurch was detached and transferred to the ecclesiastical parish of Llandaff. A further curtailment took place in August, 1921, when the chapelry of Tongwynlais was converted into a separate ecclesiastical parish with St. Michael's as the Parish Church.

CHAPTER VII.
LOCAL ANTIQUITIES.

Although, as I have shown, Whitchurch has existed for many centuries and has been associated with some events of historical importance there are few visible antiquities or structures of fame in existence to-day. It will be well, nevertheless, to place on record a note of such places or objects as exist or have existed in order that posterity with its wider range of knowledge and vision, fortified by such additional local material as may yet be discovered, can properly assess their importance in the sphere of historical knowledge.

Let us, then, commence with the Roman Era. It has now been established that Roman forts existed at Cardiff and Gelligaer, and as vestiges of a Roman road exist at points between these two stations it may safely be surmised that this road extended over the Cibwr or Cefn Onn range into Cardiff. The course of this road has, however, not yet been determined. It may have passed over Y Ddrainen (Thornhill) near Castell Morgraig, or, as some have surmised, over Rhiwbina Hill, but no proof of either route has yet been obtained.

Nevertheless, there is reason to believe that a Roman Camp or station or villa existed on Rhiwbina Hill, as, from time to time, Roman relics have been unearthed. Writing in the *Bulletin of Celtic Studies* (Vol. I, page 73), Dr. Mortimer Wheeler states:—

"In Glamorganshire, in cutting back the top of the quarry, three-quarters of a mile north of Rhiwbina, Cardiff, Roman poetry, tiles and coins have been found from time to time, but no foundations seem to have been observed. The pottery, now in the National Museum of Wales, includes second-century Samian and a fragment apparently of an early third-century Samian vessel with applied reliefs. The three bronze coins inspected are of Trajan, Antonine, and a third-century (radiate) emperor, the two latter undecipherable. It may be noted that this evidence of Romano-British occupation is one of several observed from time to time around Cardiff."

The site on Rhiwbina Hill where these relics were found is to-day locally known as Llewelyn's Quarry, but is properly named the Gelli Quarry. It stands at the end of a ridge and commands a wide view in several directions, and its situation marks it out as an obvious position for a small camp or fort or signal station, or possibly a residence.

There was a tradition at Whitchurch of the existence of a Roman Camp. In a printed document of 1871 issued by a local committee reference is made to an alleged statement by "a gentleman of the neighbourhood who lived in the time of Elizabeth" to the effect that the old church was "a small building situate on what was once a Roman encampment." In a scrap book, belonging to a member (Eli Evans) of the committee mentioned above, Whitchurch is described about 1860 as "a place eminent for its Tumulus, its Roman Fort, its Haematite, its Sheet Iron, its Tin Plates, its Pork and its Potatoes."

The supposed 'Roman Fort' was within a stone's throw across the Old Church Road from a later Norman motte castle, and on the older Ordnance Survey Maps the site is legended 'Supposed Remains of Roman Station.'

In an old Tredegar Estate map made about 1760, a copy of which I possess, there are markings which seem to indicate part of the boundaries of a rectangular camp, which includes the site of the old churchyard. The northern limit is just without the curtilage of the house known as *The Pines*, the western limit extends approximately along the drive leading to that house, and the southern and eastern limits are probably defined by Tynypwll and Old Church Road (upper part) respectively. The field outside the northern boundary was significantly named *Cae'r Moat* (the Moat Field). According to old inhabitants, where now stands a block of cottages adjoining the east side of the Central Bakery and backing to the old churchyard formerly existed a raised bank which was known as *The Mount*. In 1877-8 the Llandaff Highway Board carried out an improvement in the Old Church Road, and David Llewelyn, the contractor, in the account rendered by him to the Board describes the work as "removing a corner of *The Twyn* (mound) near the Church." These facts do not, of course, establish the existence of a Roman work in the locality, but they do seem to suggest that something very much like a military construction was at one time in being in this locality.

Adjoining the old quarry near the summit of The Wenallt is an ancient earthwork assigned by some to the Iron Age and by others to the Danish period. Here is a description of this camp written by Dr. Mortimer Wheeler, by whom a plan was prepared which is now on the walls of the National Museum of Wales:—

"On the south spur of the Wenallt, two miles north of Whitchurch, Cardiff, Dr. D. R. Paterson has discovered a small oval earthwork, about half an acre in extent. It is tilted over the brow of the hill towards the south, at a height of 600 feet above sea-level, and commands a very extensive view across the low-lying coast country. On the north it is cut off from the back of the ridge by two or more ramparts with intervening ditches, but much quarrying has obscured the outer works. An opening on the south probably marks the original entrance. The general character and site of the work closely resemble those of the westernmost 'camp' on Hardings Down, Gower."*

Dr. Paterson claimed that this camp was of Norse origin (page 75), that from it was derived the place-name Kibbor or Kibor, from the Scandinavian words *kip* (a pointed hill or jutting point) and *borg* (a fort or fortified height) or *bord* (a ridge).

Dr. Paterson's theory, however, seems unlikely. The Wenallt Camp is obviously sited for the purpose of resisting attacks up the hill from the Coastal Plain. It may be assumed that as the Norse invasion was from the sea they would first have occupied the plain and driven the British into the hill territory.

* B.B.C.S., Vol. I, p. 75.

If the Norsemen had taken the Wenallt and wished to hold it they would obviously have selected a site for a camp at a higher point better suited for repulsing attacks from the north. It seems more likely that the camp was a native military work constructed for the purpose of resisting the sea-rovers or some other earlier alien enemy making for the interior.

"Three hundred feet below the Wenallt, on a smaller but similar ridge," proceeds Dr. Wheeler, "is the motte known as The Twmpath, which is of interest as presumably a later solution of the same military problem." For a long period this mound on the Ynisyrysgallenfraith Farm was regarded as the burial place of an ancient Welsh tribal chief, but today the view is generally accepted that it was a military work of the Norman period constructed for the purpose of guarding the pass leading from the hill region into the Coastal Plain.

It was the policy of the Normans to protect their territory as they acquired it by the erection of small forts at strategic points; many of these were abandoned after more permanent works had been provided or when the need for protection had passed. Such hastily-built works were usually of the 'motte' type. The motte (*French*, a clod of earth) was a large mound of earth, on the summit of which was built a wooden keep. Mottes varied in height from 15 to 50 feet,—few, however, exceed 30 feet, and all of course were surrounded by a deep, wide ditch. The timbered keep was round or polygonal. Around the foot of the mound on the inner edge of the ditch was erected a strong timber stockade called the *palitum*, whilst often the outer bank was provided with another defence called the *herico*. This consisted sometimes of an actual hedge of thorns or brambles, but usually it was formed of stakes intertwined with osiers and prickly shrubs.

In most cases on one side of the motte outside the ditch was a large oval-shaped space enclosed by a fence or a surrounding bank and ditch, which enclosure was known as the *bailey*. This served as an outer defence in case of attack. The motte castle was connected with the bailey by a wooden bridge carried on supports from the gate of the keep to a point outside the herico. The bailey of The Twmpath, if ever one existed, has long since been obliterated as a result of farming operations, but the motte and the remains of its surrounding ditch still exist.

A comparison of The Twmpath with the mound and keep of Cardiff Castle and of other castles in South Wales, built by the Normans, shows a marked resemblance. The Welsh, however, sometimes copied Norman military methods, and where ancient works occur at points on the border-line between Norman and Welsh influences it is difficult to state definitely who were responsible for the construction. In this case, however, the balance of probability lies with the Normans, who wished to guard against the influx of the Welsh hillmen into their territory around Cardiff.

It may be well to point out here that an effort was made nearly a century ago to explore The Twmpath, on the assumption that it was a burial-mound, but without any conclusive results. The following reference to the excavation occurs in the report of the proceedings of the Cambrian Archaeological Association at Cardiff in 1849.*

"F. Fox, Esq., who had kindly undertaken to superintend the opening of the tumulus at Whitechurch (for which a special subscription of £10 had been raised) announced to the meeting the results of his excavation. It had been opened to the centre, and even further, and they had met with a black peaty matter, excessively offensive, about two feet in depth; in this there was something like a piece of iron. The grass and broom on the original surface of the ground were quite green at first, but were discoloured upon being exposed to air."

A Norman military structure of a similar type to the Twmpath seems also to have existed in the Whitchurch Old Village, but there is no evidence as to when and by whom it was first erected. It may have been built during the early period of the Norman conquest of Glamorgan, when Whitchurch was probably the scene of many hard-fought struggles between Normans and Welsh. In a later century, however, if not an entirely new structure, it was adopted by Gilbert de Clare as the administrative headquarters of his newly formed Manor of Whitchurch.

This manor was carved out of Senghenydd soon after 1266, and it may be that a motte castle was erected about the same period as Castell Coch and Caerphilly (1268-1271), but whether or not on an existing motte it is not now possible to say. It seems certain, however, that the mound, the flattened-out remains of which may still be seen in the garden of the house called Treoda in Old Church Road, was the site of a stone-built tower, which is referred to in 14th century records as Whitchurch Castle.

According to G. T. Clark the tower was circular, and its base was in the style of the castles of Fonmon and Coity. The tower is said to have been of considerable diameter, and the bas mouldings were of the Early English period. Clark, writing in 1883, states that enough remained of it a score of years previously to declare its approximate dates.†

The first authenticated reference to it occurs in a post-mortem inquisition of 1314, when mention is made of it as having been 'burnt in the war," possibly a Welsh revolt of 1294. In 1315 Edward II ordered that the "'forcelettum de Blancminster" should be put in charge of Llywelyn Bren, an order which does not seem, however, to have been obeyed. In all probability Whitchurch Tower was later restored and was the headquarters of the Lord of Glamorgan's bailiff or steward.

A record of 1348-9 mentions the "castle with a ditch around it and a barton annexed" and as late as 1440 reference is made to the "Castle and Lordship of Whitchurch with the appurtenances." If, however, as has been suggested, the Castle was one of those destroyed by Owen Glyndwr at the beginning of the 15th Century this reference may only be to its ruins.

---

* It is not clear from the extract whether the 'tumulus' was the Rhiwbina 'Twmpath' or the Castle Mound at Whitchurch.
† See *The Land of Morgan*, p. 134, also *Manorial Particulars of Glamorgan* (Arch. Camb. 1877).

No information, however, is available as to how or when it was destroyed, but there is clear evidence that it was not in use in the 16th century.

Thus John Leland the Antiquary, about 1539, wrote the following description which makes up for inaccuracy of fact in regard to distances by quaintness of spelling and phraseology:

"A 2 miles from this hille by south, and a 2 miles from Cairdif, be *vestigia* of a pile or maned place decayed at Egluis Newith in the paroch of Landaf."*

Later in the same century in 1578 Rhys Merrick stated that there "stood, in the East part of the Church an old Castle or Pyle, but now decayd, that scarce the foundacion and Rubish now remayneth. It is said that to it belonged a customary Mannour in Whitchurch."†

Another but more substantial military monument is the picturesque Red Castle which is situated on the southern edge of the Red Forest overlooking the village of Tongwynlais. This castle is an almost perfect restoration of an ancient medieval structure which had lain in ruins for centuries until the Marquess of Bute undertook its reconstruction nearly seventy years ago.

Like Whitchurch and many other small castles Castell Coch has but little recorded history, but it was not so badly ruined that its form, its details, and its dimensions could not be ascertained with a high degree of accuracy. The reconstruction was carried out with great care, and received very high praise from a leading authority on castle architecture, G. T. Clark,‡ who wrote of it:

"The restoration is very complete indeed, in excellent taste, and in strict accordance with what has been ascertained of the original structure."

Castell Coch, therefore, as it exists today, may be accepted as a typical example of a hill or border castle of the late 13th and early 14th century period.

The assumption that Castell Coch was built by Ifor Bach, the doughty little Welsh Lord of Senghenydd of the middle 12th century, is incorrect, in so far at any rate as the present structure is concerned, although it may be possible that there was an earlier Welsh stronghold on the site of which no traces have been discovered. It is more probable, however, that the native fortress, if such ever existed, was in Fforest Goch, on the eminence, a couple of hundred feet higher, which overlooks the present building. The evidence for the supposed existence of an earlier fortress in the locality is not very strong.

The reasons favouring the supposition may be summarised as follows. First the locality is on the great ridge which separates the hill country from the Coastal Plain, and G. T. Clark supposed that during the period of the Danish Invasions the Cymry had a stronghold here from which they resisted the Norse incursions into the hill territory, after they had marauded the Vale. He supposes that the warriors here

---

* *Toulmin Smith. Leland's Itinerary in Wales.*
† *Glamorgan Antiquities.*
‡ *Medieval Military Architecture.*

encamped could see the ships of the Scandinavian invaders sailing up the Bristol Channel, and that beacon fires would be lighted up on Penarth Head, and at Fforest Goch or on The Garth to summon native warriors to the defence of their territory and possessions.

Clark's theory was based on evidence of the supposed existence of a Cymric Camp in the Forest. 'Across the north-east side," he writes, "lines of circumvallation have been hewn out of the rocks, the dimensions of which show the value attached to the place, as a fortress, by the Cymry." These apparently are the traces of banks and ditches indicated on the Ordnance Survey Map as 'Intrenchments.' and which still exist above the 400 and 500 feet contour lines. They are, however, so scanty and indefinite that it is doubtful whether any certain conclusion could be derived from the closest examination of the remains.

Some writers have assumed that these ditches are the remains of Ifor Bach's stronghold. It will be remembered that after the Norman invasion of Glamorgan the Welsh were driven from the Coastal Plain into the hill districts where they were allowed to live in their own way and subject to their own laws and customs, with little interference from their foreign conquerors. In all probability they did not accept their subjugation without protest, and it seems likely that the areas adjoining the approaches to the hill territories were frequently subject to forays from the North. Whitchurch was approached from Senghenydd by passes along the valleys of the Taff and its tributaries, the Gwynlais and Nofydd, and it may, therefore, reasonably be supposed that this locality was the scene of many a hard-fought skirmish between Normans and Welshmen.

It would be the aim of the Welshmen to regain a footing in the plain, and of the Normans to retain what they had won. The Kibbor Ridge was naturally held by the Cymry and it is reasonable to suppose that they would have strongholds at vital points along the ridge for the protection of the accesses to their territories. Fforest Goch would be an ideal position for such a stronghold, as its commanding position enabled it to control not only the main gateway into Senghenydd by way of the Taff, but also the subsidiary entrance through Cwm Gwynlais.

It is an historical fact that Ifor Bach in 1158 raided Cardiff Castle and carried off Earl William, Lord of Glamorgan, with his wife and son, into the woods and held them there until his demands were conceded. Few details are available, however, of this spectacular exploit, and I know of no evidence to support the suggestion, however probable it may seem, that Ifor set forth on this deed of daring from a stronghold at or near Castell Coch, and that it was in this locality that the proud Norman family were retained in captivity.

The circumstances that led to the erection by the Norman-English Lords of Glamorgan of Castell Coch may be summarised as follows. In 1266 Gilbert de Clare, the 'Red Earl,' Lord of Glamorgan, dispossessed Gruffydd ap Rhys of his Lordship of Senghenydd, possibly because he feared that the Senghenydd Welshman showed leanings towards Llywelyn ap Gruffydd, who was aiming to unite Wales under his leadership. To safeguard still further his position Gilbert decided to build a number of new strongholds on the borders of and within the appropriated territory, at Merthyr, Caerphilly, Tongwynlais and possibly at Whitchurch.

Castell Coch was probably commenced in 1267 or 1268 and was completed some time before the Castle of Caerphilly. From the evidence obtained by examination of the ruins, however, it appears that certain improvements were carried out at a later date, e.g., the erection of a gatehouse and the thickening of the curtain wall. These additions, however, were made at no distant period—probably within a few years of the completion of the original structure. They may, indeed, have been suggested by the attack made on Caerphilly in October, 1270.

There is no record that Castell Coch was attacked by Prince Llywelyn's forces, and it does not figure in the accounts of the controversy which arose over Llywelyn's claim to the Lordship of Senghenydd. Indeed, I know of only one specific reference to it in medieval records, and that occurs in a post-mortem inquisition of 1307, in which *Rubeum Castrum* is mentioned as one of the members of Senghenydd, and the demesne of arable land (26 acres) was declared to be worth 4/4 a year or 2d. per acre, and another parcel of 16 acres was stated to be worth 2/- or 1½d. per acre, the total value being 5s. 4d. This land was seemingly that comprised within the present-day Castle Farm.

The details of its destruction are equally as meagre as those of its construction. It seems likely, with other strongholds in Glamorgan, to have been attacked (and possibly taken) by Welsh insurgents during the Revolt of 1295 and the Rising of Llewelyn Bren in 1315, but there is no record to support this assumption. Neither is there any definite evidence to support G. T. Clark's suggestion that it was put to ruin by Owen Glyndwr, who in 1404 "is supposed to have descended by this pass when he burned the episcopal palace of Llandaff and ravaged Cardiff."

When the ruins were being excavated prior to the restoration evidence was obtained showing that destruction had been effected by means of mines and fire, a fact which seemed to indicate that this took place at any rate after the invention of gunpowder about the second quarter of the 14th century. As, after the advent of Edward I to the throne, the necessity for Welsh castles for military purposes had practically disappeared, Castell Coch, like Caerphilly, ceased to fulfil its normal function, and it is probable that no attempt was made to rebuild it, after the onslaught by Glyndwr, if indeed he was the warrior responsible for its destruction.

We can, at, any rate, say definitely that Castell Coch was in ruins during the 16th century. John Leland in his *'Itinerary'* (1536-9) refers to it in the following terms:

"Castelle Gogh stondith on a high Rok of a redde Stone or Soile a 2 Miles from Landaf upper on Tave; a Quarter of a Mile from the Est Ripe of Tave."

"Castelle Gough al yn Ruine no bigge thing but high. It longith to the King and standith by Keven On."

Four decades later, in 1578, Rise Merrick wrote:

"In the Edge of a Mountaine northward standeth an old Castle or Pyle, called Castle Coch, supposed to be builded by Yvor Petit, a Gentleman issueing of Kidyvor ap Kidrich, who, as Geraldus Cambrensis testifyeth, tooke Wm. Lord of Glamorgan, etc. To whose Sonne named Sir Gilbert de Clare, his successor, gave his daughter in marriage, etc."

Thus in ruins stood Castell Coch for several centuries, providing material for numerous tales and sayings of mystery and adventure, many of them centred around the legendary figure of Ifor Bach. In the early part of last century it began to attract the attention of the archaeologists, and in 1850 it was subject to a close exploration by G. T. Clark, who published a minute description of it in *Archaeologia Cambrensis*.*

On Clark's report the following brief description of the plan of the Castle is based. Clark suggests that on account of its difficulty of access the Norman engineer rejected the site of the Cymric camp for a site "lower down the scarp, though still above the plain" where there was "a natural platform on the limestone rock, separated from the main scarp by a natural depression, and sufficiently removed from the summit to be out of reach of the military engines with which the Welsh were likely to be acquainted, or which, from their want of organisation, they were likely to be able to bring, with their forces, against the Castle."

This site was easily approached from the east by a road "which probably communicated with the old road called Roman, and no doubt Cymric, which leads direct from Cardiff to Rhiwbina." The platform was 200 yards long and 70 yards broad and the principal portion of the castle was built at its west end. On the south side of the platform the land fell away steeply for a depth of 20 or 30 feet, so forming a natural protection against attack from that quarter.

The main buildings of the castle were disposed in triangular fashion with a drum tower at each angle, but as two of the towers farthest removed from one another were connected by a semi-circular curtain wall, the general plan of the complete fortress was roughly circular.

Each of the three cylindrical towers contained three stories, the middle one of which was in line with the circular inner court, and the lowest below the level of that court. Each of the towers was roofed with Welsh stone tiles. The walls of the towers varied from 2ft. 6ins. to 10 feet thick, and the over-all diameter in each case was about 40 feet. In the walls of the towers were loop-holes for military operations. The Western Tower seems to have been used for cooking and other domestic purposes and for that reason is also today known as the Kitchen Tower.

Between it and the South Tower or Keep extended the Hall, a rectangular vaulted chamber about 31 feet by 18 feet, the outer wall of which was seven feet thick and pierced by three loop-holes. These two towers and the hall rose from the edge of the steep bank and must in those days have been impregnable from attack on that side.

The North Tower, also called the Well Tower, stood at only about 28 to 30 feet away from the Keep, as measured within the Inner Court. Adjoining the Keep, however, was another structure known as the

---

* J. S. Corbett has some useful notes on Castell Coch in *Cardiff Naturalist Society Transactions*, 1917.

Gatehouse, which guarded the main entrance to the Castle, and which is today approached by a drawbridge, the gateway itself being further strengthened by a massive portcullis.

Extending between the North Tower and the Kitchen Tower was a massive curved curtain wall about 80 feet long measured on the outer side with a chord of about 60 feet. This and the buildings referred to enclosed the Inner Court. The curtain was pierced with loops, and above was a rampart walk linking up the two towers. Further artificial protection to this part of the stronghold was provided by means of a deep dry moat which extended from the Keep around the North Tower as far as the Kitchen Tower.

Outside the castle proper was an Outer Court approximately 100 feet by 40 feet which was defended on the south side by the declivity already mentioned, and on the landward side by an extension of the moat. This outer court formed the first line of defence of the Castle and it was not until this had been captured that the defending force retired within the Castle proper.

G. T. Clark held a high opinion of the strength of this fortress. He wrote:

"No doubt, before brave men, all defences fail; and the Welsh, who certainly were not wanting in courage, did, according to tradition, more than once take this castle, probably by surprise and escalade; nevertheless, it was a very strong fortress, both by nature and art, and must have been a sore thorn in the side of the mountaineers of Glamorgan."

In 1551 Castell Coch passed with the Lordship of Glamorgan by gift of Edward VI to Sir William Herbert, afterwards Earl of Pembroke, and later, by marriage of a female descendant of the Herberts, into the Bute family. It was by the direction of the third Marquess of Bute, who took a keen interest in native military architecture, that the admirable restoration of this ancient structure was achieved. This work was carried out in 1871-2 by Mr. W. Burges, A.R.A., who also did some very fine work at Cardiff Castle.*

As G. T. Clark pointed out a substantial portion of the Early English structure still survived at the middle of last century, sufficient at any rate to enable the main elements of the building to be clearly appreciated. Every part of the original structure was represented. Two or three towers were perfect and one vertical half of the third still stood. The walls of the Hall also, as well as the vaulted chamber beneath, and the greater part of the Curtain Wall, the well, and the dungeon were all in being. The task, therefore, was not one of rebuilding but of restoration, and from the remains of the worst-damaged portions found in the moat and elsewhere, it was possible without great difficulty to detect the main details of the design, and to give expression to it in the very charming building which delights the eyes of all passers-by.

As far as it is possible to judge Castell Coch stands today exactly as it stood over six centuries ago, except for the elaborate interior

---

* For further structural details see *Archaeologia Cambrensis*, Vol. XIII, 6th Series, 1913.

decorations which, although in true medieval style and colouring, probably had no counterpart in the original building. The latter set forth details of the life of King Lucius, and over one hooded fireplace of 13th century date, are pictured the Three Fates—Clotho, Lacheses and Atropos—spinning and cutting the thread of life, and the proud motto *Avito Viget Honore.* The walls are bright with birds, animals and flowers in great variety, and exquisitely painted in their natural colours.

SHORT LIST OF SOURCES.

Archaeologia Cambrensis 1849, 1877, 1913.
Bulletin of Celtic Studies, Vol. I.
Transactions of Cardiff Naturalists' Society, 1917.
G. T. Clark: Manorial Particulars of Glamorgan.
             The Land of Glamorgan.
             Medieval Military Architecture.
Rice Merrick: Glamorgan Antiquities.
Toulmin Smith: Leland's Itinerary in Wales.

CHAPTER VIII.

THE LORDSHIP OF ROATH KEYNSHAM.

As has already been indicated the territory comprising the Parish of Whitchurch was divided amongst four medieval manors, viz., those of Whitchurch (previously and later merged in Senghenydd), Llandaff, Llystalybont (the Philog area) and Roath Keynsham.

The last-named manor came into existence as the result of gifts of land out of the Manor of Roath made by the first Gilbert de Clare, Lord of Glamorgan (1217-1230) to Keynsham Abbey (Somersetshire) which had been founded half a century or so earlier by a predecessor, William, Earl of Gloucester. The gifts included extensive lands in Kibbor, to which additional grants were later added. These gifts were confirmed to Keynsham Abbey by King Edward I in 1275.

The estates seem to have continued in the possession of the monks until the Dissolution of the Monasteries in the reign of Henry VIII, when they were taken over by the Crown and in later years sold or otherwise disposed of to lay owners. It is recorded that in 1563 some of the lands were granted by the Crown to William Morgan and William Morris, and about the same period the manor as a whole was acquired by the first Edward Lewis of Van.

Thomas Lewis of Van died seised of the lordship in 1593, and a record of 1596 shows that Edward Lewis was Lord, and held lands in demesne. The Lewis family seem to have retained the manor until late in the 17th century, when Richard Lewis between 1674 and 1680 sold it to William Morgan, M.P., of Tredegar.

The lands of Roath Keynsham were situated in the Parishes of Roath, Llanedeyrn, Llanishen, Llandaff and Whitchurch. No contemporary map is available showing the extent and boundaries of the manor, but happily in two Surveys made, one in 1650 when William Lewis of Van was Lord, and the other in 1702, when the manor belonged to John Morgan of Tredegar, the several holdings and their limits were sufficiently clearly defined to enable the late John Stuart Corbett to plot the various parcels with a fair degree of accuracy.*

The 1702 Survey is the more complete of the two. It shows that the Lordship comprised a number of detached parcels of land including at Roath large areas near old Roath Village, Pengam Farm and the adjacent moors; the greater part of the Parish of Llanedeyrn; an area in the old parish of Llandaff including the present Cardiff Cemetery; a portion of land near Gwaun Treoda (Whitchurch), and an extensive section extending from the Whitchurch boundary at Rhiwbina to the Llanishen Brook. We are not concerned here with the greater part of the Manor, but only with the area within or in the vicinity of Whitchurch.

---

* Portions of the 1650 and 1702 Survey are produced in *Archaeologia Cambrensis*, 1883, and the latter survey in *Cardiff Records, Vol. II*.
See also Manorial Map elsewhere in this volume.

Unfortunately these sections are missing from the 1650 Survey and we must rely on the 1702 Survey for our material. Let us deal first with the parcel near Treoda. The Survey reads:

"We present that one other Tenement of the said Lord of this Mannor, now in the tenure of Alice William, Widow, being parcel of this Lordship, is situate in the Parish of Whitechurch, mearing and bounding to the Common called Mynydd Buchan (Bychan), and a Highway leading from a place called Pant-bach to a place called Rydd-wathley on the East, and a Dump or Bank (of earth) on the Common called Wain Troda (Wayntreoda), which Bank adjoineth to the several Lordships of Listal-y-Bont (Llystalybont), Landaff, Sengheneth (Senhenith), and to this Lordship, on the West part thereof, the Lands of the Widow Matthews of Gabalfa (Cabalva), being part of the Lordship of Listall-y-Bont, of the South, and the land of Captain Richard Jenkins, being part of the Lordship of Senghenith, now in the Tenure of William Thomas and Henry Morgan, on the North part thereof."*

The common called Mynydd Bychan (Little Mountain), was the Great Heath which extended from Allensbank Road and the northern portion of Roath Park to Llanishen Fach Farm. Beulah Road, formerly known as Heol Nant-y-Walla, intersected the Great Heath which at this point was of narrow width, its limits being approximately Beulah Corner on the west and Tyglas Farm (Blue House) on the east.

One clause of the Survey defined the rights of tenants of Roath Keynsham Lordship to use this and neighbouring commons. Thus:—

"And we also present that all tenants of this Manor at all times of the year have, and always have had, free common of pasture for all sorts of cattle on the heaths and mountains there, called Mynydd Bychan, Wain Dyval and Wain-Treoda."

Waun Dyfal (waste mead) was the ancient name for the Little Heath which extended between Albany Road and Woodville Road. Mynydd Bychan and Waun Dyfal were enclosed by Act of Parliament in the opening years of the 18th century. Waun Treoda is Whitchurch Common. Alice Williams' land seems to have been bounded on the east partly by the Great Heath and partly by the Pantbach Road, which got its name from a still existing small farmhouse near Birchgrove. Alice Williams' land seems to have comprised a large portion of what is to-day known as the Greenclose Residential Estate.

The dump or bank on Gwaun Treoda was apparently a mound which may have served as a boundary mark for two or more of the above-mentioned four manors. It existed until the early part of the 19th century, when it was acquired as a site for a Baptist chapel, to which was given the appropriate name of Ararat. Alice Williams' homestead adjoined the common to the north-west of the Ararat Chapel and was probably the building, Tre-oda (Oda's homestead), which gave its name to the Common.

Alice Williams' land belonged to Morgan of Tredegar, and in addition to a rental to William Morgan, as landowner, she also paid him

---

* The entries in brackets are from the 1650 Survey.

a further nominal due as her Lord Feudal, as the following extract shows:—

'Alice William, widow, holdeth one tenement late of Henry Morgan Rees, adjoining to the Common called Treoda, situate in the Parish of Whitechurch, charged with a red rose, on every Midsummer Eve yearly as chief rent."

The Llystalybont Manor lay to the south-east of Whitchurch Common, and the land nearest to the common was owned or leased by the Widow Mathew—probably a connection of the Llandaff or Radyr family of that name, who may have lived at Gabalfa House near the River Taff. The land of Captain Richard Jenkins seems to have been the Spencer Estate, developed during recent years by Mr. R. N. Colley.

The land between Pantbach Road and the Philog Brook, which divided it from the Great Heath, was another Roath Keynsham holding, stretching from near the site of the modern St. Thomas' church as far as Beulah Road. This is described in the Survey as follows:—*

"We (say and) present that one other tenement of the Lands of the Lord of the Manor, situate in the Parish of Whitechurch aforesaid, now in the Tenure of Lewis Lewis, being also parcel of the Lordship and late the Land of one Samuel Edward, doth (bound and) mear to the said Common called Mynydd Buchan (Mynith bychan), the said place called Pant Bach on the South side and the said way leading to Ridd y Wathla (Rhyd y Watley) on the West, and the Lands of the said Lord of this Manor, now in the Tenure of Thomas Morgan, being in the Lordship of Senghenith (Senhenith), on the North part thereof."

The land to the north in the Tenure of Thomas Morgan was apparently the Deri Farm which extended from Beulah Corner to Pantmawr Road.

We now come to the area adjoining Rhiwbina within the Parish of Llanishen which, by reason of its contiguity, contains much matter of local interest. The Survey proceeds:

"And from thence (i.e. Rhyd-y-Walla) the said Lordship is bounded with the mears that meareth between the Parishes of Lanishen and Whitechurch (Whitchurch), until it cometh to a Brook called Castan (Cassen), in a place where the said Brook runeth between a place called Kaeyrkunrick (Kae y cunrick), parcel of the Lordship of Senghenith (Senhenith) and the lands of Richard Lewis of Corsham, Esqe, now in the Tenure of Thomas William, being parcel of this Lordship of Roath-Kensham;, and from thence to the Ruins of an old Castle called Drainan-pen-y-Graig (draynew Pen y graig), it is meared by the said Brook called Castan (Kastan), and (on) a hill called Craig Kibor (Kibber) on the north."†

---

* For the location of the several portions of the Lordship of Roath Keynsham see the following maps:—*William Rees: South Wales and the Border in the 14th Century*, and *J. S. Corbett, Manors in the Cardiff District (Cardiff Records, Vol. V.).*

† The name *Casten* appears against the Briwnant brook in a Tredegar Estate Map of 1764.

The lands in the 'Tenure of Thomas William' seem from the description to be Llanishen Fach, and some lands lying to the north of this farm possibly belonged to an ancient farm known as Dan-y-Ddraenen (Below-the Thorn), upon or near the homestead of which was later built a Lewis Mansion known as New House. Kaeyrkunrick (possibly Caeau Cynrig, Kenrick's fields), seems to have been the farm holding today known as The Graig, long the home of one of the Wride family.

The brook Castan (chestnut), so-called probably because chestnut trees grew freely on or near its banks, seems to be the Briw-nant, but the name was also possibly applied to the main stream formed by the junction of the Briw-nant and Nofydd. It was also, as has already been said, known as Nant Walla, later corrupted to Nant Waedlyd, but is generally referred to today as the Whitchurch Brook.

The old castle called Draenen Penygraig is Castell Morgraig, the ruins adjoining the Traveller's Rest Inn on the east, Draenen Penygraig (the thorn on top of the Graig or Hill) being the Welsh equivalent of the modern Thornhill. Craig Cibwr (or Kibbor) was the old name for the ridge extending from the Wenallt to Cherry Orchard and perhaps farther east.

The other boundaries of the Llanishen parcel of the Lordship are given as follows: The manor was bounded on the east by "the Lands of Sir Charles Kemeys Tynte Bart., now in the tenure of Rees John Matthew, and the brook that runneth between the land of the said Richard Lewis, Esqe, called Tyr-y-Will (Tir y Whit), and another Tenement of the said Richard Lewis Esqe, now in the tenure of William Lewis David, until it cometh to a Stone Bridge on the High way by Lanishen (Llanishen) Church; and from thence to (by) Rhyd-y-Maen Goch (Rhyd y mincoch), to a place called Gwain-y-pentrahand (Gwain y pentra) hard by the said Common called Mynydd buchan (Munith bychan), it is meared to (by) the Highway Southward; and from thence as herein (before) mentioned, to the lands of Lewis Lewis (as) aforesaid, it is meared on the South part thereof with a mount or walk (wake) there raised and now constant."

These boundaries though somewhat involved are nevertheless clear. The eastern boundary was the Llanishen Brook from the Hill Farm to a point near the Church Inn, Llanishen, and the southern boundary the highway from Llanishen to Rhiwbina, as far as Tyglas and the northern fringe of the Great Heath from Tyglas to the small homestead known as Ty'n y Coed, on the south-west boundary of Llanishen Fach.

'Tir y Will' seems by the description to be the present-day farm known as Tydraw, lying to the south of Heol Pentre Gwilym. Rhyd y Maen Goch (The ford of the red stone), elsewhere referred to as Rhyd-y-Minco, was probably near Tyglas Farm at the point where Nant y Mynydd crosses the highway. Gwaun y Pentre possibly adjoined the Great Heath near the Caerphilly—Beulah cross roads.

Apart from the place names already mentioned the Survey also mentions other tenements and lands in Llanishen Parish, viz., Llwyn Crwn, Tai Mawr, Tyr-y-mud, Barway, Tonmawr and Craig y Castell

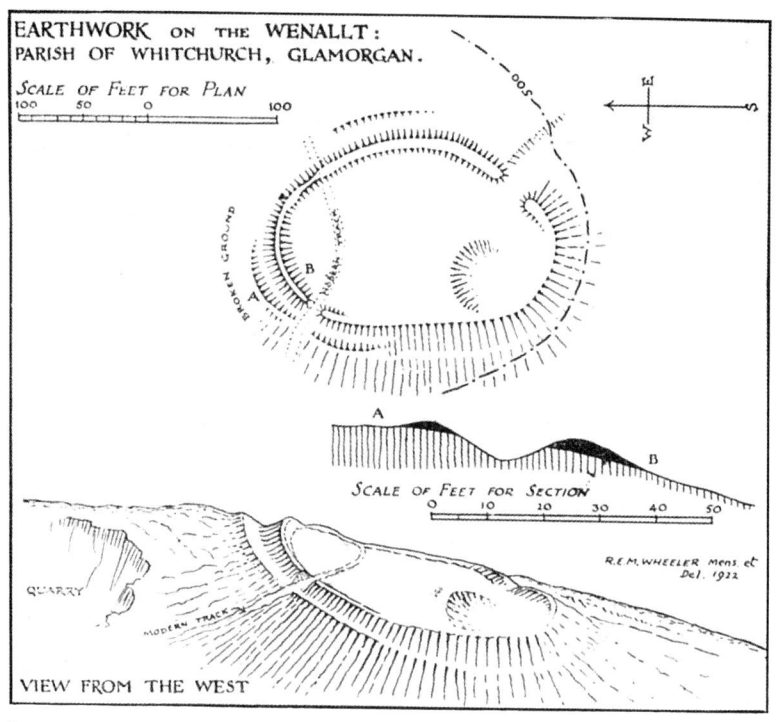

WENALLT CAMP SITE *National Museum of Wales*

THE TWMPATH, RHIWBINA *Hilda Chappell*

Castell Coch Ruins before Restoration *Cardiff Library*

Castell Coch, Tongwynlais *Cardiff Library*

(also referred to in 1650 as 'alias Blaen Ffynnon Denar neere Draynen Craig.')

Other interesting facts emerging from the Survey refer to branches of the Lewis family. Thus:

'Thomas Lewis of Llanishen, Esqe, holdeth the lands late of Jenkin Morgan Gwynne, situate in Lanishen aforesaid, now in the tenure of Thomas Lewis, under the chief rent of ¾d.'

This obviously refers to Llanishen Fawr and lands which were passed from the Gwynnes to the Lewises by the marriage of one of the sons of Lewis of Van to the Gwynne heiress.

'Mrs. Grace Lewis, widow, holdeth a certain Tenement in Lanishen, called Rhydymincoe, now in her own tenure, under the chief rent of ½d."

Grace Lewis was a daughter of Humphrey Wyndham of Dunraven and the widow of Gabriel Lewis, who had rebuilt Llanishen Fawr. After her husband's death she removed to the house called Rhydymincoe, better known to-day as Tyglas (Blue House) which she seems to have owned in her own right, subject to the payment of a small acknowledgment to the Lord of the Manor.

It appears from the Survey that at this time the Lordship comprised freeholders and tenants. The freeholders, amongst whom were Thomas Lewis, Grace Lewis, and others each paid a very small chief rent and owed 'suit of court' to the Court Leet held twice a year, when summoned. Their tenure was known as free and socage. A heriot of 5/- had to be paid to the Lord upon every exchange or alienation of free lands. Other lands were let by the freeholders (including the demesne lands of the Lord) to tenants who in addition to their ordinary rent to their landlord paid a small acknowledgment to the Lord of the Manor. These also were obliged to attend the Court Leet. Alice Williams and Lewis Lewis were probably tenants of the Lord's demesne lands.

In addition to the Court Leet, which was a civil court and dealt with pleas above 40/- and was presided over by the Steward of the Manor; there was also a Court Baron, which dealt with misdemeanours and nuisances, with questions relating to property within the Manor, debts and damages under 40/-, services, customs, heriots, chief rents, the Lord's rights, etc. It was held every three weeks if occasion required.

SHORT LIST OF SOURCES.

Archaeologia Cambrensis, 1883.
J. S. Corbett: Glamorgan Papers.
J. Hobson Mathews. Cardiff Records.
Professor Wm. Rees: South Wales and the Border in the 14th Century.

CHAPTER IX.

THE DESCENT OF OLIVER CROMWELL.

In the many accounts of the life of Oliver Cromwell considerable attention has been paid to his Welsh ancestry and a number of complicated and very divergent pedigrees are extant. Most of these go back right into the prehistoric period, but none so far as I am aware further back than Adam. Like most Welsh pedigrees they must be regarded as unreliable in the earlier stages, although some of them at any rate are probably accurate for the later steps of descent.

All of the Cromwell biographers, however, are agreed that the family was of Welsh origin. Thomas Carlyle is perhaps the only one who is not quite definite, and even he ascribed the descent of the Protector either to a Williams of Glamorgan or a family of the same name in Berkshire.

Of the Williams ancestry there can be no possible doubt—it was fully acknowledged by several members of the Cromwell family. The first of Oliver Cromwell's line to adopt the name was Richard Williams, later known as Sir Richard Cromwell. In numerous legal documents relating to his acquisition of lands at Neath, Rumney and elsewhere he is referred to as 'Richard Williams, alias Cromwell,' and similar references to 'Williams, alias Cromwell' occur in later deeds executed by his descendants including the great Protector himself.

According to Frederick Harrison the name Williams appears "in Oliver Cromwell's marriage settlement and even in the inscription over the Protector's bed when his effigy lay in state." It is also recorded that after the death of Oliver Cromwell, some members of the Cromwell family reverted to the name of Williams.

Further proof of the Welsh descent is also to be found in the coat-of-arms and private seal used both by Sir Richard Cromwell and by his great-grandson Oliver of that ilk. According to one writer,

'Although Sir Richard Williams had by royal command exchanged his own surname for that of Cromwell, yet he continued to use and display the Williams coat-of-arms—*sable a lion rampant argent*—and the historic coat was continued as the family escutcheon to the end. The crest used is a demi-lion rampant argent holding in his right gamb a diamond ring, traditionally said to allude to a jewel given by Henry VIII to Sir Richard Williams, or Cromwell, on account of his feat of arms at a court tournament."*

The Cromwell escutcheon is, in part, practically the same as that of the family of Lewis of Van, New House, Greenmeadow, etc., who regarded the Williams family as a cadet branch.† The coat of arms was that of Caredig, Lord of Powys and Ceredigion, and of his descendant

---

* H. N. Vaughan in *Cymmrodorion Transactions*, 1936.
† See Clark, *Cartae Glam*, pp. 1932-3.

Gwaethfoed, Lord of Cardigan, from whom the Lewises and the Williams are stated to have sprung. Cromwell's private seal comprised six quarterings, all Welsh, two of them being the silver lion rampant on a black background.*

It may, therefore, be accepted as undeniable that the Cromwells were partly of Welsh origin and descendants of a Williams family. There is, however, not the same unanimity in regard to the locality in which the family lived. The places usually favoured are Eglwysnewydd (i.e. Whitchurch) and Llanishen (Cardiff). Two or three writers, however, out of many dozens, offer alternative suggestions and it will be well to dispose of these forthwith.

Rush Meyrick, the historian of Cardiganshire, refers to the Cromwells as descendants of a family of Williams of "Cwm Castell in the Parish of Newchurch (i.e. ·Eglwysnewydd), Carmarthenshire," whilst Philip Yorke, stated they hailed from 'Morgan Williams of Nantchurch, Cardiganshire,' another unknown locality. That these two attributions are certainly wrong is sufficiently proved, in my judgment, by the fact that the Cromwell coat-of-arms was that of a well-known and prolific East Glamorgan family. A *Peniarth MS.*† attribution to a Williams of 'Nan Church' in Glamorgan is obviously a mis-rendering of New Church (Eglwysnewydd), in that county.

The majority of the Cromwell writings and pedigrees give Eglwysnewydd (Glam.) as the location of the Cromwell-Williams ancestors, but Leland, the Antiquary, and many who followed him, domiciled them at Llanishen. Our problem is to decide which of these two places has that honour. Not that the matter is one of very great importance, as in any case the two parishes bearing these names adjoin one another. It may be their very proximity indeed that has given rise to the confusion.

A few writers, apparently without any known authority, have given Plas Llanishen as the ancestral home, the particular reference being to the old house near Llanishen Church—since pulled down and replaced by a farmhouse, Llanishen Fawr—which was for a long period the home of a branch of the Lewis family. At the time, however, in the 15th or early 16th century, when the Cromwell-Williamses migrated to London the Lewises had not arrived at Llanishen, and the house which preceded Plas Llanishen (built by Gabriel Lewis about 1635) was then the home of the Gwyn family into which a cadet of the family of Lewis of Van married. Moreover, there is evidence showing the existence at Llanishen of an influential Williams family during the time both of the Gwyns and of the Lewises.‡

---

* The seal and arms of Oliver Cromwell are fully described in articles in *Archaeologia Cambrensis* 1859 (p. 147) and in *Cymmrodorion Transactions* 1936 (p. 45).
† Hist M.S.S. Commission. *Report on Welsh MSS*, Vol. I, Pt. II *Peniarth*, p. 908.
‡ References appear in the *Survey of the Manor of Llystalybont* (1653) to George Williams of Llanishen, in the *Roath Keynsham Survey* 1702 to Thomas Williams of Llanishen. In 1741 a Thomas Williams of Llanishen entertained Charles Wesley. An inscribed stone on the orchard wall of Llanishen Fach records that it was built in 1821 by Rev. Henry Williams.

The first of the Cromwell biographers to discuss the Cromwell pedigree was Rev. Mark Noble in a substantial life of the Protector written in 1784. He probably used the family pedigree prepared by Sir John Prestwich, in which the descent is traced from Gwaethfoed— also the ancestor of the Lewis family—through Yeban ap Morgan of New Church, i.e. Eglwysnewydd (Whitchurch) and his son Morgan Williams, who married a sister of Thomas Cromwell, Earl of Essex, of which marriage Richard Williams alias Cromwell was a product.

That Noble's Newchurch or Eglwysnewydd was our Whitchurch is shown by this note:

'Morgan Williams, a gentleman of Glamorgan, possessed of an estate worth about two or three hundred pounds a year which estate has been long enjoyed by the family of Lewis and before them by the Vaughans and now lets at £900 per annum."

This reference is, perhaps, to the Lewises of Llanishen or, more probably, the branch which was located at New House.

The Whitchurch attribution is also contained in a pedigree at the Cardiff Library, printed by the late Sir Joseph Bradney in *Llyfr Baglan*. This is very similar to that of Noble, except that Noble has wrongly duplicated two of his later entries. The *Llyfr Baglan* pedigree is likely to be fairly reliable as it is taken from a collection made by one John Williams about 1600-1607 before the Protector's time, and was to some extent based on

'The boocke of Lewis Morganwg w'ch was made of late dayes Conteynynge the pedigrees of Sir Richard Will'ms alias Crwmwell."

Lewys Morganwg lived between 1480 and 1520 and he as well as John Williams were contemporaries of the Williamses and Cromwells during the period that matters for our enquiry. Like Noble, John Williams traced Richard Cromwell from Gwaethfoed through Ievan ap Morgan of Eglwysnewydd.

It is unnecessary for us to trace the entire pedigree. It will suffice if we start with Ievan ap Morgan and his son William ap Ievan, both 15th century Welshmen whose names also occur in Noble's table. Ievan ap Morgan and his family were probably supporters of Harry Tudor (afterwards Henry VII) when he landed at Milford Haven to seize the throne of England, and some of them may have migrated to London when he became King. In the Church of St. Helen, Bishopsgate, there is a brass in memory of Thomas Willyams who died in 1495, and who, according to J. C. Hare, was a younger brother of Ievan ap Morgan.

Let John Williams now tell his story:

'The said Ievan ap Morgan dwelled in the p'ishe of newchurche w'thin a myle to Cardiff where the heire of the younger sone of the said Ievan inhabiteth at this tyme.'

'But the foresaid Will'm ap Ievan ap Morgan being a valient active younge man and, as the report in these p'ties goeth, the beast archer that in these daes was knowen, hee served Jasper, ducke of Bedford, being the lo of Clamorgan and morganwg. And afterwardes bye hime p'fered to the service of kinge Henrie the seaventh, and hee m in England w'th whome I ame uncertene but that hee had issue (yiz) morgan will'ms and Jon will'ms.'

'Morgan Will'ms ma w'th the da of walter Crwmell, sister to the Lord Crwmell, late Earle of Essexe. And they had issue Sir Richerd will'ms surnamed Sir Richard Crwmell.'

'Sir Richerd will'ms, knight, alias Crwmell, had issue Sir Henrie Crwmell, knight, and francis Crwmell now leaving."

Except for the location of the family homestead most Cromwellian biographers accept the above descent. Sir Richard Williams was the son of Morgan Williams and Katherine Cromwell and the grandson of Ievan ap Morgan, and he in turn was the great grandfather of Oliver Cromwell, Lord Protector.

From the *Llyfr Baglan* pedigree and other sources the attribution of the Williams family to Whitchurch has been derived. Whence then comes the statement that the Williamses were of Llanishen? In all probability from the following passage in John Leland's *The Itinerary* (1536-1539), wherein, dealing with Kibworth or Kibbor, he refers to

'an Hille in the same Commote caullid Keven On a 6 miles from the mouth of Remny. This Hille goeth as a Waulle overthwart betwix the rivers of Thaue (Taff) and Remny ..... In the South side of this Hille was borne Richard William alias Crumwelle yn the Paroch of Llan Isen."

The hill 'caullid Keven On' is the Cefn Onn range extending from Rhiwperra to Castell Coch, which was also about this period known as Cefn Cibwr (or Kibbor).

Here we have two statements from contemporary sources domiciling the Williams family one at Whitchurch, the other at Llanishen. Which is correct? Personally I favour Leland for the following reasons:

1. John Leland had been appointed in 1533 as 'The King's Antiquary.' He was probably a person of some consequence at Court, and may be presumed to have been on terms of acquaintanceship with most public men of the period. At the time he was compiling his *Itinerary* Sir Richard Williams alias Cromwell was a man of some importance. He had taken an active part in suppressing the Pilgrimage of Grace and was a Commissioner in South Wales for the Suppression of Monasteries. Leland probably knew Sir Richard, and, in any case, is not likely to have made any statement concerning a personality of his eminence without verification.

2. There is evidence of the existence of an influential yeoman family or families of the name of Williams at Llanishen from the sixteenth to the eighteenth centuries probably at Llanishen Fach farm, and these may well have been descendants of the same William ap Ievan ap Morgan from whom Oliver Cromwell's line sprang.

3. There is an old local tradition that the Cromwell-Williams family ancestors resided at Llanishen Fach. The present farmhouse is not a very pretentious building, is probably much less in extent than was formerly the case, and appears to be of more modern construction than the 16th century. In all probability the old house, like many more in the locality is a reconstruction.

4. Llanishen Fach has been for a long period and still is in the ownership of a branch of the Lewis family, a fact which harmonizes with

Noble's statement made in 1784   At this time the Lewis family had not acquired their Greenmeadow estate in the Parish of Whitchurch.

5. Llanishen Fach fits in with the locality mentioned by Leland "on the southe side of this hill," (i.e. the Craig Llanishen section of the Cefn Onn or Cibwr ridge), "yn the paroche of Llan Isen."

If this theory is right how did other writers come to mention Eglwysnewydd (or Whitchurch) as the location of William ap Ievan ap Morgan's residence? May there not have been some confusion in their minds arising from the fact that the two parishes adjoin?

Llanishen Fach is situated a little more than a mile from the old Parish Church of Whitchurch and about two-thirds of a mile from Llanishen Church, and the western boundary of the farm co-incides with the boundary between the two parishes. From the farmhouse of Llanishen Fach into the Parish of Whitchurch is little more than two stone-throws, and it is not a matter for surprise that some writers should have erred in assigning the Williams property to Whitchurch instead of to Llanishen. It is admitted, of course, that the foregoing reasoning is not very conclusive; at any rate the attribution of the Cromwell-Williams family ancestry to Llanishen Fach provides the only working theory that has yet been propounded.

How did the humble family of Williams of Llanishen (or Eglwysnewydd) develop into the, at one-time, all-powerful family of Cromwell? If the traditional story is well-founded William ap Ievan ap Morgan was a supporter of the Tudor interest, and he and (or) his sons may have joined Harry Tudor and possibly fought at Bosworth (1485).

Next year Jasper Tudor, who had been created Duke of Bedford, was granted the Lordship of Glamorgan, an office which he held from 1486 to 1495, and William of Ievan seems to have been rewarded for his services by means of a local appointment under Duke Jasper.

His sons, however, Morgan and John, and possibly another, seem to have sought their fortunes in London. Both of them seem early to have adopted the English fashion of permanent surnames, and became known as Morgan Williams and John Williams respectively.

Morgan Williams is stated to have received grants of land at Putney within the Manor of Wimbledon. Here he set up in business as an ale brewer and innkeeper, which business he seems later to have extended into Wandsworth, Mortlake and Greenwich. References appear to him in the manorial records of Wimbledon as having on more than one occasion infringed the regulations of that manor.

In time he became a person of some local consequence. He is reputed to have become brewer of ale to Henry VII, in which capacity he supplied the need of the Royal courts at the Palaces of Greenwich, Eltham, Nonsuch and Richmond. It is also stated that in 1575 he was a yeoman of the guard of Welshmen, with non-military duties of a semi-legal nature as his main royal service.

Brother John ap William also went to London. He is said to have entered the legal profession, in which he won some success, and also became accountant and land agent to Lord Scales, and Steward of the Manor of Wimbledon. He is referred to in contemporary documents as John Williamson and John Williams.

Old Whitchurch

In due course he married, and his daughter Joan became in 1534 the wife of Sir John Price, LL.D. of Brecon, who was a member of the Court of the Marches and played an important part in bringing about the Union of England and Wales. Price was a Commissioner for the Suppression of the Monasteries and acquired church lands. He was a celebrated Welsh antiquary and in 1573 wrote *Historiae Britannicae Defensis* in answer to Polydore Virgil. He was also joint author with Humphrey Llwyd of Denbigh of The *Description of Wales*. His best known title to fame, however, consists in his authorship of the first book ever printed in the Welsh language, viz., *Yn y Llyfr Hwn* (1555), comprising the Lord's Prayer, the Creed and the Ten Commandments.

Another 16th century Welshman of note, was Lord Williams of Thame, who was made President of the Court of the Marches by Queen Elizabeth in 1559. The late Sir Lleufer Thomas states that he was the second son of John Williams and therefore a cousin of Sir Richard Cromwell.*

A neighbour of Morgan Williams at Putney was one Walter Cromwell, who had been a blacksmith and farrier in Harry Tudor's army, but was now a brewer and fuller. He had two children, a daughter Katherine, and a son Thomas. About 1495 Morgan Williams married his neighbour's daughter, and to them was born in due course a son Richard. According to Leland's statement quoted above, Richard was born at Llanishen, and it would appear from this that, in addition to his business and property at Putney and elsewhere in the London area, Morgan Williams was also in possession of the Welsh estate and sometimes resided there.

Thomas Cromwell was only a few years old at the time of his sister's marriage, and between him and his nephew Richard there was only a few years difference in age. Young Thomas was of a very forceful character. After holding clerical posts in Antwerp and Rome he became Italian secretary to Cardinal Wolsey and later a Member of Parliament.

After the Cardinal's fall in 1531 he entered the King's service, was knighted, made Privy Councillor, and by 1534 had become a Principal Secretary of State and Master of the Rolls. Next year he was appointed Visitor-General for the Suppression of the Monasteries, and in 1536 became a Peer. In 1537 he was Vicar-General and Vice-Regent under the King in all religious matters, and was an all-powerful promoter of the Reformation. Other important offices fell to his lot, and in 1539 he was made Earl of Essex and Lord Chancellor of England. His excess of zeal for the Reformation, however, seems to have turned the King against him, and in June, 1540, he was impeached and beheaded.

With such an important man for uncle it is not surprising that young Richard Williams was able to achieve riches and a high position in the State. In order perhaps to secure greater favour with his uncle, or, as some reports suggest, at the express wish of the King, he adopted before 1536 the surname Cromwell in substitution for that of Williams.

* See *Y Cymmrodor* 1900: *Further Notes on the Court of the Marches*.

For a time, according to Thomas Cromwell's will, he seems to have been 'a servant with my lorde Marques Dorsett,' but later entered his uncle's service, and was by him appointed the South Wales Commissioner for the Suppression of Monasteries. He gained credit with the King for his services in connection with the Pilgrimage of Grace, and was knighted. He also received gifts of church lands in Huntingdonshire, which in 1542 he exchanged for monastic lands at Neath and elsewhere in Glamorgan.

The downfall of his uncle does not seem to have affected his interests. He became a Member of Parliament for Huntingdonshire, and seems to have died a wealthy man. After his death he was succeeded by his son, Sir Henry Cromwell, whose second son Robert was the father of Oliver Cromwell, Lord Protector of England.

A SHORT LIST OF SOURCES.

There exists a large body of biographical literature relating to the Cromwell family, particularly to the Protector. Most of these discuss the pedigree. Perhaps the most useful are:—

R. B. Merriman. Life and Letters of Thomas Cromwell (1902).
Noble. Memoirs of the Protectorate House of Cromwell (1784).
Waylen. The House of Cromwell.
(Brotherton & Co.). The Life of Oliver Cromwell (1724).

See also:—
J. Howell. The Cromwell Family and their Connection with Wales. (In the Red Dragon, December, 1882, and January, 1883).
Notes on Genealogy of Oliver Cromwell (Arch. Camb. 1846).

CHAPTER X.
THE STORY OF LOCAL GOVERNMENT.*

In view of the ever-increasing importance of modern local government in the life of the people it is essential in modern histories of township growth that some account should be given of the development of this important function.

Whitchurch is by far the most populous parish in the Cardiff Rural District, and is governed by three main types of local authority—County, District and Parish Councils. This tripartite system is not really ancient, as these bodies were created only after the passing of the Local Government Acts of 1888 and 1894.

At the time of their creation Whitchurch was a comparatively small township with a population of about 3,000; and a rural form of administration was perhaps not inappropriate. Today, however, it is a populous and growing suburb of Cardiff, with a population exceeding 20,000, and so closely is it linked up with that City that there are no clearly marked, undeveloped boundaries separating them. A re-adjustment of local government organisation in the near future, therefore, seems inevitable.

The civil parish of Whitchurch is a development from the more ancient ecclesiastical unit. The term 'parish' (Greek, *paroikia*) was in ancient times applied to the area served by a local priest centred at a church, or the area within which tithes were levied for the support of the church. Originally, Whitchurch formed part of the parish of Llandaff and was served by a priest from the Cathedral, part of which also served as the parish church of Llandaff. In course of time a branch church or chapel was provided at Whitchurch, which was served by a special priest, and the area allocated to that chapel was known as a *chapelry*. Whitchurch then became a chapelry of Llandaff, and in 1845, it was constituted a separate ecclesiastical parish.

After the advent of the Normans to Glamorgan in the 11th century the conquered territory within the Coastal Plain was divided into a series of manors, the boundaries of which were not always coterminous with the areas served by parish priests. Sometimes two or more manors were within the same ecclesiastical parish, whilst very large manors might comprise two or more parishes. The chapelry of Whitchurch, for example, comprised not only the manor of Album Monasterium, but also parts of the manors of Roath Keynsham, Llandaff and Llystalybont.

In the Norman and Early English periods such local government as existed was of a very rudimentary character and was mixed up with feudal practice. The manor was the economic unit, and its courts—

---
* The most complete account of the general development of our local administrative system is contained in Mr. and Mrs. Sidney Webb's *Local Government*.

Court Baron and Court Leet, especially the latter—settled business relating to land and to the observance of general laws made by the State or by the Lord Marcher, and also enforced rules of a communal nature such as the mitigation of nuisances which injuriously affected the Lord and his tenants. Many public services which, however, are today regarded as local government functions, e.g., the care of the poor, the provision of bridges, education, etc., were to some extent discharged as charitable duties by the Church.

As the centuries rolled by the Church took an ever-growing interest in the well-being of the people. At each church it was customary for the priest to hold meetings of the parishioners primarily for the transaction of church business, although extraneous matters affecting the interests of the parish were also discussed. Over these meetings the Parish Priest—in Whitchurch a Vicar of Llandaff—presided, and as he was usually the best educated man in the parish, it is natural that he exercised great influence over secular as well as over religious affairs. Such meetings were at first held in the church building, but when secular business became a general church function the church vestry was more generally used. Hence the origin of the term Vestry Meeting for a later-day local government authority.

In the 13th and 14th centuries the Church gained great ascendancy over the Manorial Courts. The local priests often championed the cause of the people against the Steward of the Manor and protected them against unjust administration of manorial laws and customs. In this way the Parish Meeting at the church came to be regarded as a general assembly of church members and adherents not merely for the transaction of church business, such as the election of church officers and the administration of church property, but also for dealing with matters affecting the general environment of parishioners.

In later years as Royal power increased and the rights and powers of manorial lords were curtailed the Feudal system gradually disintegrated, and the manorial courts were restricted to functions of an estate character and their business became merely formal. In time the wages system displaced feudal arrangements, and problems of unemployment and poverty appeared.

Under the new conditions the influence of the Church increased. The priest became a more important person than the manorial steward. The Vestry Meeting became the regular medium for the consideration of environmental as well as church business, and in time was recognised as an organ both of the Church and the State.

As early as 1555 and 1563 highway legislation was passed which associated the parish with the duty of road maintenance. Then in 1601 an Act (43 Eliz. C2) imposed statutory duties on such meetings and obliged the residents of each parish to care for the poor, aged, blind and impotent persons, and the apprenticing of poor children, residing within its limits. Provision was also made by this Act for the raising of funds for such purposes by taxing the owners and occupiers of land.

This was our first Poor Relief Act, and this was the first measure which recognised the parish as the unit for local government purposes.

From being a charitable function of the Church the relief of the poor was now made an obligatory duty of all the parishioners, and the parish started its long history as a local government unit. Under the Act of 1601 the churchwardens and overseers of the poor, who were charged with the administration of the new law, were appointed by the Parish or Vestry Meeting. The justices of the peace were also charged with the duty of seeing that the new arrangements were properly administered. This system of poor-law administration continued in being until the passing of the Poor Law Amendment Act, 1834, which extended the area of charge from the parish to a Union of Parishes and established Boards of Guardians.

From this necessarily brief account it will be seen that the civil parish was a development from the ecclesiastical parish. It was not until the 19th century, however, that our modern system of civil parishes came into being by the combination of small parishes or the sub-division of large parishes, and under these revised arrangements civil parishes ceased to synchronise in all cases with the ecclesiastical units. As has been already mentioned Whitchurch at first was a part of the ecclesiastical parish of Llandaff, of which it later became a chapelry; later the chapelry was converted into a separate ecclesiastical parish, and the new civil parish comprised the area of the latter. The ecclesiastical and civil parishes of Whitchurch were probably identical until the year 1902 when the Llandaff Yard area was detached from Whitchurch and added to the ecclesiastical parish of Llandaff. Later in 1921 the ecclesiastical parish was further curtailed by the creation of the ecclesiastical parish of Tongwynlais.

In process of time duties other than Poor Law, such as the maintenance of order, the mitigation of nuisances, the provision and upkeep of highways and the like were imposed on the parishes or on groups of parishes forming divisions called Hundreds, and various officers such as the Constable and Highway Surveyor were appointed to enforce the decisions of the Vestries. The local justices were also associated with these functions, and in certain circumstances they acted as a major authority.

The method of enforcing obligation on the different parishes was by "presenting" them (a procedure analogous with our present-day system of 'prosecution') to the Justices, who were empowered to make orders for the discharge of neglected duties. The *Glamorgan County Calendars* teem with such orders over a couple of centuries.* Here are a few examples:

1591—"The bridge of landaff insufficient in default of the townshipp of Landaff."

1593—"The bridge of Llandaff in great decaye in default of Whitchurch and Llandaff."

1727 and 1750—"The antient bridge called Llandaffe Bridge is ruinous and out of repair and ought to be repaired by Glamorgan inhabitants.'

(By this period the maintenance of bridges had become a county liability).

---

* See *Cardiff Records*, Vol. II, Chap. V.

1733—Grand Jury "present the highway leading from the ford on the road to Llandaff from the parish of Radyr to the Parish of Whitchurch to be out of repair; and that the same ought to be repaired by the inhabitants of Whitchurch."

1733—"We present Evan Thomas Howell of the P'ish of Whitchurch in the sd County for not pruneing the hedges adjoyning to the high way leading from Ton Gwinlas to fforest yssa in the sd p'ish of Whitchurch (Discharged).

1734—Grand Jury "certify that the Highway leading from the ford called Rhyd y Radir on ye River Taffe from ye parish of Radir to the church and village of Whitchurch . . . . . hath since been well repayr'd by and at ye Expence of ye Inhabitants of ye sayd parish of Whitchurch so that his Ma'ties subjects may Safely pass and repass that way."

1748—Grand Jury present upon the oath of Lewis Thomas, gentleman, the highway leading from a place called Velindre towards a dwelling house of Thomas Morgan, called late Mr. Howards, in the parish of Raddyr to be out of repair."

1798—Judge Hardinge presented portions of the highway from Llandaff to Cardiff and Thornhill Road from a place called Y Ddrainen.

1799—Judge presents the road "from a house called Maendu House to Whitchurch Brook situate in the Parish of Llandaff to be repaired at the expense of that Parish."

Parochial responsibility for highway maintenance did not result in good roads, and in the latter half of the 18th century Acts of Parliament were passed under which the care of many main roads was vested in Turnpike Trust Commissioners who erected turnpikes, chains and gates at various points and levied tolls in respect of vehicles and live stock passing through. Local roads administered by Commissioners included the Cardiff-Caerphilly Road over Thornhill, Cardiff-Tongwynlais Road through Whitchurch, and Philog-Llandaff Road (i.e. College Road, etc.) There were gates at Gabalfa, Tongwynlais and Llandaff, and a chain barrier near Radyr on the Llantrisant Road. (Hence the name Radyr Chain).

Each Commission comprised a large number of landed gentry, justices and works proprietors, resident in the district. If the income from tolls was insufficient to meet the cost of repair and the interest on invested capital the Commissioners had the right to call on the parishes for a share of the parochial statute labour or for money payments in lieu thereof, but they had no power to levy rates. The system of compulsory recruitment of local labour (including horses and carts) for road maintenance was in force until the 1830's.

The Turnpike Commission had control only of the main roads. By-roads and country lanes still remained a parochial liability and the care of these was in charge of local highway surveyors (unpaid) who could requisition the service of local residents with their horses and vehicles for a certain number of days each year. If such labour was insufficient, hired labour was employed and the cost of this and of material was borne out of parish rates.

Following the Rebecca Riots in West Wales, during which many turnpike gates and toll houses were demolished, the Government set up a Commission to inquire into the grievances of the rioters, and on the recommendation of this Commission special legislation known as the South Wales Highway Act was passed in 1844. Under this Act the various Trusts were consolidated, and their functions, assets and liabilities transferred to County Road Boards. The turnpike gates and other barriers were retained and tolls continued to be charged until 1878, when under an Act of that year they became main roads, and the cost of maintenance was charged half on the parishes and half on the counties. Under the Local Government Act of 1888 the whole of the cost had to be borne by the new County Councils.

Let us now return to the Poor Law Amendment Act of 1834, which transferred poor-law functions from the Parish Vestries and Overseers appointed by them to Boards of Guardians. New administrative units, comprising groups of parishes, adjoining market towns, and known as Unions, were set up, and for each Union a Board of Guardians was appointed. Each Board consisted at first of a number of directly elected members together with the justices of the peace resident within the Union.

The election of Guardians was in the hands of occupiers and owners of property rated at not less than £5. Each person on the register of electors had a number of votes varying from one to six according to the ratable value of his property. One vote was accorded for each unit of £50 ratable value. Persons registered both as occupiers and owners had up to 12 votes. The voting papers were delivered at the houses of the electors—in certain circumstances electors could vote by proxy— and afterwards collected. The Local Government Act of 1894 abolished ex-officio members (i.e. the local justices) of Boards of Guardians, the property qualification, voting by proxy, the plural vote, and house to house voting, and substituted voting by ballot for all parochial elections. Boards of Guardians continued in being for the administration of Poor Law until the passing of the Local Government Act of 1929. Whitchurch was a constituent unit of the Cardiff Board of Guardians, whose functions passed, so far as the administrative county was concerned, to the Glamorgan County Council Public Assistance Committee.

The Parish Vestry and the Overseers continued in being after the passing of the Act of 1834, although their powers were greatly curtailed. The duties of the overseers were restricted to the assessment of properties and rate collections, the preparation of registers of electors and a few other small matters. Other functions of the Vestry included the suppression of nuisances, provision of fire appliances, village pump, management of burial grounds, maintenance of highways and public footpaths, preservation of rights of way, administration of parish charities, and the like, but as the years rolled by some of these functions were transferred to other authorities. Police functions passed to Quarter Sessions by the Act of 1856, in 1860 their road powers were transferred to Highway Boards, in 1872 their sanitary duties were taken over by new Sanitary Authorities. In later days the Vestry ceased to be an important authority and the scope of its duties was very limited. The Vestry gave place to the Parish Council in 1894, and that body appointed the Overseers until the passing of the Local Government Act of 1929, which abolished the office of Overseer and transferred assessment and rating functions to the local authorities. Cardiff Rural District Council now performs the duties formerly discharged by overseers appointed by the Whitchurch Parish Vestry and later by the Whitchurch Parish Council.

It will be of interest now to indicate the development of our present local arrangements from the Vestry. In 1862 the highway powers of the Vestry were conferred on a new authority known as the Highway Board, which was set up by the County Road Board under the Act of 1860. The area of responsibility for local roads was extended from the parish to a Highway District (which comprised a number of parishes) for each of which a Board was constituted, comprising the justices resident in the district together with representatives, known as *waywardens*, appointed by the several vestries in the district. Whitchurch, with other parishes, was included in the Llandaff Highway District and was represented on the Llandaff Highway Board. The Highway Board appointed a salaried Highway Surveyor to supervise the roads and to carry out works ordered by the Board. Parochial liability for road maintenance, however, remained, and rates collected in any parish for highway purposes could not be spent outside the parish, except with the consent of the parishioners concerned. The Highway Board audited and certified its own accounts. The records and annual reports of the Llandaff Highway Board are happily still available, and have considerable value from the local historical point of view.

The next raid on Vestry powers occurred after the passing of the Public Health Act of 1875, a measure which was passed after a series of serious cholera and other epidemics. Under the Act the limited sanitary powers of the Vestry were transferred to a body called the Local Sanitary Authority whose area was coterminous with that of the Poor Law Union. The new local body was called the Cardiff Union Rural Sanitary Authority, and was elected each year by the Guardians representing the areas in the Union outside the borough of Cardiff passing a resolution constituting themselves the Rural Sanitary Authority. The new body was, therefore, substantially a sub-Committee of the Board of Guardians, but had its own separately appointed officials.

Local government in the late 1880's was, therefore, constituted on the following lines:—
(1) The Glamorgan County Road Board controlled the main highways and bridges.
(2) The Justices in Quarter Sessions administered justice, the police and certain other matters.
(3) The Cardiff Boards of Guardians administered the Poor Law and through its Assessment Committee dealt with appeals against property valuations for rating purposes.
(4) The Llandaff District Highway Board maintained local roads and bridges, and certain public footpaths.

(5) Whitchurch Vestry dealt with a variety of minor matters including public rights of way, etc.
(6) Whitchurch Overseers appointed by the Vestry assessed properties and levied and collected rates.
(7) In addition there was another local authority—the Whitchurch School Board—set up in 1883 under the Education Act of 1870 which managed schools provided entirely out of public funds and free from control by religious denominations. Previously local scholastic needs had been met solely at National Schools belonging to the Established Church, or at schools kept by private agencies.

This complicated system of local government had developed in a very haphazard manner, and in time its unsuitability to the changing conditions of the period came to be recognized. Accordingly steps were taken to merge the various *ad hoc* or special purpose bodies in more comprehensive authorities. The first forward step was taken in 1888 when under a Local Government Act of that year County Councils were created, to which were transferred the functions of the Road Boards, the local government powers of Quarter Sessions—police administration being made the responsibility of Joint Committees appointed by County Councils and Quarter Sessions—and other powers which had been discharged by minor authorities or which were the result of new enactments. The process of enlarging the functions of county councils by transferring to them the duties of lesser authorities has been continued down to 1930. School Boards, for example, were abolished by an Act of 1900 and Boards of Guardians by an Act of 1929, and their functions in so far as the Whitchurch area is concerned were vested in the Glamorgan County Council.

In 1894 another Local Government Act was passed which set up in those portions of counties outside chartered boroughs new directly-elected authorities called District Councils, each such council being described as Urban or Rural according to the category of the area administered by it as defined under sanitary legislation of the 1870's. Whitchurch was included within the area of the Llandaff and Dinas Powis (now Cardiff) Rural District Council. To this body were transferred the powers and duties of the Cardiff Union Rural Sanitary Authority and those of the Llandaff and Dinas Powis Highway Boards. The Board of Guardians was, however, still retained and each member elected to serve on the Rural District Council became *ipso facto* a member of the Board of Guardians. From time to time the scope of Rural District Council activities has been greatly enlarged by new legislation.

The Act of 1894 also replaced the Vestry by a new authority—the Parish Meeting in very small parishes, the Parish Council in populous parishes. Whitchurch was in the latter category and got a directly-elected Parish Council. The duties of this authority have always been of limited scope. Their main functions relate to the maintenance of footpaths, the provision of allotments, recreative spaces, and burial grounds, street lighting, library facilities, etc. Their power of appointing overseers was taken from them by an Act of 1929.

To-day the local government of Whitchurch is vested in three authorities—Glamorgan County Council, Cardiff Rural District Council and Whitchurch Parish Council—instead of in the seven separate authorities which existed in the late 1880's. In view of the enormous recent development and growth of population and the changing character of the locality and of the additional responsibilities of local government authorities the existing system of administration is scarcely suitable to present circumstances, and it seems not unlikely that Whitchurch will in the near future be either merged in the City of Cardiff or itself constituted into an area independent of the rural district with its own Urban Council.

The following is a list of the persons elected to represent Whitchurch on the County Council from the inception of that authority:

	County Councillor.	County Alderman
1889-1917	Col. Henry Lewis, J.P., O.B.E. (Greenmeadow)	
1917-1925		Colonel Henry Lewis, J.P.
1917-1931	H. Spence Thomas, J.P. (Melingriffith)	
1931-1938	Edgar L. Chappell, J.P. (Rhiwbina)	
1938-		Edgar L. Chappell, J.P.
1939-	Frederick C. Hale, J.P.	

The following is a list of representatives of the Parish of Whitchurch on the Cardiff (prior to 1922, the Llandaff and Dinas Powis) Rural District Council. Between 1895 and 1922 the number of such representatives was three. When as the result of the Cardiff Extension Order the area of the Rural District was reduced, three additional representatives were attached to Whitchurch, and after the making of the Glamorgan Review Order of 1934 the number was further extended to 10. The membership of the Council is normally determined by triennial elections, but during the World War such elections were suspended. Occasional vacancies resulting from death, resignation or other cause were filled by co-option. The periods mentioned in brackets are those during which the various members served on the Council.

Henry Lewis (1895-1903)
Thomas Williams (1895-1897)
William Wride (1895-1903)
Eli Rees (1898-1900, 1904-1906, 1919-1921)
William Evans (1904-1906)
Edward Jenkins (1901-1907)
William Jones (1907-1909)
Peter Sharpe (1907-1919)
D. Morgan Rees (1908-1909, 1913-1925)
A. H. Bullock (1910-1923)
Edmund Lewis (1910-1912)
George E. Williams (1922-   )
Edgar L. Chappell (1923-   )
C. James Hardwicke (1923-1926)

Walter Williams (1923-1931, 1932-1935)
W. F. Skinner (1924-1928)
C. H. Hockridge (1926-1935)
David Williams (1925-1930)
T. C. Warren Evans (1928-   )
F. C. Hale (1931-   )
David Davies (1934-1942)?
Edward Evans (1934-   )
R. Loveluck Jenkins (1934-   )
A. E. Ogden (1934-   )
W. S. Jones (1936-   )
T. G. Thomas (1937-   )
W. H. Rowley (1942-1944)
W. E. Gough (1944-   )

Drawing Room, Castell Coch, 1892 — *Cardiff Library*

Thatched Cottages, near Malsters' Arms, 1903 — *W. Morgan Davies*

Thatched Cottages, Merthyr Road, 1899 — J. A. Day

Thatched Cottages, Old Church Road, 1903 — W. Morgan Davies

CHAPTER XI.

DEVELOPMENT AND PUBLIC SERVICES.

Population, Growth and Building Development.

Up to the 1880's the growth of population and building development at Whitchurch were in the main associated with the extension of industry at Melingriffith and other local industrial undertakings. In 1801 the population was only 696. By 1811 this had increased to 997. In the latter year there were 228 houses, and according to Nicholas Carlisle* the amount raised in local rates at this period at 13/4 in the pound was £370 10 6. During the next forty years the increase in population was fairly steady, but between 1851 and 1861 there was a big spurt resulting in an increase of 613 in population and 126 in the number of houses. Then the development eased off, especially during the 1870's in which decade the population increase was only 30.

During the 1880's the position again improved, and during the 1890's an increase of more than 46% was recorded. This development was associated with the fact that a water supply from the Cardiff Corporation's Rhiwbina Reservoir was made available during 1892, whilst by 1894 a considerable part of the parish had been sewered into the new Rhondda main sewer. Whitchurch now began to lose its predominant characteristics as an industrial village by reason of its development as a popular suburb of Cardiff. In 1900 the population was 4,865. By 1911 this had jumped to 9,079, a percentage increase of 86. Progress during the next decade was slowed down as the result of the European War, but by 1921 the population had nevertheless risen to 11,289.

It will be of interest to indicate the localities in which development was most pronounced up to the latter date. Between the 1840's and 1860's most of Tongwynlais seems to have been built whilst there was also development in the Whitchurch Old Village and a little in Llandaff Yard. Development in the 80's and 90's was mainly in the vicinity of Llandaff Station, and the earliest streets completed under the Private Street Works Act during the 1900's were the Hawthorn, Evansfield and Hazelhurst Roads and Belle Vue Crescent, Llandaff North.

Prior to the 1880's there was no direct road access from Whitchurch to Llandaff Station. The only available route was via Velindre Road and Heoldon. Soon after the building of the new church in 1883-1884 the present Church Road was formed and building development along its length commenced. The Gelli Farm adjoining the station was also opened up for building, but it was not until the late nineties and the following decade that development in these areas became really active. Building development in particular streets proceeded usually over many

---

* Topographical Dictionary of the Dominion of Wales.

years, and final street completions did not take place for a long period after the formation of builders' roads. Thus it was not until 1909-10 that The Parade, The Avenue and Alfreda Road came under the operation of the Private Street Works Act. Heolyforlan followed in 1912, Wingfield Road in 1913 and Bishop's Road in 1915. Meanwhile in 1912 the Rhiwbina Garden Village was commenced and a number of houses were built during the next two or three years in Penydre, Lon-y-Dail, Y Groes and Lon Isa.

For a time after the War development was slow owing to the shortage of labour and materials and high costs generally. Before building activity became really brisk the area and population of Whitchurch were curtailed as the result of the Cardiff Extension Order under which Llandaff North and the Birchgrove areas were transferred from Whitchurch to the City. By this transfer the 1921 Census population fell by 3,171 to 8118. This loss, however, was soon made good as the result of the building boom which followed. By 1931 the population of the reduced parish had increased by 57 per cent. to a total of 12,733. The estimated population today is over 20,000.

Development Statistics.

From the Census and other official sources the following table has been completed, which provides a statistical basis for obtaining a more complete picture of development than that given in the preceding section:—

Census Year.	Number of Houses	Population	Rateable Value
1801	—	696	—
1811	228	997	—
1821	235	972	—
1831	264	1,184	—
1841	295	1,376	—
1851	346	1,661	—
1861	472	2,274	—
1871	585	2,722	—
1881	574	2,752	£17,009
1891	699	3,322	£23,702
1901	1,029	4,865	£29,769
1911	1,892 (est.)	9,079	£50,893
1921	2,178 (est.)	7,528*	£54,175
1931	3,126 (est.)	12,733	£81,566
1941	5,606 (est.)	18,155 (est.)	£118,842
1943	5,772 (est.)	20,000 (est.)	£121,232

Further information in regard to development is obtainable from the records of new roads made up by owners or by the local authority under the Private Street Works Act. Between 1878 and 1922 there were 40 street proposals covering 5¾ miles of street. In the period from 1922 to 1932 7¼ miles were included in 58 schemes, and from 1932 to date 55 proposals have matured covering 6¾ miles. The estimated

---
* For reduced area resulting from Cardiff Extension Order, 1922.

mileage of highways and streets (excluding back lanes) in the parish today is about 31.
External Public Services.
The strategic position of Whitchurch in relation to Cardiff and to the densely populated Taff Valley has enabled it to benefit from large-scale public services provided by the authorities and companies serving those areas, and has relieved the Rural District Council from the responsibility of carrying out less efficient local schemes. The first and most important service—water supply—is a function of the Cardiff Corporation, which, when the Breconshire Reservoirs scheme was sanctioned by Parliament, got powers of direct supply to Whitchurch residents. The Corporation has filter beds and storage reservoirs at Rhiwbina. Next comes sewerage. The provision of local sewers is a matter for the local authority and the developers of building estates. Sewage disposal is entirely a local authority function, and small-scale disposal plants tend to be costly and unsatisfactory. Soon after a piped water supply was provided at Whitchurch the Ystradyfodwg (now the Rhondda and Pontypridd) Sewerage Board embarked on a scheme for the construction of a main trunk sewer with a sea outfall, and terms were agreed by the District Council with the Board for the contents of proposed Whitchurch sewers to be discharged into the Rhondda main sewer. Some localities adjoining the City boundaries discharge into the Cardiff Corporation main sewers.

By agreement with the Corporation Whitchurch has for many years also had the benefit of Cardiff's fire protection service.* Whitchurch is also served by the omnibus services of the Corporation, in addition to those of the Caerphilly and Pontypridd Urban Councils and that of the Rhondda Omnibus Company. Facilities are also provided by the Cardiff Education Committee, under an agreement with the Glamorgan County Education Committee, enabling local students to receive technical training at its Technical College. The Corporation is a very large ratepayer at Whitchurch not only in respect of its water undertaking but also by reason of the location there of the Mental Hospital and the Greenhill Special School.

Two other important services provided by outside bodies at Whitchurch are gas, by the Cardiff Gas Company, and bulk-supply electricity by the South Wales Power Co. Ltd.

Detailed reference to some of the above-mentioned services will be made in later paragraphs.
Water Supply and Sewerage.
The Cardiff Union Rural Sanitary Authority was constituted in 1875, and Dr. F. W. Granger was appointed Medical Officer of Health. He soon got to work with zeal for the improvement of general health conditions. His annual reports during the next twelve years—he died in 1887—provide valuable evidence not only of his own ability and zeal, but also of the whole-hearted manner in which the members of the authority discharged their duties. From his Reports may be obtained a reliable estimate of sanitary conditions 60-70 years ago.

---
* Now merged in the National Fire Service (N.F.S.)

In 1875 there was no piped water supply in the village and no system of drainage. Water for domestic use was obtained from springs, shallow wells, and the Whitchurch Brook, and most of these sources of supply were often contaminated. The sanitary conveniences attached to houses were mostly foul privy middens, and slop water and household garbage were thrown upon gardens and waste spaces in the vicinity of the water supplies. In addition a large proportion of the householders kept pigs under primitive conditions in their back gardens. It is not surprising, therefore, that the water supplies were frequently polluted with sewage, so giving rise to epidemics of typhoid and other zymotic diseases.

Dr. Granger was from the first alive to the importance of pure water, and numerous warnings against the use of water from certain wells, street pumps and the brook for dietetic purposes were from time to time issued. In 1876 as a first step towards proper house drainage he urged the necessity for the provision of house drains to carry off slop water from the houses either into underground cesspits or into the street drains, and reported that the Sanitary Authority had called upon each owner to drain his property. The Authority also ordered the conversion of privies into pail closets, these being deemed more capable of being properly cleansed.

The provision of a water carriage system was, of course, at this time impracticable in the absence of a piped water supply. Dr. Granger regularly emphasised the urgent necessity of such a supply. In 1879 he wrote:

"Where the subsoil is gravel, such as under Whitchurch, parts of Llanishen and other parishes in the District, the subsoil water at a depth of 12 or 14 feet is continually, though slowly, moving onward, and although the drains and cesspools of a cottage may be situated some distance from a well, the drainage water may find its way into and contaminate the drinking supply. Even if this happened, however, the danger may not prove great all at once, but if infectious disease once manifested itself, it is probable that through the medium of the water all who drink thereof might imbibe the disease."

After a few years there was some improvement in conditions, but little could be done until a proper supply of water was available. Some unfit wells were closed, and a few public wells were provided at suitable positions. Dr. Granger reported in 1882 that Whitchurch was served by two public pumps and by private wells.

The general public were apparently not very responsive to the efforts of the authority to improve conditions, especially when these efforts affected their personal interests. They objected to the closing of their private wells and particularly to restrictions upon the keeping of pigs. In 1883 Dr. Granger reported in regard to pig-keeping:

"We have constantly to be waging war with the owners, who often resort to all sorts of artifices to delude us. They will remove the pigs immediately they are requested, but as your authority is not empowered to order the removal of the pig-sties, they are often brought back again as soon as the inspector's back is turned. They

View Eastwards from Church Tower, 1903. *W. Morgan Davies*

Thatched Cottage, Junction of Tynypwll and Penlline Roads, 1904. *W. Morgan Davies*

LAST LOCAL COUNTRY CARRIER PASSING THROUGH　　W. Morgan Davies
WHITCHURCH, 1904

FORLAN FARM, 1902, NOW THE SITE OF FORELAND　　W. Morgan Davies
AND ST. FRANCIS ROADS

are often in too close proximity to the dwellings, and are without drainage of any kind, and the leakage from the cask of wash finds its way into the house, or perchance into some well by percolation."

In 1885 the question of providing a piped water supply and proper sewerage arrangements came under serious consideration. A sewerage scheme for Whitchurch, Llandaff Yard and Maindy was prepared, with filtration works at Maindy, but as the estimated cost of this scheme was £8,500 it was deemed prohibitive. A smaller scheme for Llandaff Yard only was rejected by the Local Government Board. The matter was therefore deferred in the hope that as a result of an impending improvement in the Cardiff Water Supply some arrangement could be made for supplying Whitchurch. The Cardiff Corporation had in 1879 obtained Parliamentary powers for the acquisition of the property and rights of the Cardiff Waterworks Company, and in 1884 had been granted further powers for obtaining a new water supply from the head waters of the River Taff. The pipe line from Breconshire to Cardiff was commenced during 1885 and was completed in April, 1888. The Rhiwbina Reservoir, from which Whitchurch was to be supplied, was commenced in 1886. In 1891-2 the Corporation laid down service mains to most parts of the parish, and by 1894 practically all local residences had their supplies from the public mains.

The provision of sewerage facilities was now a practical proposition. At this time the Ystradyfodwg (now Rhondda) and Pontypridd Main Sewerage Board had in hand the construction of a trunk sewer with a sea outfall. On the suggestion of the Local Government Board the Sanitary Authority negotiated with the Sewerage Board for the right of draining into the Trunk Sewer, and in December, 1888, a formal agreement was executed under which for 35 years Whitchurch should have such right on payment of an amount of $3\frac{1}{2}$d. in the pound of ratable value. In 1894 the Sanitary Authority let contracts amounting to £6,000 for the sewering of Whitchurch into the Rhondda sewer, and during that year Dr. Pritchard, who succeeded Dr. Granger in 1887, reported the filling in of 700 cesspools, and the removal of 500 privies and 115 earth closets In the following year the work of improvement was practically completed.

1894 was, therefore, one of the outstanding years in the sanitary and development history of Whitchurch, and it was also the year in which was passed the Local Government Act under which the Rural Sanitary Authority ceased to exist and the Rural District Council was set up in its place. The estimated population of Whitchurch at this time was about 3,500. Working-class housing conditions at this period were of a low standard. During the nineties several dozen unfit houses were permanently closed and many dilapidated houses were repaired. A number of such dwellings were of the thatched roof type. Whitchurch was being tidied up to bring it into line with the improved type of building development which was now in full swing.

Treatment of Infectious Diseases.

Up to the late 1890's infectious diseases were being treated, by agreement between the Rural Authority and the Cardiff Corporation, at the Canton Sanatorium. Owing to the accommodation being needed for Cardiff residents the Rural District Council had to make other arrangements. Several sites at Whitchurch were provisionally selected for the erection of a hospital, but the Parish Council opposed on the mistaken ground that its location there would be a danger to the neighbourhood, and they asked local landowners to withhold land from the District Council.

Pending the selection of a suitable site, in 1900 provision was made in a temporary structure on Radyr Court Farm. The Tredegar Estate offered a site at Whitchurch "but some of the parishioners made such frantic demonstrations that the offer was immediately withdrawn." In 1903 another site on Tir Pwdr (*i.e.*, Ty-pant-yr-ywen) was under consideration, but as the price asked by the Tredegar Estate was deemed too high the District Council decided to build elsewhere. In 1904 they bought a portion of Colonel Hill's estate at Ely, which they exchanged with the Board of Guardians for land near the Ely Homes, and on the latter site was built the Isolation Hospital, which still serves Whitchurch and other areas in the Rural District. The building was opened in August 1907. For the treatment of cases of small-pox an arrangement was made with the Barry authority for the use of their hospital.

Gas and Electricity.

In addition to water supply and sewerage means of lighting are also necessary for quick building development. Up to the late nineties there were no gas or electricity services available locally. Gas had been laid on to Llandaff in 1892 but had not been extended to Whitchurch. The Parish Council some time after its formation in 1894 had under consideration the question of street lighting. Representations made to the Gas Company early in 1895 for the extension of the mains proved unsuccessful, and it was not until 1899 that the mains were laid and a supply made available. The terms quoted by the Gas Company for street lighting were deemed unsatisfactory and the Parish Council asked a firm of consulting engineers to prepare a scheme for the generation of electricity for lighting 82 lamps, 160 yards apart. The estimated cost of this scheme was £1,850, exclusive of buildings.

On an approach to the Local Government Board the Parish Council were informed that they were not empowered to generate electricity for lighting purposes; they therefore asked the District Council to proceed with a scheme. These representations were unavailing, and between 1901 and 1903 the Parish Council erected and maintained a number of acetylene street lamps. In September, 1903, terms were arranged with the Gas Company for gas-lighting the streets on the basis of £3 1s. 4d. per annum per lamp, standards and lamps to be provided by the Council. This figure was reduced to £2 15s. 4d. in August, 1904, and later in 1910 to £2 13s. 8d.

In 1904 the South Wales Power Company proposed to extend their electricity mains to Whitchurch, and the Rural District Council were invited to take a supply. Several years elapsed, however, before a supply was actually available. In 1910 the Velindre Road Electrical Sub-Station was built and a system of mains laid along the principal streets. In January, 1911, arrangements were made with the Parish Council to take a supply of electricity for street lamps at a cost of £2 17s. 6d. per lamp. Since that year electricity has been extended to most parts of the parish and the electrical undertaking is now one of very great importance. The number of units sold by the Council throughout the Rural District now amounts to more than seven millions per annum.

Fire Protection.

After the provision of a piped water supply by the Cardiff Corporation in 1895 the Parish Council decided to take action to deal with fires. Appliances were purchased and a voluntary fire brigade of 15 members was organised. During the latter part of 1897 the volunteers were reported to be making good progress with their drill, and a Parish Meeting was held for the purpose of obtaining sanction for the purchase of firemen's clothing, outfit and equipment. Police Sergeant Williams was in charge of the training of the Brigade, for which duty he was paid the sum of £3. He was also voted a salary of £7, later increased to £9, per annum, as captain-instructor. At first the equipment consisted of a pump, standpipe and hose, which was conveyed to the scene of the fire in a vehicle horsed by a local butcher.

The volunteer fire brigade continued in being until 1909, when the members went on strike, because the Parish Council would not provide them with a proper headquarters. This action forced the hands of the Parish Council, who provided temporary quarters off Church Road, whilst arrangements were being made for the provision of a permanent building. A site in Bishops Road was acquired at a cost of £86, and thereon was built a fire station with Parish Council offices above. For carrying out this work a loan of £900 was obtained. Improved equipment was also provided, and this was supplemented in 1914 by a Merryweather Engine costing £570.

In 1921 it was thought that the members of the Brigade, who were then commanded by Mr. W. Morgan Davies, were too old for the work, and they resigned. Police Inspector Bennett was asked to organise a new brigade, a duty which he declined to undertake. The Parish Council now decided to organise a paid brigade, the captain of which, Mr. Griffiths the butcher, was to receive a salary of £15, and each other member £3 15s. 0d. per annum. The total annual estimated cost was £71 10s. 0d. This arrangement lasted only for a short time, and the Parish Council later made arrangements with the Cardiff Brigade to service the district. The National Fire Service is now the authority responsible for local fire fighting activities.

Library Gardens.

At the end of 1899 the Cardiff Corporation were negotiating for the purchase of Velindre House and grounds for the purpose of establishing a Mental Hospital. To enable this scheme to be carried out it was necessary to extinguish a public right of way across the land from the top end of Heoldon to the Merthyr Road near the old Tithe Barn. The Parish Council expressed hostility to the proposal, and negotiations took place between representatives of the Corporation and the Parish

Council. Ultimately the Parish Council representatives, Messrs. A. H. Bullock and Edmund Lewis, agreed to withdraw their opposition, conditionally upon the Corporation presenting to the Parish Council the triangular site of about four acres adjoining the junction of the Merthyr and Velindre Roads, and constructing a new footpath along the north-western side thereof. The Corporation offered to lease the land for a period of 75 years at an annual ground rent of 10/-, subject to certain restrictions relating to demonstrations, fetes, etc. The Parish Council refused the offer, and ultimately the Corporation agreed to the terms, and obtained from the vendors an abatement of £400 from the purchase price. The land conveyance was made direct to the Parish Council.

Library Facilities.

Early in February, 1895, the Parish Council were authorised by a Parish Meeting to adopt the Public Libraries Act and to expend an amount not exceeding a penny rate. A house was rented at an annual rental of £34, excluding rates and taxes, and fire and lighting for one room. The upper part of the premises was to be used as Parish Council Offices, and the downstairs rooms were let for £10 a year to a privately organised Library Committee. The arrangement seems not to have been successful, and the library arrangement was abandoned at the end of one year.

In June, 1896, the Parish Council convened a public meeting for the purpose of discussing the provision of a Public Hall. A committee was set up to further the movement but apparently nothing resulted. After the conveyance of the Velindre Road land to the Parish Council in 1899 the Parish Council approached the Carnegie Trust for a grant for the erection of a library building on part of that site. The application was granted and towards the end of 1904 the new building, designed by Messrs. R. & S. Williams and erected by Mr. W. T. Morgan at a cost of £2,000, was completed.

Mr. H. R. John was appointed to the combined post of Librarian and Park-keeper at a wage of 18/- per week plus living quarters. Gifts of books and many donations were solicited from the general public and in 1905 the Library was opened. After a few years a demand arose for branch libraries and in the autumn of 1909 one was opened at a cottage near the Philog and another at Tongwynlais. Later a third branch was established at Llandaff North. These branches seem to have continued sporadically until 1922, when they were closed.

Whitchurch Common.

One of the most discussed questions at Parish Council meetings during a period of nearly fifty years has been the acquisition of public rights over Whitchurch Common. In 1895 negotiations were opened by the Parish Council with the agents of the Marquess of Bute, one of the Lords of the Manor. Nothing eventuated, and in 1897 the Parish Council asked Lord Bute to present the common to Whitchurch residents as a Jubilee Gift. This request also brought no result.

During the next couple of years numerous protests were being made against gypsy camping on the Common, and in April, 1899, it was decided to consult the Board of Agriculture as to the possibility of an Enclosure Scheme. On being asked by the Board to deposit an amount of £50 to cover expenses the Parish Council decided to take no action. A further approach was made to Lord Bute's Agent, and in January, 1900, Mr. J. S. Corbett intimated that Lord Bute "is disposed to meet the wishes of the Parish Council if proper arrangements can be made for keeping the Common as a recreation ground." In April of the same year Mr. Corbett stated that he had communicated with the solicitors of Lord Tredegar, who also held manorial rights, and these "had approved in principle of the transfer to a public authority subject to rights of access to his Lordship's adjoining land being provided."

The matter again hung fire, and in February, 1901, Mr. Corbett wrote that owing to the death of the Marquess of Bute nothing further could be done in the matter. "What was intended to be done," wrote Mr. Corbett, "was in the nature of a free gift and the Trustees who are at present in charge of the Estate have no power to make such an arrangement." In May, 1904, the new Lord Bute was asked to carry out the arrangement sanctioned by his father, but this representation failed.

For some years the matter lay dormant, but in 1910 and again in 1914 deputations from the Parish Council waited on Lord Bute's solicitors without success. In 1919, in response to another request by a newly-elected Parish Council, the Bute solicitors replied that Lord Bute was not prepared to hand over the Common, but was agreeable to the Parish Council planting trees thereon. In 1922 the Parish Council spent a sum of £30 on this improvement. Several efforts have since been made to prevail on Lord Bute to transfer his rights, and on the last occasion apparently Lord Bute was prepared to do so conditionally on there being no interference with the camping rights of gipsies. To this condition the Parish Council would not agree, and there the matter lies. Negotiations with the Tredegar Estate in regard to the manorial rights of the Roath Keynsham portion of the Common were more successful and these are now vested in the Parish Council.

Boundary Changes.

From time to time with the continuous growth of Cardiff proposals for extension have been made by the Corporation. The first of these affecting Whitchurch was made in 1898 and related only to a small area of about 10 acres. The next Borough Extension was made under an Extension Order of 1922. Under this order an area near Birchgrove and Caerphilly Road, together with the Llandaff North portion of the Parish, were detached from Whitchurch and added to the City. The following table gives the statistical particulars before and after the extension:—

	Before Extension.	After Extension.
Area	3,269 acres	2,907 acres
Population ...	11,289	7,528
Rateable Value ...	£58,117	£54,175

The population and rateable value lost by this curtailment was soon made good during the building boom of the ensuing years. By the Census of 1931 the population had increased to 12,733 and the rateable value in that year had increased to £78,148. By a Glamorgan Review Order made in 1934 the Eglwysilan portion of Tongwynlais, comprising an area of 469 acres, a population of 800 and an estimated rateable value of £1,500 was transferred to the Parish of Whitchurch. Exact figures are not available as to the present population of Whitchurch, but it is officially estimated at over 20,000. It is of interest to note that since the Cardiff Extension Order of 1922, up to the outbreak of War, about 3,000 new houses had been completed.

Electoral Divisions.

After the sanction by Parliament of the Cardiff Extension Order of 1922, under which Ely, Llandaff and a portion of Whitchurch were incorporated in the City the name of the Llandaff and Dinas Powis Rural District was changed to the Cardiff Rural District, and an adjustment of local representation on the Rural District Council was effected. Whitchurch got 6 members instead of 4. Under the Glamorgan Review Order which followed the passing of the Local Government Act of 1929, the area was extended by the unification of Tongwynlais and the local representation on the Rural District Council was further increased to 10 members out of a total of 39 for the district. The parish was by the same Order divided for electoral purposes into 5 wards, viz., Tongwynlais, Velindre, Eglwysnewydd, Treoda and Rhiwbina. Adjustments were also made in the County Council electoral divisions. By the absorption of Ely and Llandaff into Cardiff the total electorate of the Radyr division was greatly reduced, whilst that of Kibbor, consequent on the abnormal development of Whitchurch, had greatly increased. It was therefore decided to transfer a large slice of Northern Whitchurch (comprising the new Tongwynlais and Velindre Wards) to a new county electoral division named Castell Coch, in which the Radyr Division was merged. At the ensuing triennial election Sir Lewis Lougher was elected as its representative on the County Council.

Vital Statistics.

The vital statistics of Whitchurch have not been recorded separately from those of the Rural District, but the following comparative statement over a long period of years for the District as a whole may probably be taken as indicative of the position at Whitchurch. It will be seen from the statement that great reductions have been effected in the death rate, due largely to the improvement of sanitary conditions, and during recent years to the public services provided for the care of mothers and infants:—

Census Periods.	Population.	Birth Rates.	Infantile Death-Rates.	General Death Rates.
1875-1881	16,189	30.92	117.88	16.06
1887-1891	18,539	31.71	115.00	15.97
1892-1896	—	30.25	121.00	14.90
1897-1901	23,047	28.97	108.00	13.20
1902-1906	—	27.89	102.00	12.39
1907-1911	33,200	24.90	96.00	11.53
1912-1916	—	22.58	70.60	10.52
1917-1921	42,122 (reduced to 23,620)	19.83	75.00	11.56
1922-1926	—	18.74	60.80	10.07
1927-1931	29,046	13.97	67.50	9.63
1932-1939	(Est. 32,000)	12.31	55.40	10.75

Rateable Value and Rates.

Other evidence of the extent and rapidity of development and of public expenditure in Whitchurch is contained in the following table showing the rateable values and rate poundages levied in the parish at intervals over the past sixty years:—

	Population	Rateable Value	Rate Poundage
1881	2,752	£16,990	2/1
1886	—	21,691	2/3
1891	3,322	23,545	2/6
1896	—	25,756	3/8
1901	4,865	29,769	5/6½
1906	—	35,843	5/6
1911	9,079	50,388	6/7
1916	—	54,696	6/-
1921	11,289 (Reduced to 7,528)	54,965	15/2
1926	—	69,875	13/5
1931	13,533	78,148	13/5
1936	—	102,479	15/8
1941	20,000 + (est.)	118,842	18/0½
1943	—	121,232	16/6

SHORT LIST OF SOURCES.

Annual Reports of Medical Officer of Health.
Census Returns.
Cardiff R.D.C. Annual Financial Statements.
Llandaff Highway Board Records (Glam. County Archives).
Llandaff and Dinas Powis Sanitary Authority Records.
Whitchurch Parish Council Minutes and Correspondence.

CHAPTER XII.

THE STORY OF THE SCHOOLS.

On account of the close association over many centuries between the Chapelry of Whitchurch and the Mother-Church of Llandaff—the headquarters of religion and culture in South-East Wales—local educational history is of greater interest and covers a far longer period than that of more remote parishes. As has already been shown the religious connection of Whitchurch with Llandaff was placed on a firm and definite footing by the Concord of Woodstock (1126), although in all probability the association had been a close and binding one from a much earlier date.

Scholastic instruction was until about a century ago regarded as essentially a function of the Church working independent of the State, and it may be assumed that such educational facilities as were provided at Llandaff over hundreds of years were freely available as of right to the parishioners of Whitchurch. The educational history of Whitchurch, therefore, was until comparatively recently that of the Mother-Church.

Scholastic functions were exercised by Llandaff probably before the Norman Conquest. Bishop Bledri in 983 ordered that every priest should set up a school in connection with his church, mainly, it may be supposed, for the purpose of religious teaching. The policy seems also to have been continued by his successor, Bishop Joseph.

It may therefore be assumed that scholastic activities were an essential feature of the church organisation at Llandaff in the 10th and 11th centuries. In the 12th century also the famous Geoffrey of Monmouth is supposed to have been associated in a teaching capacity with a school at the Cathedral. Records, however, are sparse, and it is not until the 15th century that we have very reliable information.

It is definitely known that about 1470 Sir David Mathew left money for establishing a chantry which supported a priest to say mass at the Cathedral, and also "to keepe a free Scole for certeyn pore children to the number of XX." This school was in existence more than a century later, and it is recorded that one John Singer was the chantry priest and taught 20 scholars for a salary of £5 14s. 0d. per annum. In all probability, however, the chantry was wiped out in the reign of Edward VI.

Numerous entries in the *Llandaff Act Books* occur during the 17th century. About 1638 there was a contract for glazing the 'school

WHITCHURCH GOLF CLUB HOUSE, FORMERLY PENTWYN FARM *Cardiff Library*

WHITCHURCH GOLF COURSE, NORTHERN PORTION *Cardiff Library*

WHITCHURCH GOLF COURSE, SOUTHERN PORTION *Cardiff Library*

WHITCHURCH SECONDARY SCHOOL   *Glamorgan Education Committee* house.' In 1662 Thomas Jones, B.A., was Junior Vicar Choral, and in addition to ministering to the chapelry of Whitchurch, he also conducted a school for 12 boys at Llandaff. For this he received £12 per annum additional to his stipend of £20 from the Cursal Barns as one of the Vicars Choral. In the same year a sum of £5 was paid for "the rebuilding and repayreinge the schoole house," etc.

Also in 1662 Wm. Deere was paid £4

"for teaching 8 boys and girls such as neither they themselves nor their parents are competently able to pay for their such schooling and education; and these children to be chosen and approved by some of the discreetest persons there."

A record of 1691 also records the allowance to "Wm. Dear, deacon," of £4 "for giving the Singing psalmes in the Quire of this Church, over and above the eight pounds form'rly allow'd him by this Chapter for keepeing school." Five years later in 1696 the widow of Wm. Deere was awarded a benevolence of 40/- "with £4 more for teaching school at Llandaffe since the death of her husband." Edward Lhwyd also mentions the existence of a Llandaff school in 1698.

There is also evidence of the continued existence of the Llandaff school in the 18th century. In 1716 William Morgan was elected "Master of the Free School," and in 1719 Browne Willis mentions the existence of a school in a room over the Cathedral Chapter House. There are also records relating to the rebuilding of a school-house in 1727, to the appointment of Thomas Charles as Master in 1736, and in 1737 to the provision of a fives court for the use of the scholars.

In all probability the Llandaff school or schools connected with the Cathedral were maintained continuously as part of the ecclesiastical organisation right down to the setting up of National Schools in the Cathedral village in 1817, and it seems safe to assume that the facilities there provided were available to poor children from Whitchurch as from other hamlets in the Parish of Llandaff.

It is likely, however, that such facilities covered the needs of only a small proportion of the children; children of the better-to-do parishioners were probably taught to read and write, if nothing more, in small proprietary schools carried on usually in private houses, each scholar paying a small weekly fee.

The dissenting bodies which came into existence in the 17th century realised the importance of scholastic teaching as an aid to religion, and it is likely that the Puritan preachers imparted instruction in reading, so that their adherents might at any rate be able to read the Bible.

When during the Cromwellian era the Puritans were in control of the government of the country they passed in 1649-1650 the first education act in our history—"An Act for the Better Propagation and Preaching of the Gospel in Wales." Under this measure Commissioners were appointed "to provide for the keeping of schools and education for children" and to make allowances so that "fit persons of approved piety and learning may have encouragement to employ themselves in the education of children in piety and good literature." A number of schools were set up by the Commissioners in different parts of Wales, including one at Cardiff with Andrew Bancroft as master and another at St. Fagans. It was, however, perhaps hardly to be expected that such a school could be set up at Llandaff, the diocesan centre of the Established Church.

The example of the Puritans, however, was not without effect on the policy of the State Church. After the Restoration of the Monarchy in 1660 the Puritan schools were closed and repressive legislation enacted against Dissenters. Nevertheless in 1662 the Bishop of Llandaff appealed for funds for the setting up of free schools throughout his diocese, and it is likely that a number of such schools was set up by the local clergy. The Llandaff Free School already referred to may have been one of the results of the Bishop's new policy.

The attempt to repress Puritanism did not wholly succeed, and Puritan ministers and schoolmasters set up conventicles in private houses, where religious services were held and people were taught to read the Bible, if nothing more. Two local conventicle leaders were Thomas Quarrell, of Whitchurch, and John Powell, M.A., the ejected clergyman of St. Lythans.

About 1674 an ejected London clergyman, Thomas Gouge, started an important movement in Wales for the spread of Puritan principles and for teaching poor Welsh children to read and write English, with a view to their more efficient instruction in scripture. Gouge's Welsh Trust founded between three and four hundred schools in various parts of Wales, including Cardiff, Wenvoe, St. Nicholas and Michaelston-y-Fedw. I have not been able to trace the existence of a Gouge school in any part of the Parish of Llandaff.

In due course the Welsh Trust died out, and in 1699 the Society for the Promotion of Christian Knowledge (better known as the S.P.C.K.) was established by some of Gouge's followers, but with wider aims. Its efforts extended chiefly over England and between 1699 and 1737 only 12 schools seem to have been established in Glamorgan. It is likely, however, that some local Charity Schools were set up through the influence, although not under the auspices, of the S.P.C.K. In 1707 a school charity was founded at Cardiff by Jane Herbert and another in 1710 by Craddock Wells, whilst Mary Lewis made similar provision at Llanishen and Lisvane in 1728, and Mrs. Aldsworth at Eglwysilan in 1730.

The Charity School movement covered only a small area in Wales, but out of it grew the remarkable Circulating School Movement initiated by Rev. Griffith Jones, an Anglican clergyman, of Llanddowror. He collected subscriptions from sympathisers, and sent out from his training centre in Carmarthenshire a number of schoolmasters to carry on schools in various places throughout Wales for teaching men, women and children "to read God's holy word in their native British language."

The schoolmasters stayed from three to six months in each place, and then passed on to other centres, leaving their more apt scholars to carry on locally the task of teaching others. Up to Griffith Jones' death in 1761 no fewer than 3,495 such schools had been held, with an attendance of nearly 160,000 scholars. This work was continued by Madame Bevan until her death in 1779, after which the movement petered out.

Many Circulating Schools were held in Glamorgan, including the following in the Cardiff district.

1738-9, Llanishen; 1739-40, Eglwysilan (2 schools); Pentyrch; 1740-1, Eglwysilan, St. John's (Cardiff); 1741-2, Lisvane; 1742-3, Lisvane; 1744-5, St. Nicholas; 1748-9, Eglwysilan (Groeswen); 1749-1750 Eglwysilan (Groeswen); 1752-3, Roath Parish Church, Whitchurch Parish Church; 1753-4, Lisvane, Ffilocks (Philog, Whitchurch); 1754-5, Ty Bach Dan y Graig, Lisvane; Llanishen Almshouse, Groeswen (Radyr), St. Fagans; 1755-6, Llanishen Almshouse; Maesybryn (Llanedeyrn); 1756-7, Eglwysilan; 1757-8, Llanishen Village, Tongwynlais; 1758-9, Tynycae (Whitchurch); 1772-3, Mardy House (Radyr).

Out of the Circulating School movement grew the Welsh Sunday School which for the greater part of a century was perhaps the most potent educational agency in the Principality. Thomas Charles, of Bala, in 1785, tried to revive circulating schools in a movement of his own soon after Robert Raikes had begun his great work in England, and he combined with his circulating schools a religious Sunday teaching organisation similar to that of Raikes. The Circulating School idea was soon dropped, and Charles concentrated upon the task of organising Sunday Schools for the religious education of adults as well as children.

This movement was mainly connected with Methodism, but other sects copied, including the Anglican Church. Many of the Sunday Schools, especially in the early days, were ephemeral in character, and were held in private dwellings, barns, and other miscellaneous buildings, and no record of their activities is available. Later, with the setting up of regular chapels, the Sunday Schools assumed a permanent character, and they played an important part in the teaching of reading, particularly of the Welsh Bible.

Tribute is paid in the Reports of the Education Commissioners of 1847 to the valuable work of the Welsh Sunday Schools, and considerable details are given of their activities. From those documents, the appended particulars of local Sunday Schools have been derived. It should be borne in mind that the returns take into account only the

Schools which were in being in 1847—doubtless there were many other local schools which were non-permanent:—

Name and Location of School.	Date of Foundation.	Average Attendance, 1847.	Number of Scholars also attending Day Schools.
Llandaff:			
National Boys (Church)	1817	40	52
National Girls (Church)	1817	40	60
Radyr:			
Bethel (Calv. Meth.)	1822	100	6
Radyr Court (Church)	1841	26	9
Llanilltern:			
Philadelphia (Ind.) (now Taihirion)	1817	7	4
Pentyrch:			
National School (Church)	1834	43	40
Penuel (Baptist)	1829	49	3
Bethlehem (Ind.)	1829	143	22
Horeb (Calv. Meth.)	1804	65	7
Whitchurch:			
Ararat (Baptist)	1824	55	15
Ebenezer (Calv. Meth.)	1809	70	23
Penylan (Wesleyan)	1820	110	54
Llanishen:			
National School (Church)	1827	75	54
Lisvane:			
Derwendeg (Baptist)	1812	46	29
Llanedeyrn:			
Hephzibah (Calv. Meth.)	1835	59	40

Until late in the 18th century the educational agencies providing for the needs of Whitchurch parishioners were either centred at Llandaff Cathedral or connected with Dissenting bodies. It may be supposed that under such circumstances a large proportion of the local population could neither read nor write. Many of those who had learnt the arts had probably been taught by better educated neighbours or by attending small private schools conducted at their own residences by persons of limited educational attainments.

About the 1780's the Quaker ironmasters of Melingriffith, who had a great regard for the well-being of their workers, seem to have taken certain steps for the provision of scholastic facilities for the children of employees. No records of this activity are available, and one can only deduce the fact from miscellaneous entries in the works accounts. Thus an entry of 1786 records repairs by works artizans to a school building, and the membership roll of a local friendly society started in the same year is headed by 'Edward Williams, Schoolmaster.' Edward Williams (Iolo Morgannwg) lived in Llandaff about this period, and one would like to believe that he was the Melingriffith schoolmaster. There is, however, no evidence to support this suggestion.

Rhiwbina Council School	*Cardiff Library*

The "Fox" Schoolroom, 1905	*W. Morgan Davies*

TYNYPARC ROAD, 1911 — W. Morgan Davies

HEOLYFORLAN, 1911 — W. Morgan Davies

Eighteen months later the Friendly Society was joined by 'Robert Rowland, Schoolmaster.' This was the first of a long list of members of the Rowland family connected with Melingriffith Works. I have no further information apart from these entries, but they do seem to establish the fact that there was a school building and a schoolmaster in the locality and the probability is that the venture was sponsored by the Works proprietors. Mention is made also in the Heath Enclosure Award 1801 of a schoolmaster named Llewelyn Prosser who had a tenement and land at Rhiwbina.

Apart from the Melingriffith effort practically all the public forms of education have been associated with religious organisations; probably almost the only secular subject taught was reading, and this was taught for a religious purpose. Early in the 19th century the need for a more regular system of education came to be felt—although the religious motive still continued to be dominant—and as the result of the work of the educational pioneers, Dr. Bell and Joseph Lancaster, two school-promoting organisations came into existence.

These were the National Society for the Education of the Poor—an Anglican body—and the British and Foreign Schools Society—an undenominational body which co-operated with Lancaster. Both bodies were supported by voluntary subscriptions and a large number of "National" and "British" schools was set up throughout the country. In 1833 State aid for the two societies was made available for the erection of new buildings. After 1846 grants for the maintenance of schools were also given.

Both National and British schools provided a wider secular curriculum than the older scholastic agencies; writing and arithmetic, as well as other subjects, were taught in addition to reading and scripture. The voluntary system of school organization, based on charitable subscriptions, State grants and the fees of scholars, continued until 1870, when publicly-maintained Board schools first came into existence. From this period the religious motive in education became less important than the civic motive, and the teaching of scripture gradually ceased to be the primary subject of the curriculum.

The 19th century educational history of Whitchurch has associations with the Lancastrian, National and School Board forms of organization. As has already been indicated the Melingriffith proprietors—the Messrs. Harford—were much interested in the welfare of their workers. Being Quakers, also, the principles of education advocated by Joseph Lancaster fitted in most nearly with their views. Prior to the formation of the British Society Lancaster was carrying on propaganda in favour of undenominational schools. In 1806 he was at Swansea, where probably the first Lancastrian school in Wales was established.

Possibly as a result of the Swansea venture the Harfords in October, 1807, invited Lancaster to address a meeting at Whitchurch with a view to the establishment of a similar school in that locality. At this gathering a decision to set up such a school was arrived at, and a committee was set up for the purpose of furthering the movement.

Next day Joseph Lancaster issued the following letter, commending the proposed new school to the local community.

To the Heads of Families and others whom it may concern at Melingriffith Iron-Works and its Vicinity:—

Friends

After enjoying the high gratification of your company yesterday I had the pleasure of meeting in the evening a number of persons well known among you, who were interested in the success of the great and good work I had before recommended. A number were chosen as a committee, and a subscription began for the fitting up of a schoolroom and opening the school, as soon as possible. The establishment and encouragement of a Girls' School was also taken into consideration and agreed to as part of the plan.

It was with great satisfaction I met so many steady and Respectable persons. Their subscriptions do honour to their feelings as men. I am glad there are such a number of Benevolent characters among you who will interest themselves in the prosperity of the design. The Blessings of the rising generation will doubtless rest upon them. The youth will hold them in veneration, and the whole neighbourhood look up to their example and themselves witness that the labour of virtue bringeth forth pleasure.

My desire for your welfare and the happiness of your children would induce me to wait upon you all personally and request that *with one heart and with one spirit* every individual would give *according to his ability* to forward the establishment of the school, but as my Time does not admit this I address you by letter and I assure you I will gladly render you any service that lies in my power.

I hope you will encourage one another to contribute such a sum of money as will effectually establish the thing. The cheerful gifts of any, however small, will be acceptable to the fund, and by your steady support will certainly confer a lasting benefit on the place and neighbourhood.

Wishing you every blessing in your families as well as in the establishing of the school I remain your respectful and well-wishing Friend.

JOS. LANCASTER.

Melin Griffith,
12 mo 26—1807.

As a result of the appeal a sum of £53 3s. 3d. was subscribed in 1807 and a further amount of £14 in 1809. The donations came from the Harfords and a few local gentry and shopkeepers, as well as from Melingriffith workmen, and I have definite proof that the school was in being during 1808 and 1809. Both boys and girls were admitted on tickets issued for quarterly periods by Robert Rowland, the Melingriffith accountant, who acted as treasurer for the fund. During 1809 as many as 62 children attended. The school was in charge of a master.*

---

* The master's name was William Gatward. He was paid a salary of £10 per quarter. (C.L. MS. 2-665).

I cannot say how long the school was in being, but as the Harford connection with Melingriffith ceased before 1810, it is not unlikely that the school was then closed, or it may have been re-organised as a private adventure school.

It is, at any rate, improbable that the district was from this time onwards for any long period without some form of school arrangement, in addition to the facilities provided at the National Schools in Llandaff, and a local Sunday School connected with Ebenezer Calvinistic Methodist chapel. Details of local scholastic arrangements are contained in reports furnished in 1818 to a *Select Committee on the Education of the Poor*.

This information was supplied by William Davies, Senior Vicar Choral, in regard to Llandaff, whilst the Junior Vicar Choral, Thomas Lewis, returned for Whitchurch, which at the time had a population of 997 against a total of 960 for all the hamlets of Llandaff.

Two day schools and a Sunday school were reported in existence at Llandaff, all apparently connected with the National Society. In addition there were

"Two day schools at Whitchurch, at which the children are paid (for) by their parents; and a Sunday school, supported by subscription, containing 30 boys and 26 girls; the master's salary is 3/6 per week, and monitor 1/10."

"The poorer classes are desirous of possessing more sufficient means of education; and there is a National School just erected (at Llandaff) but not yet opened, for want of a proper master to instruct the children."

"At Whitchurch, the poorer classes in general have no means within themselves of educating their children, but are mostly inclined to let them receive instruction; and the Sunday school is dying for want of support."

I cannot say what kind of day schools existed. They were probably proprietary 'dame' schools, maintained by the payments of school fees by parents.

The Sunday school, however, was a subscription school, and since the teachers were paid it was probably associated with the Anglican Church; a Sunday school associated with Ebenezer Methodist chapel would most certainly not be able to pay teachers.

In 1833 was issued a further valuable Government document called *Abstract of Education Returns*: The entry for Whitchurch reveals the existence of a Day School with 24 boys and 6 girls whose school fees were paid by the parents, and of three Sunday schools, viz.:—

	Boys	Girls
Calvinistic Methodist (Ebenezer) ...	25	22
Wesleyan Methodist (Melingriffith) ...	21	14
Baptist (Ararat)	14	10

In addition "about 20 children from the parish attend the National Schools at Llandaff." There seem to have been two National Schools, one with 51 boys and the other with 67 girls. These schools also met as Sabbath Schools in the same buildings. The Master and Mistress were paid £30 and £25 respectively, and also received school fees of 6d. per month from each child.

Other schools seem at this time to have been established in neighbouring villages. A National School started in 1818 at Pentyrch had 50 girls and boys in attendance in 1833. In addition an Independent School in connection with Bethlehem Chapel (Gwaelodygarth) was set up in 1832 and served 30 children. There were also Independent and Methodist Sunday schools in Pentyrch Parish and one dissenting Sunday school but no day school at Radyr.

Further facts are contained in the *Report of the Royal Commission on the Employment of Children*, 1842. There reference is made to a school—also mentioned in the 1833 Abstract—which was kept by Thomas Phillips in a small out-building adjoining the Fox and Hounds Inn, and which is still referred to locally as *The Fox School*. Phillips seems to have started this school as a private adventure about 1821 and to have carried it on for about 35 years.

Phillips was born at Thornhill in March, 1791, and later lived at Lisvane where he attended school first at Penyrheolfelen and afterwards at Lisvane Church. He became a weaver, but, being 'a bit of a scholar,' at the age of 25 he switched over to teaching.

The 1833 Report makes, *inter alia*, the following statements in regard to local educational arrangements.

"There are in this neighbourhood (Melingriffith) many Sunday Schools in connexion with the Establishment, Welsh Methodists or Whitfieldites, Independents, Baptists, and Wesleyan Methodists, at which reading only is taught; many only obtain this type of instruction."

"In the winter evenings some schools are open for instruction, and are attended by the young people who labour at the Pentyrch and Melin Griffith Tin Works. This mode of instruction is of use to those who have had the advantage of previous day-school education, but not of much use to those who labour hard through the day, and, from fatigue or inaptitude, may remain till doomsday and not make much progress.

"There are day schools for the working population, from which they are removed early, and when once removed to continuous employment very few think of attending any kind of school afterwards. I know of no school whatever in the neighbourhood that is attended by children and young persons actually employed in labour.

"The branches of instruction commonly taught are reading, writing and arithmetic. The teachers have had no other than common day-school instruction; certainly have no education qualification and training.

"Those children who have attended this school (i.e. Phillips') have rarely been removed before 11 to labour; even the removal at that age is too early, and I certainly should recommend them being kept at school till 13 years at least, though I am not aware that the removal to work at the tin or iron works has ever operated to the injury of any of the children, for those at continuous employment appear to me as healthy and even more spirited than those who do not go to work."

"The girls employed in the tinworks are generally instructed in needlework, knitting, and reading, prior to commencing labour, at some of the small schools kept by females for that purpose."

Five years later was published the notorious *Report of the Commissioners on the State of Education in Wales*, better known as *Brad y Llyfrau Gleision* (The Treachery of the Blue Books). These Reports are of great value as a source of educational facts and statistics, but the conclusions were vitiated by the strong anti-Welsh complex of the Commissioners and their assistants. For the local reports Mr. R. R. W. Lingen, M.A., afterwards Lord Lingen, was responsible.

It will suffice if I give here very briefly a summary of the facts given in the Reports relating to the local schools. At this period there were in existence three day schools and three Sunday Schools.

Of the Village School, kept by Thomas Phillips, the visiting assistant commissioner writes:

'The master appeared intelligent and spoke English correctly. The children were orderly on the whole. This appeared to be rather an efficient school."

It was held in a building 30 f et by 15 by 10 and had accommodation for 75. There were 44 names on the book, representing two girls and 23 boys between the ages of 5 and 10, and 9 girls and 10 boys over 10. Fifteen of the children lived more than 1½ miles from the school. The subjects taught were reading, writing and arithmetic. The master was supported by school fees paid by the parents, which that year amounted to about £39.

There were also two Dame Schools. One, kept by Miss Crea, met in a building 14 feet by 12 by 9, with accommodation for 28, which was situated half a mile from the village. There were 24 children in attendance, all but two being less than 10 years of age. The average attendance for the previous year was 13 girls and 10 boys. Miss Crea opened her school in 1839 when she was 39 years old. Her income from school fees was £25 per year. The Inspector wrote of her that "she appeared to be well informed though she spoke English not quite correctly."

Mrs. Jordan's school was threequarters of a mile from the village and met in a room 13 feet by 13 by 10 which had accommodation for 28. There were actually 40 enrolled, all but 6 below 10 years of age. On the average 20 girls and 8 boys attended. Mrs. Jordan was a widow who commenced teaching when 34 years old in 1837. Her income from school fees was given as £44. The inspector reported of this school that the children "appeared orderly and the mistress somewhat intelligent, but she spoke English incorrectly."

The Llandaff National Schools for Boys and Girls, started in 1817, were kept by Mr. and Mrs. Williams, who received £50 and £40 per annum respectively for their services. Mr. Williams also acted as an agent for which he received £4 and he also received £4 as a Collector of Taxes. He was a shoemaker before he became a schoolmaster. The income of the two schools amounted to £70 from subscriptions and donations and £27 from school fees,

The total number of Whitchurch children attending school was given as 108 or 7·8 per cent of the total population of 1376. In addition 243 persons of all ages attended three Sunday Schools—76 males and 94 females under 15, and 37 males and 36 females over 15.

In addition to the two National Schools Llandaff Parish had two Dame Schools at Ely. The Sunday Schools at Llandaff were conducted at the National Schoolrooms by the master and mistress of the day school.

A vigorous controversy followed throughout Wales on the publication of the 1847 Reports, and great resentment was felt against the aspersions of the Commissioners on the Welsh people and language. The publication of the documents, however, stimulated greater interest in educational matters and quickened the efforts of the two national school-promoting agencies in the setting-up of more and better schools.

In the fifties, probably due to the retirement of Thomas Phillips,* steps were taken to set up a National School at Whitchurch. Mr. T. W. Booker, the Melingriffith Works proprietor, was the leading spirit in this movement, and he seems to have advanced by way of loan a sum of more than £1,000 for the erection of a school building.

The site selected for the structure was part of a garden in Tynypwll Road in the occupation of David Evans, and comprising an area of 1 acre 12½ poles. Its joint owners, Lord Dynevor and Edward Priest Richards (the predecessors of the present-day Wingfield and Mackintosh Estates), gifted the site, and on January 13, 1854, executed a Deed of Trust† "to the Ministers and Churchwardens of the Parish of Whitchurch and their successors" authorizing them to appropriate the land and to use it and any buildings erected thereon for ever for the purposes of

"A School for the Education of Children and Adults or Children only of the Labouring, Manufacturing and other poorer classes in the Parish of Whitchurch aforesaid, and as a Residence for the Teacher or Teachers of the said School, and for no other purpose, which said schools should always be in union with and conducted upon the principles, and in furtherance of the ends and designs of the Incorporated National Society for promoting the Education of the Poor in the principles of the Established Church."

The National School seems to have been closely associated with the Melingriffith Works, and was managed by the Vicar and Churchwardens in association with the Booker family.

Arrangements seem to have been made for the deduction from wages paid to the employees at Melingriffith Works of a weekly sum of twopence in respect of each of their children attending the National School. The children of parents not employed at the Works had each to pay 2d. every Monday morning to the Head Teacher at the school. Poundage deductions for school purposes ceased on Jan. 16, 1883.

The Melingriffith proprietors seem also to have interested themselves in a small school for juniors and infants which met in a small building (still in existence) at Penylan on the hill near the works. This was

---

* Phillips died at Pentyrch late in 1857 or early in 1858, and was buried at Whitchurch.
† Now in possession of the Glamorgan County Education Committee.

probably one of the dame schools referred to in the 1833 Report and seems to have continued in being at any rate until the establishment of the School Board in 1884. A Miss Richard appears to have been the last mistress. She was in charge as early as 1865. In its later years it became a "select academy for young ladies," and the children of working-class parents mostly attended the National and afterwards the Board School.

There were also other private schools both at Whitchurch and Tongwynlais during the sixties, seventies and eighties. Miss Eliza Brangham kept such a school in the vicinity of Whitchurch Common as early as 1855 and as late as 1888. There was a dame school in the vicinity of the present Whitchurch Library, also one at Thornhill,* another at Rhiwbina, and several at Tongwynlais. From the seventies to the nineties also Robert Small kept a school for boys at the Philog. Small is said to have previously been an assistant teacher at the National School. He had the reputation of being a good schoolmaster and his 'Academy' was popular with better-to-do people who desired a 'superior' education for their boys. A school fee of 1/- or 1/2 per week was paid in respect of each pupil.

Unfortunately the earlier log-books of the Whitchurch National School have disappeared and I am not able to give exact details of the arrangements which operated here. It seems, however, to have started as a combined Mixed and Infants' School. Although I cannot be certain of the fact I believe the school was conducted in its earlier years by Mr. and Mrs. James Walker. These people certainly held the appointment in 1865, and Mr. Walker continued to serve until September, 1883. In 1870, however, the school was re-organised into two departments, one for Boys under Mr. Walker, and the other for Girls and Infants, the latter being placed in charge of Miss Lucy Roberts.

In 1873 Mr. Walker and Miss Roberts left, and the two departments were placed in charge of Mr. and Mrs. J. Colston Meredith who came to Whitchurch from the National School, Penarth. In December, 1882, Mrs. Meredith relinquished her post and a Miss Agnes Hodges carried on in succession to her until March, 1883. Mr. Meredith now gave up his appointment and in April, 1883, the two departments were placed in charge of Mr. and Mrs. Desberough. They, however, did not remain for long, and soon after the transfer of the school to the newly formed School Board they left. This was in October, 1885.

Up to the 1860's there were no scholastic facilities at Tongwynlais, apart from a few dame schools catering mainly for infants, and older children used to attend either at the National School, Whitchurch, or Bethlehem School (Gwaelodygarth). Early in that decade through the activities of Mr. and Mrs. Henry Lewis (Greenmeadow) an Anglican Church was established and in connection with it there was started a National School. In 1865 this was in charge of Miss Elizabeth Walker. It probably met in the temporary church premises which stood on part of the site of the present Council School.

This school seems to have had a somewhat irregular existence. When funds ran short it was closed until the financial position improved.

---

* Kept by Miss Preston (Rhiwbina Farm).

For example it was opened in January, 1871, and closed in December, 1872. It was again opened in May, 1877, but in April, 1879, was closed when the Melingriffith Works failed.

During the middle of the 19th century Nonconformity was increasing rapidly in strength locally, and a majority of local residents were Dissenters. It is not surprising, therefore, that the need was felt for a school which had no association with the Established Church. After the passing of the Elementary Education Act of 1870, which authorised the setting up of publicly-elected School Boards to manage State-aided schools of an unsectarian character, a movement was initiated locally in favour of such a development at Whitchurch.

Public meetings were held, and a pamphlet* was issued over the names of Eli Evans, John Phillips and Thomas Thomas, prior to the issue being submitted to a plebiscite of the ratepayers. The balloting took place on March 17th, 1871, when a majority of electors cast their votes against the proposal.

The following extracts from the pamphlet are interesting from a historical standpoint:

"Taking a population of 2,900 provision will have to be made according to the Act for nearly 500 children, and as it is not intended to interfere with existing schools, which in our Parish (including Church Schools (240) and private schools (50)) have accommodation for about 290 children, provision would have to be made for 210 scholars, assuming the Church schools to be full, whose ages would range from 5 to 13 years.

"The cost of school buildings and land for this number we will say would be £600 involving an annual repayment of £20 for 50 years to the Government. The cost of conducting the school at 26/- each scholar per year would amount to £273 making a total of £293. This would be met as follows:

	£	s.	d.
Government grant at 13/- per head	136	10	0
School fees averaging 2d. per week	82	5	0
Rate of 1d. in £1 on £14,260 (R. Value)	89	2	6
	£307	17	6

leaving an available balance of £34 17 6. The above will include expenses of master, assistant teacher, secretary and treasurer."

The foregoing figures seem extraordinarily modest in the light of modern costs, but they had a fair relation to scholastic costs at that period. In the following extract the Nonconformist argument for the adoption of the School Board method is stated with considerable moderation:

"There was a time when the denominational public school would have been suitable to the Parish of Whitchurch and that school a Church School. But these times have passed away which will be gathered from the following observations:

---

* Remarks on the Elementary Education Act, 1870, and its Applicability to the Parish of Whitchurch, 1871.

"The first account we have of the present Church at Whitchurch was handed down by a gentleman of the neighbourhood who lived in the time of Elizabeth.

"He describes it as a small building in what was once a Roman encampment. Without doubt it was made large enough to contain all the worshippers of the Parish—the houses at the time numbering probably from 30 to 40. Such was Whitchurch Church 300 years ago, and such is Whitchurch Church now, capable of holding about 200 persons.

"There are seven places of worship in the parish and two others close upon the boundaries—in all capable of accommodating upwards of 2,000 people. These chapels are all in active operation with their Sunday schools carried out by zealous and devoted teachers, and yet, we have, in one only public elementary school, a conscience clause or time table to be offered to the children of the great majority which carries on the face of it a handicap. This would place each child under a sort of ban, causing him to be looked on as 'not one of us,' etc."

In spite of the unfavourable result of the ballot, which was influenced in the first place by the desire to avoid the small education rate involved, and secondly by the desire not to show disrespect to Mr. Booker, the chief local employer, public opinion continued to ripen and towards the end of 1882 consent for the establishment of a School Board was obtained, the first election of seven members taking place on 9th January, 1883. The population of Whitchurch by this time had increased to 3,322. Mr. Henry Lewis, Greenmeadow, was elected first chairman of the new Board.

Unfortunately the records of the Whitchurch School Board were destroyed a few years ago and I am unable to record its early transactions. In all probability the earlier months of its existence were spent in negotiations with the managers of the National Schools at Tongwynlais and Whitchurch for a transfer of premises and functions. The former school building was ultimately taken over on November 30th, 1883, and re-opened as a Board School with Mr. Benjamin Williams as Headmaster. During its first year it had an average attendance of 120. In 1900 Mr. C. H. Smith was appointed head of the school and in the following year the Castell Coch school was built by the Eglwysilan School Board, and placed in charge of Miss Edmunds.

Difficulties arose on account of the fact that the village of Tongwynlais was at that time situated within two parishes. At first children from the Eglwysilan area also attended the new school, but as this school was rate-supported only by Whitchurch residents the Whitchurch School Board in 1888 excluded Eglwysilan children. The difficulty was in due course adjusted between the two school boards and in 1894 the school building was enlarged. Four years later, however, a further dispute arose and Eglwysilan children were again shut out.

In the early eighties the Melingriffith Works was passing through troublesome times. The Booker Company had failed and the Booker family had left the district. Their successors took little interest in local civic affairs and they were also face to face with financial difficulties. The changed conditions had adversely affected the position of the Whitchurch National School, and subscriptions for its maintenance were not coming in very freely. The Managers could not make adequate provision for the needs of the district and ultimately they handed over the school to the new School Board as from October 1st, 1884.

On April 20th, 1885, the deed of transfer was executed, the signing managers being Rev. J. T. Clarke (Vicar) and Messrs. T. W. Booker, Joshua Herne, Griffith Phillips and W. D. Haddock. The deed provided that the Board were to have the use of the site and buildings from 9 a.m. to 4.30 p.m., except between 12 and 12.30 p.m., and on Saturdays, Sundays, Christmas Day, Whit-Monday, Ash Wednesday, Good Friday and Ascension Day. The deed also permitted the erection of an Infants' School upon the site.

As has been stated, the appointments to the Whitchurch National School of Mr. and Mrs. Desberough seems to have terminated in October, 1885, and new appointments were made by the School Board. The Boys' School was placed in charge of Mr. Peter Sharpe who, although fresh from college, had formerly served at the school as an assistant under Mr. Meredith. Mr. Sharpe held his appointment until March 13th, 1914, when he resigned after 37 years service to take holy orders. On March 16th, 1914, Mr. W. S. Jones became his successor and held the post until his retirement in October, 1936. The present headmaster, Mr. John Morgan, commenced duties in the same month.

In November, 1885, Miss Clara Tovey took charge of the Girls' and Infants' department. After about three years the infants seem to have been organised into a separate department under Miss J. Emily Symonds, who occupied that office from March to November, 1888, when she was succeeded by Mrs. M. Warwick, who remained headmistress until her retirement in 1913. Since the latter date there have been two heads of the Infants' School, Miss Annie Evans, who served from April, 1913, to September, 1919, and the present head, Miss S. A. Moredcai, who commenced on January 5th, 1920.

Miss Tovey appears to have been succeeded as head of the Girls' School about 1889 by Miss Annie Rees, who left in February, 1895. Between March, 1895, and July, 1902, Miss J. Edith Rosser was in charge. Then followed Miss Emily Pengelly, who held the post from September, 1902, until October, 1930. The present head, Miss Alys A. Thomas, commenced duties in December, 1930.

The School Board controlled local education from 1883-4 until their functions and property were transferred to the Glamorgan Education Committee towards the end of 1903. At the beginning of its career the system of payment of "School Pence" by parents was continued, a uniform fee of 2d. per child per week being levied. These fees were, however, abolished under the provisions of a new Education Act which came into operation at Whitchurch in September, 1891. Since this date all public elementary education has been free.

There was a considerable growth of population at Whitchurch during the School Board period, the increase between the Census years

1881 and 1901 amounting to no less than 80 per cent. Extended school facilities therefore became necessary, and the Board had to face up to a substantial building programme. The old National School buildings had to be re-modelled and considerably extended. In 1884 the school was re-arranged—the girls and infants were brought to the lower floor and the boys accommodated upstairs. Additional building was undertaken at this period and again in 1894.

A few years later in 1896 a new school was built at the Heath (Birchgrove) and in 1899 another at the Hawthorn (Llandaff North). Even this additional accommodation did not meet the needs and a new Infants' School was built at Glanynant. This was opened on July 25th, 1902. This is the building to-day used as a Girls' Department.

The equipment at the various schools, however, was not of a high order, if one may judge from the entries of Head Teachers in the school log books and the reports of Government Inspectors. At times supplies were so short that the children were required to provide their own slates, pens, etc. In September, 1884, the Inspector reported of the Whitchurch school that "writing is bad and no wonder when proper slates have been supplied only during the last six weeks. Fragments have been used before. All slates should be properly ruled."

In November of the following year Miss Tovey complained of the dirty state of the school. There were only three dirty maps on the wall and apparatus and stationery were scarce. In the nineties Mr. Sharpe made frequent strictures regarding the inadequacy of desk accommodation, and in 1901 complained of a lack of nibs, exercise books and drawing books.

With the opening of a separate school for infants at Glanynant in 1902 it was thought that local scholastic facilities would suffice for many years. Population growth, however, was greater than ever and between 1901 and 1911 there was an increase of no less than 86 per cent. The Glamorgan Education Committee had therefore, in addition to improving the standard of staffing and equipment, to face up to a large building programme. Plans were prepared for the extension of the Heath and Hawthorn schools and for the erection of a new Infants School at Whitchurch and the provision of new accommodation at Tongwynlais. The latter was opened in 1914. The new Glanynant Infants' School came into use in May, 1916, and the previous Infants' School was converted into a Girls' School.

Post-war development at Whitchurch proceeded at a very rapid rate. Although the area and population of the Parish was greatly diminished as the result of the absorption of the Birchgrove and Llandaff North areas into the City of Cardiff, the rate of development was maintained and the population of the reduced area was at the Census of 1931 considerably greater than that of the undivided parish in 1921. The need for further school accommodation was recognised and in 1929 the Rhiwbina Mixed and Infants School was opened under the head-mastership of Mr. T. Pugsley. This is the largest elementary school in the County of Glamorgan.

Still the need grew and, as part of the scheme of re-organisation recommended by the Hadow Committee, a new central mixed school for children of eleven years and over was built and opened in June, 1939, and placed in charge of Mr. Stanley Chivers, M.A. This stands on a site of 18 acres, part of which was proposed to be used for a new Junior Boys' School to take the place of the obsolete National Schoolroom situate in Tynypwll Road. This project, however, had to be temporarily abandoned, following the outbreak of the present War.

An organised system of public secondary education is of fairly modern date. In Wales it commenced with the passing of the Welsh Intermediate Education Act of 1889, which provided for a system of State-aided secondary schools in each Welsh county. Considerable discussion took place as to the number and location of such schools in Glamorgan, and it was not until May, 1896, that the county scheme for the establishment of 13 schools was approved.

It had, however, been decided some years previously that two such schools should be established at Barry and Penarth and that Whitchurch children should be accommodated at the latter school. In 1892 a building fund was opened with a subscription of £1,000 and the gift of a five acre site by Lord Plymouth. Further sums were contributed by other persons, and the County Council made a grant of £5,000.

Plans for a school to cost £7,000 were prepared and in August, 1894, the foundation stone of the building was laid by Lady Windsor. A School Governing Body was appointed in 1896 and on January 20th, 1897, the two departments of the Penarth Intermediate School were opened. Accommodation was provided for 120 boys and 80 girls. There was not, however, at first a great demand for places, and the numbers actually enrolled for the first year were 52 boys and 36 girls. Penarth Schools were enlarged in 1910.

The rapid growth of population at Whitchurch led to a demand by the Parish Council for the local provision of secondary school facilities. Further representations were made in 1919 after the European War, but as the Cardiff City Council were at this time considering a proposal to include Whitchurch within the city area the Glamorgan Education Committee deferred consideration of the matter. The Committee, however, provided a new Secondary School at Caerphilly which local children were allowed to attend as an alternative to Penarth.

This arrangement met local needs only for a few years, however, and, following the extraordinary building development of the twenties and thirties, the demand for a local secondary school again became clamant. A decision to proceed with the erection of a school was made in 1934, and a site of 21 acres was duly acquired. Financial difficulties now arose consequent on the economic depression, and for a period the Education Committee, although they admitted the urgency of the position, were unable to proceed. After a time, however, the consent of the Board of Education was obtained for the erection at an estimated cost of £32,000 of a secondary school to accommodate 320 boy and girl pupils, and this building was formally opened by the Right Hon.

Lord Portal on November 17th, 1937. Mr. A. J. Richard, M.A., was appointed Headmaster.

The new school proved inadequate to meet the needs and a proportion of scholars requiring secondary education have still to attend at Penarth. Extensions of the Whitchurch School are proposed but the outbreak of the World War has caused the execution of these to be delayed.

SHORT LIST OF SOURCES.

Abstract of Education Returns, 1833.
F. A. Cavenagh. The Life and Works of Griffith Jones.
David Evans. Sunday Schools in Wales.
Griffith Jones and Madam Bevan. Welch Piety (1737-1776).
M. J. Jones. The Charity School Movement.
L. S. Knight. Welsh Independent Grammar Schools to 1600 (1920).
L. S. Knight. Welsh Cathedral Schools to 1600 (Cymrodor, Vol. 29).
L. S. Knight. Origin of the Welsh Grammar School (Cymrodor, Vol. 31).
L. S. Knight. Welsh Schools from A.D. 1000 to A.D. 1602 (Arch. Camb. 1919).
Melingriffith Documents (deposited by me at National Library of Wales).
Report of the Commissioners of Enquiry into the State of Education in Wales (1847).
Report of Select Committee on the Education of the Poor (1818).
T. Shankland. Sir John Phillips, the S.P.C.K. and the Charity Movement in Wales.
Various Local School Log Books.

CHAPTER XIII.

HISTORIC MELINGRIFFITH.*

Probably no other industrial undertaking in South Wales has been worked without break for as long a period as the Melingriffith Tinplate Works. It is situated at or near the site of an ancient corn mill which in medieval times was a manorial mill of the Lordship of Senghenydd and, at a later period, of its member the Manor of Album Monasterium. The name *Melin Griffith* (*Griffith's Mill*) was probably derived from Gruffydd, son of Ifor Bach, who was Lord of Senghenydd during the latter part of the 12th century.

The mill was in operation intermittently for many centuries. In 1695 it was leased, with a 2 acre field called *Cae Vellyn*, by the Dowager Countess of Pembroke to John Mathew, of Splott, and was described as being in a 'ruinous' condition. It was probably put in commission by the Mathew family, for in a similar document of 1715 the adjective 'ruinous' does not appear.

This mill was driven throughout its existence by water directed along an artificial course from the Taff at Radyr Weir, and this method of obtaining power has been and still is in operation at Melingriffith Works.

The earliest reference I know to an ironworks undertaking at this point occurs in an *Ewenny Priory document* of May, 1749. This records that Rees Powell, of Llanharan, agreed to lease for 21 years to Richard Jordan and Francis Homfray, both of Staffordshire, "a water corn grist mill called Velin Griffith and a forge in the parish of Whitchurch." In an unexecuted draft lease for a period of 200 years by William Powell to Richard Jordan mention is made of forges erected on the site of a water corn grist mill called Melin Griffith and *a forge erected nearby by Rees Powell*. It seems clear from these documents that an ironworks enterprise was founded by Rees Powell, of Llanharan, probably before 1749.

The Jordans disposed of their interest in the property to a Bristol firm called Reynolds, Getley & Co., in 1765. Amongst the partners of this firm were ironmasters of the name of Harford, who were well-known Bristol Quakers. By 1786, if not earlier, the ownership of the undertaking was in the hands of Harford, Partridge & Co., a firm who were later associated with other South Wales ironworks undertakings, including Ebbw Vale.

In the early years of the 19th century a young man named Richard Blakemore—a relative of the Partridges—was at Melingriffith, and by

---

* As I have related at great length the history of the Ancient Mill and tinplate works in a previous work, *Historic Melingriffith*, only a brief outline need be given in this chapter.

1810 the works was acquired by the firm of Richard Blakemore & Co., with Blakemore as managing director. Under his direction the enterprise prospered exceedingly. He acquired the Pentyrch Forge and opened collieries in that neighbourhood, and built a railway linking up Pentyrch and Melingriffith.

Blakemore was a bachelor, and in 1820 he adopted a nephew, Thomas William Booker, who in time succeeded to the business and traded as T. W. Booker & Co. The enterprise continued to prosper, and Mr. Booker's three sons, Richard, Thomas William and John Partridge, who lived at The Pines, Velindre, and Greenhill respectively, were given an interest in the concern. In due course T. W. Booker, Senior, entered Parliament and the management of the undertaking was vested mainly in his second son, T. W. Booker, Junior. In 1858, T. W. Booker, Senior, who had three years previously on his uncle's death adopted the additional surname of Blakemore, died, and the three sons inherited.

The eldest son Richard was of dissolute habits and took very little interest in the business, and upon the second son fell the heaviest responsibility for the management. Considerable extensions were made to the new works, and additional mills were built and side-line industries for the manufacture of wire and red ochre were established.

Financial difficulties, arising partly from depressed conditions of trade following the Franco-Prussian War, were encountered, and in 1872 outside capital had to be obtained. The partnership was converted into a limited liability company under the title of T. W. Booker & Co., Ltd., and the property was disposed of to the new company for the sum of £425,000. A number of outside directors joined the Board and T. W. Booker was made Managing Director. At this period Melingriffith comprised 12 mills and had an annual output of 10,000 tons of sheet iron and 100,000 boxes of tinplate.

The new company was handicapped not only by the trade slump, but to a far greater extent by the development of steel manufacturing processes during the seventies. Steel was a superior basic commodity than iron for tinplate production. A scheme for the conversion of Pentyrch Works for the manufacture of steel by the Bessemer Process was prepared, but the company were unable to face the enormous cost. Pentyrch, instead of being an asset, soon became a liability.

To add to its troubles certain of the firm's customers failed to pay their debts, and involved the undertaking in a substantial loss. Then in 1878 the West of England and District Bank, which had made heavy advances to T. W. Booker & Co. Ltd., also failed, and its liquidators called upon the company to repay its loans. This it was unable to do, and a winding-up order was made against it.

In July, 1881 the Booker undertaking was put up for sale as a going concern, but no bid was received, and attempts to dispose of the property by private treaty also failed. Ultimately the Melingriffith section was leased to the Cardiff Iron and Tinplate Co. Ltd., with James Spence as managing director, and the Pentyrch section was closed down.

During the 1880's depressed conditions continued in the metallurgical industries of South Wales. In 1885-7 Melingriffith operated only intermittently, and in November, 1887, it suspended operations and the Spence company went into liquidation. In June, 1888, the Melingriffith and Pentyrch properties were sold in lots by public auction. Melingriffith Works and railway and 39 freehold cottages were bought by Richard Thomas, of Lydbrook, for the very low sum of £12,000, plus £10,500 for machinery and plant.

A new company, the Melingriffith Company Ltd., was incorporated with a capital of £40,000, the chief shareholders being Sir William T. Lewis (afterwards Lord Merthyr), Richard Thomas and E. P. Martin. Richard Thomas became managing director. The new syndicate began working under favourable conditions. It had acquired the property at a knock-out figure and was not saddled with the obsolete and unremunerative ironworks at Pentyrch. In addition it had an advantage over competitors in the form of cheap water power.

Under Richard Thomas' skilful management the works were completely reorganised and improved. The enterprise prospered exceedingly, and in 1898 the total capital was raised to £70,000 and in 1918 to £100,000 by the issue of bonus shares.

In due time Richard Thomas acquired and developed other undertakings and founded the well-known concern, Richard Thomas & Co. Ltd. Melingriffith, however, continued as a separate private company and was under the directorship of Richard Thomas until 1916. The control then passed to his sons, and Mr. Spence Thomas was managing director when in 1934 the works was sold to Richard Thomas & Co. Ltd. Tinplate manufacture was temporarily suspended and during the recent World War the buildings and plant were used for war-time purposes.

AERIAL VIEW OF MELINGRIFFITH WORKS

HEOL-Y-DERI, RHIWBINA, 1903   W. *Morgan Davies*

HEOL-Y-DERI, RHIWBINA   *Cardiff Library*

CHAPTER XIV.
THE GROWTH OF DISSENT.

On account of its close association over centuries with Llandaff, movements inimical to the Established Church do not seem to have secured great support at Whitchurch. The locality, nevertheless, had some associations with the Puritan and later Nonconformist developments from which sprang the various dissenting sects which loom so large in the modern religious life of Wales.

It will be recalled that in 1638 two Cardiff clergymen, William Erbury and Walter Cradock, were turned out of the church by the Bishop of Llandaff for declining to comply with Archbishop Laud's order to read the *Book of Sports* in the parish church. These two men later became Puritan ministers and from the efforts of these and like dissentients later developed antagonism to the Established Church.

During the Cromwellian regime an attempt was made to bring the State Church under Puritan influence, and clergymen who were not sympathetic to Puritan ideas were replaced by others, and the funds of certain parishes sequestrated for use in others to which Puritan ministers had been appointed. Thus the tithes of Llanedeyrn, Llancarvan and Whitchurch and the rectorial funds of Eglwysilan were alienated for the maintenance of John Miles, the newly-appointed Baptist minister of Ilston (Gower).

After the Restoration of the Monarchy many Puritan clergymen in their turn were deprived of their livings, and a series of statutes was enacted against persons who were hostile to the Established Church. Amongst those so deprived of their offices was Rev. John French, of Wenvoe, who, later, in 1696, founded the first regular local dissenting church at Womanby Street, Cardiff.

During the decades following the Restoration Nonconformists met for worship at conventicles in private houses, barns, etc., and were ministered unto by dissenting preachers. Many such conventicles were organised locally at Llanedeyrn, Lisvane, and especially in the Caerphilly district at Waunwaelod, Tyfry, Gwaungledyr and Craig-yr-Allt, and these were served for a time by John Powell, an evicted clergyman from St. Lythan's, and Thomas Quarrell, a former clergyman in Montgomeryshire. The latter seems to have lived at Whitchurch, but served mainly the conventicles in Llanedeyrn, Lisvane, Bedwas, Eglwysilan, Gelligaer and Mynyddislwyn.

By the Declaration of Indulgence of 1672 (Charles II) the penal laws against dissenters were suspended, and later the passing of the Toleration Act in the reign of William of Orange enabled dissenting churches to be established legally.

A number of independent churches were founded in South Wales, including Womanby Street Church (now Trinity Congregational), Cardiff, the minister of which also served a smiliar church at Watford. While all such churches were independent of the Established Church they did not always agree in their tenets or in their system of church government. In time the two great denominations known as Congregationalist (or Independent) and Baptist came into being, but it was not until late in the 18th century and in the early part of the 19th century that these largely increased in number.

The granting of religious freedom by the removal of restrictions against Dissent seems to have lessened the desire for dissent, and, although a number of Nonconformist causes were established, it was not until the great Methodist Revival of the fourth decade of the 18th century that the seeds were sown of a movement which was many years later to sever a large body of religious people from the Established Church.

The Revival started about the same time in Wales as in England. In England it was led by the brothers John and Charles Wesley and George Whitfield; in Wales by a group of young men which included Howell Harris, Daniel Rowlands, William Williams (Pantycelyn) and others.

In the 1730's Womanby Street Chapel (Cardiff) together with another Independent Church at Watford were in charge of Rev. David Williams, at whose invitation in 1738 Howell Harris visited Cardiff and Watford for the purpose of conducting religious services. In addition meetings were held, amongst other places, in the house of Thomas Williams, Llanishen (probably Llanishen Fach Farm).

In 1739 George Whitfield came to Cardiff at the invitation of Howell Harris, and these two Revivalist leaders preached at the Shire Hall. A week after this Howell Harris held a preaching service at Whitchurch. This is the only recorded engagement at Whitchurch of Howell Harris, but during the next 30 years he frequently preached in the neighbourhood —at Cardiff, Gabalfa, Llanedeyrn, Lisvane and Pentyrch.

Charles Wesley also was early on the scene. In November, 1740, he preached from the pulpit of Llanishen Church. On a return visit in July, 1741, he dined at Llanishen and preached to a society which had been formed there, together with others "chiefly predestinarians," probably a contingent from Watford. It would appear that theological differences had already rent the following of the revivalists but not yet to such an extent as to sever them into the two classes of Arminian (or Wesleyan) and Calvinistic Methodists.

Later in the year Charles Wesley paid another visit. He preached at a house which stood at the corner of Mill Road, Llanishen, and during the same visit he attended a "revel" at Whitchurch which lasted a week and at which, "many local clergy and gentry" were present.

Such revels were common in Wales in the early days of Methodist propaganda. They were survivals of festivals connected with the patron saints after whom the local churches were named. The name given to such celebrations was *Gwyl Mabsant* and the festivals usually synchronised with the saint days.

In time the Gwyl Mabsant degenerated into a pleasure fair or feast. The programme included rustic sports, singing competitions, dancing, cock-fighting, etc., and the various inns vied with one another in providing entertainment for their patrons in the form of feasts, harp and fiddle music, dances, wrestling and fighting matches and the like.

These 'revels' were much deprecated by the Puritans and later by the Methodists, and the revivalists frequently attended such gatherings in order to denounce the practices associated with them. In 1742 a notable Methodist Convention was held at Watford which was attended by four Welsh and three English evangelists. There was discussed a variety of matters affecting doctrine and also the furtherance of the Methodist mission. The revivalists were mostly connected with the Established Church, and few of them, at first at any rate, desired to break away from that church or to found new sects. The societies which they formed were for the purpose of deepening spiritual life within the somewhat formal practice of the church.

Sometimes local clergymen identified themselves with the societies and helped to spread evangelical teaching and practice. Most clergymen, however, were hostile or indifferent. Whilst the Wesleyans at a fairly early date started to organise separately the adherents to their faith and to provide their own chapels and their own special ministers, the Calvinistic Methodists were more reluctant to break away from the Mother Church. They continued their association with that church, and although they held independent services they used to attend the parish church for communion.

In cases where the clergymen were godly, clean-living men, earnest and sincere in religious profession and practice, devout Methodists respected them and felt little desire to leave the church. Many clergymen at that time, however, were of less noble character and discharged their offices in a very perfunctory manner, with the result that earnest Methodists felt repulsion at partaking communion from their hands.

In time, therefore, the demand grew for specially ordained, independent Methodist ministers, and, after long controversy, in 1811, the demand was conceded, and so the way was prepared for the complete severance of Calvinistic Methodists from the Established Church.

Not only did the Welsh Methodists take a different line from the English Methodists; before the middle of the eighteenth century even the latter became disunited in points of doctrine. Whitfield, like the Welsh Methodists, favoured the Calvinistic doctrines of election and predestination, special redemption and preservation in grace, whilst the Wesleyans accepted the more liberal Arminian tenets which provided for salvation for all. In Wales the Whitfieldites were lost in the Calvinistic Methodists.

SHORT LIST OF SOURCES.

T. Bowen. Dinas Caerdydd a'i Methodistiaeth Galfinaidd (1927).
J. Hughes. Methodistiaeth Cymru (1851-6).
T. J. Humphreys. Hanes Methodistiaeth Wesleyaidd yng Nghymru (1900).
J. Spinther James. Hanes y Bedyddwyr yng Nghymru (1893-8).
J. Austin Jenkins. The History of the Early Nonconformists of Cardiff (1891).
H. Elvet Lewis. Nonconformity in Wales (1912).
Thomas Rees. History of Protestant Nonconformity in Wales (1883).
Rees and Thomas. Hanes Eglwysi Annibynol Cymru (1871-5).
John Roberts. Methodistiaeth Galfinaidd Cymru (1931).
Tawelfryn and E. Bush. Hanes Ymdaith Cynulleidfioliaith (1904).
J. Williamson. History of Congregationalism in Cardiff and District (1920).
David Young. The Origin and History of Methodism in Wales (1893).

CHAPTER XV.

EBENEZER AND TABERNACLE METHODIST CHURCHES.*

Although there was probably a Calvinistic Methodist society at Whitchurch towards the end of the eighteenth century the first organized church, meeting in its own chapel, does not seem to have been formed until 1808. This church was known as Ebenezer and was situated near the Ashgrove Farm in Pantmawr Road. The building was about eighty years later converted into a row of three cottages which still exist and are today locally known as Providence Place.

Unfortunately, no records of this early church are available, and I am unable to give particulars of its founders or of the circumstances connected with its early history. In all probability it was established by adherents of Methodist Churches in neighbouring townships, who had been attracted to reside at or near Whitchurch by reason of the development of the Pentyrch and Melingriffith Iron and Tinplate Works.

Such information as I have been able to obtain has been gleaned from references in periodical and other literature of the period and from an unpublished essay by Mr. J. Rees Jones of Whitchurch.

That the church was not connected with the Parish Church of Whitchurch in any way is practically certain, for it may be assumed that the Vicars Choral of Llandaff who served Whitchurch at this period had little sympathy with the Methodist movement.

Happily there was a local vicar who was definitely of Methodistical tendency. This was the Rev. Daniel Jones, who from about 1780 held for 32 years the cures of Penarth, Lavernock and Radyr. He had come to reside at St. Fagans in 1780, where he kept a day school in a little Methodist chapel in that village, and it is recorded that he fraternized with the Methodist preachers of the period who came to preach at that chapel. He not only entertained the visiting preachers at his home, but he himself used to preach at Methodist gatherings and to attend the monthly denominational meetings.

Prior to 1811, it will be remembered, practically all the Methodist preachers were ordained clergymen, and the Methodist churches relied mainly on these for such functions as the administration of the Holy Sacrament. This practice continued in Glamorgan until 1818 in which year Bishop Marsh of Llandaff presented an ultimatum to clergymen of Methodist tendencies in his diocese that they must either give up Methodism or leave the Church. I do not know whether the order was generally obeyed but certainly some local clergymen, including Howell Howells, of Trehill, seceded to become Methodist preachers.

---

* For the general background of the Methodist movement in Wales see J. Hughes: *Methodistiaeth Cymru*, and Rev. John Roberts: *Methodistiaeth Galfinaidd Cymru*.

Daniel Jones, it is recorded, used to hold special services at the Parish Church of Radyr, at which he administered the Lord's Supper to Methodists belonging to societies or churches at St. Fagans, Radyr, Pentyrch and Whitchurch, but I am unable to say when this practice ceased.

The only official information I have relating to the Ebenezer meeting place is contained in a denominational return of 1882 which states that the Ebenezer premises were held on a lease of 999 years from 1808 at a yearly ground rent of 7/6, and that the chapel had seating accommodation for 200. Ebenezer seems to have continued in being as a separate church until 1867, when it was merged in a new church, near the centre of Whitchurch, today known as Tabernacle. Ebenezer Chapel, however, was used for Sunday School purposes for many years later. Ebenezer never had a regular pastor. Like most early Methodist churches it relied on exhorters, prayer leaders and lay preachers for the conduct of services and the delivery of discourses, with the exception of one Sunday a month when, after 1818, regularly ordained ministers of the Methodist denomination officiated and administered communion.

The number of ordained Methodist ministers at this period was very small. In 1818 there were only about five such ministers serving the 28 or 29 Methodist chapels in the county of Glamorgan. These were Howel Howells, of Trehill (St. Nicholas), Hopkin Bevan, of Llangyfelach, Richard James, of Pontrhydyfen, David Williams, of Merthyr, and Richard Thomas, of Llysworney, all of whom, except Howells, were ordained in 1811 or later.

Of these, Howel Howells had been a clergyman. The *Cwrdd Misol* (Monthly Meeting) also approved, after careful investigation, a number of laymen to act as lay preachers or exhorters. Amongst these was one Edward (or Edmund) Phillips of Whitchurch, and it may be assumed that this man was responsible to the denomination for Ebenezer. The church was a Welsh church throughout its existence, although possibly occasional English services were also held. There were probably about a dozen Methodist churches in East Glamorgan at the time Ebenezer was started and many others were founded in succeeding years. In 1821, for example, a Methodist church was established at Fforddlas (Radyr), which 20 or so years later was transferred to Bethel, Morganstown.

Ebenezer, like other Methodist churches, was served at different times by some of the leading preachers of the denomination, including such well-known pulpit giants as Edward Mathew, of Ewenny, Howell Howells, of Trehill, and William Evans, of Tonyrefail, and it is from the biographies of some of these preachers that I have been able to collect the meagre details relating to the early local Methodist cause.[*]

William Evans kept detailed diaries of his numerous engagements, and Eglwysnewydd (i.e., Whitchurch) figures often in his itineraries. Soon after his recognition as a minister of the denomination he preached on September 27th, 1818, at Cardiff, Eglwysnewydd, and Caerphilly in morning, afternoon and evening services respectively. For many years

---

[*] See especially J. J. Morgan: *Cofiant Edward Matthews, Ewenni,* and W. Evans: *Cofiant William Evans, Tonyrefail.*

the linking up of Whitchurch and another local centre with Cardiff was a common practice of the Methodist preachers.

A Sunday School seems to have been organised from the inception of the church. A Government Committee reported in 1818 that there was a Sunday School at Whitchurch 'containing 30 boys and 26 girls.' This probably met at Ebenezer. Another government report of 1833 records that the Methodist Sunday School comprised 25 males and 22 females. Still another Government report stated that Ebenezer Sunday School was started in 1809 and that in 1847 it comprised 70 scholars of whom 23 attended day school and 40 were able to read the scriptures.

A feature of Methodist Sunday Schools at the period—it still lingers in some Welsh counties—was the assembly of neighbouring schools at one centre for a festival, known as *Cymanfa Holi'r Pwnc*, at which the several schools collectively recited passages of scripture and were questioned on scriptural matters by a denominational leader. This catechetic method of teaching was exceedingly popular, and the festivals attracted large congregations. Such a festival was held at Ebenezer in November, 1828: several neighbouring Sunday Schools joined in and Rev. William Evans was the catechiser.

An important local event was the holding of the denominational monthly meeting at Ebenezer on August 12 and 13 of 1829. At this meeting the Rev. John James (Penybont)—afterwards well-known in Methodist circles throughout Wales—was accepted as a preacher.

By the 1830s the setting up of new churches seems to have become the responsibility of the denomination. A Cwrdd Misol held at Trehill in October, 1831, gave consent for the erection of a chapel at Penmark, and a later meeting decided that the financial responsibility for an estimated expenditure of £3,127 should be shared by 28 existing churches in Glamorgan. The amount allocated to the several churches ranged from £600 by Cardiff to £20 each by Pentyrch, Bethel and Ystradmynach. Ebenezer's quota was fixed at £45. Each church was expected to raise the allocated amount within a period of four years.

William Evans was an active Temperance advocate. He addressed a temperance meeting at Ebenezer on January 10, 1838. He also collected for the London Missionary Society and in 1843 a sum of £1 7 0 was credited to that society from Ebenezer.

In course of time the number of regularly ordained Methodist ministers increased, and each church got a greater variety of preachers. Here, for example, is an extract from a scheme for 1857 covering fifty churches. The allocations to Ebenezer were as follows:—

Jan. 25.	Feb. 22.	March 22.	April 26.
Benjamin Evans,	William Jones,	Evan Harris,	Evan Williams,
Llantwit Major.	Cwmavon.	Merthyr.	Taibach.
May 24.	June 28.	July 26.	Aug. 23.
	Edward Mathews,	David Roberts,	Benjamin Evans,
	Ewenny.	Cowbridge.	St. Fagans.
Sept. 27.	Oct. 25.	Nov. 22.	Dec. 27.
William Evans,	David Davies,	John Jones,	B. Evans,
Tonyrefail.	Pontrhydyfen.	Bridgend.	St. Fagans.

It would appear that by this year the visiting preacher spent the whole of the Sabbath at the station assigned to him.

In the later fifties there was a great deepening of religious fervour throughout Wales which led to the great Revival of 1858-1860 and the formation of numerous Nonconformist churches, many in Glamorgan. The Methodists took an active part in this important religious awakening, and the Methodist denomination shared in the great numerical increase which took place in church membership throughout the Principality.

Locally the Revival seems to have been anticipated by a feeling of antagonism, which was made manifest at Whitsuntide 1858, to the bad influence of Llandaff Fair. To counteract this nine local Methodist churches marched in procession through the streets of Cardiff and afterwards met in Seion Chapel,* Trinity Street, at a largely attended *holi'r pwnc* festival. Included in the visiting schools was that of Ebenezer.

The Revival seems to have had a profound influence locally and led to the formation during the immediately succeeding years of many new local churches. Two of these were offshoots of Ebenezer. There were the churches of Gilgal, Llandaff, founded on September 26th, 1859, and Hermon, Tongwynlais, which dates from December 17, 1860. The leader of the Gilgal detachment was a flourishing Llandaff builder named Job Davies, whose name still survives in a terrace of dwellings called Job's Row in old Church Road. So ardent was Job Davies in his support of Gilgal that this church was playfully dubbed by Mathews of Ewenny as "Job's Chapel of Ease."†

Many of the adherents of Gilgal were employed at the College Iron Works which about this time was owned and worked by a well-known Methodist preacher, Rev. Richard Lumley. The withdrawal from Ebenezer of a considerable part of its membership, which was largely drawn from adjoining villages, must have weakened the church considerably and may have been a reason why its removal to a more central situation was desirable. At any rate in 1866 it was decided to build a new Methodist Chapel at Whitchurch, into which Ebenezer would be merged. This chapel was christened Tabernacle and was opened in July, 1866.

---

* On the site of which Cardiff Central Library now stands.
† Gilgal was the youngest and smallest of the local Methodist churches, but it was proud of its activities. At Welsh Sunday Schools the recitation of passages of scripture, religious poems, etc., by scholars was a feature, and in 1862, according to *Y Drysorfa* of that year, about 6,700 items were recorded at the Gilgal School. The following particulars of the year's output throw an interesting light on Sunday School practice at this period:

Biblical chapters...	...	...	...	...	516
Verses from Bible	...	...	...	...	5,927
Number of hymns	...	...	...	...	73
Chapters of *Hyfforddwr*	...	...	...	...	2
Chapters of *Rhodd Mam*	...	...	...	...	11
Ten Commandments	...	...	...	...	32
The Lord's Prayer	...	...	...	...	6
Addresses (own Composition)	...	...	...	15
Passages of Poetry	...	...	...	...	28
Dialogues	...	...	...	...	5
Other Recitations	...	...	...	...	58

Little information is available as to the circumstances which led to this development or regarding local Methodist personnel at the time. The leading families at Ebenezer at this period seem to have been those of Thomas Evans, of Whitchurch, and John James, of Llandaff North. Descendants of both these families are still connected with Tabernacle.

Thomas Evans seems to have been a retired ironfounder from Pontypridd. He was locally known as 'Thomas Evans y Gaseg Felen,' i.e., Thomas Evans of the Bay Mare. For fifteen years he rode this mare to hounds and to preaching engagements. It is stated that he played a leading part in negotiations for a site for Tabernacle and in the organisation of building operations. According to local report much of the building material and haulage was given free by members and sympathisers, and the actual building was carried out by a local contractor, William Evans.

It is of interest to record that the whole of the building used at Tabernacle was carried out by members of one family associated with the church. Mr. William Evans' son-in-law (Edwin Williams) erected the organ chamber and re-seated and re-furnished the chapel, whilst Mr. Taliesin Williams, his grandson, built the schoolroom.

The transference from Ebenezer to Tabernacle was evidently made with the consent of the Cwrdd Misol, for at a meeting of that body held at Treforest on October 25-26, 1866, "brethren were appointed to visit Eglwysnewydd to deal with the case of one of the elders who was in financial difficulty, and also to negotiate with the owner of the site of the church with the object of acquiring the freehold so as to enable the chapel to be converted into dwelling houses, in view of the fact that a new chapel had been erected on a more convenient site."

I cannot say whether these negotiations were opened, but if so they were evidently not successful for it was not until many years later after the premises had been disposed of to a local resident that the conversion was carried out. I have been informed, but have no definite knowledge on the point, that for ten years or so after the opening of Tabernacle occasional religious services and a Sunday School were held at Ebenezer.

It will be convenient at this point to insert the following details relating to Ebenezer and Tabernacle, extracted from a return of denominational assets made to the General Meeting in 1882:—

	Ebenezer.	Tabernacle.
Leasehold or freehold	Leasehold...	No title.
Present landowner ...	Mr. Brookes	—
Date of Lease	1808	—
Length of Lease	999 years ...	—
Erection or extension of chapel to present size ...	1808	1866
Seating capacity	200	350
Ground rent	7/6	—
Amount spent since beginning of 1873 to date in building or renovation	£20	£320
Amount of debt 1881	—	£710
Value of chapel and appurtenances ...	£250	£1,100.

From this return it appears that Tabernacle was, like many other Methodist meeting houses, built on a site which had been given or leased verbally by the landowners without the execution of a protecting deed. Further reference was made to this defect in a report of 1883 in which mention was made of Lord Bute as the apparent owner. It was decided that steps should be taken to acquire a satisfactory title. These negotiations apparently came to nought. I have been informed locally that the nominal owners—the Mackintosh Estate—were unable to guarantee a valid title, owing possibly to some objection from Lord Bute, the Lord of the Manor. Legislation in due course protected churches in this position, and in 1912 the freehold of the site was acquired.

Tabernacle was opened with special services in 1866, at which sermons were preached by the Methodist divine, Edward Mathews, of Ewenny, and the well known Congregationalist stalwart, Rev. William Williams (Caledfryn), of Groeswen. The church started with a membership of 30, a debt of £600 and unbounded faith. Soon the number of members increased to 60 and by 1870 to 71. In the latter year the Sunday School comprised 123.

The first deacons of the new church were
Thomas Evans (Y Gaseg Felen).
John Dew (Caerphilly Road).
David Evans (The Brook).
William Thomas (Y Ddraenen, i.e. Thornhill).
Daniel Evans (Brynderwen).
Evan Morgan.
John James (Llandaff North).

The last-named was also Precentor and for 25 years acted as Sunday School Superintendent.

Other prominent workers in the church at this time were Thomas Williams (Tyclyd), Mrs. Catherine Lewis (Radyr) and Mrs. Evans (Ashgrove).

As in the case of Ebenezer the new church of Tabernacle had no regular pastor, and relied mainly on the activities of its own personnel and local lay preachers. At this period Rev. Samuel Drew carried on a preparatory school at Llandaff for intending ministers, and his students used to practice the preaching art on the congregations at Tabernacle.

It was not until 1875 that Tabernacle became sufficiently strong numerically and financially to warrant the appointment of a regular pastor. In that year the Rev. David Evans, B.A., responded to a call from Tabernacle and commenced a ministry which lasted for about 18 years.

David Evans was a native of Brecon and for a time worked as a bank clerk in that town. He was, however, much attracted to the ministry and studied at Trefecca. He was the first Trefecca student to receive the degree of B.A. (London). He commenced preaching in 1856, but it was not until August, 1862, at the Lampeter Association meetings, that he was ordained as a regular Methodist preacher. He held pastorates at Montgomery, Blaina (Mon.), and Broadmead Welsh Church, Bristol, prior to his coming to Whitchurch.

Soon after his advent to this locality the Melingriffith Works company got into difficulties, with the result that there was much unemployment and poverty in the neighbourhood which badly affected the financial condition of local churches. In 1884, therefore, Mr. Evans gave up the paid pastorate of Tabernacle, but continued to exercise an unofficial fostering care over the church until in 1893 it was once more in a position to support a minister.

Mr. Evans died at Whitchurch in 1899 at the age of 63. His funeral sermon was preached by Dr. J. Cynddylan Jones, who was himself closely associated with Tabernacle from 1894 until his death in 1931. Cynddylan paid a high tribute to Mr. Evans, whom he described as "A Violet in the Shade." This was an apt description of Mr. Evans who was frail physically and of a retiring disposition. He was not a 'popular' preacher but he possessed a sterling character and was thoughtful, earnest and sincere.

He was greatly interested in education, and in addition to serving on the local School Board he was for many years prior to his death a member of the Council of Cardiff University College. He was much interested also in denominational matters and was one of the founders and active leaders of the Monmouthshire and Glamorgan Presbytery. He strongly favoured the founding of English Calvinistic Methodist churches. He is best known in his denomination for his services as Joint Editor of *The Treasury* and later as Editor of the *Christian Echo* (c 1881) and of *The Monthly Tidings* (1889).

Tabernacle's second regular pastor was a younger and less experienced man and "a complete contrast in temperament and outlook to his predecessor." He was Rev. W. Tudor Jones, who had been educated at Aberystwyth and Cardiff. It soon became evident that his theological views clashed with those of the orthodox leaders in his church, and these differences of opinion in time led to such unpleasantness that in 1898 Mr. Jones resigned his pastorate. In the following year he was admitted to the Unitarian Ministry at Swansea. In later years Mr. Jones pursued his studies in Germany and elsewhere and has attained some fame as an authoritative writer on philosophical subjects.

Considerable statistical information is available in connexional records from 1882 onwards and in the Church records from about 1894. In 1883 the church comprised 53 communicants and 28 children with a total congregation of about 200. There were 12 teachers and 96 scholars attending Sunday School, and the attendance at Band of Hope was about 40. The church debt at this period was £710 whilst church assets were returned as of the value of £1,250.

There were, however, signs of growth, and ten years later in 1893 the number of communicants was given as 72 whilst the Sunday School had grown to 148. The total receipts for this year came to £171 or nearly double the amount received ten years previously.

As in other Welsh churches of the locality at this period the use of the vernacular at church services proved to be a considerable handicap to progress. English was rapidly displacing Welsh as the home language, and migrants to Whitchurch were mostly from English districts. In

Old Whitchurch

the late eighties a system of bilingual services seems to have been introduced but this was not a practicable solution of the difficulty, and gradually Welsh services were reduced in number. By 1894 the transition had proceeded to a stage that one Welsh service only was held on Sunday mornings at 10 a.m. followed by an English service at 11.15 a.m. All the other services were conducted in English.

In 1895 the Welsh Sunday morning service was discontinued, probably from want of support, but as a sop to those who still clung to the old language a Welsh week-night service was held during the summer months only. This concession does not seem to have met with much appreciation, and from 1896 onwards Tabernacle has been an all-English church. It continued, however, to make returns to the Cwrdd Misol until 1899, when it transferred to the English District.

During Mr. Tudor Jones' ministry the need for a Methodist place of worship seems to have been mooted at Llandaff North. The first call was for the establishment of a Sunday School and one was apparently started in 1897. Next year ordinary services were started and a demand was made for the erection of a branch chapel. Tabernacle assumed responsibility for this erection. I do not know what cost was incurred on this project but in the returns for 1900 Tabernacle's debt was given as £500. Hawthorne Road Methodist church was incorporated in 1898-9.

In due course Tabernacle Church cleared the debt and transferred Hawthorn Road to the Forward Movement. Some idea of the strength of Hawthorn Road in the early years is given in the Calvinistic Methodist annual for 1901. According to this Hawthorn Road church comprised 29 communicants and 20 children and candidates, with a total congregation of 159. The total collections amounted to £38 8 7 and the debt is given as £500.

The later history of Tabernacle is centred around the faithful and devoted service of its third pastor, Rev. John Viner, which commenced on September 1, 1900, and continued for 38 years. Mr. Viner was born at Lisvane of Somerset parents who later removed to Pontlottyn, where he spent his boyhood. At the age of 18 he joined a Welsh Calvinistic Methodist church in that town and acquired a knowledge of the Welsh language. Having decided to become a minister he attended a preparatory school at Pontypridd and later proceeded for training to Trefecca. His first and only pastorate was that of Tabernacle.

During Mr. Viner's first year the church building was renovated, one gentleman making a gift of £200 towards the cost. During 1902 a sum of £500 was paid off the Church debt, leaving a balance of £392. Further improvements, however, soon became neessary. In 1903 a better system of lighting was installed, and in 1909 an organ was provided. The cost of the latter was cleared during the following year as the result of a very successful bazaar.

The most substantial building scheme was started in 1929. In that year the freehold of adjoining premises was acquired, and on this site a spacious schoolroom, with classroom, kitchen, offices, etc., was built, and the old schoolroom converted into a vestibule and minister's parlour. These works cost about £2,500.*

When Mr. Viner commenced his pastorate the church comprised 70 members, and the Sunday School numbered 150. Under his earnest and tactful direction the church grew in numbers and prosperity, especially after the Revival of 1904. By 1905 26 new members had been enrolled whilst the Sunday School had increased to 217. The income of the church from collections had also increased by nearly 50 per cent. Moreover the church became very active in a variety of directions and during his pastorate almost every known form of subsidiary society seems at one time or another to have been tried out at Tabernacle, e.g. Adult Bible Class, Band of Hope, Christian Union, Christian Endeavour, Sisterhood, Red Cross Society,. Girls' Guild, Home Fire Girls, Literary and Debating Society, Mutual Improvement classes, Lecture Courses, etc., all witnessing to the pulsating life of this active Church.

At the time of Mr. Viner's retirement in 1938 there were 207 communicants at Tabernacle and a total congregation of about 300. The Sunday School comprised 20 teachers and 154 scholars, with an average attendance of about 126. The total collections during 1939 amounted to £635, including about £370 towards the Ministry. The church debt in 1939 was returned as £1,187 and the value of assets covered by insurance at £4,730. The debt is today below £500.

In accordance with the system of the Presbyterian (C.M.) Church government is in the hands of a small body of elders elected by the church. At the time of the founding of Tabernacle in 1866 there were seven such elders. By the early years of the present century they had dwindled to three, and in 1902 the Church decided to appoint a Committee to support the elders in their declining years. This unusual development, however, was carried on until 1933 when the orthodox system of government was again introduced and new elders appointed.

An unusual feature of the membership of Tabernacle has been the inclusion of many ordained ministers who have selected Whitchurch as their place of residence. In this connection mention may be made of
        Rev. J. Cynddylan Jones, D.D. 1894—1931.
        Rev. E. Norman Jones. 1897—1907.
        Rev. Dr. Griffiths. 1921—1925.
        Rev. D. H. Williams, D.D. 1934—
        Rev. Henry Rees. 1935—1939.
Of these Dr. Cynddylan Jones was the best known. He was a great personality, a great preacher, a great divine and author, and the most powerful influence in contemporary Welsh Methodist life.

Mr. Viner lived but a short time to enjoy his retirement. He died on June 23, 1940. The following estimate of his character by a member of his church is a fitting tribute to his memory:

"In regard to the pulpit he prepared his sermons carefully, and revealed in them the fruit of much reading, deep thinking and fellowship with God. His voice was pleasant and had a tender and appealing

---

* I am indebted to Mr. Iorwerth Howell, Secretary of Tabernacle Church, for most of the facts and figures ralating to the church during recent years.

quality. His whole demeanour was reverent, and he certainly created an atmosphere conducive to worship and the acceptance of the Gospel. While it can be said of him, that as a preacher, he declared 'the whole counsel of God,' the pre-eminent note was that of comfort."

Personally he was characterised by genuine and profound humility. His humility however, was not abject or servile, but always combined with dignity."

His successor, Rev. Rheinallt Nantlais Williams, B.A. (Wales and Cambridge) commenced his service at Tabernacle in 1939. During the recent World War he became an Army Chaplain, and served with the British North African Forces. He has been awarded the O.B.E. (Military Division) "for gallant and distinguished service."

CHAPTER XVI.

HERMON CALVINISTIC METHODIST, TONGWYNLAIS.

During the fifties of last century the iron and tinplate works at Pentyrch and Melingriffith were flourishing, and there were indications of extensive developments which might result in a considerable increase of population. The population of the parish of Whitchurch and the adjoining hamlet of Rhydyboithan increased by 37 per cent. during this decade, and there seemed good prospects of continued growth. Local religious leaders were therefore justified in supposing that there would be an added need for new chapels, and each denomination was anxious to ensure provision for its own adherents. Then in 1859 occurred the great religious revival which spread throughout Wales and had a profound influence on Welsh people.

At this period Calvinistic Methodists resident at Tongwynlais were connected with the Churches of Ebenezer (Whitchurch) and Bethel (Morganstown), and under the influence of the Revival and with a confident belief in the growth of their village, they deemed it an opportune time to establish a cause in their own locality. These local pioneers of Methodism—most of them members of Ebenezer—met in a cottage at the northern end of Queen Street, later demolished to make way for the construction of the Cardiff Railway, and this cottage, which they christened Y Deml (The Temple), became the first home of the church today known as Hermon.

In the following year they embarked on the venture of building a permanent place of worship and the structure known as Hermon Chapel was opened on December 17, 1860. The site was at the south end of Queen Street and formed part of the estate of Mr. C. H. Williams, of Roath Court. Apparently the first lease was a short one, for, according to a connexional report of 1882, the current lease was stated to be for a period of 99 years from 1876 (not 1860) and the ground rent was given as £3 16 0.

The first building, which had seating accommodation for 350, had two front entrances between which stood the pulpit—the congregation thus faced the doors. The floor of the chapel sloped upwards into the entrances and the seats at the back of the building were on a level with the pulpit. This very unusual arrangement was apparently unsatisfactory and twenty years or so later a reconstruction scheme was carried out. The floor of the chapel was levelled, the pulpit was placed at the opposite end, a gallery was constructed and the seating re-arranged.

According to the return already mentioned an amount of £700 was spent on the structure between 1873 and the end of 1880, the bulk of which was probably in respect of the works above described. The recorded debt at the end of 1880, however, was only £250.

It was about this time that the church decided to extend a call to its first pastor, Rev. W. D. Morris. Previously it had depended on the services of lay preachers and visiting ministers. After a few years service Mr. Morris left to take charge of a church in the Aberdare Valley.

Few details are available regarding the history of the church prior to the eighties. No minutes are extant and the connexional records prior to 1882 are not readily accessible. The return for the latter year shows that there was a congregation of about 150, inclusive of 58 communicants and 27 children, whilst the Sunday School comprised 14 teachers and 119 scholars. In that year the church debt was £250 whilst the collections for the ministry amounted only to £33 3 9.

During the eighties industrial depression fell on the district. The Booker company failed towards the end of the seventies and their lands and industrial undertakings were sold by auction. Pentyrch Ironworks was closed down and never re-opened, and many local workers were obliged to leave the district. By 1888 the membership of Hermon had dropped to 34, whilst the Sunday School attendance had shrunk to less than 40. The position did not improve much during the nineties, the membership varying during that period between 35 and 40 and the total congregation between 60 and 70, meeting in a chapel containing seating accommodation for about 400. The Sunday School attendance averaged below 40. The income of such a small church in a relatively poor area was low,—in the eighties it was usually less than £100 and in the nineties it seldom rose above that figure.

It is not surprising therefore that the church could not afford to maintain a regular pastorate; as in its early days, it continued to rely on the services of local preachers and visiting ministers On special occasions leading preachers of the denomination, such as Edward Mathews of Ewenny and William Evans, of Tonyrefail, occupied its pulpit.

In addition to its other handicaps the church was for some years hampered by debt,—not a large one to a flourishing church, but a heavy one to a poor struggling church. Between 1882 and 1898 this was reduced from £250 to £170. During the next couple of years a great effort was made to lessen the amount, and by the end of 1900 the outstanding liability had fallen to £50. The receipts for 1900 were returned as £206 13 11 as compared with £94 in 1898.

Hermon, like most others in Whitchurch, had started as a Welsh church, and for the first 40 years of its existence it was affiliated to the East Glamorgan *Cwrdd Misol* (Monthly Meeting). Its pioneers were all Welsh-speaking, and throughout its history most of the church members belonged to a few faithful families. Unfortunately, although Welsh was the language of the church, the home language was mostly English, and in time the young people and children found it difficult to follow services conducted in the Welsh language.

As in other Whitchurch churches the elders and leaders resisted the tendency to supplant Welsh with English with the result that many of the younger people transferred their allegiance from Hermon to other churches in the locality which had "gone English."

In due time the Welsh 'diehards' of Hermon had to bow to the demand for the admission of English as the language of the church. At first a compromise was agreed on. Welsh services were held on Sunday mornings, whilst the evening services were in English. As the elders and leaders of the church were all Welsh in language and thought it was a trial to them to conduct the evening services in what to them was a foreign language, and the English of the *sêt fawr* gave great amusement to the younger members of the congregation.

The tendency towards Anglicisation, however, at last proved too strong and during the European War there was a complete change-over from Welsh to English. The church, however, still retained its affiliation to the *Cwrdd Misol* until 1923 when it transferred to the East Glamorgan English Presbytery.

Although Hermon, like other Whitchurch causes, benefitted for a short time from the effects of the Revival of 1904 the language difficulty was a hindrance to its development, and during the first decade of the present century the story was one of continuous decline. In 1900 the church comprised 41 communicants and a congregation of about 70, and the Sunday School averaged about 39. By 1908 the number of communicants had fallen to 34, the congregation to 64, and the Sunday School to 20. The decline continued during the next decade. In 1912 the number of communicants was only 13, the congregation about 40, whilst the average attendance at Sunday School was only 14. During this year the church income was £55 16 7. In 1915 the membership increased to 14, but the congregation declined to 25, whilst the Sunday School average was raised to 20.

During this period the financial difficulties arising from a declining membership were accentuated by a relatively heavy debt which had been unwisely incurred during the year or two following the 1904 Revival. The original debt was wiped off during this time of quickened activity, but in 1906 the church embarked on a doubtless much-needed scheme of renovation which included the building of a vestry, alterations to the ceiling, the provision of new lighting arrangements and some ornate interior decoration, and which involved an expenditure of about £450. This was a big venture for a church comprising only 39 members with a total income during 1906-7 of only £126.

Following the Revival the church had extended a call to the Rev. T. J. Jones, who held the pastorate jointly with that of Bethel, Morganstown, from about 1905 until 1917.

The above-mentioned debt may have been one of the causes of the continued decline. In addition the church sustained during 1907-11 severe losses among its membership due to deaths and removals from the district. In 1910 the Senior Deacon, the Secretary, and the Treasurer, on whom the burden of church business mostly fell, died within a few months of one another, and in 1911—12, as has been mentioned above, the membership fell to about a dozen.

It seemed likely, therefore, that the church would have to be disbanded. This unhappy ending, however, was averted by the effort, of one family, that of the late William Thomas, secretary and deacon,

COED Y WENALLT, CORPORATION PARK   *Cardiff Library*

WENALLT ROAD FROM THE DERI   *Cardiff Library*

NANT CWM NOFYDD *Cardiff Library*

WHITCHURCH BROOK NEAR RHIWBINA HALT *Cardiff Library*

who had died in 1910. Mr. Thomas left a widow and 10 children, the eldest a girl student at Cardiff University College, and the youngest a child of two. All these children had been attached to Hermon, although Mrs. Thomas was herself a member of Ainon Baptist Church.

On the death of her husband who had been devoted to Hermon, Mrs. Thomas transferred her membership to the Methodist cause in order to retain her children's interest and her husband's association with the church. From now onwards the story of Hermon is bound up with the life of the Thomas family. One of the sons, Mr. Wilfred Thomas, then a pupil at Pontypridd Intermediate School, became Secretary, another son, Mr. Gwilym Thomas taught himself music in order to play the church organ, while, later, another brother, Mr. Frank Thomas, became Treasurer. In addition, the daughter, Miss Gwen Thomas, B.A., often conducted the services when no preacher was available, and became an able lay preacher whose services were much in demand at other churches in the neighbourhood. Upon this faithful family fell the task of keeping the church alive until better times returned. It was a common experience for visiting preachers to discover at the close of morning services that the congregation had consisted entirely of the members of one family.

In 1912 the church lost the services of Miss Gwen Thomas who left to take up a teaching appointment at Ebbw Vale. The Thomas family, however, still carried on. About this time the *Cwrdd Misol* appointed a committee of the ministers and deacons of two Cardiff churches— Pembroke Terrace and Crwys Road—to help Hermon in its struggle by arranging for a regular pulpit supply, especially on Sunday evenings. This assistance helped the church greatly, and a slight improvement was recorded up to the outbreak of War, when the Church Secretary, Mr. Wilfred Thomas, and a few other young men who had begun to take interest in the affairs of the church were called on to join H.M. Forces. Fortunately, however, by this time Miss Gwen Thomas had returned to the district and she shouldered much of the responsibility for the church's welfare.

In 1917 Rev. T. J. Jones relinquished his oversight of the church and the *Cwrdd Misol* asked Rev. Lewis Mendus, B.A., the minister of Park Church, Treforest, to assume temporary pastoral supervision. Services continued to be held regularly on Sundays and on one weeknight. Towards the end of the War period, however, great difficulty was experienced by Hermon and other local churches in obtaining Sunday 'supplies,' and an arrangement was therefore made with Bethesda Congregational Church, under the leadership of the late Mr. Evan Anthony, for the temporary amalgamation of the two churches in order to meet the shortage of preachers. A united service was held on Sunday mornings at Hermon and on Sunday nights at Bethesda. Each church, however, maintained its identity in regard to financial matters.

After the restoration of peace Rev. E. L. Mendus severed his connection with Hermon on his transference to the pastorate of Grangetown Forward Movement Church. The joint arrangement between Hermon and Bethesda continued for a time after the end of the war. In June, 1919, Mr. Wilfred Thomas returned home from war service and the two churches now went their separate ways. Mr. Thomas' services, however, were available only for a short time as he soon left for college to complete his training for the scholastic profession. During 1920 Hermon passed through another critical period. Miss Gwen Thomas had married and left the district and the church was now without a leader. For two or three Sundays no services were held.

Mrs. Thomas, however, was still undaunted. She prevailed on some members of the *Cwrdd Misol* to get things going again. Tabernacle Church, Whitchurch, were asked by the Monthly Meeting to release one of its officers, Mr. John Williams, for the time being to guide the church at this difficult period. Mr. Williams attended sometimes two services a Sunday as well as one week-night. The Church prospects were, however, by no means bright. The membership was still only about 12, and even Dr. Cynddylan Jones, with his wide experience of the difficulties of churches, had no solution to offer to the problem with which Hermon was faced.

At the end of 1920 Mr. Wilfred Thomas returned and once more assumed the duties of Secretary and active church leader, and from this time the little church entered upon a new lease of life. Mr. Thomas and his little band of devoted workers were faced with financial problems arising out of the existence of a debt of £375 and the necessity of carrying out repairs to the chapel structure. They decided to make no outside appeal or organise any secular efforts to obtain funds. They took the view that the church was first and foremost a spiritual organisation and that its members should be prepared to meet liabilities out of their own resources. As an indication of the magnitude of the task which they had set themselves it should be stated that in 1920 the number of members was only 17, the total congregation only 23, whilst the Sunday School attendance averaged only 16. The total income for the year was only £69.

Soon, however, conditions commenced to improve. In addition to the forceful help of Mr. John Williams, the Church had the advantage of the assistance of Dr. Griffiths, a retired Khasia Hills missionary who had settled at Whitchurch. Dr. Griffiths undertook the visitation of members and the conduct of the weekly church meeting. His services were given without remuneration, and he soon endeared himself to the little flock. By the end of 1921 the membership had increased to 21, by the end of 1922 to 30, and by the end of 1923 to 43.

During these three years of revival the church became active in various directions. A sisterhood was organised by Mrs. Dr. Griffiths with Mrs. Wm. Thomas as Treasurer, a Band of Hope was conducted by Mr. Wilfred Thomas, and the number of weeknight meetings was increased from one to four. The Sunday School also increased from an average of 16 in 1920 to 36 in 1921 and to 60 in 1923. With increased membership the financial position improved. The income for 1921 amounted to £152, or more than double that of the previous year.

A hopeful spirit now prevailed in the church, and the question of a permanent pastor came up for consideration. After consultation with another pastorless church—Trinity, Taffs Well—it was decided in October, 1923, to invite Rev. W. D. O. Jones, Maesteg, to become their joint minister. Mr. Jones accepted and has served the two churches with great fidelity ever since.

Under his guidance the church has consolidated its position. In the latest official returns available—that of 1939—the number of communicants is given as 57, the congregation as 115, whilst the Sunday School comprises 14 teachers and 92 scholars. The total collections during the year amounted to £169 of which £125 was for the maintenance of the ministry. The church debt has been reduced to £170 without any recourse to outside help. The freehold of the church has been acquired during recent years. The church property is today valued at £1,200.

CHAPTER XVII.

WHITCHURCH METHODIST CHURCH.

Although the earliest records I have been able to examine of a Wesleyan Methodist Church at Whitchurch date back only to 1839 it seems certain that there was some kind of Wesleyan society here many years before. It is known that both John and Charles Wesley paid frequent visits to Cardiff, and the latter on at least one occasion conducted missions at Whitchurch.

Wesleyan Methodism during the 18th century made little progress in South Wales, mainly, perhaps, because its preachers carried on their evangel in English, a language which at that period was not generally spoken or understood in the locality. In, and for some years after, 1765 the Glamorgan Circuit extended from Chepstow to Llanelly, but as the number of societies increased it was sub-divided. Thus in 1796 two circuits were created, the Cardiff Circuit covering Monmouthshire and East Glamorgan and the Swansea Circuit covering West Glamorgan and Carmarthenshire. The total membership of the Cardiff Circuit in 1797 was only 236, whilst Swansea had 164.

The need for Wesleyan preaching in the Welsh language was at last realised, and in 1796 a bilingual missioner, John Hughes, was placed in charge of the Cardiff Circuit. From this time forward Welsh ministers were attached to the Glamorgan circuits, with the result that more rapid progress was recorded, although at this period Wesleyanism was regarded with some hostility by other dissenting sects.

By 1805 the membership of the Cardiff Circuit had increased to 309, and growth now became more rapid; by 1808 a total of 562 was attained. Apparently a number of Welsh societies came into being probably as the result of the activities of Griffith Owen, William Evans and Griffith Hughes. Amongst local Welsh societies formed at this period were those at Cardiff, Caerphilly, Ely, Lisvane, Machen, Llantrisant, etc. In 1812 a Cardiff Welsh Circuit seems to have been formed, but this was united in 1814 with the English Circuits as part of the South Wales division. Another change was effected in 1817, when all Welsh Wesleyan churches were organised into a Welsh division.

Few Welsh chapels appear to have been built to house the Welsh societies. There seems to have been established a Welsh chapel at Caerphilly (and presently another at Llandaff) in 1816, and one at Lisvane in 1822. The first Welsh Wesleyan Chapel at Union Street, Cardiff, was not built until 1838; prior to this year the Welsh Wesleyans used the English Chapel in Church Street, which was rebuilt in 1829.

It is probable that there were Wesleyan causes at Ely, Llandaff and Melingriffith before 1829. These were 'societies' which met in the homes of some of the members, usually for Bible reading and prayer, interspersed by occasional preaching services conducted by the circuit ministers or by lay preachers. The society at Melingriffith probably started as a Welsh cause, but it is likely that it soon became bilingual. The local leader is said to have been Christopher James, a shopkeeper at Heoldon, who had previously been a carpentry contractor at Melingriffith.

He was a man of great personality and character, and from him sprang a line of Jameses who played an important part in the commercial life of Merthyr Tydvil and Swansea. Amongst these were his grandsons, Justice Milbourne James (1807-1881) and C. H. James, M.P. (1817-1890). Some members of the James family are still leading figures in legal circles at Merthyr.

Christopher James was born in 1752 and died at the advanced age of 85 in 1837. It seems unlikely that he would have become the pioneer of a new cause after the age of 60, and it may therefore be supposed that the Melingriffith cause was in existence as early as the year 1812, although it may not have become a regularly organised church until many years later. The Wesleyan society members were probably associated with the Parish Church and their adherence to Methodism was extraneous to ordinary church activities; they belonged to the 'society' for the intensification of their religious life much in the same way as modern church members belong to such bodies as the Oxford Movement.

No definite information is available regarding the inception of Wesleyan Methodism at Melingriffith. A Government Report of 1847, however, mentions that the Penylan (or Melingriffith) Sunday School was founded in 1820, and it seems likely that a regular society existed before that year. Another Government return made in 1833 reports that at that period there were three Sunday Schools at Whitchurch belonging to the Calvinistic Methodists, Baptists and Wesleyans respectively. The last-mentioned comprised 21 males and 14 females.

We now come to such church records as are available. For the privilege of examining these I am indebted to Mr. T. W. Phelps of Kelston Road, who has been connected with the local Methodist cause for more than seventy years. These records include, *inter alia*, an almost complete range of hymn sheets printed for use at anniversary meetings held in connection with Melingriffith Wesleyan Sunday School, commencing on May 19, 1839. The hymns and the other printed matter are in the English language, a fact which seems to indicate that the cause from this date onward at any rate was primarily English. The 1839 hymn sheet mentions that the occasion was the first anniversary; from this one may deduce that the church and Sunday School were founded in 1838. The Government returns already mentioned, however, refer to Sunday Schools existing in 1820 and in 1833. May it not be that 1838 marks the year in which the Wesleyan 'Society' was constituted into a permanent church worshipping in its own regular meeting house?

This meeting house, according to local tradition—I have seen no records of the fact—was the small building which still stands on the hill known as Penylan, overlooking Melingriffith Works. It may originally have been an outbuilding connected with the old Penylan farmhouse, but it had long been in the ownership of the works proprietors who allowed the Wesleyans to use it rent-free, as nearly all of them were Works employees.

Tradition has it that in the earlier years the new church maintained some connection with the Parish Church. As late as the forties of last century, it is said, the society met for a service in its own chapel at 9 o'clock on Sunday mornings, and at about half-past ten the congregation used to march in procession to a service at the Parish Church. On Sunday afternoons and evenings they again worshipped at their own chapel. Apparently, whilst the church services were ordinarily conducted in English, on special occasions such as anniversary meetings, Welsh services were also held, and in the late 1850's the records refer to Melingriffith as being English and Welsh. Anniversary and other special services, it is said, used to be held at the 'Finishing Room' of the Works.

Of course the little church had no regular pastor. One of the Cardiff Circuit ministers exercised general oversight and conducted devotional services at regular intervals, probably once a month, whilst on other Sundays the church was served by local preachers or else prayer meetings were held. An effective lay preacher during the 1850's— "Thomas Phillips of Melingriffith"—seems to have been in charge of the church, and regularly preached both in English and Welsh.

After a dozen years or so the first meeting house was found to be too small, and steps were taken to secure more ample accommodation. On December 1, 1851, a church meeting appointed a committee "to act and propose things concerning the new chapel at Melingriffith." The following were appointed to serve on that committee, viz., Morgan Lewis, William David, Daniel Jones, Edward Jones (chairman), Thomas Thomas, John Thomas (secretary), John Smith, James Jones, Semei Stanfield, Samuel Humphreys (Treasurer), John Lewis and William Thomas. Most, if not all, of these persons were officials or workers employed at the Melingriffith Works, and their names seem to indicate that they were mostly of Welsh extraction. It is of interest to note that the descendants of some of these persons have been associated with the church down to the present day. The Lewis family in particular have always been prominent leaders, and it is claimed that five generations of this family have been connected with the cause.

Scarcely a stone's-throw away from the first meeting-place was a larger structure, possibly a barn, which seems to have been placed free of rent at the disposal of the church. This building belonged to the Bookers of Melingriffith Works, and it was a condition of the letting that the plans for the adaptation of the building had to be approved by James Powell, who at this time was the Works Agent.

Two sets of plans for adaptation were submitted to the committee by Semei Stanfield and John Thomas. After some discussion the plan of John Thomas was preferred "if Mr. Powell did approve of." Mr. Powell was apparently not in agreement with the committee's decision, and it was not until May, 1852, that his sanction was obtained.

The committee seem to have been divided as to whether the old pulpit should be used or a new one made. One of the members had concluded negotiations for the purchase of a pulpit from a Cardiff church, "which was not at all agreeable with the committee." The expression of disagreement led to the withdrawal of one of the members from the committee. Ultimately, however, the transaction was confirmed and in November two of the committee members went to Cardiff to pay £4 to Wm. Luke Evans, churchwarden of St. John's, for the pulpit in question.

In June, 1852, tenders were received for the internal wood-work of the chapel, with the exception of the pulpit and the communion table, but including panelling and moulding work and the flooring joists in the singing pews and inside the communion seat, and that of John Emmanuel, Llanishen, in the sum of £102 was accepted. The unsuccessful tenderer, Evan David, was given the work of flooring the body of the chapel and putting in and painting windows. Of course, there were bound to be extras. Emmanuel's account included items for a new porch, roofing gutters to stable and other minor works, and the total came to £121 16s. 0d. Evan David's bill was for £5 5s. 0d. A further sum of £10 5s. 6d. was paid for chandeliers and sconces, whilst Thomas Mills, of Caerphilly, charged £5 7s. 6d. for a clock which the Sunday School presented to the church. Much of the building material used was given by the Melingriffith Works proprietors.

The committee delegated to members the collection of funds for defraying the cost. The collecting books are still available and show a total collection from members and friends amounting to £80 14s. 0d., of which £27 6s. 0d. was collected by Morgan Lewis. At the opening services a further amount of £18 7s. 1d. was collected. The little church was now in debt. In February, 1853, the amount was £32. During the year efforts were made to clear this, but not with complete success, and in January, 1854, a special meeting of members was convened to deal with the matter, and the record of the meeting reads: "Every member came forward nobly in the present moment so that the deficiency was made up."

The official name of the church was Melingriffith Wesleyan Methodist Church, but it was also variously referred to in the records as Melingriffith Wesleyan Society, Melingriffith Society of Wesleyans, and Penylan Chapel Society.

The new chapel was opened by special services on two week-ends in December, 1852, and was evidently intended to serve Welsh as well as English worshippers, for whilst the first week-end service was in English, the two services on the next week-end were mostly in Welsh. The following is the order of service:—

Sunday, Dec. 12, 1852. English Services.
10 a.m. and 6 p.m. Rev. Hugh Carter (Merthyr Circuit).
2 p.m. Rev. E. Fice.

Saturday, Dec. 18, 1852. Welsh Service.
7 p.m.   Mr. David Davies.
         Rev. Henry Wilcox.
Sunday, Dec. 19, 1852. Welsh Services.
10 a.m. Rev. Henry Wilcox.
6 p.m.   Rev. Thomas Jones.
2 p.m.   Rev. Henry Wilcox.
         Rev. G. Follows (English Sermon).

On Christmas Day a special Tea Meeting was held at the new chapel, and various commemorative addresses were delivered.

During the fifties and sixties the Church and Sunday School seem to have maintained their bilingual character. Entries in Sunday School accounts in 1853 and 1855 relate to the purchase of Welsh testaments. In 1864 church anniversary services were conducted in Welsh in the morning and in English in the afternoon and evening. In 1861 and in 1866, and possibly later, the church contributed to the funds of both the English and Welsh Circuits. In the late 1860's the process of Anglicisation at Whitchurch was developing rapidly and, although I have no information on the matter, it seems unlikely that Welsh services survived far into the seventies.

The Sunday School seems from its inception to have been a very live department of the Melingriffith church, and the financial records show that it contributed substantial sums to church funds. In the early fifties Semei Stanfield was Superintendent and he seems to have held the office for nearly thirty years. Other active workers were Thomas Thomas (who was Secretary in the fifties), T. J. Lewis, John Lewis and J. M. Lewis. Sunday School income was derived from an annual donation of £5 from Mr. T. W. Booker (which was regularly paid from 1857 to 1872) and the proceeds of collections at anniversary services. In addition a tea meeting (*te parti talu*) was held annually at first on Whit-Tuesday and later on Good Friday, and the profits on these functions, which averaged about £10, were handed over to the funds of the church.

The Melingriffith Wesleyans seem to have had the blessing of the Booker family. Their patronage was evidently appreciated, and in 1856 and 1860 presentations of Bibles were made by the church to Mr. T. W. Booker (Blakemore), M.P., and to his daughter respectively, the latter on the occasion of her marriage to Rev. Cyril Stacey.

At both the old and the new meeting houses the leader of singing was John Smith. For many years, as was usual at early dissenting churches, there was no instrumental accompaniment. Later John Smith seems to have organised an orchestra, the string instruments for which were made by himself. Smith and James Jones were the leading players. Later the orchestra gave place to a harmonium. This was probably the instrument purchased for £4 10s. 0d. in 1883 by the Sunday School.

In 1881 the meeting house was renovated by Charles Shepherd at a cost of £83 8s. 6d., the cost being met by special collections. Of the total amount collected T. J. Lewis was responsible for £37 8s. 0d., obtained mostly from Cardiff Wesleyans, including John Cory, Richard Cory, Lewis Williams and the Herne family. The reopening services, with the usual tea meeting, took place on June 8, 1881.

The Wesleyan Methodists occupied their second meeting house for more than forty years. Whitchurch during this period developed very considerably, and the need became felt for a larger building on a more central site. The old chapel had seating accommodation for 150 only and was well away from the developing portion of the parish.

Early in 1893 steps were taken to provide a fund for the erection of a new chapel. Subscriptions were obtained from well-to-do Wesleyans resident in Cardiff and these were supplemented by the proceeds of lectures, tea meetings, sales of work, etc. The lead in raising money for this purpose was taken by Messrs. Robert Davies, John Lewis and Wm. Thompson, all of whom were officials at Melingriffith Works. By January, 1894, an amount of £132 had been collected. A building committee was now formed and a body of trustees appointed to deal with the business of the church and to establish a proper relationship with the Wesleyan connexion. Mr. T. J. Lewis was appointed Secretary, and Mr. Robert Davies, Treasurer, whilst Rev. W. H. Clogg of Roath (Wesley Circuit), acted as the first Chairman. The first trustees included the three persons named, together with Messrs. E. R. Moxey, J.P., J. Walter Hibbert, J. C. Parkyn, Lewis Williams, John Rogers, J. N. Kestell, John Lewis (Accountant), William Williams, John Lewis (Shearer), John Morgan Lewis and E. Huzzey.

Mr. Charles Jones (Architect) was instructed to prepare plans for a chapel with seating accommodation for 250 and a schoolroom for 100 children. The tender of Mr. Henry Davies for erecting the building (£900) was accepted at the end of April, by which time a sum of £400 had been raised. The site selected was near the junction of Merthyr Road with Velindre Road. A foundation stone-laying ceremony took place on June 29, 1894, and the new chapel was opened in April, 1895.

The cost of the building, equipment and various incidental expenses, originally estimated at £1,119, was considerably exceeded, and, according to particulars furnished to the connexional headquarters, the final figure was £1,330. Of this amount a sum of £1,000 had been locally collected. The Wesleyan Chapel Committee made a grant of £40 and a loan of £60 towards the deficiency, subject to the remaining debt being wiped off within a period of ten years.

A couple of years later, in April, 1897, the church purchased an organ for £63. This instrument continued in use until 1911, when it was replaced by a new organ costing £300, part of the cost being borne by Mr. Andrew Carnegie.

The Church and Sunday School were now fast expanding, and in May, 1900, further extensions became necessary. Additional land was acquired and plans prepared for the erection of classrooms. These were built by Messrs. Saulter & Sons at a cost of £262. In 1905 more land was leased and plans were under consideration for the enlargement of the chapel. A building fund committee was set up with Mr. W. R. Davies as Secretary and Mr. Frank Wills (Rhiwbina) as Treasurer, and steps taken to raise the necessary funds. A substantial contributor was Sir J. Herbert Cory, who in later years further helped the church with great liberality.

In 1911 the tender of Mr. H. Gummer, in the sum of £675, was accepted for extending the chapel frontwards to Penlline Road. There was of course much additional expenditure on the installation of electric lighting, structural adaptations to accommodate the new organ, additional seating, etc. The new buildings were opened on Dec. 6, 1911, whilst the new organ came into service in the following February. The total debt outstanding on the completion of the works was only £175, and in 1916 the debt was wiped out by another gift of £72 from Sir J. Herbert Cory. Two years later, in 1918, the freehold of the land was acquired for the sum of £192, of which amount Mr. T. J. Lewis raised £167.

Further building expansions and improvements were undertaken in 1924, and in 1929 the question of erecting a new schoolroom came under consideration. To enable the latter work to proceed it was deemed necessary to reduce the church liability in respect of a mortgage on the minister's house in Velindre Road, held by Sir Herbert Cory. Of the total amount of £650 a sum of £100 had been repaid in 1923. Sir Herbert was again approached and agreed to reduce the amount outstanding by £250.

It was not until 1935 that the scheme for building the proposed new schoolroom, with accommodation for 200 scholars, was proceeded with. The plans were prepared by Mr. A. G. Lynham, F.R.I.B.A., and a contract was entered into with Mr. H. C. Parker (Cardiff) to erect the building.

Since 1905 the following resident ministers have served the church:—

1905-07 Rev. Harold Chappell.	1923-25 Rev. W. J. T. Small.
1907-10 Rev. J. Newton Davies.	1925-29 Rev. T. O. Beswarick.
1910-13 Rev. T. Ewbank.	1929-32 Rev. E. Nicholas.
1913-16 Rev. J. A. Findlay, M.A.	1932-35 Rev. J. R. Rushton.
1916-19 Rev. T. J. Evans.	1935-41 Rev. H. Wilkinson.
1919-22 Rev. A. B. Duncalfe.	1941- Rev. S. J. Martin, B.A.
1922-23 Rev. W. Withers.	

The membership of the Melingriffith Wesleyan Church in 1894 was only 45. The present membership of the Whitchurch Methodist Church is 211, with an additional number of 10 juniors.

CHAPTER XVIII.

AINON* AND SALEM CHURCHES, TONGWYNLAIS.

One of the oldest East Glamorgan Baptist Churches is Tonyfelin, Caerphilly, founded in 1784 as a daughter church of Hengoed. Its pastor was Rev. Griffith Davies. The church drew its membership from many miles around, including some from Tongwynlais. Griffith Davies carried out mission work in outlying villages and in 1822 commenced preaching at the homes of Thomas Jones (Eos Glan Rhymni) and Edward Williams at Tongwynlais.

Services were later held in the club-room of a local inn kept by David Miles. To these gatherings the pastor was accompanied by some of the more zealous members of the church. Griffith Davies was succeeded at Tonyfelin in September, 1826, by the afterwards famous Rev. Christmas Evans, and the latter seems to have continued the mission at Tongwynlais. Under his influence the little band of Baptists at Tongwynlais rented a dwelling in Mill Road as a meeting-place. This was opened on September 29, 1827, and here, in addition to regular prayer meetings, occasional special public services were held. At the opening service in this meeting-house Christmas Evans and five others officiated.

Christmas Evans did not remain long at Tonyfelin. In the autumn of 1828 he received a call to the pastorate of Tabernacle Church, Cardiff, and the great preacher has himself recounted how he decided to accept the call and made his famous covenant with himself whilst returning home from Tongwynlais over Caerphilly Mountain. Rev. John Jones, of Llandyssul, served Tonyfelin after the departure of Christmas Evans for the next three years, and during his pastorate the Baptists of Tongwynlais seem to have organised themselves into a regular church. In 1830 Jones baptized a number of adherents at Tongwynlais probably in the river.

The need for better and more permanent accommodation now came to be felt, and in 1831, according to a Church record, a perpetual lease of a chapel site was obtained from C. C. Williams (Roath Court) and Rev. Wyndham Lewis (New House) on the exceptionally favourable terms of a ground rent of 1/- every 999 years. This may have been for only part of the present church site for later denominational records show that a ground rent of £3 per annum was paid. At a more recent date the freehold of the site was acquired. The building of the chapel

---

* This account of Ainon has been largely based on official church records placed at my disposal by the Church Secretary, Mr. Ebenezer Davies. Some of the facts relating to the first two decades are from *Hanes y Bedyddwyr* (1839) by David Jones.

was commenced in 1831 and the opening services were held on April 24 and 25, 1832. The officiating ministers were Revs. William Williams, R. Prichard, William Jones, William Thomas, J. Edmunds and T. Thomas. The new chapel had seating accommodation for about 400. In 1851 it was enlarged to accommodate 600.

The church continued to be regarded as a branch of Tonyfelin until June 12, 1838, when it was constituted an independent unit with a membership of 41. On the latter date Rev. Morgan Evans was ordained as the first pastor. Amongst those who participated in the ordination services were Revs. D. Edwards, O. Michael, J. James, D. R. Stephens, W. Jones, D. Davies, D. Jones and T. Thomas.

Morgan Evans was the son of Richard Evans, an influential Caerphilly shopkeeper, and commenced preaching in 1832. In addition to being a good preacher he had literary tastes and won prizes at eisteddfodau under the *noms de plume* Cynfelyn and Morgan Mwynfawr. He died at the age of 35 in 1841. At this period Ainon had 53 members and a Sunday School of 77.

Mr. Evans' successor, Rev. John Thomas, came from Llantrisant on December 9, 1842, but remained at Ainon scarcely two years. During his short pastorate a daughter church seems to have been established at Llantwit Fardre. It may have started as a Sunday School. An 1844 denominational return states that in 1844 Ainon had 72 members and two Sunday Schools comprising 13 teachers and 100 scholars.

For some time apparently the church was without a pastor, and then in 1846 began the five years' pastorate of Rev. William Lewis who died at Tongwynlais on Dec. 13, 1851, and was buried at Ainon graveyard. A short time before his death the Baptist Association meetings or *Cymanfa*—then regarded as an event of great importance—was held at Ainon, which had recently been enlarged, and the denominational letter to the churches on 'The Consistency of the Christian Character' was from the pen of Mr. Lewis. This *Gymanfa* was one of the most successful in the early history of the Baptist cause in South Wales. The preaching services drew a crowd, it is said, of 10,000, from far and near. A platform was erected in the open air and the leading preacher was the Baptist stalwart Rev. David Jones of the Cardiff Tabernacle.

At the time of Mr. Lewis' death the combined membership of Ainon and its Llantwit Fardre branch, named Salem, was 130, whilst the attendance at the two Sunday Schools amounted to 150. In the following year Salem (Llantwit Fardre) seems to have been incorporated a separate church with a membership of about 50. After the secession Ainon's membership dropped to about 85.

In June, 1853, Rev. Daniel Jones ("Silver Tongue") began what was perhaps the most useful pastorate in Ainon's history. Daniel Jones was born near Llandovery and ministered to several churches at Cwmsarnddu, Liverpool, and Felinfoel before coming to Tongwynlais. In addition to being an eloquent and effective preacher he was also a poet of some merit and won many prizes at eisteddfodic competitions. He also published a collection of Welsh hymns suitable for use at Baptist services.

During his ministry there was a considerable influx of population to Tongwynlais resulting from industrial development at Pentyrch and Melingriffith, and many of the incoming population were monoglot English. Some of the English Baptists expressed a desire for religious services in their language, and on March 4, 1860, separate English devotional meetings were started in a room rented from Edmund Thomas of the Lewis' Arms. The English branch held prayer services here on Sunday mornings, and in the evenings lay preachers from Cardiff attended to preach. The minister served the branch church on two Sabbath days each month.

The Baptist cause at Tongwynlais was now pulsating with life, due in part possibly to the influence of the great Revival of 1859. By 1860 Ainon had 160 members in all whilst the Welsh and English Sunday Schools had a total of 32 teachers and 280 scholars.

After a time the English Baptists felt themselves strong enough to justify the provision of a chapel of their own. A plot of land in Queen Street (then known as Ivy Street) was accordingly leased from the Executors of Charles Crofts Williams, of Roath Court, at an annual ground rent of £3 for 99 years commencing February 2, 1858. Building work commenced in 1862 and in August of that year was granted to Morgan Morgan, Tongwynlais (Lock-keeper), Thomas Thomas, Tongwynlais (Grocer), and Solomon Lewis, Aberdare (Builder), the lease of the plot of land on which these persons "have erected and built a Chapel or tenement for celebrating Divine Worship by the congregation of English Baptists." It is of interest to note that the original lease of Ainon Chapel was also granted to Morgan Morgan, the Lock.

In November of the same year the opening of the new chapel, which was named Salem, was celebrated by special services in which the following ministers officiated, viz., Revs. Nathaniel Thomas (Tabernacle), Rees Griffiths (Bethany), Edward Jones (Penuel), David Davies (Ararat), — Bailey (Canton), and Edward Roberts (Pontypridd), in addition to several Cardiff lay preachers. Welsh sermons were delivered at Ainon, and English sermons in the new chapel on the Sabbath, and Welsh and English sermons at three meetings on the following day.

Whilst this important development was maturing Rev. Daniel Jones, now 75 years old, was in a bad state of ill-health, and on December 28, 1862, his very successful pastorate which extended over $9\frac{1}{2}$ years was ended by his death. His funeral at Ainon was attended by between 50 and 60 ministers and a very large body of laymen of all classes. Rev. W. Williams (Caledfryn), of Groeswen, conducted the obituary service in Welsh whilst Rev. D. Davies, D.D., preached an English sermon.

Ainon's next call was to a young man, William Jones, then a student at Pontypool Academy. This was given in July, 1864, and Mr. Jones accepted, conditionally on his being allowed to complete a fourth year's course at college. The condition was agreed to, and it was not until May 21, 1865, that Mr. Jones commenced his joint pastorate of Ainon and Salem. On this date he baptized six adherents of Salem. As usual the Induction Services extended over two days and several ministers officiated both at the Welsh and English chapels, the services being attended by very large congregations.

As Morgan Morgan, one of the lessees of the Salem chapel site, died in 1866 it was deemed wise to safeguard the business position by vesting the property in a body of 15 trustees representing the two churches. In August the trustees were duly elected and their names and the conditions appertaining to the trust were embodied in the Salem Trust Deed dated August 4, 1866. The following list of the first trustees throws considerable light on the humble character and social position of the persons who were associated with the two churches, viz. :—

> Thomas Thomas, Pentyrch Works, Hammerman.
> Solomon Lewis, Aberdare, Builder.
> James Israel, Pentyrch Works, Coker.
> Rees Richards, Tongwynlais, Brickmaker.
> David Tyler, Tongwynlais, Finer.
> William Williams, Tongwynlais, Furnaceman.
> Richard Francis, Walnut Tree Bridge, Platelayer.
> Thomas Evans, Walnut Tree Bridge, Smith.
> Edward Morgan, Castell Coch, Labourer.
> Thomas Llewellyn, Morganstown.
> Joseph Coslett, Pear Tree Cottage, Labourer.
> William Thomas, Rubinah Quarry, Contractor.
> Thomas James, Tongwynlais, Woodward.
> Michael Lyons, Tongwynlais, Policeman.
> Alfred Gough, Tongwynlais, Labourer.
> John Davies, Tongwynlais, Collier.

In addition to being humble working men many of them were unlettered,—no fewer than nine of them could not write their own names. All the signatures and marks were witnessed by the pastor, Rev. Wm. Jones.

It will perhaps be of interest to quote passages from the Trust Deed. The chapel, it is stated, was "erected at the expense of the Particular or Calvinistic Baptist Denomination . . . . . for promoting the worship of Almighty God by Protestant Dissenters of the Denomination aforesaid." The Deed prescribes that the number of trustees must not be less than five nor more than fifteen, that all Trustees must be members of a Baptist Church, and only "men members" of the church are permitted to participate in their election or in the transaction of financial business. Women members are, however, permitted to vote for the appointment or dismissal of pastors.

The most interesting portions are those relating to church doctrines. It is stipulated that the premises must be used and enjoyed as and for "A place of Religious Worship by Protestant Dissenters of the Denomination of Particular or Calvinistic Baptists who do and shall maintain the Doctrines of one Living and True God, three equal persons in the Godhead—the Proper Deity and the real Humanity of our Lord Jesus Christ—the Sinful State of Man by Nature and by Practice—The Free Justification of the Penitent Sinner by Faith in the Atoning Sacrifice of Jesus Christ—the Regeneration, Conversion and Sanctification of the Soul of Man by the Spirit and Grace of God—The Moral Law a Rule for the Conduct of all Believers—The Resurrection of the Dead and Future Judgment—The Eternal Happiness of the Righteous and Everlasting Misery of the Wicked.

"And those only who do and shall practise Baptism by Immersion in Water in the Name of the Father and of the Son and of the Holy Ghost, to such only as are of years of understanding upon their own Confession of Repentance towards God and of Faith in our Lord Jesus Christ, and also such other persons of the Faith and Practise aforesaid as shall be hereafter united to the same Society and attend the Worship of God in the said Chapel."

No person was to be allowed to partake of the Lord's Supper unless he had been previously baptized by Immersion, and no person was to be elected or to continue as Pastor "who does not maintain and teach the before-mentioned Doctrines and Practice Baptism in manner aforesaid."

The 1866 Trust Deed records that the property was subject to an Equitable mortgage debt of £200 due to Charles Henry Williams. The Solomon Lewis, of Aberdare, was probably the builder of Salem Chapel.

Rev. William Jones served the two causes faithfully from 1865 to 1874 and was held in high esteem in the locality. He was not only a popular preacher but also had literary qualifications and contributed several articles on religious subjects to *Y Greal*. Mr. Jones left Tongwynlais to serve Nebo, Ebbw Vale, where he was inducted on May 17, 1874.

The sixties was a period of intense Nonconformist growth in Whitchurch. In addition to Salem the new churches of Hermon (1860), Bethel (1865) and Tabernacle (1866) were established, whilst an Anglican cause was also started at Tongwynlais (1860). It speaks well for the devotion of the adherents of Ainon and Salem that they were able to maintain a relatively large membership in face of the competition of the new churches. In 1865 their total strength was 177 whilst the Sunday Schools comprised 18 teachers and 230 scholars. The number of members in 1870 was 169 or only eight less than five years earlier.

After the departure of Mr. Jones a unanimous call was given to Rev. Joshua Thomas, of Pyle, who accepted and commenced his pastorate on the first Sunday in January, 1875. The Induction meetings however, were not held until March, and no fewer than eleven ministers participated. A Church meeting held on this occasion set up separate diaconates for the Welsh and the English churches.

In December, 1875, it was decided to carry out renovation work at Ainon. The cost of this work amounted to £500.

Joshua Thomas served Ainon and Salem for $5\frac{1}{2}$ years with considerable success, and during that period baptized no fewer than 131 members.

The combination of two churches using different languages under the same pastor, however, was not altogether satisfactory and ultimately the partnership suffered the fate of all such bilingual associations in South Wales. The English section complained that it was not receiving a fair share of the pastor's ministration, and at last in November, 1880, Salem with its 100 or so members, decided to secede from Ainon and continue as a separate church. The minister cast in his lot with the secessionists, and in the 1881 Report to *Cymanfa* it is recorded that "The Rev. Joshua Thomas has resigned his charge of the church at Ainon, Tongwynlais, and taken the oversight of the English church at the same place."

In June, 1881, the vacant pulpit at Ainon was filled by Rev. W. Roderick who had held pastorates at Rhyl and Clwtybont since 1875, and who served Ainon until December 30, 1887, when he returned to Rhyl. During the first year of his ministry the *Cymanfa* again met at Ainon

The relative strengths of the two churches at the time of their dissolution are indicated in the Conference returns of 1881. These show that Salem took 103 members, leaving 88 at Ainon. By 1883 the position had become stabilized, and both churches had made progress. The 1883 statistics are as follows:—

	Ainon.	Salem.
Membership	114	112
Sunday School—		
Teachers	12	18
Scholars	90	180

The secession of Salem naturally gave rise to financial difficulties. At an Ainon Church meeting held in February, 1881, under the chairmanship of James Israel, it was decided to hold a conference of representatives of the two churches with a view to obtaining a satisfactory financial adjustment. The meeting was apparently held, for the report of a later church meeting in September records that Ainon had agreed to hand over the deeds of Salem conditionally on the latter church assuming responsibility for half the debt (viz., £80) of Ainon.

Some arrangement on these lines was accepted, and Salem seems to have paid over a sum of money in exchange for the deeds. The Ainon deacons who completed the transaction do not, however, seem to have satisfactorily accounted to their membership, for in February, 1886, a church meeting resolved that they (i.e. the deacons in question) "were not to have their places until they had given a satisfactory account to the Welsh church for the money they had received."

Henceforth we must treat Ainon and Salem as separate churches and record their histories separately. The eighties were a difficult period in the history of Whitchurch following the failure of the Booker undertakings at Pentyrch and Melingriffith in 1879. The permanent closing down of Pentyrch Ironworks led to the removal of many workers from the district whilst the fitful working of Melingriffith under the management of the Liquidators and James Spence during the greater part of the succeeding decade greatly lowered the economic standards of those who remained. Ultimately in 1888 the enterprise was acquired at a low figure by Richard Thomas and industrial conditions gradually became more stabilized and prosperous.

The effects of the worsened economic conditions on Ainon's position may be gathered from the following statistics of its membership during the middle eighties, viz., 1883-4, 114; 1885, 102; 1886, 93; 1887, 87.

WHITCHURCH BROOK LEAVING CWM NOFYDD *Cardiff Library*

WENALLT RESERVOIR *Cardiff Library*

THE OLD BUTCHERS' ARMS SEEN HERE BEFORE RECONSTRUCTION *Cardiff Library*

HEOLYFELIN, RHIWBINA *Cardiff Library*

Nevertheless during the difficult period the church debt was reduced between 1882 and 1887 from £160 to £120, possibly as the result of the contribution by Salem.

It was the economic factor in all probability which led to Mr. Roderick's departure in 1887. For the next 2½ years Ainon was without a pastor. During this period the former pastor, Rev. W. Jones, of Ebbw Vale, seems to have lent some assistance, and in September, 1888, he baptized nine members in the River Taff, an event which perhaps accounts for Ainon's increase of membership to 94 in that year.

At last, in May, 1890, Rev. G. J. Williams, of Pontypridd, accepted Ainon's call, but did not commence his ministry until October. The prospects were not rosy but Mr. Williams' advent seems to have quickened activity. As usual, his induction was made the occasion for preaching services which extended over five days.

Six months later, however, the new minister fell sick and for four months was unable to attend to his duties. On medical advice he retired from the pastorate on December 27, 1891. According to the church records he baptized during his short ministry 18 members, 11 in the chapel and 7 in the river Taff. In 1892 twelve members forsook Ainon for the Taffs Well cause and 88 names only were left on the church registers.

For another 3½ years the church was again without a minister. In 1894 the number of members was only 80, whilst the Sunday-school comprised 7 teachers and 90 scholars. The church during this period was apparently served by a lay preacher. Then on May 12, 1895, Rev. R. A. James took charge, but his stay also was short; he left in 1898. By this year the membership had fallen to 76. It should be noted in passing that during the latter year Tabernacle (Taffs Well) was founded by Mr. John Thomas (grocer), a member of Ainon.

In 1899 Rev. John Onfel Jenkins accepted a call to Ainon. Mr. Jenkins had previously held pastorates at Crickhowell, Rhayader and Risca extending over a period of nearly 20 years. He served Ainon until 1905, when he removed to Penuel, Penarth. Under his ministry the church membership increased from 81 in 1900 to 147 in 1902. During the same period the Sunday-school increased from 11 teachers and 90 scholars to 17 teachers and 165 scholars. The corresponding figures for 1905 were 162 church members and a Sunday-school comprising 18 teachers and 160 scholars.

It was during the period of Mr. Onfel Jenkins' pastorate that the conversion of Ainon from a Welsh to an English church took place. The transition was a gradual one, beginning with the introduction of English sermons, but ending up with the entire elimination of Welsh. The association of the church with the East Glamorgan *Cymanfa*, however, continued for some years. The growth of Ainon during this period can probably be largely attributed to the change of language.

Next came in 1905 Rev. Henry Jones, who had been educated at Bangor and had held a pastorate at Maesyberllan since 1898. His ministry at Ainon was the longest, with one exception, in the history of the church. It lasted until 1916, when Mr. Jones accepted a call to churches at Trelewis and Nelson. Mr. Jones' stipend at Ainon was £8 per lunar month.

Having regard to the gradual weakening of all churches just before and during the first great war Ainon seems to have maintained its position very well during Mr. Jones' pastorate. The official records show that in 1916 the membership was still at the relatively high figure of 124, with a Sunday school membership of 190.

After the departure of Mr. Henry Jones Ainon was again without a minister until 1923, when Rev. A. C. Turtle, a native of Swansea, who had held pastorates at Waunarlwydd (1906-1919) and Llanbradach (1920-1921), took charge. Mr. Turtle's pastorate at Ainon was a very active one. He was a man of energy and business capacity, and during his period of service a debt of £40 was wiped off, a site for a new Sunday school purchased, the freehold of the chapel site acquired at a cost of £75 and a considerable fund accumulated towards the cost of erecting a proposed Sunday school. This fund to-day amounts to about £400.

Mr. Turtle ultimately resigned his pastorate in 1935 to take up a business appointment in Cardiff, and he was succeeded for a time by Mr. T. H. Lovegrove, who had previously acted as an assistant to Mr. Turtle. Mr. Lovegrove, however, soon left for Chard, Somerset, and Mr. W. Metson, a young man from Porth, who had passed the Baptist Union examination, was ordained probationer pastor of the church by Mr. Turtle. He left in August, 1938, to become pastor of Longcross Street Church, Cardiff, and is now serving as a chaplain in H.M. Forces. Next, in September, 1939, Mr. H. O. Williams was ordained pastor of Ainon, but he remained for a short time only. At the present time the church has no pastor.

During recent years Ainon's membership has again fallen to a comparatively low level. According to the Baptist Handbook the number of members in 1940 was only 80, whilst the Sunday school consisted of 12 teachers and 85 scholars.

Like its mother church, Salem's story, subsequent to its separation from Ainon, has also been one of struggle and varying prosperity. Neither church has been able, on account partly of the stunted development of Tongwynlais, to fulfil the hopes of its founders, who planned for far larger congregations than have been available. Unfortunately, owing to the absence of church records for some periods, I am unable to give such full details as are available in respect of the mother church. Through the courtesy of Mr. David Williams, who has been secretary of Salem for more than 25 years, I have had access to most of the existing records.

Soon after its secession, in 1883, Salem embarked on a scheme for the enlargement of the chapel building. The pastorate of Rev. Joshua Thomas continued until 1889, when Mr. Thomas retired and took up residence at Pontypridd. During his stay at Tongwynlais he seems to have interested himself in public affairs and served a period of six years as a member of the Radyr and the Eglwysilan School Boards. Later he became a member of the Pontypridd School Board and also of the Pontypridd Board of Guardians. He died in May, 1905.

Mr. Thomas was succeeded by Rev. Charles Rees in 1893. Mr. Rees came from Blaina (Mon.), where he had held a pastorate since leaving Llangollen College in 1887. His stay at Tongwynlais, however, was but a short one and in 1896 he left for Abercarn, where he ministered until 1924.

Mr. Rees' ministry in its early days seemed to be a promising one. In 1894 the church membership was returned as 117, with a Sunday school comprising 15 teachers and 160 scholars. There was, however, some amount of dissension within the church and, according to local report, some unpleasantness also arose between Mr. Rees and some of the members arising out of the will of William Martin, made in November, 1895, who bequeathed his property to the Salem church trustees, the proceeds to be devoted, so it is said, to the erection of a vestry. As a result of the dissension Mr. Rees resigned in about three years' time and took charge of a church at Abercarn, where he remained until 1924. The effect of these internal disturbances on the church was very damaging and in 1895 the membership dropped to 84 and the Sunday school to 9 teachers and 90 scholars.

For a time the church was served by a Cardiff Baptist College student named Richard Arnold Jones. Then came in April, 1897, Mr. J. S. Dennis, a student from Aberystwyth. He was ordained at Salem in the following month. Rev. R. D. Phillips, Cilfynydd, presided, Rev. T. Williams, of Aberystwyth College, delivered the charge to the pastor and Rev. C. Rees (Abercrave) the charge to the church. Mr. Dennis' stipend was fixed at £6 per lunar month, with four clear Sundays free each year. It may be well to note here that this was not an unusual stipend for this period and for many years later, although some later pastors at Salem received as much as £9 per month. At no time probably in its history has the church been able to pay a salary exceeding £10 to its minister.

Internal dissensions still continued and leading officials of the church threatened resignation. The atmosphere was not very encouraging to a young minister, but he was a very good preacher and seems to have made himself very popular, and when in August, 1898, he resigned and left for a 'foreign land' the church presented him with a sum of £20 in token of their appreciation of his services.

In 1899 both Ainon and Salem, between which churches still existed a measure of antagonism, had new pastors, the Rev. Onfel Jenkins ministering to the former and Rev. Frederick J. Durston to the latter. Mr. Durston arrived in June. During the preceding months efforts were made to wean back to the church some former officers and members who had forsaken their allegiance or had lessened their interest in the church.

Rev. Onfel Jenkins' pastorate at Ainon was a very popular one and this, combined with the disharmony at Salem, militated against the success of the latter. There seems to have set in an exodus from Salem to Ainon, and in November, 1889, the Salem church meeting decided that "transfer letters shall not be granted to those who are seeking membership of Ainon for the reason that they have not dealt honourably with the church." In spite of this decision the drift from Salem continued.

The fact that at this time Ainon was in process of conversion from Welsh to English probably had much to do with the transference of membership. I have been informed—but have been unable to verify this statement—that at one notable service at Ainon no fewer than 50 persons —most of them from Salem—were admitted into membership. In time the relations between Mr. Durston and some of the church members became strained and in October, 1900, the pastor resigned and removed to Pontypridd where he ministered at The Temple until 1916.

The next pastor of Salem was Rev. D. B. Johns, a minister of 36 years standing, who served the church from May, 1901, until September, 1908. Mr. Johns had held pastorates since 1864 at St. Mellons, Risca, Cwmavon, Swansea, Pontypridd and Merthyr, and in 1908 he left Salem for Cilfynydd.

Mr. Johns, like several other former Tongwynlais ministers, was interested in literary work, and under the *nom-de-plume* Periander wrote several devotional books and English translations of well-known Welsh hymns, a history of the Welsh Church, and an account of the family of Lewis, of Greenmeadow.

As far back as April, 1899, the question of building a schoolroom had been under consideration by the Church, and in December of that year a lease was obtained from the Roath Court Estate at a ground rent of 12/- per year of a plot of land at the rear of the church. Later a further lease of land to give access to this plot was secured. On this site during the period of Mr. John's ministry a schoolroom was built at a cost of £150. In December, 1896, the Trust Deed of 1866 came under review. Some of the original trustees had died; others had ceased their connection with the church. A new list of trustees was prepared by the church and embodied in a legal memorandum. Four of the original trustees only continued to serve in that capacity. In March, 1902, a further revision was made and the legal memorandum of that date contains 18 names. Of these eighteen two only occur in a new list of nine trustees appointed in April, 1941.

Under Mr. John's ministry the church seems to have become more stable. Between 1900 and 1906 the membership increased from 90 to 128, although Sunday School attendance had dropped from 143 to 129. During this period also relations between Ainon and Salem became more friendly and the pastor of Ainon on one occasion occupied the pulpit of Salem. When, however, Salem was temporarily closed for renovations it was from Hermon rather than Ainon that the church sought hospitality. On Mr. John's departure in August, 1908, he was presented by the church with an illuminated address and a purse of gold.

Following Mr. Johns came Rev. W. H. Jones, a young man who had served a church at Ystrad for about three years. He came to Salem in 1910 and left in June, 1916, to take charge of a church at Llanhilleth, which he served until 1923. Subsequently he held pastorates at Chadderton, Bethel (Cardiff) and St. Mellons.

During his stay at Tongwynlais he studied for a time at the Baptist College, Cardiff, and during 1915 he undertook a preaching tour for the Y.M.C.A. at various troop camps in the Midlands. He was very popular with young people and, although the church membership in 1915 was returned as only 88, the Sunday School in this year, attained the abnormally high figures of 11 teachers and 195 scholars.

In March, 1916, Mr. Jones accepted a call to Llanhilleth, and in order to retain his services the church offered to increase his salary to £8 per lunar month. Mr. Jones treated this offer as a renewed call and a deputation from Salem was sent to Llanhilleth to ask that church to release him from his acceptance. Llanhilleth, however, seem to have pressed their claim, and on July the retiring pastor was presented by Salem with a gold watch and his wife with a silver tea service as a token of appreciation of their 5½ years services.

Later in the year an effort seems to have been made by the Baptist denominational authorities to combine Salem and the Baptist church at Nantgarw under the Sustentation Scheme into a joint pastorate under Mr. Jones, but as Salem could not undertake to contribute an amount exceeding £70 a year to the fund the proposal did not mature.

After 1916 both Ainon and Salem were without pastors and in 1919 the possibility of a combined pastorate for these churches seems to have been considered in certain quarters. In December, 1919, Salem extended a call to Rev. A. E. Turtle, but possibly because of this suggestion negotiations with Mr. Turtle terminated abruptly. In July, 1920, Ainon formally invited Salem to give consideration to the possibility of a joint pastorate. This proposal was, however, rejected.

In August, 1922, a call was extended to Rev. J. D. Hughes, a pastor of many years' experience, who served the church faithfully until, on account of advancing years, his retirement in April, 1928. He was presented with a testimonial by the church, and still resides at Tongwynlais.*

In 1930 Ainon, of which Mr. Turtle had been pastor since 1923, was making preparations for the celebration of its centenary. Amongst other things it had in mind the erection of a Sunday School building on a plot in Queen Street, but did not want to proceed with this project if there was any prospect of the reunion of the two churches. Through Mr. Turtle an approach was made to Salem. The proposal was duly considered, but Salem thought no good purpose would be served by the discussion of such a proposal at that time.

For many years after the retirement of Mr. Hughes Salem was without a pastor. At last in October, 1941, a call was extended to Rev. J. W. Evans, of Rhayader, a minister of many years standing, whose recognition services were held on May 6th, 1942.

In due course, no doubt, the mother and daughter churches of Ainon and Salem will be reunited. It is not for outsiders to meddle in their affairs, except as a matter of public interest to point out that the combined strength of the two churches in 1941 is less than that of Ainon alone

---

* He died in July, 1945.

a couple of years before Salem was founded. The official figures* are set forth in the following table:—

	1860 Ainon.	1941 Ainon.	1941 Salem.	Total.
Date of Foundation	1838	1838	1880	—
Seating	600	600	400	1000
Membership	196	83	102	185
Sunday School—				
Teachers	32	12	12	24
Scholars	280	85	110	195

* From the *Baptist Year Book*.

CHAPTER XIX.

ARARAT BAPTIST CHURCH.

The Baptist form of religious dissent dates back locally to the 17th century, and the first Baptist church established in South Wales was set up at Ilston in Gower under Puritan auspices in 1649. During the 18th century other Baptist churches were established, including one at Castleton. From the Castleton cause sprang about 1742 the Bethesda Baptist Church, Bassaleg, which became the mother church of Lisvane, Capel Gwilym and Ararat.

In the early part of the nineteenth century the Baptist churches at Lisvane, Tabernacle (Cardiff) and Tonyfelin (Caerphilly) drew their membership from many miles around, and it is probable that some Whitchurch Baptists were connected with each of these churches. In view of the distance of Whitchurch from these centres regular attendance was not practicable and local Baptists used to meet for devotional purposes locally at the dwellings of some of the members.

In the northern edge of Whitchurch Common formerly stood a farmhouse called Gwauntreoda Uchaf, once the patrimony of the notable family of Yorath Mawr, and this house or one of its out-buildings was the most usual place for local Baptist gatherings. Regular prayer meetings and occasional preaching services were held there, and members of the Lisvane Church used occasionally to visit them and help to strengthen the faith of local adherents.

After a time the faithful group resolved that the time had come to establish a regular local church as a branch of Lisvane. This was about 1824. The site selected for the new meeting-house was a mound on Whitchurch Common which was a well-known manorial boundary landmark. I have no information as to how the group got consent to appropriate land from the common for the purpose, but it seems certain that the new chapel was named Ararat because it was built on the mound, on the analogy of the hill on which Noah's Ark rested. The story of Ararat has been admirably told in an essay written by the late Rev. Luther Jones on the occasion of the Church Centenary, and upon that essay the present account has very largely been based.

Here in due course the first Ararat chapel was built for the use of Welsh Baptists of the locality. In spite of its scriptural name, however, the church was better known for many decades as Capel Wauntreoda, or more commonly, *Capel y Waun.*

Although started under the auspices of Lisvane, since the latter was still a daughter church of Bethesda, that church probably had some jurisdiction over Ararat until it was constituted an independent church in 1828. At any rate a contemporary writer mentions that a meeting place was built here in 1824 "under the guardianship of Bethesda."*

The new church was dedicated at a preaching session in which Revs. David Saunders (Merthyr), John James (Pontrhydyfen), Evan Jones (Castleton), William Jones (Cardiff), and John Jordan David (Carnarvon) took part.

In 1828 Ararat received its letter of release from Lisvane, and at a Glamorgan Baptist *Cymanfa* (or Conference) held at Cowbridge in the following year the church was admitted to membership of the East Glamorgan Association. At the same meeting John Williams, of Lisvane, who had given proof of his talent and fidelity, was admitted to the ministry.

Prior to 1829 Ararat had relied for ministration upon visiting ministers and lay preachers, amongst whom was John Williams, and the latter was now appointed pastor. His induction took place at another *Cymanfa Bregethu* (Preaching Festival) in which the special preachers were Revs. Thomas Thomas (Croesyparc), Christmas Evans (Tabernacl), William Jones (Bethany), Evan Jones (Castleton) and David Evans (Cadoxton).

At this time the church comprised 73 members, but under the guidance of the new pastor the church grew apace. The Association reports show a membership of 100 in 1833 and 105 in 1834, whilst there was a much larger congregation. Apparently, however, the membership was not maintained, for the annual return for 1840 gives the membership as only 71.

Ararat seems to have attached importance to Sunday School work from its inception, and this tradition has been well maintained to date. A Government Education Report of 1835 mentions that Ararat Sunday School comprised 14 males and 10 females. This is probably an under-statement, and perhaps refers only to juniors. The denominational report for 1840 mentions that the school consisted of seven teachers and 50 scholars. Sunday School records go back to 1838, in which year Thomas Bryant was Superintendent and Eli Evans, Secretary. Rules prepared for the conduct of the school at this time show that great emphasis was placed on the memorizing of passages of scripture, a striking feature of Welsh Sunday School practice.

As a result of the growth of the church it became necessary in 1836 to extend the accommodation, the enlargement being effected by the construction of a gallery.

Rev. John Williams served the church until his death in 1840. His service seems largely to have been a service of love, for the stipend which the little church could afford was not very large. This is how a contemporary Baptist historian wrote of him:

"The minister is in comfortable worldly circumstances, for which reason the church and congregation are receiving service at a quite low cost; but perhaps this may not be an advantage to them in the future."†

---

* D. Jones. Hanes y Bedyddwyr (1839).
† Ibid.

Possibly lack of finance or the desire to secure another well-circumstanced pastor was the reason why nearly four years were to elapse before a successor was appointed. On January 3, 1844, a new minister, Rev. David Davies, was inducted, and he served his people faithfully for 20 years. The statistical records show that the church membership increased from 71 in 1840 to 136 in 1860. The Sunday School in the latter year was more than double that of 20 years earlier. Mr. Davies is stated to have baptized 114 members during his pastorate.

The continued growth necessitated a further enlargement of accommodation. In 1851 the chapel was rebuilt at a cost of £600, seating accommodation being provided for 320, and a vestry also was added. This little building was neat and unpretentious, albeit a not unpleasing architectural unit, and was a well-known landmark in the locality until its displacement in 1915 by the more showy structure in use today.

In 1865 came to Ararat as pastor a young student, Rev. Thomas Thomas, from Pontypool college, who served the church for ten years and then resigned to take up the pastorate of Mount Carmel, Caerphilly. He died in 1908 and was buried at Ararat.

Early in Mr. Thomas' pastorate there seems to have been some difficulty at Ararat, possibly owing to difference of opinion over the demand by a small minority for the use of English as the language of public worship. This demand was strongly resisted and a small number are said to have seceded to establish with other English Baptists in the locality the church today known as Bethel. The secession does not appear to have weakened the church very much for in 1868 the number of members returned was 112 or only 24 fewer than in 1860, whilst the Sunday School suffered a loss of only 24 scholars. By 1870 the membership had recovered to 146 and the Sunday School numbered 115.

The next minister, Rev. D. E. Jenkins, came to Ararat straight from collegiate training at Llangollen in 1876. His stay, however, was brief; in 1880 he left to take over the pastorate of Llandaff Road Baptist Church, Cardiff, where he remained until 1889.

Up to the last year of his ministry the baptism of new members took place in the Whitchurch Brook near Cornel-y-Waun Farm, where a pool was formed by the construction of a temporary dam. The pastor and his novitiates entered the water, whilst the congregation assembled on the banks. This arrangement was not satisfactory under all weather conditions, and in 1879 an indoor baptistry was provided at the church, the supply of water being drawn from a tank in which roof water was collected.

In the late seventies the language difficulty again gave rise to discussion, which in 1878 ended in a decision that English should be used at evening service for an experimental period of six months. The change apparently commended itself to a majority of the members, and was made permanent; during the next thirty years Ararat was a bilingual church.

Another innovation of this period which the older church members also lamented was the introduction of instrumental music into church services. Up to 1878 hymn books were not in general use, and the congregation, led by an unaccompanied choir, used to sing words read out to them by the preacher, a couple of lines at a time. In the year mentioned Tom Day, the choir leader, introduced a concertina during choir rehearsals and a portable piano during anniversary services. Strong criticism of the innovation was made by a section of the church but ultimately the new arrangement was approved, and the harmonium continued in use until the installation many years later of a pipe organ.

In 1880 Rev. James Gomer Watts, of Cwmbellan, became pastor and during this year the membership was returned as 120, with a Sunday School comprising 14 teachers and 120 scholars. Some differences seem to have occurred between the minister and a section of the members and Mr. Watts left in 1883 to take over the pastorates of the Baptist Churches at Glascoed and Pontnewynydd. According to the 1883 report the church membership fell to 70 and the Sunday School to a total of 85.

For nearly two years the church was without a pastor. Then in August, 1885, the vacancy was filled by the appointment of Rev. James Bevan, of Witton Park, who served the church faithfully until his death at the age of 53, in November, 1899. Mr. Bevan's ministry was a great success. He was held in great reverence by his church and in the highest respect by the entire neighbourhood. He took a great interest in local education and for many years served as a member of the Whitchurch School Board.

One of the most notable events of his ministry was the holding of the Welsh Baptist Association meetings at Ararat on July 29 and 30, 1887. At these meetings in addition to the business conference there were five devotional services in which the 'stars' of the denomination preached to large congregations drawn from far and wide. So great was the assembly that Ararat could not accommodate it and the services took place in the open air in a field at the rear of the church.

As many as 10 preachers took part in the Association services, but this feast of eloquence was not unusual in the history of the church. For example, in March, 1853, four services were held at Ararat in connection with the church's anniversary and, according to *Seren Gomer*, in its following May issue, no fewer than twelve separate sermons were delivered, of which only two were in English.

The progress of Ararat at this period was rapid and the accommodation of the chapel was strained to its limit. The church therefore decided to lease at £2 10 0 per annum an acre of additional land from Lord Tredegar for the purposes of building extension. For financial reasons building operations were not proceeded with for some years, but steps were taken to raise a building fund to which additions were made from year to year.

Two years after Mr. Bevan's death in 1900 he was succeeded by Rev. David Gyfelach Hughes, of Dolau, Radnorshire, who, after four years service, accepted, in 1906, a call to Pontypridd. During Mr.

Hughes' ministry the language question again came under discussion. Since 1878 the practice had been to conduct the morning service in Welsh and the evening service in English. Whitchurch was becoming ever more anglicized and attendance at morning services steadily shrank. It was therefore now decided to abandon the Welsh services and Ararat became all English.

The change seems to have had a beneficial result on the strength of church membership. The records for 1905 show that the number of members was 150 or more than double that returned in 1883, whilst the Sunday school comprised 16 teachers and 160 scholars.

The next pastor of Ararat was Rev. T. Deri Jones, B.A., of Penydarren, who accepted a call in 1910. Mr. Jones strongly pressed the need of providing increased accommodation for Baptist worshippers, although the building fund had as yet attained a total of only about £500. The church seemed inclined to act on his advice to rebuild, but at this point Mr. Jones left in 1913 to undertake a pastorate at Abersychan.

The building scheme, however, was not dropped. A year or so later constructional work was begun. First, a schoolroom was built to accommodate the church whilst the chapel was being rebuilt. Then work on the main building was proceeded with. The foundation and stone-laying ceremony took place on October 14, 1914, and although progress was to some extent hampered by conditions arising out of the European War the contractors, Messrs. E. Turner & Sons, were able to complete the work in time for opening services to be held on April 5, 1915.

The new chapel, which was designed by the late Sir Beddoe Rees, cost £3,000, and had seating accommodation for 650 persons or about double that of the old building, whilst the schoolroom, divided into class-rooms for Sunday School purposes, accommodated 200.

According to the denominational records of 1915 Ararat had 131 members and its Sunday School comprised 17 teachers and 160 scholars. The Church had also one recognised lay preacher.

It was now felt that the church should again have a regular pastor, and in 1916 another young man, Rev. W. Emlyn Jones, accepted a call. His ministry, however, was of short duration; within two years he accepted a call to Dalston Junction, London.

In May, 1919, the new pastor, Rev. Luther Jones, a native of Carmarthenshire, who had received his training at the Baptist College, Cardiff, and who had held pastorates at Tonyfelin, Caerphilly (1912-1915) and Beulah, Dowlais (1915-1919) now came to Ararat. His advent was at a time when Whitchurch was on the eve of extraordinary development. In the course of a very few years many hundreds of houses were to be built in the vicinity of the Church and a great increase of population was imminent. Mr. Jones died during 1944, and towards the end of that year the pastorate was offered to and accepted by Rev. W. George Evans, B.A., B.D., of Baker Street Church, Aberystwyth. Mr. Evans was inducted pastor of Ararat in April, 1945.

Resulting from this extraordinary development Ararat has prospered exceedingly and additional buildings have been erected to meet the needs of the Sunday School and other auxiliary activities of the church. According to the denominational record for 1941 the present chapel provides seating accommodation for 700 and has a total membership of 344, whilst the Sunday School comprises 57 teachers and 295 scholars.

CHAPTER XX.

BETHEL BAPTIST CHURCH.*

Up to the sixties of last century Welsh seems to have been the mother tongue of most of the residents of Whitchurch, and with the exception of the Parish Church and the Wesleyan chapel services at places of worship were conducted mainly or wholly in the Welsh language. Monoglot English Baptists, Methodists and Congregationalists connected themselves with the English churches of their denominations at Cardiff.

About the period mentioned an Anglicizing tendency made itself felt in the local Welsh churches. The younger adherents were being taught English at the National School, and gradually they became more proficient in that language than in their mother tongue. Many of the immigrants attracted to the locality by the developing industries at College Road, Melingriffith, and Pentyrch also were English, and for all of these there was no religious provision by their own particular sects.

A clash seems to have taken place between the older Welsh leaders of the respective churches and the younger generation regarding a demand for the carrying on of religious services in the English language. It is not unnatural that the older folk resisted the demand vehemently, with the result that in some cases the younger people broke away to form new churches or joined other denominations which conducted services in English, with the consequent weakening of the Welsh causes.

According to local report such a clash seems to have taken place at Ararat in the early sixties, with the result that some members apparently left that church to join with local English folk who belonged to Bethany Church, Cardiff, for the purpose of starting a Baptist cause at Whitchurch.

On May 8, 1865, a deputation from Bethany Church came to Whitchurch to discuss with the local people the question of establishing an English Baptist church. The deputation comprised Rev. Rees Griffiths (Pastor) and Messrs. Thomas White (an Inland Revenue Officer), James Ward (Roath Castle), Edwin Osborne and David Llewelyn. After some discussion it was decided to constitute such a church and the Rev. Rees Griffiths formally approved the new venture. The first members of the new cause, as given in the minutes of that meeting, were David Richards, William Beake, John Hammett, —. James, —. Richards and W. Beake. For permission to inspect these minutes I am indebted to Mrs. Thomas (Heoldon), in whose possession they are.

---

* An account of this church appeared in an article in the *Evening Express* (Cardiff) June 30, 1902.

Four days later, on May 12, the first church meeting was held, when John Hammett was appointed Secretary and David Richards Treasurer. David Richards was also apparently appointed the first deacon. At this meeting two additional members, John Rosser and Peter Wells, were admitted. On May 14 "Sisters Rosser and Robbins" were baptised in the Whitchurch Brook adjoining the Common. These were the first baptisms into the new church.

The little group met at first in a small thatched cottage in Merthyr Road, but soon removed to a barn which they rented adjoining Whitchurch Common. After a couple of years the little church built at a cost of £200 a small chapel on a site to the rear of the present-day Bethel Chapel, which was leased from the Penlline Estate. This little building was opened in 1867.

In January, 1867, Mr. Hammett, who had left the neighbourhood, was succeeded as Secretary by Phillip Lewis, who for many long years was a leading pillar of the church. In December, as the result of a ballot, he was elected a deacon. In April, 1867, a baptismal service was held at which nine new members were baptised.

Up to this time the church had no pastor. It depended for its ministry on local lay preachers and deacons from Bethany and other churches, with occasional baptismal and other services conducted by Rev. Rees Griffiths. Amongst others who assisted the church in the conduct of services were Thomas White, Price Jones, David Llewelyn and Alderman Dr. Thomas Rees, of Cardiff.

At length in June, 1868, at the ninth church meeting, it was decided to invite Mr. Neville Harris, of Cardiff, to become pastor of the church without a guaranteed salary. He accepted, and on July 5, 1868, his ordination services were held, at which Revs. Rees Griffiths (Bethany), Nathaniel Thomas (Tabernacle), and T. Price (Aberdare) officiated. Mr. Harris' pastorate, however, was of short duration; on December 6 of the same year he tendered his resignation, probably because his income was insufficient to provide for his proper sustenance. During his pastorate the church applied for and received membership of the Glamorgan and Carmarthen English Baptist Association.

From this experience it seemed clear that the church could not yet afford a full-time, paid pastor, and for the next thirty years the church relied as before on the ministration of lay preachers and visiting ministers. The church seems during a considerable portion of this time to have been under the watchful care of William Morris, a grocer of Duke Street, Cardiff, who was an active lay preacher and who in later years had charge of Llandough Baptist Church.

In November, 1869, William Jones was admitted to membership, and he and his family rendered yeoman service to the church during the following half century. A Sunday School started in the early days of the church seems to have failed. Through Mr. Jones' efforts, however, it was restarted and under his earnest guidance it became a regular feature of church activity.

In later years Mr. Jones' sons took an active interest in church affairs, and one of them, Sidney Jones, acted as Secretary for more than thirty years On his retirement from this office in February, 1921, he was presented with a gold watch and chain as a token of appreciation of his long and faithful service. The late Mr. J. W. Hobbis took over the duties of Secretary from Mr. Jones and carried them on until his death in 1942.

The Richards family also served the church well. As we have seen, David Richards was the first treasurer and first deacon and acted in those capacities for many years, and he and his two sons, John and Gwilym, were important leaders of the church. Gwilym Richards followed his father as treasurer and after many years handed over the duties to the late Edmund Lewis.

In the early eighties the need for increased accommodation was felt and approaches were made to prosperous Cardiff Baptists for financial aid. In 1884 a Building Fund was started with a donation of £50 by Richard Cory, to which members subscribed a further sum of £20. To this fund additions were made from time to time.

Ten years later, in 1894, the new chapel was built at a cost of £1,024, on the portion of the site immediately in front of the original meeting-house. The builder was G. Griffiths, of Cardiff. The new building had seating accommodation for 350 as against 150 in the old chapel. The opening services were held on October 10, 1894 and were conducted by Revs. Dr. Edwards, Charles Davies (Tabernacle), R. O. Johns (Tredegarville), C. H. Watkins (Splott) and G. Owens (Porth). At this period the church comprised 42 members, whilst the Sunday School consisted of 7 teachers and 70 scholars. The first baptisms in the new chapel took place on October 28, 1894, when W. Morris officiated.

On October 17, 1894, the Quarterly Meeting of the Glamorgan County Association of Baptists was held at Bethel.

The ministry was still in the hands of unattached friends and it was not until 1896 that the matter of appointing a paid permanent pastor seems seriously to have been considered. In that year the church on two occasions decided "to go in for a minister." A call was extended to a prospective pastor in May, 1896, which was declined. As the total income of the church in 1896 was only £84 and the expenditure was a little in excess of this amount it is perhaps not surprising that some difficulty was experienced in obtaining a suitable candidate. The church had in 1895 purchased a small organ and had also spent £55 on heating apparatus, and some members felt that the debts so incurred should be discharged before they entered on further commitments.*

Again in 1897 and in 1898 consideration was given to the matter and in the latter year a call was extended to a young student who now occupies a prominent place in the Welsh Baptist denomination. This call also was declined. In October, 1899, the church decided to invite Rev. John Arthur Jones, of Porthcawl, to accept the pastorate. Mr. Jones, although a native of Aberystwyth, had spent his boyhood at

---

* Details relating to the period (1884-1899) were obtained from an old minute book lent to me by Mr. Harman Lewis.

Pentre (Rhondda Valley) and when only fifteen years of age preached his first sermon at Hermon Chapel in that town. He decided to enter the ministry and was educated for that vocation first at Pontypridd Academy and then at Pontypool College, and on March 30, 1896, was ordained at Porthcawl.

Mr. Jones, who was popularly known in Whitchurch as "John Arthur" commenced his ministry at Bethel on the first Sunday of 1900. He was then a young man of 25. The terms of his appointment included a fixed stipend of £90 per annum and four free Sundays. The Church seems to have received an annual contribution of £10 towards this stipend from the Baptist Augmentation Fund. The recognition services were held on June 22, and were conducted by Rev. J. Meredith Jones (Newport) and Rev. W. E. Winks (Cardiff), whilst a large number of speakers addressed an evening meeting presided over by W. Morris. At this time Sidney Jones was Secretary and Edmund Lewis, Treasurer.

Mr. Jones was a very able and thoughtful preacher, and soon became very popular especially amongst young people. Under his energetic ministry the church took on new life and soon witnessed a substantial increase of membership. In a newspaper article of June, 1902, it is stated that since Mr. Jones' advent the membership of the church had increased by about 92 to a figure at that date of 170, whilst the Sunday School then numbered 200.

To cope with the development of the church it was early seen that further accommodation would be needed. In spite of outstanding liabilities the church decided in 1900 to erect galleries and generally renovate the building. This work was carried out by E. Turner & Sons (Cardiff) at an estimated cost of £540. A Building Fund Statement at the end of 1901 shows a total expenditure of £628.

A good deal of the money for carrying out this work seems to have been lent interest free by members of the church. Now began an active campaign for the clearance of the debt. The first big effort took the form of a bazaar held in 1901 which yielded a sum of £186 for this purpose. In association with the event a special collection was organised and in all a total sum of £387 was raised. The total amount left to be raised at the end of the year was £115. By the end of 1903 the debt had been reduced to £75 and six months later it fell to only £15. This debt apparently was in respect of monies borrowed on note of hand, and did not include a permanent mortgage of about £400 on the church buildings.

The church continued to grow steadily. During 1904 there was a net gain in membership of 28, and the financial receipts for the year amounted to £180. The energetic efforts of the pastor were appreciated by the church and his stipend was raised to £110 in 1901, £120 in 1904 and £130 in 1905. These amounts do not appear very large today, but they were well above the average of the remuneration locally paid to ministers forty years ago. By 1906 the membership had risen to 200 whilst the Sunday School comprised 14 teachers and 260 scholars.

Mr. Jones terminated his connection with Bethel in 1913, having accepted a call to Penuel, Bangor. During the next couple of years

RHIWBINA HILL FROM NEAR THE TWMPATH *Cardiff Library*

CWM NOFYDD AND GELLI QUARRY. CEFN CARNAU IN DISTANCE. *Cardiff Library*

THATCHED COTTAGES AT THE PHILOG *Cardiff Library*

CWM Y MWYALCHEN COTTAGES, THE PHILOG *Cardiff Library*

Bethel was without a pastor, and during this period, in June, 1914, further renovation work was undertaken. At length on September 16, 1915, a new pastor, Rev. Edward Roberts, M.A., B.D., of Cardiff and Mansfield College (Oxford) took charge. This able young man was a native of Llanelly, and Bethel was his first pastorate. He served the church until March, 1924, when he resigned to become minister of Tabernacle, Newbridge (Mon.), where he remained 12 years until 1936 in which year he became a tutor at the Cardiff Baptist College.

During Mr. Roberts' ministry further building extensions became necessary. In 1920 the freehold of the church was purchased for the sum of £130, and in the same year a new schoolroom was built at an estimated cost of £650. This building was opened on Jan. 1, 1921. In addition to its building effort the church during this year raised a sum of £263 for the Baptist United Fund. A drop in membership to 161 in 1920 was largely regained by 1924 when the church membership was returned as 192.

Two years elapsed before the appointment of a new pastor, Rev. Ceulanydd E. Jones, who commenced, on April 4, 1926, a ministry which extended until his sudden death in 1942. Mr. Jones was educated at Spurgeon's Baptist College, and had held pastorates at Mount Zion, Blaengarw (1917-1922), and Bethany, Treherbert (1922-1925) before coming to Whitchurch. His period of service coincided with that of enormous local building activity and population growth, a development which, combined with the pastor's efficient service, had had a profound effect on the prosperity and success of the church. By 1933 the membership had increased to 286; the present membership is 340.

To cope with the growth additional accommodation became necessary, and in 1927 a further expenditure of £1,000 was incurred in pulling down the old vestry and building an organ chamber, classrooms and a small detached Primary Room. In addition a pipe organ costing £700 was purchased. The completion of these works was signalized by special services held on November 2, 1927.

Towards the end of 1944 a call was extended to and accepted by the Rev. W. E. Mathias-Williams, of Hanbury Road Baptist Church, Bargoed, whose induction services were held at Bethel on December 7, 1944.

An active worker in the interests of Bethel was the late Mr. J. W. Hobbis who, from 1921 until his death in 1942, acted as Secretary and general business manager of the church. It was largely as the result of his energetic and whole-hearted efforts that Bethel has met with such a large measure of success. The removal of the Secretary and pastor by death within such a short space must have inflicted a heavy blow on the church.

CHAPTER XXI.

BEULAH CONGREGATIONAL CHURCH.

Watford Church was closely associated with the Methodist Revival of the 1740's, and from it sprang a daughter church at Groeswen, which in the early years of last century drew its membership from many miles around, including some from the parish of Whitchurch. At this period its pastor, Rev. Griffith Hughes, used to conduct services not only at Groeswen chapel but also in farmhouses at a considerable distance from Groeswen. He is known to have preached at 'Rhiwbynau' Farm in 1812 and again in 1815, and at other times he conducted services at Briwnant and neighbouring farmhouses and frequently until the 1830's he held meetings on Sunday afternoons at Tonyrywen Farm (Caerphilly Road).

William Lewis, of Tonyrywen, and his wife were zealous members of Groeswen, as also was their daughter, afterwards Mrs. George, of the Deri. It seems likely that Griffith Hughes had the intention of establishing a branch cause in the Parish of Whitchurch, but he died in 1839 before his plan could mature.

Other Congregational causes beside Groeswen and Watford were established in the district. These included Ebenezer (Cardiff), an offshoot of Womanby Street, Taihirion (Llanillterne) and its daughter churches at Pentyrch and Gwaelodygarth, and doubtless some Whitchurch families were connected with these. As, however, these places of worship were so far away from Whitchurch it is likely that local Congregationalists used to meet for worship occasionally in one another's homes, and local ministers doubtless attended at times and preached.

Wauntreoda Isaf (or Cornel y Waun) seems to have been a regular venue for such gatherings. In the 1830's it was tenanted by Mr. and Mrs. Griffiths, both of whom were devoted members of Ebenezer and generous subscribers to its funds. It is stated that Mrs. Griffiths, who died in 1848, bequeathed a sum of £400 to causes associated with that church, of which at that time Rev. Lewis Powell was pastor.

The Griffiths family seems to have been succeeded at Cornel y Waun in the forties by Edward and Mary Daniel, who had removed there from New Inn, Monmouthshire, and these also became associated with Ebenezer. This zealous and faithful couple were held in very high regard by their fellow religionists, who joined with them in establishing a Congregationalist cause in their own locality. This cause probably started at Cornel-y-Waun, and it is known that at the services held at the farmhouse during their tenure Rev. John Jones, pastor of Bethlehem (Gwaelodygarth), frequently officiated. In later years the Daniels removed to Tir Hwnt (now Tydraw) Farm near Pentre Gwilym on Thornhill Road and it may be on account of their impending removal that the centre selected for the new cause was in the locality then variously known as Nant y Walla, Rhyd y Walla, or Rhyd Nant y Walla, a name rendered in the first trust deed of Beulah as 'Nant Rhyd Walter.'

Amongst the early members of the Congregationalist cause promoted by the Daniels were William and Ann Brown of Bethlehem, William and Mary Roberts of Bethlehem, Edward Roberts of Watford and William and Martha David of Peterston-super-Ely. After much deliberation a small dwelling house, which had previously been used for the purposes of a smithy, was rented as a meeting place for £4 10 0 per annum. The site of this house today forms part of the site of the Beulah Schoolroom.

In this little meeting house, which was named Beulah, in the early days a Sunday School was held in the morning and Welsh preaching services or prayer meetings were held on afternoons and evenings and on certain week nights. The first sermon was preached there on Christmas Day, 1848, by Rev. John Jones of Bethlehem and Rudry, and he seems to have been entrusted with the oversight (without remuneration) of the new church whilst in its formative stage. In 1849 he was appointed pastor, an office held jointly with the pastorates of Bethlehem and Rudry. It seems, therefore, correct to say that Beulah was a daughter church of Bethlehem.

The need for more suitable meeting accommodation was soon felt. The raising of funds was a much more difficult task than in later days. The chief—almost the only—means was to hold a public tea-party (*te parti talu* as it was then called), for which a charge was made. On Whit Tuesday, 1849, such a party was held, followed by a public meeting. The proceeds of this function were devoted to the making of a pulpit and benches to equip the old house, extra funds being obtained by way of loan from members.

The first pulpit was of rather an interesting type and merits a few words of description. It was a kind of arm-chair, behind which was a step or small platform on which the preacher stood, whilst the top portion of the long chair back ended in a reading desk. In the arm chair sat the *blaenor* or chief deacon so as to keep the pulpit quite firm. He had, however, another function than as a mere makeweight. To him was entrusted the important task of ensuring that the sermons were in accord with the theological principles and theories then favoured by the denomination. For this reason he was termed *Ceidwad yr Athrawiaeth* (The Guardian of Doctrine).

The remuneration of visiting preachers in those days was generally very low, but the exact amount paid to any individual depended somewhat upon the extent to which he had satisfied the ceidwad. A story is told of the ceidwad offering the small sum of one shilling in payment of the services of a certain preacher, Rev. J. Evans (Maerdy). The latter enquired what the money was for? The reply was that the sermon was not worth more than a shilling. Whereupon the preacher rang the coin on the table. The ceidwad asked, "Why do you do that?" "Because" was the reply, "I want to make sure that the shilling is a good one; a man who can be mean enough to offer me a shilling for a sermon may also be mean enough to give me a *bad* shilling."

Although the church in its early days was small proceedings were not always harmonious. William Brown* was a man of strong character, who disagreed with the views of one of the early pastors and was anxious to secure his removal. At one of the after-meetings, known as the *Seiat* (the society), he strongly criticised the minister's sermon and complained that he received no spiritual food from such preaching.

Whereupon another old deacon rose up and said, "At our house we have a cupboard to keep our bread, and it happened that bread put therein soon became unfit to eat. After some time I told my wife we had better buy our flour at a different shop. 'No,' she said, 'I will give the cupboard a thorough cleaning and limewash it well.' This was done and although we bought the same flour, the bread afterwards kept nice and sweet. And I advise you, William Brown, instead of complaining of the spiritual food, to clean your cupboard and whitewash it out with the grace of God: you can then depend upon it that the food will be good and nourishing."

The adapted cottage served the needs of the little church for a couple of years. Then the members felt justified in embarking upon a building scheme. A lease for 999 years at 20/- a year was obtained from William Howell as from Nov. 15, 1850, of the site adjoining the cottage for the purposes of a chapel and graveyard. A few months later on March 26, 1851, an appeal for subscriptions was made on behalf of the Church by "J. Jones, Minister, and Edward Daniel and William Russell, deacons." This brought in a sum of £38. Building work on the new chapel was put in hand and on Whit Tuesday, 1851, the opening services were held. The cost of the building was £138.

Through the courtesy of Mr. William Phillips,† of Llanishen Fach, I have been permitted to examine the first lease and the first trust deed of Beulah and it will be of interest to give the substance of these documents here. On November 15, 1850, the owner of the chapel site, William Powell, Labourer, granted to Thomas John, Farmer, and his assigns a lease for 999 years at an annual rent of 20/-.

"All that piece or parcel of ground lying and being near a certain brook called Nant rhyd Walter (about 15 perches) . . . . with liberty and authority . . . . to erect and build or cause to be erected and built thereon a chapel or meeting house as a place of worship to be called the Welsh Independents and any other building he may think proper thereon."

A week or so later Thomas John, in consideration of the sum of 5/-, conveyed this lease to Edward Daniell and other trustees duly appointed by the church. The following is a list of the Trustees:

Edward Daniell, Whitchurch, Yeoman.
William Brown, Whitchurch, Tin Packer.

---

* There was also a William Brown, a man of strong individuality, connected with the Tabernacle C.M. Church in its early days; probably the same man. He died at the age of 80 in July, 1891, and was buried at Beulah.

† Other official records were also lent me by Mr. Phillips; also some by Mrs. Thomas Samuel (Whitchurch).

Old Whitchurch

William David, Whitchurch, Labourer.
George Pike, Pentyrch, Forgeman.
William Russell, Pentyrch, Forgeman.

After reciting the particulars of the lease and the transaction between Thomas John and Edward Daniell the nature of the Trust is defined. The following are the relative points relating to the use of the land and the management of Church affairs:—

(1) "The said Trustees shall build a meeting-house or chapel and other offices on the said piece of ground and to be used, occupied and enjoyed as a place of Public religious worship for the service of God by the Society of Protestant Dissenters of the Denomination called the Welsh Independents and attend the worship of God in the said Meeting House and to be used for no other purpose whatever and also to permit a part of the said piece of ground to be used as a Burial Ground to the said Meeting house and that none other than those members or communicants shall be buried therein belonging to the said Meeting house.

(2) "And also that there shall be a Committee to consist of thirteen Members being communicants of the said Society and that all propositions made by them are to be carried by a majority of the said Members."

(3) The Trustees shall be empowered by a majority of the *Men* Members present at a properly convened meeting to raise funds by way of Mortgage.

(4) "The Trustees shall permit to officiate at the said Meeting house such person or persons of the aforesaid Denomination as the said members or the major part of them, *Men* . . . . shall from time to time elect to officiate as their Minister . . . . according to the usual order and custom of Societies of Protestant Dissenters of the Denomination aforesaid."

(5) "The said Trustees shall have power to receive all subscriptions towards the welfare of the said chapel and shall apply the same towards the welfare of the said chapel according to the proposals made and carried by a majority of the members at a meeting convened for that purpose."

(6) The number of acting Trustees to be not less than five; additional trustees to be elected by the *Men* Members bringing the number up to thirteen. Only subscribing members of at least 12 months standing to be elected as Trustees by a duly convened meeting.

The deed was registered with a Chancery representative at Cardiff on December 5th, 1850, and later on February 4th, 1864, enrolled in the High Court of Chancery pursuant to a new Act of Parliament passed in 1862.

After a few years Mr. Jones gave up the Beulah ministry and he was succeeded by Rev. William Russell, who was already a recognised local preacher and had been ordained at Machen. He seems to have had charge of a chapel at St. Bride's as well as Beulah until August, 1857, when he was deprived of speech through a paralytic seizure. He continued, however, to attend Beulah and after his death many years later at Tongwynlais, he was buried in Beulah graveyard. He was 70 years old at the time of his death on May 17, 1891.

During the next two and a half years the little church was without a pastor. In 1858-9, a religious revival broke over South Wales and the local church felt its influence. Beulah seems to have been more affected than its neighbours and a substantial increase of adherents followed. In 1860 the total membership increased to 49. Soon a call was extended to John Lloyd James, a young man from Carmarthen College. Mr. James was ordained on February 2nd, 1860, and served the church until October, 1869, when he accepted a call to Capel Ivor, Dowlais.

Rev. Lloyd James had a taste for writing, and became well known as a bard under the nom-de-plume *Clwydwenfro*. Whilst at Beulah he wrote a history of the Independent Conferences and also a *pryddest*. In later years he published a number of Welsh books, and was a frequent contributor to the denominational magazines. In his day the remuneration of ministers was very low. As was then customary there was no fixed stipend, and Mr. James seems to have been supported by collections for the minister made once a month. From an examination of some odd cash books of the period I find that Mr. Jones' ministerial income during the years 1865, 1867 and 1868 amounted to £22 3s. 0½d., £19 12s. 1d. and £23 7s. 8½d. respectively.

Soon after Mr. James' advent it was decided to extend, renovate and beautify the little chapel and in September, 1860, a contract was made with John Emanuel, of Llanishen, for the sum of £210 to carry out the work. By March, 1861, the building was completed, and Mr. James preached therein for the first time. On April 28th special preaching services were held to celebrate the formal opening.

Prior to the undertaking of this work special efforts were made to clear the debt on the old chapel. An account dated January, 1860, records the result of a special appeal for funds for this purpose. The total collection of £23 18s. 10d. represented contributions by 29 members, the amounts ranging from 2/6 to £2 15s. 4d. Supplementary funds for the new chapel were obtained by way of loans on the security of promissory notes bearing interest at 5 per cent. In 1864 the total amount of the debt was £215, the lenders including Llewellyn Howell (£10), J. Davies (£10), John Davies, Taihirion (£20), Mrs. Ann Jenkins (£40), William Williams (£50) and John Phillips, Groeswen (£80). Records of later years show that amounts were paid off as the funds came in. By 1871 the debt was reduced to £125, a considerable achievement for those days. At this period, it may be noted, the active church officials were Enoch Daniel, Secretary, and D. Nicholas, Treasurer.

It may be of interest to record here the remuneration paid to visiting preachers during Mr. James' pastorate. The amounts paid ranged from 1/- to 5/- in addition to hospitality. I do not know on what principle the remuneration was made, but regular ministers of note probably got the higher rates. Thus Lewis Powell (the retired minister of Ebenezer), John Jones, of Bethlehem, and Dafis, Llantrisant, got 4/6 per Sunday, whilst ministers of lesser note received lower fees. Students from Carmarthen and Bala were uniformly paid 1/6.

In some cases ministers who had a supplementary income, e.g., by working a small holding, were paid on the lower scales. Thus the well-known preacher, Dafis Taihirion, was at one time paid 1/- only for his services. The story is told that after one payment of a shilling he was invited to pay a return visit. He expressed regret that he had no more shilling sermons left but had a supply of half-a-crown sermons. The hint was duly taken and later payments to him were at the half-crown rate.

In the late fifties and sixties there was considerable development at Llandaff Yard consequent on the opening of the College Ironworks and as some Congregationalists lived in that locality, and members of the Daniel family were apparently associated with that undertaking, a branch Sunday School was opened about 1856 in a loft of one of the Works buildings. Occasional Welsh and English preaching services and prayer meetings were also held there. The Works had a chequered career and at times when the Works were closed the Sunday School lapsed, to be again re-opened when work was resumed. The Sunday School was in being in the 1870's and early eighties, and there still live persons who attended the school at that period.

After Mr. James' departure in 1869 great interest was taken in the affairs of the church by John Phillips, of Cornel-y-Waun, and the energy and zeal which he put into the work of organizing the church during the next twenty-five years greatly increased its strength and influence. Mr. Phillips came to Whitchurch from Garth, Eglwysilan, in 1863. He was an active member of Groeswen and continued his connection with that church until 1869, although for some years previously he was an occasional attendant at Beulah and rendered it financial assistance.

Mr. Phillips was elected Treasurer of Beulah on October 10, 1869, in succession to David Nicholas, and held that office until his death in June, 1894. In addition he served as a deacon, as precentor and also as Sunday School Superintendent, and he also lodged and entertained visiting preachers. He was in fact the main pillar of the church, and in addition an influential local citizen who for several years represented the parish on the Board of Guardians.

Mr. Phillips threw himself whole-heartedly into the work of the Church. His first effort was to wipe out the outstanding debt. Through his activity not only was this done but soon steps were taken to effect improvements in the building. The Church income was soon raised to a much higher level, so enabling better remuneration to be made to resident ministers and visiting preachers. The following statement of receipts during the years immediately before and after his accession to office are sufficient evidence of this fact: 1864, £48 19 4; 1865, £50 17 5; 1867, £36 17 3; 1868, £38 7 4; 1869, £67 8 11; 1871, £114 1 7; 1872, £113 9 4; 1873, £69 18 3. This increase was brought about not only by higher contributions by members of the congregation and of the *Seiat* with special efforts on the occasion of anniversary services, but also by the holding of tea meetings, lectures, concerts and eisteddfodau. Throughout his connection with the Church he was a generous subscriber, and also lent money freely when the need arose.

From about October, 1869, the fees paid to visiting preachers show a substantial increase. They now ranged from 12/- to £1, or from four to five times the sums previously paid, for ordinary services, with still higher rates to anniversary preachers. Well-known preachers visited the church during the periods when the pastorate was vacant and, possibly for this reason, the church membership showed a substantial increase. According to a church record for 1869-70 there were 71 members, of whom 26 were men and 45 women.

Three years after Mr. James' departure, in 1872, a young Cardiganshire man, a student of Brecon College, W. Meuryg Rees, received a call and was ordained at Beulah on July 4. His stipend was fixed at £52, not a large sum but more than double that paid to his predecessor. The occasion of his induction was one of considerable local importance, and a series of services was held extending over several days. In all, nine ministers officiated, the leading preacher being Professor Morris, of Brecon.

Mr. Rees started with promising prospects. He preached not only at Beulah but also in English at the College Road Sunday School. He was, however, a man of delicate constitution and after two years service died of consumption at his mother's home in Treherbert on June 3, 1874, and was buried at Groeswen.

In 1875 the little church was again improved and the works, including a new pulpit, cost about £100. When this work had been finished a call was extended to the Rev. D. Gwernydd Rees, of Witton Park, Durham, a native of Landore, Swansea. Mr. Rees accepted the invitation and commenced his ministry on the first Sunday in January, 1876. The induction services however, did not take place until February 6 and 7, when the Rev. Thomas Rees, D.D. (Swansea) W. J. Nicholson (Groeswen) and several other ministers officiated. In the following year Mr. Rees also accepted a call to the pastorate of Watford Church, and he continued to serve the two churches until his resignation of Beulah in March, 1917. He resigned Watford in 1919.

As has been shown the stipends of Beulah ministers like those of most Welsh ministers until very recent times were always small, and even in those days of relatively high money values scarcely adequate for the maintenance of a minimum standard of life. Mr. D. G. Rees' commencing salary was at the rate of £6 per calendar month, an amount which was paid until April, 1877 when, probably by reason of his acceptance of the pastorate of Watford, the rate was reduced to £5 per calendar month or £65 per year, an amount which continued for the greater part of the 40 years' ministry. It should be stated that for about ten years between 1898 and 1907 the late Sir Herbert Cory (then resident at Tynyparc) made an annual subscription of £12 towards Mr. Rees' stipend.

About the latter year some difference seems to have arisen between the pastor and a section of the church partly on account of the formation of a branch church at Llandaff North, and in June, 1909, the church decided on financial grounds to supersede the fixed salary method by that of the monthly ministerial collection. Mr. Rees declined the new terms and resigned. Later, however, he withdrew his resignation and a ballot of members was taken "to decide whether he is to remain as our Pastor or not." 24 decided in his favour, 8 voted against, 4 declared neutral, and 22 members did not vote. The salary received by the pastor from monthly collections during the last eight years of his service averaged £58.

By 1878 the debt on Beulah was again cleared and the time was now ripe for further developments. In this year the church was registered for the performance of marriages. First, and as a preliminary to a further building programme, it was decided to acquire the ownership of the chapel site and, in January, 1899, negotiations resulted in the transfer by Edmund Howell of the freehold for the large sum of £175 to Messrs. John Phillips and D. Gwernydd Rees, the trustees appointed in 1850 being by this time either deceased or aged. The position was regularized in December, 1885, by a further conveyance of the land to a newly-created trust comprising the following eight members:

        John Phillips, Farmer.
        Rev. D. G. Rees, Pastor.
        Wm. Llewelyn, Agent.
        Thomas Nicholas, Furnaceman.
        William Thomas, Mason.
        Joseph Llewelyn, Woodman.
        John Jones, Tinman.

all of Whitchurch, and David Harry Davies, Merchant's clerk, of Llandaff Yard.

The terms of the trust deed were substantially as in the earlier deed of 1850.

After the acquisition of the freehold a scheme was adopted for the taking down of the old cottage and the erection of a new vestry and caretaker's cottage. This was carried out by direct labour and a detailed account of 1879 shows that the total cost amounted to £193.

As the income of the church during 1879 was only about £136 and the sum in hand was small further loans had to be raised to meet the expenditure of £368 on the freehold and new building. An amount of £332, bearing interest at 5 per cent, was advanced on the security of promissory notes by Miss Mary Ann Price, Penyrheol (£50); Edmund Thomas, Rhiwbina (£50); John Davies, Glanynant (£60); John Phillips, Wauntreoda (£22), and the Blwch Elian Lodge of True Ivorites, Eglwysilan (£150). It speaks well for the little church that by 1888 the whole of these loans were repaid, the last £130 being raised by a special collection during the last year.

Accommodation, however, was still cramped, and on November 12, 1889, a church meeting was held for the purpose "of discussing whether, having regard to the fact that the present building has become quite insufficient to accommodate our present congregation and also to its very dilapidated condition it is not advisable for us to have a new chapel built." The decision of the meeting, which was attended by 30 members, was in favour of a new building, and it was resolved to negotiate with Mrs. Hares, Cardiff, for the acquisition of a site adjoining the chapel. Her terms, however, proved to be unacceptable, and at a later meeting it was decided to approach Rev. D. Griffiths, Congregational Minister, Bristol, for the sale or lease of a plot of ground owned by him and his wife on the opposite side of the road, then in the occupation of Frederick Williams, one of the church members.

Mr. Griffiths agreed to lease 436 square yards of this land to the Church for 999 years as from February 2, 1890, at an annual ground rent of 30/- for the erection within a period of nine calendar months of a chapel costing not less than £800, and for the purposes of the lease the following were elected Trustees, and their names appear in the deed, viz.:—

Rev. D. G. Rees (Pastor)   S. D. Griffiths (Water Inspector)
John Phillips (Farmer)   Daniel Jones (Tin Doubler)
John Davies (Platelayer)   Thomas Evans (Traveller)
E. M. Thomas (Insurance Agent)   Joseph Salmon (Tin Roller)
Philip Philips (Farmer)   John Jones (Tin Assorter)
D. W. Rees (Clerk)   John Evans (Mason)

The trust clauses follow the model of the earlier deeds.

Steps were taken to raise funds for the new undertaking and in December, 1889, a sub-committee consisting of Rev. D. G. Rees and Messrs. John Phillips and James Langford was appointed with power "to determine the size and kind of new chapel we are to have and to arrange all things."

Mr. Edwin Williams, builder, of Whitchurch, was asked to prepare plans for the chapel for submission to the local authority, and he was expressly instructed that the building was to be at least one foot longer and one foot wider than Tabernacle, at that time the largest chapel in the Parish.

On January 6, 1890, the idea of building by lump-sum contract seems to have been rejected and the following resolution was adopted: "Resolved that Mr. James Langford do all the woodwork connected with the chapel, he being unable to give an estimate of the cost, and the Committee and Church are quite willing to accept his bill as it stands when the work is finished." Further, "John Evans to do the mason work."

It was doubtless thought that as Messrs. Langford and Evans were members of the church the cost would be less than if the work was let out to the lowest bidder. An ordinary building contract also would not conveniently admit of voluntary contributions of material, labour and haulage by members and friends, and it seems that John Phillips and possibly others had promised to assist in this way.

Building operations were commenced in March, 1890, and memorial stones were laid by John Phillips and J. G. Marychurch, of Cardiff. Money offerings towards the building fund included £50 by Mr. Phillips, £10 by Mr. Marychurch and £84 collected from members and friends by the pastor.

It seems to have been the original intention to take down the old chapel and utilize the materials in the new building. Happily, however, Dr. W. T. Edwards, a prominent Cardiff congregationalist, dissuaded the church from this course and himself contributed an amount equivalent to the estimated value of the materials which might have been used, viz., £25.

On February 22-25, 1891, the formal opening of the new chapel took place, and special services were held at which the following amongst other ministers officiated, viz., Revs. D. G. Rees, D. Griffiths (Bristol), W. J. Nicholson (Swansea), C. Tawelfryn Thomas (Groeswen), D. Evans, B.A. (Whitchurch), J. Bevan (Ararat), J. Taihirion Davies and J. Williamson, M.A. (Cardiff).

At the public meeting held on February 25, over which Dr. W. T. Edwards, J.P., presided, Mr. J. Phillips, the church treasurer, stated that the new chapel had cost £1,240, exclusive of gifts of free labour and haulage, the value of which was estimated at £175. Towards the cost a total sum of £565 had already been raised by freewill offerings of members of the Church and outside sympathisers.

The church was therefore left with a deficit of about £700. This was further increased later in the year by the expenditure of £80 in adapting the old chapel for the purposes of a school and assembly room and effecting necessary repairs. Loans amounting to £750 were made by Mrs. Russell, John Phillips and John Davies. By the time of the Treasurer's death in 1894 the debt had been reduced to only £300.

At the time of the opening of the new chapel the church had 112 members enrolled, whilst the total congregation was about 200 and the Sunday School numbered 160. The total annual income amounted to £156 and the assets of the Church were returned as worth £1,500.

The increase in membership was mainly due to the increase of population, but also partly to the fact that by this time the church had largely changed over from Welsh to English. In fact, in 1891, only Sunday morning services were entirely Welsh. The afternoon Sunday School, except for one class, and the evening service were conducted in English.

The switch-over from Welsh to English in the morning service took place in October, 1898, when it was decided that for an experimental period of three months morning sermons should be preached in English. On December 29 of the same year the church decided to make this arrangement permanent.

The church, however, was still regarded as Welsh and continued its affiliation to the East Glamorgan Welsh Association. Ultimately in 1904 Beulah transferred to the East Glamorgan English Congregational Association and two years later in 1906 the spring meetings of that body were held at Beulah.

In June, 1894, the Church sustained a severe loss through the death after a long illness of its most active member, John Phillips. Throughout his connection with the church he was held in the highest esteem and on the occasion of his second marriage in May, 1882, he was presented by the church with a congratulatory address, his portrait in oils, and other gifts, in recognition of his many services to the church. The address was signed on behalf of the church by Rev. D. G. Rees (Pastor) and Messrs. W. David, David Nicholas and Thomas Wride (Deacons) and Thomas Lovell (Secretary).

Many stories are still told by old people to illustrate the dominant personality of John Phillips. He ruled the church sternly but with great ability, and to his forceful character Beulah owes its development at this period. On one occasion during 'big meetings' he stopped the preacher during his sermon to correct inattentive listeners seated in the gallery. One of these was his own son Phillip. What shame that lad must have felt when his father called out: "Phillip, if I catch you talking and playing again you will have your behind warmed tonight."

Thomas Wride of Blue House, also, was somewhat of a character. Although not much of a musician he fancied himself as a leader of the singing. On one occasion the minister (Rev. D. G. Rees) drew his attention to the fact that a hymn was being sung out of tune. "Oh," said Thomas Wride, "it doesn't matter; it'll surely come right in the end."

In an obituary notice of John Phillips in a Welsh denominational magazine the Pastor wrote of him:

"After many years of experience the writer can say that he was a man of great sincerity, active and enlightened, of broad and liberal views, possessing a strong intellect, a lively spirit, a warm heart, and always bent on doing good."

After his death the office of treasurer was taken over in August, 1894, by his daughter Miss A. E. Phillips, who, upon her marriage to her cousin, Mr. William Phillips, now of Llanishen Fach, relinquished the office to her husband. Mr. William Phillips was appointed treasurer in August, 1895, and held the office until 1925. It is of interest to note that a grandson of John Phillips in the person of Mr. Lyn Price (Bridge House) today holds an analogous office, that of Financial Secretary of the Church.

Rev. D. G. Rees was held in high esteem by the Church throughout his long ministry, in spite of occasional differences to one of which reference has already been made. He also had the respect of the parishioners generally and served as one of their representatives on the Whitchurch School Board throughout the existence of that body. The church showed their appreciation of him in 1901, when, on the completion of his 25 years of service, they presented him with an illuminated address and a purse of gold. In acknowledging the gift Mr. Rees stated that throughout his connection with the church he had missed only two and a half Sundays through illness, had preached at over 1,500 services at Beulah and had received 320 persons into membership.

In the early 1900's there was considerable building and growth of population at Llandaff North and some members of Beulah resident in that locality together with other Congregationalists desired to establish a branch church near their homes Amongst these were Messrs. Morgan Watkin (a deacon of Beulah), W. C. Shail and C. F. Pitman. The movement was strongly supported by Rev. D. G. Rees who, from time to time conducted devotional services at the Hawthorn Infants' School.

In November, 1903, Beulah appointed a committee comprising the following members for the purpose of selecting a site for a new meetinghouse, viz., Rev. D. G. Rees and Messrs. Thomas Samuel (Village Farm), John Evans (College Road), John Jenkins (Kingsland Road), — Howells (Evansfield Road), Wm. Phillips (Treasurer) and S. D. Griffiths (Secretary). In the annual report of Beulah for 1903 the Pastor reported that "as a church you have unanimously decided to support me in my desire to start a new cause at Llandaff Station which is, I am glad to say, with God's blessing, progressing very favourably."

In March, 1904, arrangements were made for a lease for 99 years (with the option of purchase) of land in Belle Vue Crescent and a local Building Committee (with Mr. E. F. Pitman as Secretary) was formed, and Mr. W. C. Shail was asked to prepare plans. In due course a building contract was entered into for an amount of £685 and in May, 1905, the new chapel, named Christchurch, was opened.

At this period there was an outstanding debt on the mother church and a request for a contribution of £100 made by Christ Church was turned down, and a resolution adopted that Beulah would assume no further liability for the daughter church until its own debt had been cleared. Nevertheless Mr. Rees continued to exercise oversight over Christ Church until the first regular pastor, Rev. Lewis Richards, arrived in 1906. It was felt, however, that Beulah had a moral responsibility to help the new cause and in November, 1908, Beulah agreed to make a payment of £80 to Christchurch and raised a loan to meet the obligation.

The opening of the Llandaff North church did not materially affect the prosperity of Beulah as, owing to the substantial development which was taking place in Whitchurch at this period, many Congregationalists settling in the locality joined the older and better known church. The effect of the revival of 1904-6 also was favourable to religious development and the churches with a Welsh tradition probably were more influenced by this upheaval than those of more English character.

Referring to the Revival Mr. Rees, in his letter to the church at the end of 1904, said:

"His good spirit has been with us, and as the year was drawing to its end we were given strong proof that He was at work in our midst. The series of special prayer meetings which were held at the vestry were well attended and great spiritual fervour began to be manifested in our midst.... and thanks be to God He has sent showers of blessings upon us; the desire of our heart has been granted, by the earnest and strenuous spiritual life amongst our members, especially amongst our young people. Today we have a strong band of young people filled with the spirit of God, and working their utmost for the glory of God in the salvation of souls."

A year later in his message for 1905 he further wrote:

"As a Church we cannot forget the year of 1905; it was amongst the years of God's right hand. 'The Lord hath done great things for us; whereof we are glad'. Showers of blessings descended. Some of the converts have lost their first love, but others are still faithful and consistent members—true followers of the Master."

The development due to building activity and the influence of the Revival, however, does not appear to have been permanent as will be seen from the following statistics of membership:—1903, 114; 1904, 121; 1905, 143; 1906, 178; 1907, 166; 1908, 147; 1909, 134; 1910, 109.

In 1907 the debt on Beulah was completely wiped out, and the debt of £80 shouldered in respect of Christ Church in 1908 was the only outstanding liability for a few years. In 1912 steps were taken by Professor H. S. Jevons and his associates to develop the Rhiwbina Garden Village, and it seemed likely that a big influx of population would lead to a greatly increased membership. This hope, however, was only partly realised, for the outbreak of the Great War delayed the full realisation of the planned programme.

Possibly in anticipation of this development in 1914 Beulah embarked on further expenditure amounting to £320 in enlarging the old premises and adapting the main room for the purposes of the Sunday School and for holding various meetings, and in providing an electricity supply for lighting the church. The renovated premises were re-opened in December, 1914.

The burden of caring for the churches of Beulah and Watford was towards the middle of the War period proving too great a strain on the revered pastor who had now attained the age of seventy and in September 1916 he gave notice of his intention to give up the pastorate. On Sunday, March 4, 1917, he preached his farewell sermon. His retirement was made the occasion for a further recognition—the fourth during his lifetime—of the merit of his work, and on March 7 a public meeting was held at which he was presented with an address and a wallet containing treasury notes to the value of £80. Although his 41 years service as pastor was ended, however, Mr. Rees continued to reside at Rhiwbina and was associated with his old church until his death in 1933.

Prior to 1915 the property of Beulah was vested in two sets of trustees appointed by trust deeds of 1885 and 1890. Of the persons so appointed six were dead, three had left the district, and others on account of advancing years were unable to take an active interest in the affairs the church. At a church meeting held in May, 1915, under the chairmanship of the senior deacon, Mr. T. Samuel, it was decided to appoint trustees for the old and the new premises. Three of the old trustees, viz., Rev. D. G. Rees, John Evans and Sidney D. Griffiths were re-appointed, and fourteen additional trustees were selected to serve with them, viz. :—

  James Henry Hicks, Tinplate Worker.
  Thomas Hicks, Tinplate Worker.
  John William Jenkins, Commercial Clerk.
  Margaret Ann Jones, Spinster.
  Wm. Samuel Jones, Schoolmaster.
  David Llewelyn, Quarry Owner.
  Ernest Victor Parsons, Builder.

Elizabeth Ann Phillips, wife of Wm. Phillips.
Edward John Price, Poor Law Clerk.
Sarah Hannah Price, wife of E. J. Price.
Theodore Salmon, Tinplate Worker.
George Edward Samuel, Assistant in Corn Stores.
William Hamer (Llanishen), Gentleman.
David Williams, Colliery Proprietor.

The signatures of the new trustees were witnessed by Messrs. T. J. Roberts (Secretary) and William Phillips (Treasurer).

After the retirement of Mr. Rees in 1917 Beulah was without a pastor for 2½ years, and, owing to the effects of the Great War including the withdrawal of young men for services in the forces, the membership was small and the financial position unsatisfactory. The Church could not well maintain a minister whilst it was hampered by debt and in 1918 a special effort was made to remove this handicap. In addition to a sum of about £135 raised within the church itself a further amount of £170 was raised by special donations from outside friends. Of the last amount the English Congregational Board contributed £50, Sir William James Thomas a like amount, Mr. J. C. Meggitt £30 and Mr. T. W. David £10.

The debt was in this way cleared and the Church was now in a position to consider filling the ministerial vacancy. As, however, the total membership was only about 120 it was felt that for a few years at any rate the Church could not, unaided, pay a minister at a rate adequate to meet the increased cost of living which followed on the war, and the Congregational Board undertook to make an annual contribution not exceeding £50 to the ministerial fund.

In the summer of 1919 a call was extended to and accepted by the Rev. Samuel Jones who commenced his ministry on the second Sunday in August of that year, although the formal Recognition Service was delayed until October 20. At this service the special preacher was Rev. D. Ewart James (Southend) whilst Revs. R. E. Salmon, D. G. Rees, John Williams (Saundersfoot) and others also took part.

Mr. Jones was born at Kidwelly in 1876, and was educated at Carmarthen College. Before coming to Beulah he had held the following pastorates viz., Llantrisant and Castellau (1904-7), Brynteg, Abertillery (1907-1911), Zion's Hill, Haverfordwest (1911-1919). He started his ministry at a salary of £265, which was later raised to £300 and subsequently stabilised at about £270.

The new minister came to Beulah at a time when Whitchurch was about to change from a more or less self-contained village depending largely on local industries into a rapidly growing suburb of Cardiff. As I have indicated the development of Rhiwbina had commenced before the Great War. In the 1920's hundreds of new houses were built, and Beulah from being more or less a rural church on the outskirts of Whitchurch soon became surrounded by a considerable urban community, and as it was the only Congregational church in the parish with the exception of Bethesda, Tongwynlais, it also served the needs of persons of that denomination who settled in the other developing areas of Whitchurch.

In 1918 the membership of the Church was about 120 whilst its total income was only about £200. The advent of the new population led to a great increase in the number of members and adherents and to a relatively greater increase in church income. At the time of the pastor's death in 1940 the membership was about 200 whilst the sum of the various Church funds was in the vicinity of £600.

The strength of the church would doubtless today have been much greater but for the fact that other denominational churches were opened within a short radius, viz All Saints Church, Rhiwbina Baptist, Rhiwbina Methodist and Bethesda Gospel Hall.

During Mr. Jones' ministry one substantial structural scheme was embarked upon. Instrumental music in the form of an American organ had been introduced into church services in 1882. In 1905 one of the church members, Mr. Llewelyn Langford, proposed that the Church should acquire a pipe organ and offered a donation of £100 towards the cost. As, however, the church was at that time in debt and was also involved in some liability in regard to the branch church at Llandaff North the proposal was rejected and it was not until 1925 that the provision of such an instrument became practicable.

The project was now taken up with enthusiasm, and Mr. T. Alwyn Lloyd, F.R.I.B.A., was commissioned to prepare a scheme for the erection of an organ chamber and new vestries and the consequent adaptation and renovation of the premises. The work was carried out by Messrs. Ben Thomas & Co. Ltd. and on completion an organ was purchased and erected. The total cost of the scheme was about £2,200. The raising of funds for the discharge of this obligation was left mainly to a committee of ladies, and it speaks well for their zeal and energy that by 1934 the entire debt so incurred was fully discharged.

Mention should be made here of the part played by two of the oldest deacons in the service of the church. Reference has already been made to the fact that in August, 1895, Mr. William Phillips (now of Llanishen Fach) took over the duties of church treasurer after the death of his father-in-law John Phillips, an office which he faithfully discharged until his resignation a few years ago. At the same period both he and Mr. T. Samuel, who also served as Precentor, were elected deacons. Mr. Phillips still holds this office and Mr. Samuel served until his death in September, 1927. It is true to say that these two gentlemen during their long connection with the church carried on the tradition of devotion and loyal service to the cause which had been started by the Daniel family and carried on by David Nicholas, Thomas Wride, David Evans, John Phillips, to mention only a few of the active leaders of Beulah in olden days.

In 1928 it became necessary again to appoint new trustees and in September of that year a further deed was prepared vesting church property in the following members, viz. :—Amelia Davies, W. Morgan

Davies, John D. Duncan, William Hamer, Annie Hicks, D. J. Hicks, W. T. Hicks, R. D. Hughes, W. S. Jones, D. Llewellyn, W. Parry, William Phillip, J. L. Shenton, E. V. Taylor, Ben Thomas, W. C. Upward.

During the past twenty years Beulah in addition to its regular pastorate, has had the advantage of the membership of several retired ministers who have rendered services as occasion required. Rev. D. G. Rees (the venerated pastor) continued his connection with the church until his death. Other local retired ministers who were members or otherwise assisted the church were Revs. E. Jones Williams, Iona Williams and Edward Morgan. So far as is known one minister of religion only was nurtured in the church, viz., Rev. George Llewelyn (of Rhiwbina Hill). He preached his first sermon at Beulah in August, 1911, and in 1916 the Church provided him with a measure of financial assistance to enable him to study at New College.

During recent years Beulah has greatly increased in numbers and influence. Its pastor, Rev. Samuel Jones, was a man of great sincerity and tact and always aimed to maintain peace within the church and good relations with the world outside. Although not of a robust constitution he was nevertheless rarely sick, and it came as a shock to his church and to the local community when, after a short illness, he passed away on May 12, 1940. The high regard in which he was held by his church is well expressed in the following extract from a tribute paid by his diaconate:

"A true Christian gentleman has joined his Maker, and his life will always be a fragrant memory. During his long service to the Church he was loved by all and he will always be remembered for his loyal devotion, his kind consideration for others and his earnest desire at all times to co-operate in a kindly manner with all the officers, organisations and members forming the Church he loved so much."

A call to the church was accepted by Rev. Elfed Jones, the young minister of Ramah Welsh Congregational Church, Treorchy, and on Nov. 8, 1941, special induction services were held. It is in keeping with the tradition of the church that Mr. Jones like all his predecessors at Beulah commenced his career in the Welsh pulpit. And one may hope that although the language of Beulah is now English the Welsh spirit which has hitherto suffused the church will still continue to inspire its work.

The new ministry gives promise of continued development for the church. During 1942 no fewer than 26 new members were admitted, bringing the total up to 234. The number on the registers on December 31, 1944, is given as 198. The financial position also shows improvement and the income from members' contributions during 1943 amounted to more than £700. A Junior Church has been formed, and there are other flourishing church activities.

It should be added that the present chief officers of the church, in addition to 13 deacons, are Messrs. R. S. Randell and W. M. Jones (Joint Secretaries), Miss Doris Price and Mr. D. Lyn Price (Joint Financial Secretaries), and Mr. O. C. Bugler (Treasurer).

Note.—In addition to material obtained from individuals and from church records much information has been derived for this chapter from published writings, of which the following are the most important:

Rees & Thomas. *Hanes Eglwysi Annibynol Cymru*, Vol. II (1871), Vol. V (1891).

Williamson. *History of Congregationalism in Cardiff and District* (1920).

Evening Express, Dec. 24, 1891, *Round the Churches, Beulah*.

CHAPTER XXII.

BETHESDA CONGREGATIONAL, TONGWYNLAIS.

The Congregational church which met in the little chapel of Taihirion on the Llantrisant Road in Llanillterne Parish was the mother of many churches, including that of Bethlehem, Gwaelodygarth (founded in the first quarter of last century), which drew its adherents mainly from families connected with Pentyrch Ironworks. About 1842 Bethlehem came under the charge of Rev. John Jones, who had been pastor at Rudry and Watford, and Mr. Jones occupied the pastorate until his death in 1872. During a considerable part of this period he also exercised a watchful care over two daughter churches, of Beulah (Rhiwbina) and Bethesda (Tongwynlais).

In the 1850's many Congregationalists resident at Whitchurch and Tongwynlais were adherents of the Gwaelodygarth church. With the industrial development of Pentyrch and Melingriffith there occurred at this period a considerable increase of population at Tongwynlais, and this fact, coupled with the influence of the Great Revival of 1859, encouraged the local adherents of Bethlehem to establish a Congregational church nearer their homes. In 1859 they hired a suitable room and worshipped there until June, 1861, when a new and commodious chapel, specially built to meet their needs, was opened. This building, which provided seating accommodation for between 300 and 400 people, is said to have cost £800. The promoters had failed to acquire a freehold site and had therefore to accept a 99 years' lease expiring about 1957.

For many years the new church, which was named Bethesda, was managed as a daughter church of Bethlehem, and Rev. John Jones gave up his pastorates of Rudry and Beulah in order to serve the new cause, which he did until his death in 1872.

At the time of the founding of Bethesda great hopes were entertained of the rapid development of Tongwynlais. About the middle of the sixties, however, the proprietors of the Melingriffith and Pentyrch undertakings got into financial difficulties, and under Bank pressure the concern was organised as a public company in the early seventies. This decade, however, was one of serious trade depression, whilst the discovery of the process of steel-making put the ironworks at a great disadvantage. By the end of the decade the new company failed, and Pentyrch ironworks was closed down. Many local residents had to leave the district, and Bethesda, with other neighbouring churches, sustained a loss of membership.

About this period also Welsh as the home language was being displaced by English. A section of Ainon Welsh Baptist Church had started an English branch—Salem—whilst a local Anglican cause had also been founded for English people. The English churches were attracting adherents from the Welsh churches, which were thus tending to become weaker. A Congregational denominational historian writing in 1872 expressed the view that if the services at Bethesda were conducted in the English language the attendance would greatly improve, as most of the younger people of the locality were fonder of English than of Welsh. Bethesda at this time, as in later periods, was a weak church, and at no time has it ever attracted regular congregations comparable with its accommodation or been financially strong.

After the death of Rev. John Jones, Bethesda was served for short periods during the seventies by two pastors. First came Rev. J. H. Morris, of Llanharan, who held the joint pastorates of Bethesda and Canton. As he was a man of delicate health he resigned after a short period and a few years later, in 1881, emigrated to America. The next minister was a young man, Rev. Morgan Hopkins, a native of Cwmllynfell. He was born in 1850, entered Carmarthen College in 1871, and then served a Congregational church at Aberavon for five years before coming to Tongwynlais.

His pastorate here, however, was only of short duration; in little more than a year he died at the early age of 32, and was buried at Groeswen. Mr. Hopkins had literary gifts and translated into Welsh "From Log Cabin to White House" and Secker's "Wedding Ring." His ministry, though short, was a fruitful one, and the church was in a promising state at the time of his death. This revival may have been partly due to the fact that during his ministry, in 1879-80, the church changed over from Welsh to English.

In due course Mr. Hopkins was succeeded by Rev. Thomas Anthony, who had been trained at Bala and had been ordained minister of Bethesda'r Fro in May, 1878. He came to Tongwynlais in 1882. Bethesda was now a regular English church, and had joined up with the East Glamorgan Congregational Association. Under his guidance the membership more than trebled itself. It was not, however, even then a strong church; its membership in 1884-5 was only 63, although the congregation on Sunday evenings often numbered 250. After a time Mr. Anthony accepted a call to Mountain Ash, and was succeeded by Rev. A. R. Ezard who, however, left in 1889 for Hannah Street, Cardiff, where he remained until 1891, when he went to Brecon.

For a time the church was without a pastor. Rev. D. Gwernydd Rees (Beulah) exercised oversight of the church for a period and later Rev. J. H. Walker, of Christ Church (Penarth) discharged a similar duty. A church without a resident pastor, however, tends to weaken. In 1891 the number of members fell back to 45 and the Sunday school to about 60, whilst the church was burdened with a debt of £250.

After a time, in January, 1894, a new pastor, Rev. D. R. Morgan, of Wooton Bassett, a native of Rhigos, came to the church. Mr. Morgan was the father of the eminent soldier-scholar, Brigadier-General J. Hartman Morgan, K.C., M.A., Professor of Constitutional Law at University College, London, who, during his father's pastorate, served as a Sunday school teacher at Bethesda. Mr. Morgan left Tongwynlais in 1898 to take charge of a new English chapel at Llanbradach, from which place he removed later to Ystrad Rhondda.

Since 1898, Bethesda has had no regular pastor and relies on the ministrations of visiting pastors, lay preachers and theological students. In the early period Rev. Gwilym Jones, of Christ Church (Penarth), exercised general oversight and subsequently other local ministers have rendered similar service. At first the membership fell rapidly and debts accumulated. For many years past, however, the position has become stabilised. In 1928 the church comprised 56 members and a Sunday school of 6 teachers and 60 scholars, and similar figures applied ten years later. All the members are drawn from six to eight families, and it is to the loyalty of these families that the church owes its continued existence.

In spite of its limited membership the church in 1932 built a useful and spacious vestry, and is today entirely free of debt. The membership during recent years has varied between 45 and 60, whilst the Sunday school totals also range between the same limits. In addition to the Sunday school the church has a Young Peoples' Society and a Band of Hope, whilst a week-night prayer service is also a regular activity.

SHORT LIST OF SOURCES.

Rees & Thomas. Hanes Eglwysi Annibynol Cymru.
Williamson. History of Congregationalism in the Cardiff District.
Various Church Records.

CHAPTER XXIII.

RECENTLY FOUNDED CHURCHES.

I have dealt in preceding chapters with the older churches of Whitchurch which were for the most part founded half a century or more ago. Since the European War Whitchurch has undergone a building boom and has developed from a village into a township of fair size. To meet the needs of the new population several new churches have been provided, and in this chapter it is proposed to give the salient facts about each, and to conclude with a general summary of past religious development and a statistical statement relating to the present-day position.

ST. TEILO'S ROMAN CATHOLIC CHURCH.

The present Catholic Parish of Whitchurch was formerly part of the Parish of St. David's (Cardiff). On account of the inconvenience of attending at Cardiff catechism classes for children were conducted at Whitchurch in 1923 by a local school teacher, Miss Rogers, at the home of her parents and in other private residences.

As the numbers increased the need for more ample accommodation was felt and an approach was made by local Catholics to Canon Hannon of St. David's. Arrangements were made for the use of the Island Cottage Schoolroom, and here from June, 1923, the classes were held under the general direction of Father Kinsella. The expenses of these meetings were borne by the Whitchurch Catholics.

After a time notice to vacate the Island Cottage schoolroom was received, and the Catechism classes were transferred to the old schoolroom connected with the Fox and Hounds Inn. Here, in February, 1924, was sung by Cannon Hannon the first Mass in Whitchurch since the Reformation. There were about 21 persons present at this meeting. Soon the membership increased and the services were transferred to the skittle alley.

In due course arrangements were made for the provision of a permanent meeting place. A near-by site was bought by Archbishop Mostyn, and the present church hall was erected with funds largely provided by St. David's. It was opened with the singing of Low Mass by the Archbishop on April 14, 1925.

For a time the church was served from St. David's, usually by Father Kinsella. At length Whitchurch was made a separate parish, the first priest being Father Phelan, who in 1936 was succeeded by Father McCormack. The present priest, Father Probert, came in 1941. There are now about 300 members of the church, and funds are being collected for the erection of a new church building.

RHIWBINA METHODIST CHURCH.

As I have already shown Wesleyan Methodism is one of the oldest of the dissenting causes located in the parish of Whitchurch. There was also at one time another Wesleyan Church located at the junction of Caerphilly Road and Beulah Road, but this was later merged either in Llanishen or Birchgrove or both. The chapel was converted into a dwelling which was demolished a few years ago in connection with a Corporation road improvement scheme.

Whilst the Whitchurch Wesleyan Church was within the Wesley Circuit, the churches at Llanishen and Birchgrove were grouped with Roath Road, and when in September, 1925, Rhiwbina Wesleyans desired the establishment of a church in their locality it was to the Roath Road Circuit they turned for guidance. Mr. A. L. Goldsworthy, the Circuit Steward, met a local group at a preliminary meeting to discuss the possibility of founding a new church, A further meeting held a fortnight later was attended by about 30 people, including the Rev. Wynne Owen, pastor of Llanishen and Birchgrove, and other representatives of Roath Road Church Quarterly Meeting.

Mr. J. C. Ashe was appointed Secretary and Mr. J. N. Strong Treasurer of a new church, of which Mr. Wynne Owen was to have charge. Arrangements were made for services and a Sunday School to be held at the Rhiwbina Recreation Hall. The opening services were held on October 25, 1925, Rev. Charles Feneley, Superintending Circuit Minister, officiated in the morning, and Rev. Wynne Owen in the evening, whilst Mr. J. C. Ashe had charge of the Sunday School. The new church was equipped with reading desk, organ, hymn books, etc., through the gifts of mmbers and friends.

Soon the need for a permanent meeting place was realised. A site was acquired on a 99 years' lease on the Brooklands Estate, and Mr. M. T. Seymour was commissioned to prepare plans for a chapel thereon. The building was erected by Messrs. Ben Thomas & Co. Ltd., and was formally opened by Sir William Seager on September 21, 1927, the devotional service being conducted by Rev. Charles Feneley. On the following Sunday Sacramental Services were held, at which the Revs. Peter Rock (successor to Mr. Wynne Owen), Wynne Owen, and Clement W. Harper officiated.

The following is a list of ministers who have served the church from its inception to the present time: Rev. Charles Feneley (June 1926), Rev. R. C. Stonham (September 1929), Rev. D. N. Heap (November 1932), Rev. C. F. Guy (July 1936), Rev. A. J. Smeaton (November 1936), Rev. Kenneth C. Forrester (February 1940), Rev. Bertrand Noel (December 1941), and Rev. J. Mostyn, B.A. (September, 1945).

Like all Wesleyan churches, Rhiwbina was united with other Methodist churches under an amalgamation scheme adopted in the early thirties and is now known as Rhiwbina Methodist Church. The church has been a very 'live' body throughout its short history. The chapel as seating accommodation for 200, and its present membership is 48.

BETHESDA HALL (TYNYPARC ROAD).

During the summer of 1930 a Tent Mission was held on the site of the present Monico Cinema under the auspices of the Plymouth Brethren. The Mission proved a success and many of those associated with it decided that a permanent mission hall should be provided. Arrangements were made for the holding of services on Sundays and on two week-nights at the Scouts' Hut, Rhiwbina. The first service was held on Sunday, November 23, 1930. Messrs. Ernest Marsh (Caerphilly Road) and Francis Barnett (Kelston Road) were appointed Secretary and Treasurer respectively of the new church.

The membership increased rapidly, and steps were taken to erect a new meeting place. In answer to prayer a substantial amount of financial assistance was obtained, and within a couple of years of the holding of the Tent Mission a new hall was built on a site in Tynyparc Road to the designs of Mr. J. C. Harvey (Architect). This building was opened on February 13, 1932, by a well-known local business man, Mr. James Armer. During the following week a series of special services were held.

The membership increased rapidly from 28 at the commencement to approximately 85 in 1936. In the latter year the hall was enlarged to give a seating accommodation of 220. This was opened on September 19, 1936. Two years later a lesser hall was built with accommodation for about 100.

The present membership (1943) is 178, and there are over 150 children regularly attending Sunday School. The church is a self-contained unit and bears its own financial liabilities. At the present rate of response from its members it is expected that in about four years the hall will have been fully paid for, and the church freed from debt.

RHIWBINA BAPTIST CHURCH.

The Baptist denomination is easily the largest in the Whitchurch area; it has five churches as against two each under the auspices of the Congregationalists, Methodists and Welsh Presbyterians (or Calvinistic Methodists) respectively. The youngest of the local Baptist causes—that at Rhiwbina—was founded in 1934, a previous effort initiated by Mr. I. T. Austin in 1931 having failed to obtain the blessing of the Cardiff and District Baptist Board.

Early in 1934 the Board again investigated the position, and a meeting of local Baptists expressed a strong desire for the establishment of a church. A committee, with Mr. W. W. Jones (of Ararat Church) as Secretary, was formed to canvass the district, and more than 60 persons stated they were prepared to join such a church. At a further and more formal meeting, which was attended by Professor T. W. Chance and the Rev. Gordon Hamlin (Bethany) the willingness of the Baptist Board to incur financial obligation was announced, and a formal resolution in favour of constituting those present into a church was passed.

A preliminary committee of five persons:—Messrs. I. T. Austin (Chairman), W. J. Bolter, T. W. Lewis, G. Nowell, W. W. Jones

(Secretary), was appointed, and arrangements were made for the church to meet on Sundays at the Rhiwbina Council School. The first service was held on May 6, 1934, Professor T. W. Chance officiating. On May 24 a Sunday School was opened. On July 3 formal incorporation meetings were held, in which the following persons participated, viz., Professor T. W. Chance (President), Mr. T. J. Eynon (Vice-President), Mr. Ivor Shea (Secretary), Mr. Sam Fisher (Treasurer) respectively of the Cardiff and District Baptist Board, and Revs. Luther Jones, Ceulanydd Jones, Ebrard Rees and others. At this meeting the covenant of fellowship was signed by the church members. The following church officers were appointed: Professor T. W. Chance, Moderator; Mr. W. W. Jones, Secretary; and Mr. W. J. Bolter, Treasurer.

After a time it was decided to proceed with the erection of a meeting place. A site in Lon Ucha was leased for 999 years from the Welsh Town-Planning and Housing Trust Ltd., and Mr. T. Alwyn Lloyd was commissioned to prepare plans for a school hall, and a contract was entered into with Mr. J. L. Jeans (Roath). The foundation stone was laid on December 4, 1935, and on April 8, 1936, the chapel was formally opened. The cost was approximately £2,500. The care of the church for a period of two years was entrusted to Rev. Samuel Jones (Gabalfa).

In May, 1941, the church decided to appoint a permanent minister, and extended a call to Mr. Cyril Hewitt Jones, B.A., a late student of Rawden College, Leeds. This was accepted, and in August Ordination and Induction services were held, the charge to the minister being delivered by Dr. A. C. Underwood, Principal of Rawden College, and the charge to the church by Professor T. W. Chance.

In 1943 Mr. Jones resigned his pastorate for the purpose of becoming an army chaplain, and for a time the church was in the temporary charge of Rev. J. T. Phillips, late of Cwm (Ebbw Vale) and Ystrad Rhondda. Towards the end of 1944 a call was given to Rev. Penry Davies, B.A., of Brynmawr, who was inducted minister in December of that year.

The chapel hall has seating accommodation for about 200, and the present membership of the church is approximately 80.

REHOBOTH, TONGWYNLAIS.

Rehoboth (Tongwynlais) is the meeting place of one of the "Assemblies of God in Great Britain and Ireland." It is a small corrugated iron building removed from Peterston-super-Ely and re-erected on a site in Market Street, Tongwynlais. It was opened in March, 1935, with a ten days' mission. The pastor is Mr. John Edwards.

A SUMMARY OF CHURCH DEVELOPMENT.

Before concluding this chapter it may be of advantage to summarise some of the salient points of local church history. It will have been noted that at the beginning of last century there existed at Whitchurch one church only—St. Mary's Parish Church, with seating accommodation of about 300, all the services of which were conducted in English.

The first dissenting church, Ebeneser Calvinistic Methodist, commenced in 1808, and a Wesleyan 'Society' was probably started soon afterwards. Both these bodies held services in Welsh. Then in the 1820's the Baptists established Welsh causes at Ainon and Ararat.

The period 1820-1880 saw the rise and fall of the Booker industrial enterprises at Melingriffith and Pentyrch, during which time the population of Whitchurch was nearly trebled. A need for further religious facilities developed, and there were established new causes by the Wesleyan Methodists at Melingriflth (bilingual), by the Welsh Independents at Beulah and Bethesda, by the Welsh Calvinistic Methodists at Tabernacle (replacing Ebenezer), and Hermon, whilst the Baptists founded English causes at Salem and Bethel. In addition St. Michael's was established as a chapel of ease of St. Mary's Church, its services being conducted entirely in English.

After the Booker failure Pentyrch Works was closed and Melingriffith worked only fitfully. There was a considerable migration of population, and prosperity diminished. During the earlier half of the eighties (1884-5) the new parish church of St. Mary's was built to replace the older structure. A few years later local industrial conditions improved, and there also became evident a tendency for Whitchurch to develop into a residential suburb of Cardiff.

Between 1890 and 1895 new and larger chapels were built to replace the older structures by Beulah (1891), Bethel (1894), and the Wesleyan Methodists (1895). The only other development of importance up to the outbreak of the European War was the establishment of St. Thomas' Mission Church in 1911.

Then about 1920 started the great building boom which has led to an increase of nearly 200 per cent. in the total population. In addition to the establishment of All Saints' Church, Rhiwbina, as a chapel of ease to St. Mary's, there have been erected during this period a Roman Catholic Church at Whitchurch, and at Rhiwbina new chapels for Methodists and Baptists, and the Bethesda Hall for Plymouth Brethren.

It should also be noted that, with the exception of the Parish Church, there existed in 1859 eight churches in all in Whitchurch. Of these six were all Welsh, one was bilingual, and one only English. Then in 1860 two English churches (St. Michael's and Salem) were started at Tongwynlais, and during the eighties and nineties there was a tendency for the Welsh churches to 'turn English.' Bethesda gave way in 1880; other churches during the next decade tried to compromise by becoming bilingual. The latter policy, however, was not a success. Two Welsh churches and Melingriffith bilingual abandoned Welsh in the 1890's, and another two turned over in the following decade, whilst the last of them (Hermon) changed over during the European War.

Many residents of Whitchurch are connected with Welsh churches in Cardiff, and during recent years their number has shown a substantial increase. A demand has grown up for facilities enabling the local Welsh-speaking inhabitants to worship in the vernacular, and during the winter months of the last two or three years Welsh services have been held both at Whitchurch and Rhiwbina at the close of English services at local chapels. This is a War measure, but many Welsh residents hope it may lead to the establishment of permanent Welsh cause in the locality.

It may be convenient for readers if some of the chief facts relating to the various churches in Whitchurch are assembled together in tabular form. It will be seen from the table that there are now 18 separate meeting-places in the area, providing seating accommodation for about 6,000 persons out of a total population of approximately 20,000. The number of members or communicants about 3,000, but the congregations, of course, in the aggregate probably exceed 4,000, or one-fifth of the population.

The population of church-going people considered in this way seems extraordinarily small. It must be remembered, however, that there are two, sometimes three, Sunday services, and that many people put in one attendance only each Sunday or attend even more irregularly. In addition there are Sunday Schools attended mainly by children, but also by a fair proportion of adults. In the aggregate, therefore, it is probable that nearly half the total population are connected more or less closely with the several churches.

WHITCHURCH CHURCH STATISTICS.

	Date of Formation.	Date of Building.	Accommodation.	Membership.
ANGLICAN.				
St. Mary's Parish Church	14th Cent. (?)	1885	—	500
St. Thomas	1911	1913	—	200
All Saints	1931	1931	—	200
St. Michael's Parish Church	1860	1877	—	—
ROMAN CATHOLIC.				
St. Teilo's	1923	1925	—	300
BAPTIST.				
Ainon	{ 1827* 1838	1832	600	83
Salem	{ 1860* 1880	1862	400	102
Ararat	1824	{ 1828 1915	700	345
Bethel	1865	{ 1867 1894	—	340
Rhiwbina	1934	1936	200	80
WELSH PRESBYTERIAN (CALVINISTIC METHODIST).				
Ebenezer } Tabernacle }	1808† 1866	— 1866	— —	— 207
Hermon	1859	1860	—	60

	Date of Formation.	Date of Building.	Accommodation.	Membership.
CONGREGATIONAL.				
Beulah	1848	1891	—	225
Bethesda	1859	1861	—	56
METHODIST.				
Melingriffith ⎫	1838†			
Whitchurch ⎭	1895	1895	—	150
Rhiwbina	1925	1927	200	48
PLYMOUTH BRETHREN.				
Bethesda Hall	1930	1932	220	178
ASSEMBLIES OF GOD.				
Rehoboth	1935	1935	—	12

* Branch Church.
† Later merged in the Church bracketed with it.

CHAPTER XXIV.

RHIWBINA: ANCIENT AND MODERN.

The suburb of Rhiwbina is a development of the past thirty years. Until recently it was regarded as the area within the Parish of Whitchurch, north of the Cardiff Railway between the Golf Course and the eastern parish boundary. The limits, however, were never clearly defined, and today its extent may perhaps be regarded as coterminous with the Rhiwbina Ward which was created for electoral purpose about ten years ago, although contiguous areas within the limits of Cardiff are also so described. The Rhiwbina Ward includes not only the above mentioned area but also the area south of the railway up to and including both sides of Tywern and Tynyparc Roads between the parish boundary and the Whitchurch Brook.

Prior to 1910 Rhiwbina was for the most part purely agricultural in character, although a few small villas occupied by townspeople were already in existence. The name Rhiwbina was applied to the farm on the summit of Rhiwbina Hill with the contiguous small hamlet in the vicinity of the Cardiff Corporation reservoir and filter beds. The reservoir was built on part of the Rhiwbina Farm, and one large meadow extending from the reservoir southward to the lane leading to Rhyd Nofydd still forms part of that holding. Adjoining the hamlet on the west and south to Pantmawr Road was the ancient farm known as Pantmawr.

From Rhyd Nofydd lane to the Beulah Chapel on the east side of the highway known today as Rhiwbina Hill and Heolyderi extended another farm known as The Deri which was probably so-called from the ancient lightning-blasted oak-tree which is a well-known landmark in the locality. The Deri Farm extended from Heolyderi to the eastern parish boundary which divides it from the ancient parish of Llanishen (now merged in Lisvane), and also marks the western limits of the old Llanishen Fach Farm. The portion of the Deri on Rhiwbina Hill is bounded on the east by Nant Nofydd, beyond which extending to the Wenallt Road was the small holding known as Ynys-yr-ysgallenfraith. In addition some outlying portions of the Deri adjoining the present-day Wenallt Reservoir were in Cwm Nofydd and extended from Nant Nofydd to the Wenallt Road.

The land on the west side of Rhiwbina Hill and Heolyderi, south of Pantmawr Road, formed part of Greenhill Mansion—a Booker residence built on the site of an old farm known as Pwll-Wenci (Weasel's Pool)— and of Tynycaeau Farm, which extended from Tynyparc to the public footpath now known as Lon Fach. West and north of these two farms were the lands of Pentwyn, now part of the Whitchurch Golf Course.

The land lying between the Wenallt Road and Nant Briwnant from Nant Nofydd as far as the Briwnant Lane formed part of the Graig Farm. Land on both sides of the Beulah Road belonged for the most part to Tynycoed, a small holding a little to the north-east of the Butcher's Arms, and to Pantyrywen (also known as Tir Pwdr) near the Monico Cinema.

The Whitchurch Brook in the vicinity of Beulah was known as Nant Walla or Wathle (corrupted by Ordnance Survey plotters to Nant Waedlyd) and the little hamlet lying between Beulah and the Deri Mill and Butcher's Arms was known as Rhyd-y-Walla, or as Rhyd Nant Walla; and it was not until the Cardiff Railway adopted the name Rhiwbina for their halt that this locality came to be known by the upland hamlet name.

Near Tynyparc Farm there were two small flannel factories and some fields owned and worked by a weaving family named Lewis, and connected with these was a cluster of small cottages forming the hamlet of Tynyparc. To the west of the Lewis property extending to Heol-y-Forlan were the lands of Glanynant Farm, which farm seems at an earlier period also to have been known as Y Forlan.

Apart from a stretch of fairly level land between Tynyparc and the Rhiwbina School ranging from 130 to 140 feet O.D., the greater part of the area rises steadily northward. At the Deri the height is about 196-199 feet above sea level. From this point the land rises fairly steeply, as the following O.D. figures show: Pantmawr Road 250; Filter Beds, 353; Woodhill, 430; Coedwigdy, 487; Blaengwynlais, 574. The rocks are of the old red sandstone series, mostly of a marly character, possessing a fair degree of fertility.

Local conditions were on the whole favourable to agriculture, and although during recent years farming has mostly been in the direction of stock-feeding and dairying, at one time much of the land was arable, and the Deri Mill which stood near All Saints' Church was kept busy grinding locally-produced corn. Several smithies in the locality— e.g., one at the junction of Pantmawr Road and Rhiwbina Hill (Efail Jervis), another where Beulah Schoolroom now stands—were also fully occupied in meeting the requirements of local farmers.

Before describing the transition of this sparsely occupied agricultural district into a populous residential suburb it will be well to dispose of the more remote historical matters relating to the locality. Apart from an early ringed camp on the Wenallt —possibly of the Iron Age,—a Norman Motte on Ynysyrysgallenfraith Farm, a supposed battlefield near Tynycoed, and some finds of Roman coins at the old Gelli Quarry (Rhiwbina Hill) there is little of archaeological interest to report, and few particulars are available relating to the ancient homesteads of the locality. The ruined medieval Castell Morgraig at Thornhill is outside the limits of Rhiwbina although contiguous thereto.

One of the oldest of the ancient homesteads undoubtedly is the Rhiwbina Farm, which for centuries was the home of a family of Morgan— a cadet branch of the Morgans of Tredegar. There seems to have been a farmstead at this point for more than nine centuries. In the *Book of*

Llan Dav—a 12th century compilation of records relating to Llandaff Cathedral and Diocese—there is an interesting document relating to this property which by reason of its great topographical interest merits mention here.

The document in question is headed *Riu Brein* and dates from the period of Bishop Joseph (circa 1040). According to this record Rhiwallon, the son of Rhun had stabbed a friend and member of the household of Bishop Joseph, for which crime he was expelled from the district and excommunicated. After a time he made up his quarrel with the Bishop and was pardoned conditionally on his renewing his peace with the relatives of the wounded man and making a grant of lands to the Church.

With the consent of King Hywel and of his son Meurig
'he gave Riu Brein, the land of his inheritance, with all its liberty, and the third part of the wood Ynispeithan, to God, and to Saint Dubricius, St. Teilo and St. Oudoceus, and to Bishop Joseph and all Bishops of Llandaff for ever, and with all its commonage to the inhabitants, in field and in woods, in water and in pastures, and without any service to any mortal man besides the Church of Llandaff and its Pastors."

For our purposes the interesting portions of the charter are in the topographical descriptions given. First the boundaries of Riu Brein are 'From the Rhyd Lydan (broad ford) on the Annovydd, along it as far as the Istleidog, to the Pwll of Cincenn's kiln, to the Crug Glas (green knoll or mound), to the high road as far as the ditch, along it as far as Weun Wen, along it as far as the forest of Ina."
Apart from the similarity of the names Rhiwbina and Rhiwbrein the mention of the broad ford on the brook Nofydd and of the forest or grove of Ina seem to indicate the identity of the two places with one another. The description of the woods of Ynispeithan, which almost certainly adjoined Riu Brein supplies more positive proof. Thus:
'The boundary of this forest, together with the forest which belongs to Ynis Bradwen, is: From Aber Gwngleis (now *Ton Gwynles*), on the Tav as the Guynles leads upward to its source. From its source across to the source of Nant Ddu. Along the Nant Ddu downwards, till it falls into the ground before reaching the Tav. From that place to the Tav, along the Tav, with its fish, downwards as far as Aber Gwngleis, where the boundary began."

The Gwngleis, Gwynles or Gwynlais brook, a tributary of the Taff, seems to be the brook leading from Blaen Gwynlais at the extreme end of Rhiwbina Hill between Fforest Ganol and Fforest Fawr into the Taff at Tongwynlais. Nant Ddu (the Black Brook) is the old name of the stream which rises near the Black Cock Inn and Black Brook Colliery and flows through Cwm Brynau between Craig yr Allt and Fforest Fawr into the Taff at Taffs Well. The forest included within the limits thus defined is that today known as Fforest Fawr or Fforest Goch, otherwise Castell Coch Woods, and it would appear that anciently the north-western section formed part of the property known as Ynis Bradwen (situated probably near Taff's Well) and the south-eastern section to Ynis Peithan.

In all probability the wood of Ynispeithan would be in the vicinity of Riu Brein and it may be surmised that Ynispeithan itself was the property now known as the *Ynis* which stands near the left bank of the Taff below Castell Coch. Near this locality in later days was the river ford known as Rhyd-y-boithan (perhaps previously Rhyd Ynispeithan), from which an old electoral division for the south-western part of Eglwysilan—the hamlet of Rhydyboithan—took its name.

In later records in the *Book of Llan Dav* the name Riu Brein occurs in three lists of places belonging to Llandaff contained in Bulls of Popes Honorius II and Calixtus II, in each case in immediate association with other properties known as Caer Castell and Penniprisc. The conjunction of these names seem to suggest proximity, but there is no definite evidence relating to their location. The name Cae'r Castell (Castle field) used to occur locally at Whitchurch (near the Norman motte), at Mynachdy, near Rumney Bridge, and also adjoining Castell Morgraig, but there is nothing to identify the Llandaff Book name with either of these.

In the *Book of Llandav* in a charter, also of Bishop Joseph's time, Penniprisc (Pen y Prysg, head of the thicket or wood) is referred to as "Villa penn-i-prisc, that is, Difrin Anouid." Duffryn Anouid may be the same Cwm Nofydd referred to in the Riu Brein record, lying between Rhiwbina Hill and the Wenallt, although it should be noted there is also a Cwm Nofydd near Rhydygwern and Rudry. The boundaries of Penyprysg in the Llandaff charter are as follows:

"The boundary of Dyffryn Annovydd (*now? Cwm Nofydd*) is from the well of Derguist as far as the Allt, along it as far as Rhiw Tinuil, to Pwll yr Julenn, to the Garn Lwyd leading upwards opposite to the Crug Ri, to the Gaer as far as the Annovydd, along it as far as the Buddinn."

Such terms as Dyffryn (valley), Allt (hill or declivity, e.g. Wenallt), Rhiw (slope), Pwll (hollow), Garn (Carn, rocky mound, e.g. Cefn Carnau) and Crug (mound) are names associated with hilly country, and therefore fit the situation of land in or near Cwm Nofydd. I have no proof of any kind, but I surmise that Penyprysg was somewhere in the locality of Thornhill.

As I have already said Rhiwbina Farm (which I believe to be the ancient Riu (or Rhiw) Brein was the home of many generations of a cadet branch of the family of Morgan of Tredegar. The Morgan family was a very prolific one, and threw off many branches, all of which, however, trace their descent from Cadifor, the great Welsh Lord of Dyfed who died in 1084. A fifth descendant from this chief was Llewelyn ap Ifor who married Angharad the daughter and heiress of one Morgan Meredith of Tre Deigr (Tredegar, near Newport) who was of the line of another famous Welsh prince, Rhys of Deheubarth.

The eldest son of this marriage, Morgan, inherited the Meredith estate, and founded the family of Morgan of Tredegar. The second son Ivor founded the Wernycleppa branch in the same neighbourhood and is widely known amongst literary Welshmen as Ifor Hael, the great patron of the celebrated poet Dafydd ap Gwilym. A third son was

Philip of Bedwellty, from whom through his eldest son David was derived the ancient house of Lewis of St. Pierre (near Chepstow).

Philip of Bedwellty's second son Gwilym, who was born before 1440, became the ancestor of the family of Morgan of Rhiwbina and Cefn Carnau. G. T. Clark has traced the pedigree of this family, but as it is obviously incorrect in certain particulars I do not propose to deal with it in detail.*

I cannot say when the first Morgan settled at Rhiwbina, but towards the end of the 16th century a Henry Morgan certainly lived there. A *Llandaff Act Book* record of 1612 shows that "Henry Morgan of Rubinay, gent" owned properties at Llandaff, and a Survey of Senghenydd made in 1630 records that Castell Coch was at that time in the tenure of Henrie Morgan of Riwrbyne Esq."

The Rhiwbina Morgans intermarried with highly-placed local Welsh families such as the Morgans of Black Friars (Newport), the Herberts of Coldbrook, the Mathews of Llandaff, and the Thomases of Duffryn Ffrwd, and they seem to have been numbered amongst the lesser gentry of the period.

The last male of the direct line seems to have been Thomas Morgan described as "of Rhiwbina and Cefn Carnau", who died about 1748, leaving a daughter Elizabeth, and a grandson Thomas who had married a daughter of Thomas Williams of Llanishen. The latter died without issue, and the Rhiwbina property passed to his aunt Elizabeth. This Elizabeth had married Thomas Lewis of New House, eldest son of Thomas Lewis of Llanishen, who was Sheriff in 1757 and died in 1764. The Morgan family of Rhiwbina was thus merged in the Lewises of New House, and the Rhiwbina property passed in time, after her death in 1767, to Elizabeth's younger children.†

J. A. Bradney, in his *History of Monmouthshire*, gives a pedigree which connects Sir Thomas Morgan (one of Cromwell's generals) and Sir Henry Morgan, of Jamaica (Buccaneer Morgan) with the Morgans of Llangattock Lingoed, and derives their descent from the 17th century Henry Morgan, of Rhiwbina, referred to above. Some competent critics have cast serious doubt on Bradney's table, and the validity of Bradney's claim must therefore be regarded as in dispute.

Let me now deal with the transformation of the sparsely populated agricultural area above described into the present-day suburban community. Up until about 1910 there were in the locality only a few residences inhabited by city workers, and four of these, viz. Coedwigdy, Woodhill, Willsden and Brooklyn were in the upland hamlet.

At Rhydywalla there were two or three small residences in addition to farms and a few cottages. About this period the Cardiff Railway was opened and direct train connection with Cardiff was established. The time was now ripe for development.

Between 1909 and 1912 a speculative builder named Llewelyn Langford, of Whitchurch, built a few small semi-detached villas on the west side of Heolyderi near Beulah Chapel. His operations,

---

* *Limbus Patrum Morganiae (Glamorgan Genealogies).*
† Ibid.

however, were slow and spasmodic, and it was clear that development along the lines contemplated by him would be on a very limited and halting scale.

At that time the Chair of Economics at the University College, Cardiff, was held by Professor H. Stanley Jevons, M.A., son of the eminent Professor W. Stanley Jevons, a leading British political economist. The local professor, who lived at Woodhill, Rhiwbina, had for years been interested in questions of social reform, and he resigned his chair at the University College in order to devote himself to the task of organising reformed housing schemes in South Wales. His idea was to establish new villages based on co-operative ownership and laid out in accordance with Garden City principles, largely on similar lines to the co-partnership suburbs at Ealing, Hampstead and elsewhere.

In 1911 he founded the Housing Reform Company Ltd., mostly with his own capital, for the purpose of promoting Garden Village Societies which would build and own houses to be let to their members. The first society was to operate in the Cardiff district, and early in 1912 was registered, under the Industrial and Provident Societies Act, the Cardiff Workers' Co-operative Garden Village Society Ltd. The signatories to the Society's constitution were Charles Thompson (Llandaff), D. Lleufer Thomas, Miss Lilian Howells, J. T. Clatworthy, Fred Stibbs, H. Stanley Jevons, Edward Black and Wilfred J. Hinton.

After inspecting several locations this Committee ultimately decided that the Pentwyn Estate (a possession of the Jenner family) of 110 acres, extending from Rhyd-y-walla (now better known as Beulah Corner) to the Pentwyn Farm house (now the Whitchurch Club House), was the most suitable one on which to commence operations.

The interest of a number of Cardiff citizens, some of whom were prospective tenants, was enlisted, and in May, 1912, the first meeting of shareholders of the new society was held, over which Mr. J. T. Clatworthy presided. At this meeting it was decided to accept the recommendation of the provisional committee, and to proceed forthwith to purchase 10 acres at £200 per acre and to secure an option on a further 20 acres at £220 per acre. The shareholders also strengthened the committee by adding the names of J. D. Morgan (afterwards Sir David Morgan) and H. Bull.

It was also decided to instruct the late Sir Raymond Unwin, Britain's most eminent town-planning architect, to prepare a development plan for the entire estate of 110 acres. Finances for the scheme were to be obtained as to one-sixth by the issue of shares bearing interest at 5 per cent. to intending tenants, as to another one-sixth by the issue of 4½ per cent loan stock to investors, whilst the balance was to be raised by way of loan from the Public Works Loans Commissioners.

The preliminary arrangements took up much time, and it was not until late in the year that the project took definite shape. In the summer of 1912 I joined Professor Jevons as Economics and Literary Assistant and also to carry out publicity work in connection with his various social and business schemes, and, although I did not take up residence at Rhiwbina until July, 1914, I was conversant with all the activities connected with the early history of the scheme. When the preliminaries were completed Mr. A. H. Mottram, A.R.I.B.A., was appointed Architect to the Housing Reform Company Ltd., and in the autumn of 1912 plans for the development of the estate and the erection of houses were in active preparation.

The Provisional Committee was soon superseded by a committee constituted in accordance with the Society's rules, which, I believe, comprised the following members: Messrs. J. T. Clatworthy (chairman), F. Stibbs, D. Morgan Rees, J. D. Morgan, Archer Blyton, W. J. Gruffydd and E. W. Rees. Upon the first section of 10 acres it was decided to commence with a scheme of 34 houses, viz. 22 three-bedroomed houses in Y Groes, to let at rents ranging from 5/6 to 8/9 per week and 12 houses containing four bedrooms in Lon-y-Dail to let at rents ranging from £28 to £45 per annum. Some difficulty was experienced in getting satisfactory tenders, and ultimately an arrangement was made with Mr. J. O. West, of Hampstead, to carry out the work by direct labour on a commission basis.

On March 8, 1913, I visited Rhiwbina with Professor Jevons and a few friends for the purpose of participating in a simple ceremony of digging the first sod. Building proceeded apace and on July 19th of the same year a well-attended opening ceremony was held on the Village Green. Sir (then Mr.) Lleufer Thomas presided over the proceedings, the late Lord Plymouth unveiled the date panel on No. 7 Y Groes, whilst Lady Stafford Howard unveiled the sun dial on the adjoining house. Speeches were also made by the Lord Bishop of Llandaff, Sir Stafford Howard and the late Mr. H. Avray Tipping (a famous authority on country house and garden architecture).

During 1913 and 1914 building development proceeded, not without some difficulty, and Professor Jevons and his associates had periods of great anxiety. The Society's second venture comprised 18 houses in Lon Isa, whilst Professor Jevons had two built for himself in Heol-y-Deri.

The second scheme was carried out by Mr. J. O. West as contractor with Mr. Ben Thomas as Clerk of Works. Side by side with the Society's own scheme, a further scheme of 18 houses on the south side of Penydre (at that time called Homfray Road) was carried out for and at the expense of Mr. H. Avray Tipping. The total number of houses built upon the Estate before and during the War period was 72. Unfortunately the financial strain proved too much for the Housing Reform Company which, towards the autumn of 1914, was forced into liquidation.

Professor Jevons left Cardiff for Allahabad to take up an appointment as Professor of Economics, and the local society were in a position of considerable difficulty. Happily the Welsh Town Planning and Housing Trust Ltd., which had been founded with similar objects to those of Professor Jevons' organisation by Mr. (afterwards Lord) Davies in 1913, and which had Mr. G. M. L. Davies as Secretary-Manager and Mr. T. Alwyn Lloyd as Chief Architect, came to the rescue and provided financial assistance, secured by mortgage on the Society's 52 houses.

It also took over the land options, and later acquired Mr. Tipping's private venture.

By this time, however, the War was well advanced and further building was prohibited by the Government. After the War, building operations were in course of time resumed with the aid of government loans and subsidies, and the Society embarked on further building schemes in Penydre, Lon-y-Dail, Lon Isa and Heolyderi, which were carried out by Rogers and Davies Ltd., and by the ill-fated National Building Guild.

The Garden Village experiment had given a good start to the development of Rhiwbina, and during the building boom of the 1920's speculative builders took up adjoining areas of land at Rhiwbina, not under the Garden Village Society's control, and building activity now proceeded apace. Rogers and Davies Ltd. acquired and developed the east side of Heolyderi from Beulah Corner to the Deri Farm and also an estate between the Cardiff Railway and Tywern Road, as well as small areas in Beulah Road. Ben Thomas & Co. Ltd. operated on Rhiwbina Hill, Pantmawr Road and part of the Wenallt Road. Gage and Davies, and Maynard Brothers developed Tynyparc Road and lands extending northward to the Cardiff Railway. In addition several builders worked on a smaller scale on other sites in the locality. Nevertheless it was Professor Jevons and his associates who visualised the possibilities, and but for their pioneer efforts the Rhiwbina suburb may have today been only in an early stage of development.

To cope with the requirements of the considerably added population consequent on these developments a new mixed school was provided by the Glamorgan Education Committee whilst new Anglican, Methodist and Baptist meeting houses were later built to serve members of these denominations.

CHAPTER XXV.

LOCAL ESTATES AND THEIR OWNERS.

Whitchurch is not, and apparently never has been since medieval times, dominated by one big landowner, residing in a mansion within its limits. It has, therefore, never had a local 'squire', although the term was applied at one time to the tenant-owner of Greenmeadow. 'Squire' Lewis was not the only landowner, nor even the chief landowner, in the locality. At Whitchurch proper the Bookers, of Melingriffith, were the leading personages and they occupied the largest houses—Velindre, Greenhill and The Pines—but not one of them seems to have been known as 'Squire'. *Master* or Mishtir Gwaith (Works Master) were the terms by which the Bookers, of Velindre, were most often known.

The land at Whitchurch belonged for the most part, during the nineteenth century, to a number of big estates, but much of it was later disposed of in relatively small parcels to lesser landowners and builders. It will be of interest to record some details of the more important of the larger estates.

Mountjoy Estates Ltd.

The principal Cardiff landowner, until the recent transfer of the urban estates to Western Ground Rents Ltd., was Mountjoy Estates Ltd., representing the Marquis of Bute. In so far as Whitchurch is concerned the Bute interest is practically non-existent except that Lord Bute is still Lord of the Manor of Senghenydd, of which Whitchurch forms part, and exercises control over Whitchurch Common. How did this Scottish family come to possess such vast possessions in South Wales? In the first place by marriage with earlier owners, followed by inheritance, and in the second place by subsequent extensive purchases.

In 1547 and 1550 King Edward VI conferred on Sir William Herbert (afterwards in 1557 created Earl of Pembroke) extensive manors in Glamorgan, including those of Miscin, Glynrhondda and Senghenydd, together with towns and castles which had formerly belonged to the Norman Lordship. These possessions continued in the Herbert family for several generations.

Upon the death of Philip, Earl of Pembroke and Montgomery, in 1674, the titles of the principal estates passed to his brother, but the Welsh properties were bequeathed to his daughter, Charlotte Herbert, who had married as her second husband Viscount Windsor. Lady Windsor died in 1733 and her husband in 1738. Their son, Albert Hickman, second Viscount Windsor, now inherited. He married Alice Clavering and both he, and after his death in 1758, his widow, granted several important leases to the industrial pioneers who founded ironworks at Dowlais, Melingriffith, Hirwaun and elsewhere and laid the foundations of an enormously increased fortune for their line.

Viscountess Windsor died in 1776, leaving two daughters, the elder of whom, Charlotte Jane, married John, Lord Mountstuart, who later became first Marquess of Bute. The family estates had been added to from time to time by purchase. A few years ago the Bute family were said to have been owners of estates aggregating 117,000 acres.

Plymouth Estates Ltd.

Another important estate, which does not, however, now own much, if any, land at Whitchurch, is that of the Earl of Plymouth. This estate was also acquired in the main by marriage and inheritance. An early 16th century man of ancient Welsh lineage, Edward ap Lewis, settled at Van (Caerphilly) and laid the foundations of one of the richest and most influential families in Glamorgan, some of the male descendants of which were until recently associated with Greenmeadow, and a female representative of which is still connected with New House.

Edward Lewis and his descendants acquired large estates in the Taff and Rhymney Valleys, at Llanishen, Whitchurch, Radyr, St. Fagans, Penmark and other places in Glamorgan, as well as by marriage, properties in the counties of Wiltshire and Buckingham. The senior branch of the family of Lewis of Van had residences at Cardiff as well as Caerphilly, and in 1616 Sir Edward Lewis purchased St. Fagans Castle (and lands) from Sir William Herbert and expended much money on their improvement. The last male heir of the senior branch of the Lewis family, Thomas Lewis, had no son, and upon his death his property passed to his only daughter, Elizabeth.

In May, 1730, this wealthy heiress married Other Archer Windsor, third Earl of Plymouth, and elder brother of Herbert Hickman, Viscount Windsor and Mountjoy, referred to above, who inherited the Herbert properties and passed them to the Bute family. Elizabeth Windsor (née Lewis) died in 1732, leaving an heir, Other Lewis Windsor, fourth Earl of Plymouth (1731-1790). It was this Earl who, in 1763, granted a lease of lands at Merthyr upon which the famous Plymouth Ironworks were built.

With the rapid industrial development which proceeded during the 18th and 19th Centuries the wealth of the Plymouth family vastly increased. After two generations of male heirs the succession was broken, and the possessions passed to a female representative of the Windsors, who married into the Clive family. The title was later revived. The present Earl of Plymouth, the fifth of the new creation, **is the modern** representative of the Windsor-Clive family and the **inheritor of** the vast possessions of the family of Lewis of Van. The **total area** of the Plymouth Estate is said to exceed 30,000 acres, of which 17,000 acres are in Glamorgan.

The Tredegar Estate.

The family of Morgan of Tredegar are of ancient Welsh lineage and derive their descent from Cadivor, Lord of Dyfed. Through the marriage of a scion of the house, Llewelyn, Lord of St. Clears, in 1332, to Angharad, the beautiful heiress of Sir Morgan Meredydd, Lord of Tredegar (a descendant of Rhys, King of South Wales) two ancient royal houses were united, and from this union sprang the modern house of Tredegar (*Tre Deigyr*—Teigr's homestead, near Newport). In the 16th century the main line petered out; and a cadet branch, Morgan of Machen, succeeded to the Tredegar properties.

Additions to the combined estates were made from time to time by marriage and by purchase. Late in the 18th century the senior male line of the Machen branch also died out, and the estates passed to the female representative of a junior branch, Jane, daughter of Thomas Morgan of Rhiwperra. Jane Morgan had married in 1758 Sir Charles Gould, and on his elevation to the baronetage in 1792 this gentleman changed his name by royal licence from Gould to Morgan. Jane Morgan died in 1792, and Sir Charles Morgan in 1806. Their son, the second Sir Charles Morgan, Bart., now inherited the combined estates. He died in 1846 and his son, Sir Charles Morgan Robinson Morgan, succeeded.

Sir Charles was created Baron Tredegar in 1859 and died in 1875. He was succeeded by his son, Godfrey Charles, second Baron Tredegar, who was created first Viscount Tredegar in 1905. This was the famous soldier who distinguished himself at Balaclava during the Crimean War. He died without issue in 1913 and was succeeded by his nephew, Courtenay Charles Evan Morgan, son of Colonel F. C. Morgan, third son of the first Baron. Upon his death in 1934 the present Lord Tredegar acquired the family's very extensive estates, which are situated mostly in Monmouthshire, Breconshire and Glamorgan.

Most of the Tredegar lands in and near Whitchurch were probably acquired by purchase. In the 17th century, for example, between 1674 and 1680, William Morgan, of Tredegar, purchased from Richard Lewis of Van the Manor of Roath Keynsham, which, after the Dissolution of the Monasteries, in the 16th century, had been acquired by the Lewis family. It was by this transaction and others that a considerable area of land at Whitchurch and Rhiwbina came into the possession of the house of Tredegar. Under the Heath Enclosure Award 1801, also, several parcels of land, including between 20 and 30 acres lying between Beulah Road and Tywern Road at the Caerphilly Road end, were added to the Tredegar Estate.

Wingfield and Mackintosh.

The Wingfield or Castell-y-Mynach estate comprises lands mostly in the parishes of Pentyrch, Llantrisant and Llantwit Fardre, which descended from the Mathew family to those of the Jenkins and Talbots of Hensol and subsequently to the Rices of Dynevor, from whom they passed in the female line to the present owner, Colonel Wingfield of Barrington Park (Gloucestershire).

A portion of Colonel Wingfield's Welsh inheritance in the Taff Valley at Llancaiach (properly Glancaiach) and Merthyr is associated with that of the late Mrs. Mackintosh of Cottrell, and the joint estate is locally known as that of Wingfield and Mackintosh.

The estate seems to have originated in the following manner. Edward Prichard, who was Royalist Governor of Cardiff in 1645 during the Civil War period, and later became a supporter of Parliament, owned extensive lands in the Glancaiach and Merthyr districts. The estates passed in due course to his grandson, Edward Prichard. In the absence of a male heir, upon the latter's death in 1662, his two daughters, Jane and Mary, each inherited a half share in the property.

Mary Prichard married David Jenkins of Hensol, and her interest passed in due course to its present holder, Colonel Wingfield. Jane Prichard married a Berkshire gentleman, John Wightwick, and she sold her interest to one Michael Richards of Cardiff, from whom it descended in due course to the late family of Mackintosh of Cottrell.

There is only a small portion of this joint estate in Whitchurch parish, the largest parcel being the Rhiwbina Farm.

The Mackintosh Estate.

Apart from the joint estate just mentioned there is a separate Mackintosh Estate, to which a considerable area of local land belongs. This estate seems to have evolved in the following manner. A late 17th century Cardiff alderman, William Richards, had two sons, Michael and William. From the latter was derived the Windsor Richards family, with which later were linked up the Homfrays of Penlline. The elder son, Michael Richards (1672-1729) married Mary Powell of the then prosperous family of Energlyn (Caerphilly). It was this Michael Richards who purchased a moiety of the Llancaiach property. He appears also to have acquired lands in the Cardiff district. The name of a second Michael Richards (son of the first), in association with that of Lord Talbot of Hensol, appears in the first lease of Cyfarthfa to Anthony Baron and William Brownrigg in 1765. The area covered by this lease exceeded 4,000 acres.

The next heir of the Richards family, John Richards (1734-1793) succeeded to the property in 1771. He was twice married, and had two sons—the heir, John Richards (1768-1819), who married Catherine Jones of Fonmon, and Edward Priest Richards (1768-1819), who was County Treasurer of Glamorgan. John Richards was succeeded by his son John Mathew Richards (1803-1843), who lived in and probably built Plasnewydd (Roath), the building now known as the Mackintosh Institute.

Upon the death of this gentleman, without issue, the estates passed to Alderman Edward Priest Richards, a well-known and influential Cardiff lawyer, who later held the appointment of Town Clerk of Cardiff from 1836 to 1856. He also lived at Plasnewydd and married Harriet Georgina Tyler, daughter of Sir George Tyler of Cottrell. The only child of this marriage, Harriet Diana Arabella (whose names were bestowed on streets built upon the Cardiff estate), married in 1880, The Mackintosh of Mackintosh, chief of the Clan Chattan. Both Mr. and Mrs. Mackintosh recently died, leaving no issue. From this brief account it will be seen that the present-day Mackintosh Estate is the old estate of Richards of Roath. This estate owns lands in the parish of Whitchurch.

Homfray of Penlline.

Another local estate, that of Homfray of Penlline, also formerly belonged to a branch of the 17th century family of Alderman Richards, founded by his younger son, William Richards (1674-1731), who was succeeded by another William Richards (1718-1752), and then by John Richards (1746-1824), of the Corner House, Cardiff. Like his cousins of the Plasnewydd branch, this John Richards was also a very influential Cardiff citizen. He held important public offices, including that of Constable of the Castle and Manor of Cardiff from 1792 to 1817.

He was one of the promoters of the Act of 1801 for the Enclosure of the Great and Little Heaths, comprising about 1,040 acres of common land. He married Mary Burt of Wenvoe, and their only daughter and heiress, Anna Maria Richards, married John Homfray of Llandaff, second son of Sir Jeremiah Homfray, of the famous family of ironmasters associated with Penydarren, Tredegar and Ebbw Vale, who, in 1847, purchased Penlline Castle from the Gwinett family. By this marriage the Penlline Estate, comprising lands at Cowbridge, Cardiff and Whitchurch came into being. Colonel R. R. Homfray of Penlline Castle is the present owner.

Another local estate which also derives from the Richards family is that known as the Stacey Estate, from which Stacey Road, Cardiff, got its name. This estate came into existence through the marriage of Rev. Thomas Stacey, Rector of Gelligaer, to Mary Ann Richards of Roath. This gentleman seems later in 1854 to have lived at St. John's Vicarage (Cardiff).

Williams of Roath Court.

Another well-known local estate having Whitchurch interests is that of Williams of Roath Court. This family commenced with Charles Williams, a tanner of Caerleon, about the middle of the 18th century, whose great grandson, Charles Crofts Williams, married in 1836 his cousin, Blanche Phillips of Llantarnam, and settled at Roath Court. This gentleman took an active interest in the public life of Cardiff, became an Alderman, and was several times Mayor. The city records show that in 1835 he purchased from the Corporation a considerable area of land which had been allotted to the Borough under the Heath Enclosure Award. This land was in the vicinity of Albany and Richmond Roads.

His heir, Charles Henry Williams (born 1837), married Millicent Herring of Cromer, and had four children and lived at Roath Court, whilst his brother, George Crofts Williams, settled at Llanrumney (properly Glanrhymney) Hall. Charles Henry Williams was succeeded by his son, Charles Crofts Williams, who had married Rosa Thomas, of the wealthy Ystradmynach family of that name.

Lewis of Van and his Cadets.

At one time the various branches of the influential family of Lewis of Van, a 16th century foundation, were amongst the most important landowners of Glamorgan. I have already shown how the estates of the main line passed into the possession of the present Lord Plymouth.

The possessions of the family of Lewis of Llanishen, some of which were obtained by illegal enclosures of the Great Heath and some by awards under the Heath Enclosure Act of 1801, were disposed of to the Marquess of Bute after the death of Wyndham Lewis in 1835.

Another branch of the Van family, via Llanishen, was that of Lewis of New House. This branch commenced in the earlier half of the 18th century with Thomas Lewis, a younger son of the Llanishen family, who married Elizabeth, daughter and heiress of Henry Morgan of Rhiwbina. Thomas Lewis was a very shrewd business man and was one of the founders of the famous Dowlais Ironworks, with which he and some of the descendants were associated for more than a century.

By the marriage of Thomas Lewis' heir, Rev. Wyndham Lewis (1774-1838), of Cefn Carnau and New House, with Mary Price, of Parc y Justice, considerable lands at Pentyrch, Llanillterne and Tongwynlais came into the family possessions. The Tongwynlais and Parc lands seem to have passed to Henry Lewis, third son of Rev. Wyndham Lewis (who settled at Pantgwynlais or Greenmeadow). These lands, except the Tongwynlais portions, still form part of the Greenmeadow Estate, of which Captain Harry Lewis is the present owner. The old residence of Greenmeadow has recently been demolished and the lands in its vicinity sold.

A fourth son of Rev. Wyndham Lewis of New House and brother of Henry Lewis of Greenmeadow, was the well-known Wyndham Lewis, M.P. (1780-1830), who represented Cardiff in the House of Commons from 1820 to 1826, and later was a colleague of Benjamin Disraeli in the representation of Maidstone from 1835 until his death in 1838. Two years later his widow married Disraeli, and in 1862, she became the Viscountess Beaconsfield.

A third son of the first Henry Lewis of Greenmeadow, and nephew of Disraeli's colleague, was the Wyndham Lewis (1827-1871) who settled at the Heath. A portion of land had apparently been illegally enclosed from this common before the passing of the Heath Enclosure Act and a house built thereon. This, with the Allensbank woods adjoining, was allotted to Henry Hollier, one of the Enclosure Commissioners, or a relative, and in later years it was purchased by W. Price Lewis of New House, one of the Dowlais Works proprietors.

279½ acres on both sides of the new Heathwood Road were allotted under the Enclosure Act to the Cardiff Corporation, and parts of it were disposed of from time to time in order to raise funds for various purposes. In the 1840's money was required for the erection of a town hall and law courts, and in 1849 the Corporation sold 157 acres near Heath House to Wyndham William Lewis, nephew of the late W. Price Lewis, for £3,100 or less than £20 per acre. Actually W. W. Lewis did not enter into possession of this property until August, 1859.

Wyndham W. Lewis of the Heath was twice married, his second wife being Maud Williams, of the Aberpergwm family. He left two daughters, Annie Mary Price Lewis (1851-1911), and Charlotte Eleanor Wyndham Lewis (born 1871), widow of the late Colonel W. Murray-Threipland, of Caithness and New House, Llanishen. Much of Mr.

Wyndham W. Lewis' Heath Estate, with the New House property, is now in the possession of Mrs. Murray-Threipland and her son. Part of the Heath Estate and some other lands apparently passed by bequest to the family of Clark of Talygarn. G. T. Clark, the eminent military antiquarian and genealogist, was for a long period the managing director of the Dowlais Ironworks. He married Ann Price Lewis (1819-1885), sixth child of the first Henry Lewis of Greenmeadow, and settled at Talygarn. Part of the Greenmeadow and Heath lands came into her possession. Upon her death her son, the late Godfrey L. Clark, succeeded. In addition to lands at the Heath the family also formerly held lands at Rhiwbina, including part of the Wenallt, now a Cardiff Corporation park. The present representative of the family is Mr. Wyndham Clark.

SHORT LIST OF SOURCES.

The material for this chapter has been derived from a variety of sources, but mainly from:

G. T. Clark. Limbus Patrum Morganiae et Glamorganiae (The Genealogies of Glamorgan).
Debretts' Peerage, etc.
Landed Gentry.
John Lloyd. Early History of the old South Wales Iron Works.
Thomas Nicholas. The History and Antiquities of Glamorganshire and its Families.
Who's Who.
W. P. Williams. A Monograph of the Windsor Family.

CHAPTER XXVI.

LOCAL PLACE NAMES.

Few subjects arouse greater interest among residents in any particular neighbourhood than the origins of local place names. Almost everywhere a proportion of such names is not easy of explanation, and numerous and ingenious are the speculations of folk etymologists in regard thereto. During the past thirty or forty years the study of place nomenclature has been raised almost to the rank of a science, and popular speculation has been proved to be quite unreliable.

The English Place-Name Society has made many valuable surveys and has demonstrated that guesses at solutions of different names are often far off the mark. In Wales, also, much valuable work has been done during the recent years and considerable progress has been made in philological knowledge, and in scientific method for the elucidation of hidden meanings.

The vast majority of Welsh place names, based as they mostly are on local physical features and characteristics, admit of easy solution, although it is often unsafe to accept seemingly obvious solutions as absolutely correct. In most localities a proportion of place names has changed their form so greatly over a series of years that their interpretation is not easy, and for their solution we have to look to scholars who have made a special study of etymology and phonetics.

In the Parish of Whitchurch there are many examples of place-names of obscure meaning, e.g., Rhiwbina, Philog, Heoldon, Nant Walla, and although in this chapter some suggestions will be submitted relating to most local names it must be understood that they are offered only in a tentative manner.

The usual method now pursued in the elucidation of place names is to assemble as large a number of forms as possible spread over a long period of time, and to study the changes of form and particularly of pronunciation. Standardised spelling is a product only of recent years. In past years each person spelt a name as it sounded to him, with the result that many names were expressed in writing in dozens of different forms, the earliest forms differing radically from the modern standard form. Sound changes are claimed by scholars to proceed according to definite phonetic laws, and it is for this reason that only specialists in phonetic knowledge can be relied on for safe guidance in the interpretation of obscure names.

The modern name of the parish of Whitchurch is English in origin and means *white church*. The Welsh form of this name would be *Eglwyswen*, but this form does not appear to have ever been generally used even when the population was overwhelmingly Welsh. The Welsh name in common use was *Eglwysnewydd*, which means *new church*.

I have already pointed out that the most ancient known name for the locality was *Ystum Taf* (or in a contracted form Stuntaf), which means *the bend in the Taff*. The name used in medieval manorial documents, which were usually couched in Latin, was *Album Monasterium*, the first instance of which I can trace was in 1295. During the 14th and 15th centuries this Latin form was in general use, but occasionally records were made in the Norman-French form *Blancminster* (Blancmoustier or Blancmoster), and in English as Whitminster, Whitland and in various forms of White Church, viz., Witechurche (13th cent.) Whitchurche (1376), Whytchurch (1385), Whytechurche (1441), Whittchurche (1535-6).

It may be that Album Monasterium—translated by some writers as White Monastery—indicates a monastic origin. On the other hand *monasterium* (sometimes Anglicised as *minster*) may mean simply a *church*, and the name in its present form, Whitchurch—applied to a large number of places in different parts of the country—may well have been derived from the medieval practice of whitewashing churches. If this is so, since the name has been in use at least from the 13th century, there must have been a church building in the locality at that early date.

The Welsh name on the other hand is of more recent origin. *Eglwysnewydd* indicates the erection of a new church apparently to replace an older structure. This was perhaps the old parish church in the Old Church Road which was unfortunately taken down in 1904. The first use of the Welsh name which I know of was by John Leland in 1536-9, although, of course it may well have existed before his time.

Tongwynlais is probably a fairly recent name although one of its elements, being associated with a local stream, is of very ancient origin. The first mention of the stream name that I know is in a record of the 11th or 12th century in the *Book of Llandav*, in which there are three references to *Gungleis* as the name of a tributary of the River Taff.

It seems from this that the present-day form *Gwynlais* is the proper from and not *Gwynlas* which has sometimes been used. The following examples of spelling forms in use within a short period of only fifteen years will serve to show how loosely orthography was formerly treated. They have been taken from the Whitchurch Parish Church registers Tongwynlas (1835, 1837, 1840), Tongwainlas (1838, 1839) Tongwyrddlas (1844, 1846, 1847).

The form *gwynlas* is often used in South Wales as synonymous with *gwyrdd* (green), whilst *ton* is a common word for unploughed or lay land, e.g., a grass meadow. Hence the name Greenmeadow from the mistaken Welsh name form *ton gwynlas*. This mansion was built on the site of an ancient farm known as *Pantgwynlais*, the hollow or depression near the brook Gwynlais.

The misnomer is perhaps not surprising as the form *gwynlas* was in frequent use at and before the period at which the change was made. Thus Ton Gwinlas (1733), Tongwynlas (1757), Pant Gwenlas and Tu (ty) Gwenlas (1760), and Tongwynlas (1828). On the other hand I have noted the forms Tonn Gwenglais (1591) and Pant Gwaunlais (1879). In the records of Ainon Church (1850-1870) the form Tongwynlas is very general.

The term *clais* (*glais* or *lais*) appears commonly in stream names of Celtic origin. It generally applies to a stream in a narrow place, and is often used in combination with other elements of a descriptive character, e.g., Dulais and Dowlais (black brook), from which possibly the Manx Douglas and English Dawlish are also derived, Morlais (the great brook), and the form Gwynlais (white or possibly bright, sparkling stream) with which we are here specially concerned. Tongwynlais therefore seems to mean 'the meadow land on the banks of the sparkling stream.'

The locality north of the Gwynlais brook until a few years ago belonged to the Parish of Eglwysilan and formed part of the Hamlet of *Rhydyboithan*, which I have also seen in a record of 1793 spelt Rhydybythel and Rhydybyther. *Rhyd* means 'ford' and Rhyd-y-Boithan means the Boithan Ford. This ford may have been over the brook at Tongwynlais, but more probably was over the River Taff near the locality today known as the *Ynis*.

It will be recalled that in the *Book of Llandav* an early 11th century record refers to the wood of Ynispeithan, which was the south-eastern portion of Fforest Goch (the red forest), and in all probability Ynispeithan itself was a property on the bank of the River Taff.

Ynis is a Welsh word meaning 'island' and also land on the banks of streams which are liable at times to be isolated by floods, in other words, 'a river or marsh meadow.' In addition to the house known as The Ynis in this locality there is a farm a little to the south on the right-hand bank of the Taff known as *Cilynys* sometimes locally pronounced as Gelynis or Glynis.

Rhydyboithan seems therefore to be connected with Ynispeithan of the Llandaff record—a name possibly compounded of Ynis (a meadow) and Peithan (possibly a personal name, or it may mean 'level open land'). If this speculation—for it is no more—is correct, Ynispeithan may mean either Peithan's River Meadow or 'the river meadow in the plain'.

In a letter written to T. W. Booker in 1830 by William Price of Tongwynlais, the latter's address (now The Ynis) was given as *Ynis y Llewod Duon*—the river meadow of the black lions. I cannot explain the latter name, but I surmise that it has relation to the coat of arms of a previous owner. The emblem of the local Mathew family was that of Gwaethfoed—a black lion rampant on a silver background. Incidentally this William Price was probably a relative of the Prices of Parc yr Ustus who owned Pantgwynlais before the Lewis family, and members of which also occupied a residence shown on Bowen & Kitchen's Map of Glamorgan (1760) as Tu (i.e. Ty) Gwenlas, which seems to have been the tenement today known as Ivy House. The name Ynis y Llewod Duon also occurs in Whitchurch Parish Registers as late as 1852.

Cilynys is the Tudor farmhouse on the western bank of the Taff near Tongwynlais, but in Radyr Parish. If this form is correct it seems to be compounded of two elements, *Cil* (meaning a nook, recess, or retreat) and the form *Ynys* as above, thus meaning an isolated retreat in a water meadow. This was the form used on the O.S. map of 1830 and is still used on the modern map. In a Melingriffith Works record of 1774 it is spelt Cylynnis.

Locally, however, the name is frequently pronounced Clynis or Glynis, which is probably a contracted form of Cilynys. I have, however, heard it suggested that the proper spelling form is Celynis or Gelynis, and that the name comes from *clynis* or *clun yr ynis*. Clun, as in Pontyclun, also means a water meadow, in which case the two elements are pleonastic to one another. There is a farm called Clun yr Ynis in Carmarthenshire. On the whole, however, the orthodox spelling form seems the more probable.

The few other Tongwynlais place names seem to present no special difficulty. *Castell Coch* and *Fforest Goch*—the Red Castle and the Red Woods—go back for centuries. The castle probably got its name from the colour of the stone from which it was built, and the forest possibly from its association with the Castle, but more probably from the autumn tints of the foliage of the beech trees of which in olden times it seems mostly to have consisted.

The forest, however, seems in earlier times also to have borne another name. Rice Merrick, writing in 1578, refers to it or the hill on which it stood as *Cefn y Vid* and in Bird's Cardiff Directory of 1829 Castell Coch is mentioned as the boundary of an ancient forest called *Cefn y Fud*.

Now *Cefn* means ridge, whilst *Vid* may be a mutated form of a Welsh name meaning a quick-set hedge or the land enclosed by a hedge, and also is a mutated form of an old term *mid* which meant an enclosure, a field or place of combat or tournament. There is also a Welsh word *bidwal*, meaning an encampment. It may be, therefore, that the word *Fid* is from a word meaning hedge as in *Fidlas* (green hedge, Llanishen), *Fidgelyn* (holly hedge, near Cilfynydd) and *Fid Fedw* (birch hedge, near Brithdir), or it may be a variant of *mid* (a place of combat), or a curtailed form of *bidwal*, meaning the Camp Ridge or the Ridge of the Battlefield. Either of these explanations would fit the local circumstances, but at present they must be regarded merely as speculations.

A well-defined district of Whitchurch immediately adjoining Cardiff is the *Philog*, a name which has never been satisfactorily explained. Obviously the *ph* is an Anglicised form of the Welsh *ff*. I have searched the Church Registers, Highway Board and School Records and other ancient documents and have found the following name-forms:

Ffilocks (1752, 1753)
Fillog (1798, 1828)
Ffillog Brook (1809)
Philog (1822, 1885)
Fillock (1819, 1827, 1829, 1831)
Phillocks (1835)
The Phillock (1858)
Filocks (1850)
Fylog (1862)

Filog (1865, 1867, 1868, 1883)
Fullog (1867)
Fillawg (1874)
Tulog (1877)
Ffulog (1884)
Philog Bridge (1888)

Whilst the name has been standardised in its present form only during the past half century it will be noted that one example of the form occurred as early as 1822. Correct spelling was not a strong suit in olden days. Four different forms occur in the Church Registers during a period of 20 years after 1820, whilst four other completely different forms occur in the Highway Board returns between 1862 and 1884.

It does not seem safe to venture any definite solution on forms of so modern date. When earlier records are available it may be possible to fix the meaning with some degree of accuracy. At the present all that can be done is to suggest the possibility of the name being derived from one of the following Welsh words, all of which are more or less archaic, viz. :

Ffilog or fillock, a young mare or filly
Ffulawg, a wanton or loose girl
Ffuliog (adj.), full of bustle, hurrying
Ffyliog (adj.), overgrown, gloomy

If the name was originally a stream name either of the two last-named descriptive terms might apply. The forms given, however, do not seem to fit in with these words. There was, I am informed, formerly an old cottage near the brook to which the name was also applied, and it may be that there was a field name in the same locality, e.g., Waun y Ffilog—the mare's meadow, from which both the stream and the locality derived its name. I have, however, not been able to discover such a name. Until such a name is found the suggestion must remain a mere speculation.

Adjoining the Philog is Whitchurch Common, known over many centuries as Gwaun Treoda. *Gwaun* or its mutated form *Waun* is a common Welsh name for an open space, usually rough grassy land, such as a moor. The element *tre* in *Treoda* means a hamlet or a homestead, whilst Oda is probably a personal name. The name Treoda occurs as far back as 1578 in the forms Troda, Treoda and Treada. According to some pedigrees it dates back to the 13th century when the property was supposed to be in the possession of the family of Yorath Mawr, a descendant of Iestyn ap Gwrgan and Ifor Bach.

The name also occurs in the Roath Keynsham survey of 1702 in the form *Wain Troda*, in a Tredegar Estate map of 1761 as *Waun Treodre*, and in the Heath Enclosure Award of 1801 as *Waintrodda*. In the Boundary Commission Report of 1832 the common is referred to as *Gwaundu Rhoda*. The old farmhouse known as Wauntreoda formerly existed a little to the north-east of Ararat Chapel. The present farmhouse on the south-west of the Common was formerly known as Wauntreoda Isha (Lower) and later alternatively as Wauntreoda Court and Cornel y Waun (Corner of the Common). In the 1860's the name was commonly rendered Wauntrodau.

No evidence is available regarding the identity of Oda. In 878 a Danish attack on the northern shores of the Bristol Channel led by Hubba was reputed to have been defeated by a levy under a leader called Odda, and it has been suggested that this was the person from whom Treoda derived its name. No evidence of this assumption, however, is available, and it is best to suspend judgment on the matter.

Perhaps the most intriguing name in the parish of Whitchurch is that of *Rhiwbina*. The name of the suburb follows that of an ancient farmhouse near the summit of Rhiwbina Hill which was for centuries the home of an important family of Morgan, a cadet branch of the Tredegar family. This property is mentioned in an 11th century record in the *Book of Llandav* as *Riu Brein*, and it seems likely that the modern name has in some yet unascertained way been derived from this source. In the record mentioned there is a reference to the grove of Ina as one of the boundaries and Ina has been identified by authoritative writers with a Welsh female saint of that name.

Several attempts at a solution have been made, none of which, however, are satisfactory. One theory is that Rhiwbrein was a contraction of Rhiw-bre-ina, meaning 'the hill slope of Ina', but it is contended by some competent critics that the derivation of Rhiwbina from this form is philologically impossible. The late Rev. D. G. Rees (Beulah) used to derive the name from Rhiw-pynnau,—the slope of the burdens, the latter element referring to the burdens carried by packmules which used to take this route conveying iron from Caerphilly Forge to Melingriffith and Cardiff. Another interpretation of Rhiwbina was 'the pine-tree slope'. In view of the fact, however, that an analogous name Rhiwbrein was in existence centuries before the ironworks era and prior to the introduction of pine-trees to this country neither of these interpretations can be accepted.

So far, I have been able to collect the following name-forms relating to the locality.

Riu-Brein (circa 1040)
Rubinay (1612)
Riwrbyne (1630)
Riw beine (1677)
Riw'r beine (1677-8)
Riw'r Beyne (1677)
Rhiwbine (1708)
Rhywbeina (1735)
Rhywbina (1821)
Rubina (1739, 1745, 1766, 1777, 1791, 1831, 1840, 1841, 1872)
Rhewbina (1790)
Rhiwbina (1789, 1790, 1860),
Rhubeina (1838)
Rhubina (1844, 1847, 1849, 1870)
Rhiewbyna (1868)
Rhiwbynia (1860)
Rhywbanau (1856)

Riu brein might well change to Rhiw'r bein and Rhiw'r bein might easily be connected with Rhiw'r byne or Rhiw'r beine. Rhiw undoubtedly means slope, declivity or hill, but what is the meaning of the element *beine, byne,* or *bine*? I know of no satisfactory explanation of this form and until one is found the meaning of the name must remain obscure. Nor does there seem to be any probable connection between this form and Sant Ina of the Llandaff record. For the present the discussion must rest.

A mile or so nearer Cardiff than the old Rhiwbina was a hamlet known alternatively as *Nantwalla* (the Walla brook), *Rhydwalla* (Walla Ford) or *Rhyd Nantwalla* (Walla Brook Ford). This was near the locality today known as Beulah Corner, where the brook marked on the O.S. maps as Rhyd y Waedlyd Brook crosses the highway. *Rhyd y*

Waedlyd (bloody ford) was probably the ordnance surveyor's interpretation of Rhyd-y-Walla, and may have been suggested by the tradition that a great battle was fought in the locality.

The brook name Nantwalla probably applied to the Whitchurch Brook from time immemorial although I have not seen any instance of the name prior to 1702. Nantwalla commences near the Deri Farm where its two branches *Nant Nofydd* and *Briw-nant* meet. In the 18th century Briwnant was known as *Nant Castan*, 'castan' being the Welsh interpretation of 'chestnut.' This name probably arose from the prevalence at one time of chestnut trees along its banks.

I have been able to note the following examples of the use of the names Nant Walla and Rhyd Walla.

Ridd y Wathla (1702)
Rhydwarthla (1832)
Rydwarlla (1834)
Rhydd Wathley (1702)
Rhyd y Watley (1702)
Pont Rhyd y Wathla (1761)
Rhydwathla (1761, 1802)
Rhydywathle (1872)
Reed Wathla (1801)
Rhyd-Wallau (1847)
Rhydywalla (1847, 1866, 1888)
Rhydywalle (1860)
Rhydwalter (1862)
Ralph Warthla (1888)

Nant Waedlyd (1850)
Nantygwalor Bridge (1866)
Nantywalla (1868)
Nantywathle (1872)
Nant Walta (1874)
Nantrewaltha Bridge (1880)
Nantywalta (1866)
Nantwalla (1868, 1880)
Nant y Watla (1884)
Nanthydwathle (1872)
Nantrhydwalter (Beulah Trust Deed 1848)

The corruption of Wathla or Walla to Waedlyd seems to have taken place about the middle of last century—at any rate the first appearance I know of the name was on Rammell's Map of Cardiff 1850—but the latter name does not seem to have been commonly used by local residents.

A Welsh Nonconformist church historian writing in 1872 mentions a theory that Walla or Wathla or Wathle was a corruption of *Gwaedle* (bloody place) a name given to the near-by location of a supposed battlefield during the Cromwellian period.

In fact Nant Walla and Rhydywalla were commonly used until about 1910 when the opening of Rhiwbina Halt, on the Cardiff Railway, led to the extension of the Rhiwbina hamlet from the hill to the plain. Beulah Road was adopted by the Llandaff and Dinas Powis Rural District Council as a new name for Heol Rhydywalla as late as 1915.

Rhyd is the Welsh name for *ford*. What is the meaning of the element *walla* or *wathla*? The late Dr. Paterson, who made an exhaustive survey of Danish influences on Glamorgan place nomenclature suggested that the word is a derivative of an old Norse word *vadel*, *vaedill*, *vathill*, or *waethel*, ford, and that the name indicates an early Danish settlement in the locality.* If Paterson's theory is correct Rhydwalla is a pleonastic word compounded of a Welsh and a Norse element, both of which are equivalent to the English word *ford*. There is some ground for belief that Dr. Paterson has carried his Danish

---

* *Archaelogia Cambrensis* (June, 1921).

theory too far. It seems hardly likely that a settlement would have been made in those early days so far from the sea and so near the hill territory, and it would seem wise to suspend judgment in respect of this name, which has so distinctly a Welsh form and sound, until stronger evidence is available.

Two other names indicating districts of the Parish of Whitchurch are *Velindre* and *Melingriffith*. Both these words contain the Welsh word *melin*, a mill, and have references to a manorial mill on the left bank of the River Taff, so-called, it is believed, after Gruffydd ab Ifor, a 12th century Lord of Senghenydd. The element *tre* or *tref* in the name Velindre means a homestead or a hamlet. . Velindre was the name of the mansion of the Booker family which took the place of a farmhouse of the same name. The site is now included within the limits of the Mental Hospital. *Velindre Road* took its name from the old house.

It will have been noted that with the exception of the parish name Whitchurch all the names referred to have a Welsh form and origin. This characteristic also applies to practically all the older farm and street names in the district. and during recent years the Cardiff Rural District Council as a matter of policy have tried to maintain the Welsh tradition by utilizing old farm, field and other names relating to the locality in connection with new streets. A number of non-Welsh names were submitted by landowners and builders prior to the adoption of this policy, but during recent years the majority of new streets have been given names which relate to local topographical or other characteristics.

In the remainder of this chapter I propose to explain as far as I can the meanings of the farm and other names in use at the present time. A glance at a map will suffice to show that practically half of Whitchurch on the north side has not yet come under building development. It will, therefore, be convenient to deal with names in this area first.

Hill and stream names are usually the oldest in existence today. In the northern portion of the parish are the south-western scarps of a ridge known in medieval times as *Craig Kibbor* or *Cibwr*. From *Drainen-pen-y-Graig* (today better known as Thornhill, so-called after some ancient thorn tree or trees which no longer exist), westward extends *Twynau Gwynion*, the western slope of which constitute the Cardiff Corporation park, *Coed-y-Wenallt* (i.e. Wenallt Woods).

Twyn is a Welsh word for mound or hill and *gwyn* means white. These words compounded in plural form give us Twynau Gwynion or white hills. The adjoining spur *Wenallt* likewise is compounded of *wen* (a feminine form of *gwyn*) and *allt*, a wooded hill slope, and the name may be interpreted as the white wooded hill slope. The name Wenallt or in reversed form *Alltwen*, occurs freely throughout Wales, and is probably derived from the tints of flowers and foliage growing thereon.

Between Twynaugwynion and a more northerly ridge, *Cefn Carnau* (*Cefn*, ridge; *carnau*, stony mounds or rocks) lies the valley of *Cwm Nofydd*, an ancient name mentioned in the *Book of Llandav* in the form *Annouid*, the meaning of which yet remains to be determined. In Cwm Nofydd (*Come Nowith*, 1718), is an old farm of the same name, and a farm called Wenallt, and also there existed there until recently two tenements known as *Castell y Briwydd* and *Castell Nadda*. A field adjoining the last-mentioned tenement still bears the name *Cae Nadda*.

The latter structures were not military in any sense of the term and the term *castell* (castle) was possibly applied to them in satirical intent or perhaps in the figurative sense of an Englishman's home being his castle. Castell y Briwydd appears in an old estate map (circa 1800), but in an earlier map of 1761 it is referred to as Castle Brewer. *Briwydd* is a Welsh word meaning 'bedstraw.' In Cardiff Rural District Council reports of 1923-4 the property is called Castell Ffrwd, (i.e. the castle near the stream source).

Castell Nadda, also known as the Cwm, was a small bytake of the Rhiwbina Farm. I have not seen it mentioned in any record, and the name was given me by old inhabitants of the locality. Possibly the old name was Castell Adda, i.e., Adam's castle.

On the Rhiwbina ridge separating Cwm Nofydd from Cwm Gwynlais is a locality called *Bwlch y Cwm* (the Cwm pass), and some nearby cottages are called *Tan y bwlch* (below the pass). A small farm and a quarry in the same neighbourhood are called *Gelli*, whilst an adjacent modern house is named *Coedwig-dy*. Both the terms Gelli and Coedwig denote woodland, and could appropriately be described in English as The Grove or Copse.

Both slopes of Cwm Gwynlais consist of forest land. The farm near the source of the Gwynlais brook is called *Blaengwynlais*, *blaen* being a term meaning extremity. A short distance northward lies another farm called *Penybryn*, the 'hill summit.' This is spelt *Penybrin* in a Fonmon document of 1637.

Near the southern end of *Fforest Ganol* (the middle forest) lies *Coed Cefn Garw* (the woods on the rough stony ridge),,which gives its name to an adjoining quarry. Then nearer Tongwynlais on the east side of the valley, opposite the entrance to Castell Coch, lies a farm called *Ty Isaf* (the lower house). The farm immediately below Castell Coch is appropriately termed the Castle Farm.

The land east of Twynau Gwynion falls away sharply towards a shallow valley, which is drained by the *Briwnant* brook which serves as the boundary between the Parishes of Whitchurch and Llanishen. Two farms Briwnant and Briwnant Isaf (i.e. Lower Briwnant) derive their names from the brook. The name *Briwnant* literally means 'broken brook' and is perhaps so called because its banks are broken up by the swift flow of its waters. The course is characterised by sharp, short windings and much debris is carried down during periods of flood.*

Briwnant Isaf in 1761 contained about 39 acres and in 1800 about 36. Among its field names were *Erw'r Ffynnon* (the well enclosure) *Cae Bach* (little field), *Crofft Awst* (the August croft), *Cae Gwyn* (the white field), *Cae wrth y Ty* (field near the house), *Wern* and *Cae'r Wern* (*Gwern* a swampy meadow), *Arles* (alders), and *Gwaun Syr Edward* (Sir Edward's meadow). One of the fields in 1761 was called *Cae Tinker*, i.e. the tinker's field. Tinker was a favourite name for a horse in South Wales, and it may be that Cae Tinker was called after the horse which usually grazed therein.

* Or it may be a corrupted form of *Brwd Nant* (the hurrying brook) or *Bron Nant* (the brook rising on the breast of a hill).

Adjoining Briwnant Isaf formerly existed a small holding which is marked on the O.S. map as *Glanynant* (Brookside) but in 1800 bore the name *Ddwy-erw-anwyl* (the beloved two acres or fields).

We now come to the *Graig Farm*, the home of several generations of the Wride family. *Craig* means rock but is also commonly used to denote a hill side. I have not a complete list of field names on the farm and some of those I have are seemingly modern English substitutes for older Welsh names. These include Four Acre, Lily, Clover, Barn, Wood and Pool fields. The Welsh names are *Waun Gwlyb* (wet meadow), *Caeglas* (green field), and *Cae'r Draenen* (thorn field).

On the Llanishen side of the Briwnant brook boundary extending towards the Thornhill Road are *Deri Duon* (black oaks), near *Pentre Gwilym* (Gwilym's hamlet), *Pant Ysgawen* (elder-tree hollow), *Parc* (the park), *Ton Ysgubor Wen* (White Barn meadow) and *Llanishen Fach* (The Lesser Llanishen Farm).

The *Rhiwbina* Farm extends down to *Rhyd Nofydd* (the ford over the Nofydd brook) near the residence called Brooklyn where it joins up with the lands of a formerly larger farm—the *Deri*—which extended to Beulah Corner.

Amongst the Rhiwbina Farm field names are *Cae'r Fforest* (the forest field), *Cae'r Pant* (the sunken field), *Cae'r Llwyn Bach* (the field near the little copse), *Tire'r Ysgallog* (the thistle lands), *Tire Maen* (the stoney lands), *Pum Erw* (the five acres), *Chwech Erw Coed Newydd* (the plantation six acres), *Cae'r Graig* (the hill field), *Cae Noa* (?Noah's field). The two fields south of the Rhiwbina Reservoir are known as *Cae'r Celynen* (the holly field) and *Cae'r Efail* (the smithy field).

Between the upper section of the Deri and the Wenallt Road east of the Nofydd Brook lies a small holding with the elongated but charming name *Ynisyrysgallenfraith* (the water meadow of the speckled thistle). This occurs in the Whitchurch Parish Registers in 1853, as *Ynys yr Ysguthan fraith* (the river meadow of the spotted wood pigeon). The former name by which the farm is still known is, however, probably the correct form.

The *Deri* (Oak Tree) and a near-by cottage, *Bryn Derwen* (Oak Hill) obviously took their names from the ancient lightning-blasted oak which has been for centuries and still is one of the best-known landmarks in the Cardiff district. In addition to the land already described, to the Deri were attached some fields in Cwm Nofydd north of Ynisyrysgallenfraith, adjoining the Rhiwbina Reservoir. The names of Deri fields taken in succession from Rhyd Nofydd to Beulah Corner—most of which have been built over during recent years—were *Cae'r Efail* (the Smithy Field), *Cae'r Bont Garreg* (the stone bridge field), *Dwy Erw Uchaf* (the upper two acres or enclosures), *Pump Erw* (the five acres), and *Erw Pont Rhydwalla* (the Rhydwalla bridge enclosure).

East of the brook in the locality of the Butchers' Arms were the lands of *Ty'nycoed* (the woodland homestead) near which was an old cottage called *Tygwyn* (white house). In the field adjacent to All Saints' Church formerly stood the ancient *Deri Corn Mill*. Some fields adjoining Beulah Road on the south also belonged to Ty'nycoed, while others in Llanishen Parish now merged in Cardiff belonged to a holding known as *Penygroes* (the end of the cross roads). Near this tenement formerly existed a well-known spring known as *Ffynnon Hoba* (the swine well).

From the Deri and the Deri Mill and the adjoining brook and ford have been derived a number of modern street names, viz., *Maesyderi* (the oak meadow), *Lon y Deri* and *Lon-y-Dderwen* (oak lane), *Heol Derlwyn* and *Heolyderi* (Deri Road), *Heol-y-Felin* (Mill Road), *Min-y-Nant* (brook side), *Gernant* (near the brook), *Lonyrhyd* (ford lane), *Glanrhyd* (ford bank). A street leading from Rhiwbina railway bridge is appropriately named *Heolybont* (bridge road), and an adjoining street *Caerhys* (Rhys' field) perpetuates an ancient field name.

South of the hill towards the north of Rhiwbina is another ancient farm *Pantmawr* (great hollow or lowland), from which Pantmawr Road takes its name. This property at one time belonged to the Lewises of Van who disposed of it about 1760 to the family of Morgan of Tredegar, to whom it still belongs. In 1761 it had an area of about 83 acres, including woodland and a small bytake known as *Ty'r Efail* (the smithy land). The latter took its name from an ancient smithy which formerly stood at the junction of Pantmawr Road and Rhiwbina Hill and was known as *Efail John Jervis* (John Jervis's smithy). The bungalow, "Nestleton," now occupies the site of the old smithy.

Among the Pantmawr field names were *Tair Erw'r Berllan* (the orchard three acres), *Dwy Erw'r Ysgubor* (the two acres or enclosure adjoining the barn), *Tair Erw'r Nany Morse* (Nany Morse's three acres), *Pump Erw Grobos* (the crab-apple five acres or enclosure), *Pump Erw'r Daure*, *Cae Coch* (the red field), *Dwy Erw Grinion*, *Cae Gelynen* (the holly tree field), *Cae Cerrigog* (the stony field), *Tair Erw'r Graig* (three acres on the hillside), *Dwy Erw'r Ffawydden* (the beech-tree two acres) and *Cae'r Lloi* (the calves' field).

To the west of Pantmawr is a farm known as *Ffynnonwen* (the white or sparkling spring). At one time it was known as Pantbach (little hollow), but, perhaps in order to avoid confusion with another farm of the same name in the Parish, the name was changed over a century ago to that which the farm now bears. The spring was probably near the farmhouse, although some people connect the farm name with the prolific spring which issues from the foot of the Graig alongside the footpath leading from Rhiwbina to Greenmeadow.

Among the field names of Ffynnonwen were *Hendre* (the old homestead), *Cae'r Coed* (wood field), *Pedwar Erw'r Dderwen* (the oak-tree four acres), *Cae'r Lloi* (the calves' field), *Tair Erw* (three acres), *Cae draw'r heol* (the field across the road) and *Cae'r Marl* (the marly field) The last named field was probably so-called by reason of the marly nature of the soil. This characteristic probably accounts for the name *Pant-y-Marl* (the marly hollow) which still applies to an old near-by cottage at the entrance to the Whitchurch Golf Course.

The land to the south of Pantmawr Road adjoining Rhiwbina Hill, now forming the upper section of the Golf Course, seems at one time to have formed a separate holding, the homestead being in the extreme south-east corner adjoining the Rhiwbina Hill access to the

Long Wood. The boundary wall of this old homestead still stands. I have heard old inhabitants say that this farm was formerly known as *Pwll-y-Wenci Fach*. In 1760, however, it was a small holding containing six enclosures totalling 23 acres and was known as *Tir Bess* (*i.e.* Bess's land). The field opposite Efail John Jervis was called *Cae'r Efail*. By 1800 Tir Bess had been added to Ffynnonwen.

The Whitchurch Golf House was formerly the homestead of *Pentwyn Ucha Farm*, the lands of which extended eastwards towards Heolyderi and southward to the public footpath leading from Beulah towards Whitchurch Railway Station. In 1761 it belonged to a family named Jones (possibly of Fonmon). Pentwyn Ucha may be translated "the upper hilltop farm."

Scarcely a stone's throw from Pentwyn on the opposite side of Pantmawr Road stands a farm-house known as Ashgrove. It comprised lands on both sides of the western end of Pantmawr Road; the southern portion extended as far as the Mental Hospital entrance, and there were also four enclosures adjoining the present-day Pantmawr Cemetery.

Ashgrove was known in 1760 and in 1800 as *Pentwyn Isaf* (lower Pentwyn), and comprised about 57 acres. Amongst the field names were *Cae'r Ynn* (the field of the ash-trees), whence the modern street name Pantyrynn, *Cae'r Barra* (the bread field, that is, the cornfield), *Cae'r Coed* (the woodland field), *Saith Erw'r Ysgubor* (the seven acres near the barn), *Berw pwll* (possibly the water-cress pool), *Dwy Erw'r Ysgubor Ddegwm* (the two acres opposite the tithe barn). The old tithe barn formerly stood adjoining the entrance to the Mental Hospital.

The inn known as the Hollybush is of ancient origin—it was certainly in being in 1828—and probably took its name from a near-by tenement known as Llwyncelyn. The new street name *Pantycelyn* (hollytree hollow) perpetuates this ancient name in a modified form.

Where now stands Greenhill—a residence built by a member of the Booker family—at one time stood a farmhouse called *Pwll-y-Wenci* (the weasel's pool), which was called after a still existing pool in its vicinity which continues to be a popular haunt of weasels and stoats. The ancient name is perpetuated in a new cul-de-sac street called *Lon-y-Wenci*.

South of the Greenhill estate where two new streets—*Heolycoed* (woodland road) and *Heolybryn* (the hillside road)—have been developed during recent years, lies the Rhiwbina Garden Village, which was commenced on Pentwyn land in 1912. There, largely as a result of the influence of one of the founders, Professor W. J. Gruffydd, all the new streets bear Welsh names, none of which, however, arise from local associations. These names are *Lon Ucha* and *Lon Isa* (the upper and lower lanes), *Heolwen* (the white way), *Lon-y-Dail* (the leafy way), *Y Groes* (the crossway), *Pen-y-dre* (the end of the village), and *Lon Fach* (little lane).

Adjoining Rhiwbina Halt is an old farmstead known as *Ty'nycaeau* (the homestead in the fields), from which the local street name *Heol Tynycae* is derived. On the south-west fringe of this farm formerly existed a woollen factory or mill carried on by the Lewis family. The street name *Maesyfelin* (mill field) is called after this mill, whilst the adjoining road *Heolynant* is so called from its proximity to the brook.

Tynyparc Road got its name from a very ancient homestead, recently demolished, known as *Ty'nyparc* (the homestead in the park), the lands of which probably formed part of the demesne of the mediaeval lords of the manor of Whitchurch. The portion of Tynyparc Road extending from the farmhouse towards Pantbach Road is probably of fairly modern construction—it is not at any rate shown on Yates' Map of Glamorgan (1791), and may have been made after the establishment of the factory. Old inhabitants inform me that the extended section of Tynyparc Road was formerly known as *Heol-yr-wyddfa*, a name which apparently means 'the road leading to the loom place.' This seems to be confirmed by an entry in a Llandaff Highway Record of 1878 which refers to this road as Heol y Wrytha (this form being apparently a misspelling of *wyddfa*).

On the east side of Pantbach Road—so called from an old farm *Pantbach* (little hollow)—in continuation of Heol yr Wyddfa is Tywern Road. This takes its name from a farm called *Tywern* (the house in the swampy land) which, however, in the older O.S. maps is called *Tir Winch*. *Winch* is a term frequently used in Glamorgan to denote wet or marshy land, and may be regarded as synonymous with the term *wern* (a mutated form of gwern). The old approach to this farm was from Caerphilly Road. The highway terminated at the Philog stream, from which a footpath continued to the Pantbach Road. Tywern Road did not apparently become a through road until about fifty years ago.

A recently developed building estate known as the Homelands formed part of a farm known as *Ty Pantyrywen* (yew-tree hollow house) which was alternatively known as far back as 1764 and until quite recent years, as *Tir Pwdr* (rotten land). This farm in the 18th century comprised eight enclosures, in addition to the house and garden, and extended from *Rhydywalla* to a point a little south of St. Thomas's Church, its eastern boundary being the stream. Beyond the stream was the Great Heath or Mynydd Bychan, part of which, however, adjoining the modern Phoenix Brickworks, seems to have been encroached on prior to the Enclosure Act of 1801. The modern road known as *Llwynbedw* on this estate is the Welsh form of Birchgrove.

Amongst the old field names of Typantyrywen were *Cae'r Barra* (the bread or corn field), on part of which today stands the Monico Cinema, *Waunfawr* (the great meadow), *Dwy Erw Bodor* (Pwdr), (the rotten two acres), and *Dwy Erw Isaf* (the lower Two Acres).

West of Pantbach Road and south east of Tynyparc extending to the Whitchurch Common were the lands of *Gwaen* (*Gwaun* or *Waun Treoda Uchaf*) Farm, the homestead of which was in the immediate vicinity of Ararat Chapel. In 1760 this farm comprised 10 enclosures with a total area of about 49 acres. This land during recent years has been developed as the Greenclose Estate.

Amongst its field names were *Cae Gwyn*, (the white field) whence Caegwyn Road, *Dwy Erw Gofion* (possibly the two acres of the smiths),

Tair Erw Meinon (perhaps the stony three acres), *Pedair Erw Mynydd* (the four acres near Mynydd Bychan), *Pedair Erw Pwdr* (the rotten four acres), *Wyth Erw* (the eight acres), and *Caeau Garwon* (*geirwon*) the rough fields.

At the south-west corner of Whitchurch Common stands an old homestead known to-day as *Cornel y Waun* (at the corner of the common) or Wauntreoda Court, but which in the 18th century bore the name *Wauntreoda Isaf* (Lower Wauntreoda). In 1760 it comprised enclosures on both sides of the brook and had an area of 47½ acres. Amongst its field names were *Gadda Hir* (perhaps 'cae, da hir' the long good field, the long cattle field), *Chwech Erw* (the six acres), *Tair Erw Graig* (the hillside three acres), *Saith Erw* (the seven acres), *Tair Erw* (the three acres), *Erw Llefrith* (the sweet milk enclosure), *Dwy Erw'r Felin* (the two acres adjoining the mill, i.e. Little Mill). Some remains of the Little Mill still exist. It was worked in 1837 by a miller called John Harding.

Until about half a century ago, Whitchurch village proper comprised two distinct divisions known as the Old or Upper Village (in the vicinity of the old church and schools) and the Lower Village in the Merthyr Road. Much of the area in the village was in the nature of accommodation land farmed out to different people—tradesmen and others—but having no separate farmhouses and farm buildings. *Pentref* (or the Village) Farm—the home of one of the Wride families—comprised lands in the Lower Village with outlying portions in College Road and elsewhere. Some living residents of Whitchurch recall Barry Wride cultivating his land with ploughs drawn by black oxen.

Near the Upper Village in Tynyparc Road stood as now the *Glanynant* (Brookside) Farm. This farm extended westward as far as the Whitchurch Library, and seems to have comprised lands owned by the Morgans of Tredegar and by the Richards family. On the 1760 Tredegar Estate map Glanynant is denoted as *Foreland* from which the modern street name Foreland Road has been derived. Foreland was an anglicised form of *Forlan* (itself possibly a mutated form of the Welsh *Morlan*) which gave its name to *Heol-y-Forlan* sometimes today stupidly called New Station Road.

The name Forlan is a very intriguing one, for which a satisfactory solution has not yet been obtained. In two Ewenny Documents of 1679-1680 and 1690-1, mention is made of an area of 30 acres forming part of a tenement called *The Furlongs* in the Parish of Whitchurch and which appears to refer to the Glanynant Farm of today. The name may be an Anglicised form of *Y Forlan*, a name which also applies to a farmstead on the Lesser Garth. In its unmutated form the term also occurs in farm names *Morlanga* at Merthyr Tydfil and near Peterston-super-Ely, *Morland*, a field at Boverton, and at other places in several South Wales counties.

I have heard several theories advanced in explanation of the Whitchurch name:

 1. That it comes from *Mor* (Norway) or *Moerr* (a portion of the Norse coast) followed by *land*. This is advanced as additional evidence of a Scandinavian settlement in the locality.

2. That morlan is compounded of *mor* (an accentuated form of *mawr*, great or big, and *lan* meaning upland. This explanation might well explain the Garth name but seems hardly applicable to flat level land such as that in Whitchurch, although Mynydd Bychan (little mountain) at a similar level is not far away.

3. That the name comes from O.N. or O.E. *mor* (moor or heath) applied to wet land by the water side, plus *glan*, river bank.

Morlan, normally means seashore and is frequently used by Welsh people today in the reversed form *Glan-y-mor* on the brink or bank of the sea. Obviously this interpretation does not apply to the Whitchurch name. Is it possible that the term *morlan* was also occasionally used to denote not only the seashore but also the sides of rivers and streams? If so it would be the exact equivalent of Glanynant, a name which exactly fits the land with which we are dealing. In 1760 the two fields alongside the Whitchurch Brook were known as *Dwy Erw Glanynant* (the two acres by the brook side) and *Cae Glanynant* (the brookside field), and the field name Glanynant seems to have been substituted for Y Forlan as the farm name early last century.

5. The most likely theory is that the original form of Forlan was Furlong, a name which was Latinised in medieval times to Furlongus and subsequently Cymricised to the present form. In the Middle Ages land was not usually enclosed, and cultivation was based on what is known as the 'three field system.' Large areas of land were divided into three large divisions or 'fields' and farmed on a three years' rotation; winter corn, spring corn and fallow. Two-thirds also of the land was always under the plough, and the field in fallow was generally used as common pasture.

Each field was subdivided into smaller divisions called *furrows* (a term derived from 'furrow long') or 'shots'. The holdings of the several tenants were scattered over different furrows, each of them having a series of parallel strips of an acre or half acre in extent, each strip being one furlong in length.

The name 'furlong' still exists in field names in many parts of the country, and in the 14th century the modern village of Penmaen in Gower was known as Worlangus (or Forlangus). Many modern farm names, e.g., Forlan (Pentyrch), Morlanga (Peterston), etc., may well have been derived from the 'furlong' element of the medieval system of cultivation.

In addition to the two field names mentioned above there were on *Y Forlan*, *Dwy Erw Uchaf* (the upper two acres), *Dwy Erw Nesaf* (the next two acres) and *Tair Erw* (three acres), the three comprising a block of nine acres of land bounded on the west by the footpath leading from Heol-y-Forlan towards Rhiwbina. This group of fields viewed on the O.S. map closely resembles a Welsh harp (telyn) and were known to local farmers as *Erwi'r Delyn* (the harp-fields). Hence the application of the name *Cae-Delyn* to the new street adjoining Whitchurch Station.

Other field names were *Erw Bach* (the small enclosure), *Erw Pellaf* (the farthest enclosure). Three fields abutting on Heolyforlan north of The Pines and the ancient churchyard were Cae'r Moat (the moat field, adjoining a supposed Roman camp), *Dwy Erw* (two acres) and *Dwy Erw*

Heol y Forlan, whilst two others west of them adjoining Ty-nypwll Road and the county high road were known as *Dwy Erw Feinon* (possibly the stony two acres) and *Pump Erw* (five acres).

Ty'nypwll Road took its name from the still existing farm of *Ty'nypwll*. This name occurs in an Ewenny Document of 1714 as *Ty yn y Pwll* in association with another tenement called *Ty du* (black house). Ty'n is probably a contraction of *tyddyn* (homestead) and Ty'nypwll probably means the homestead near the pool. Ty'nypwll lands extended across to the west side of Penlline Road (so called after the name of the estate).

Its lands marched with those of an ancient farm indicated on a map of 1791 as *Rowldon* (i.e. Yr Heol Don). The farmhouse still stands at the northern end of Heoldon and took its name from that of the road which was an ancient lane, probably a mere cart track, passing through a series of green fields over which a public right of way had been acquired. From its northern end the right of way continued across Velindre Road and then by means of a footpath across three fields to a point near the old Tithe Barn, by the Mental Hospital Lodge. The latter footpath was diverted to points nearer the cross roads at the request of the Cardiff Corporation in return for a gift of land to the Whitchurch Parish Council for the purposes of a public library and recreation ground.

Now what is the origin of the name Heoldon? *Ton* is a common component of Welsh place names and means 'meadow land.' Can it be, therefore, that Heol Don means the road across the green meadows and is equivalent to the common Welsh road name Heol-las or Ffordd-las meaning the green road or way? The name seems analogous to a Caernarvonshire name *Y Donnen Las*, the green surface. Or may the element *don* in the local name be associated with the Welsh word *doniog*, meaning 'bestowed,' 'given' or perhaps 'dedicated?' There is also a third alternative that it may have come from a word *ton*, meaning a wave, this term being suggested by the corrugated character of the road in question. It has also been suggested to me that there was an ancient word *don* meaning 'upper,' and that Heoldon means the 'upper road' to distinguish it from the older and lower road which runs past Melingriffith. Until more data is available in regard to ancient forms, however, the exact meaning of the name must remain a mystery.

The Velindre Road led from the Cross Roads towards Melingriffith, and near the entrance to the Works a branch forked in a north-westerly direction along the left bank of the River Taff to the Fforest Farm near which there was a ford giving connection by a public right of way to Radyr. Near this point the ford was also approached by another but more involved cart road across the Fforest Farm from Tongwynlais. Both these roads seem to have borne the name Heol y Fforest. It seems likely that the *Fforest* Farm was at one time mostly woodland.

From Melingriffith the Velindre Road continued past *Tymawr* (Great House) and Primrose Hill to Llandaff North where it connected with two river crossings to Llandaff and Radyr, one over Llandaff Bridge and the other across the ancient Radyr Ford. The land between Heoldon and the river belonged to the foregoing Tymawr Farm—once the home of a branch of the Mathews of Radyr, ancestors of a former Lord Llandaff—

Penylan (upland), and *Gelli* (The Grove). Tymawr (Great House) still stands, although its lands have been mostly developed.

Penylan ceased to be a farmhouse many decades ago, and was converted into workmen's cottages which were demolished at the instance of the Cardiff Rural District Council some years since. In 1760 it was a holding of about 31 acres, comprising nine enclosures, some of which bore the following names:—*Erw'r Fforest* (the Fforest enclosure), *Caeau Heoldon* (the Heoldon fields), *Tair Erw* (three acres), *Crofft* (the croft, adjoining the house), *Graig* (the hill field) and *Cae'r Ty Mawr* (the field near Tymawr). In a Fonmon Castle document of 1637 mention is made of a messuage and lands at Whitchurch called the *Crofte* and the foregoing field name suggests that Penylan may at one time have been known by this name. I have evidence that the Joneses of Fonmon at one time owned land in this locality. Penylan was, however, known by that name in 1714.

South of Penylan and abutting on Heoldon and its continuation towards Llandaff—the Taff Vale railway had not then been constructed — were eight fields comprising 26¾ acres belonging to Gelli, the farmstead of which was in the vicinity of Llandaff Station. Amongst the field names were *Cae'r Ffawydden* (the beech-tree field), *Cae Tymawr* (the field adjoining Tymawr), *Gelly* and *Dan y Gelly* (below the Gelli). Llandaff Station and the adjoining shopping centre now stand on the last-named field.

The land north of Velindre Road extending towards Tongwynlais, now the property of the Cardiff Corporation Mental Hospital Committee, seems formerly to have belonged to the Bookers of Melingriffith. In addition to the private lands of Velindre House were farm holdings known as *Tyclyd* (the warm, sheltered or comfortable house), *Llwyn Mallt* (Maud's Grove) and some minor tenements such as *Pwll-helyg* (willow-pool) and Pendwyallt.

Pendwyallt (summit of two wooded hill slopes) seems to have been a cottage holding attached to Tyclyd. In a map of 1760 the homestead is denoted as *Ty Poeth* (the hot house), but in a will of 1708 it is called *Pendowallt*. It appears in the Church Registers of 1846 and 1848 as *Pendwall*. In the 18th century the holding comprised about 16 acres distributed over five enclosures, all on the east side of the Merthyr Road adjoining Pentwyn Isaf land. The farmstead however, was on the west side of the highway and still stands. Among its field names were *Dwy Erw* (two acres), *Dwy Erw Uchaf* (the upper two acres), *Tair Erw* (three acres) and *Tair Erw Bellaf* (the further three acres).

Llwynmallt is a very old farm It appears in Fonmon Castle documents in several forms, viz , Loyne Mallt (1652), Llwyne Mallt (1697), Lloyne Mallt (1697), Lloine Malt (1698), and Llwyne Mallt (1698). It comprised an area of 70 acres, and in connection with it reference is made to two closes of land (11 acres) called *Kae John Kett* (John Kett's field) and *Kae yr ywen issa* (the lower yew-tree-field), but I am unable to indicate their position. Mallt is a Welsh female personal name equivalent to the English Maud or Matilda, and Llwyn Mallt would appear to mean 'Maud's grove.'

CHAPTER XXVII.

ANCIENT LOCAL FOLKLORE.

People of the Cymric race have ever been prone to belief in the supernatural, and for this reason Welsh legendary folklore has much interest for students of local history and sociology. In the more rural and isolated parts of Wales many people still believe in black and white magic, in death omens, in ghostly visitations, in demonology, but it is probable that in highly industrialised areas such as Glamorgan the spread of popular education has, except in rare cases, dissipated such beliefs, although a generation ago they were freely held by a substantial proportion of the population. Even the Cardiff area provided examples of various forms of superstition, and in this article I propose to record some of the 'old wives' tales' that were freely told and accepted as truth in the days of long ago.

Throughout Wales people used to believe in the *Cwn Annwn* (Dogs of the Under World), which were supposed to be sent from Hell to seek corpses. They were usually encountered by credulous people at dead of night, and generally after a death in the locality. The *Cwn Annwn* were spirit hounds which belonged to Arawn the Grey Huntsman, King of the Hell Abyss. They were sometimes said to have been seen, but more frequently only heard, by highly imaginative people in remote places, and they hunted, sometimes singly but usually in packs, either led or driven by their demon master, or occasionally by a ghostly hag known as *Mallt y Nos* (Maud of the Night).

The Neath, Rhondda and Taff Valleys were favourite hunting grounds of these fearsome visitants, which often appeared on the eves of religious festivals and rent the night stillness with horrible howls. In some localities the appearance of the *Cwm Annwn* was regarded as an augury of imminent disaster, sickness or death to those who saw or heard them or to some important family in the neighbourhood.

Fforest Fawr, the woods adjoining Castell Coch, was supposed to be a popular resort of these terrible and mysterious demons, and numerous tales were locally rife concerning them. Usually the *Cwn Annwn* of Castell Coch were under the control of *Mallt y Nos*. She was supposed to have been a Norman lady of the Conquest period who had, whilst living, such a passion for hunting, that she once declared that if there was no hunting in heaven she would prefer to go to Hell. For this rash declaration her soul was cursed, and she was condemned to hunt for all eternity.

She was reputed to have repented bitterly of her ancient sin, and her piteous wailing as she bemoaned her fate was clearly heard above the howls of the demon hounds as they hunted in the Fforest. Not far from Castell Coch, near the road to Whitchurch, stands a farm called *Llwyn Mallt* (Maud's Grove), and I have heard it suggested that some credulous people believed that this homsetead derived its name from the Norman lady.

One version of this local legend mentions the dogs as flying through the air, in which case they were known as *Cwn Wybyr* (Sky Hounds). In another version the Fforest hound was a seven-headed creature which used to pursue ghostly wolves in the Greenmeadow woods. In quite recent times a spectral hound—a huge black beast with fierce glaring eyes—was represented as prowling the locality of Greenmeadow and Llwyn Mallt, to the terror of passers-by. This was probably the alleged "fierce, foul and awful apparition," which, on one occasion in 1860, is said to have so badly frightened the members of the Melingriffith Band returning from a supper at Greenmeadow that they threw away their instruments and scattered for their lives. The spectral hound belief was probably an attenuated survival of the *Cwn Annwn* superstition.

Another local ghostly visitant, whose appearance was supposed to foreshadow death, was a weird spectral hag known as *Gwrach y Rhibyn*, which may be regarded as a Welsh equivalent of the Irish *banshee*. This creature also appeared in various parts of Wales. Dr. Gwyn Jones describes the spectre as the 'roof ghost.' In Cardiganshire, it seems, *rhibyn* is the term given to the ridge of a roof, whilst *gwrach y rhibyn* was the name applied to the roll of fern and straw laid along the ridge to form a core for the saddle of a thatched roof.

The spectral *Gwrach* was a dark ugly form, with long black hair and sunken, piercing eyes, and clothed in flowing robes. The creature also had wings which she flapped against the window panes of the houses which she haunted. During her flights around the houses she gave vent to fearsome howls and weird screeches.

Spectral hags of this class were reputed to frequent the Nant-y-Gledyr swamp near Caerphilly Castle, also St. Donats Castle and Beaupre. A local *Gwrach y Rhibyn* used to appear, according to popular belief, at Llandaff just before the death of members of a family called Llewelyn, which, it was said, occupied the Cow and Snuffers Inn for a period of three hundred years. The flying screeching hag, after completing her evolutions around the inn, finally disappeared through one of the inn windows.

A mysterious spectral animal, somewhat akin to the Scottish *kelpie*, was the ubiquitous *Ceffyl Dwr* (Water Horse). This picturesque creature was reputed to frequent banks of rivers and streams and marshy meadows. Sometimes its appearance was believed to herald death by drowning. In other cases, having enticed an unwary person to mount its back, it soared into the sky and disappeared into thin air, casting its rider to destruction. It was commonly believed that nobody but a clergyman could ride a water-horse with safety.

These creatures were supposed to be plentiful in the Vale of Neath and also in Duffryn Golych south of St. Nicholas village. I have also heard vague rumours that a *Ceffyl Dwr* used to frequent the banks of the Taff between Gwaun-Treoda and Mynachdy and of neighbouring streams, and it has been suggested that the name Philog (or filiog) was derived from some fancied connection with the water horse, an archaic Welsh word *ffulawg* apparently being a term for a young mare or filly.

Perhaps the most interesting as well as the most widespread and popular of the old folk tales of Wales were those relating to the appearances of weird, ghostly bodies of various colours and forms. The most general of these beliefs was in the *Ladi Wen* (the White Lady). Belief in the *Ladi Wen* was fairly common a couple of generations ago and in my boyhood the *Ladi Wen* and the *Bwci Bo* were fearful creatures who used to be on constant prowl for naughty boys.

The Ladi Wen used to be mentioned in our childish songs; one of these songs I well remember. It ran as follows:
Ladi Wen ar ben y pren,
Yn naddu coes ymbrelo.
 Mae'n un o'r gloch,
 Mae'n ddau o'r gloch,
 Mae'n bryd i'r moch gael cinio.
The following is a rough translation of this verse "The white lady is on the tree top, cutting an umbrella handle. It's one o'clock; it's two o'clock; it's time for the pigs to have dinner."

I also remember the consternation amongst children of my age and locality when the report went around that a *Ladi Wen* had made frequent appearances in the neighbourhood. Women and children and indeed many men were terrified by the supposed appearance, and some of the braver men of the locality set themselves the task of way-laying the ghost. After attempts extending over several nights they succeeded in their quest, and great relief was felt when the *Ladi Wen* proved to be a well-known local character nicknamed Twm Pwnch, who had clothed himself in his mother's night-dress and made sudden appearances before timid people, with a view to hoaxing the community. Twm was severely chastised for masquerading as *Ladi Wen*, and for many years afterwards, and possibly even today, nearly half a century later, the following couplet was sung by the children of the district, viz.:
'Twm Pwnch y Ladi Wen,
Crys i fam a cwshwn ben.'
'Cwshwn ben' was the colloquial term for the then fashionable woman's bustle—cushion or Grecian bend.

Practical jokes of the Twm Pwnch class were not uncommon in those days. The tale is still told at Tongwynlais of such a joker who in 1876 terrorised night wayfarers near Coryton by suddenly appearing and making fearful leaps into the air, shrieking horribly as he did so. An organised effort was made to catch this terrible creature, and ultimately a capture was effected, the culprit proving to be a local mischief-making body who had fitted springs to his heels. Needless to say this 'Spring-Heel Jack' met with the same reward as Twm Pwnch.

The general theory underlying the appearance of spectral ladies—whether white or grey or green or black in colour—was that the spirit of a dead woman, more or less beautiful, was held in bondage by an evil influence, and that her manifestations to human beings was for the purpose of appealing for aid to release her from her thraldom.

Such release could be effected by certain charms such as the kiss of a new-born babe or the firm hand-clasp of a pure-minded man. The unfortunate ladies, it was said, used to beckon or make similar signs to human beings for help, but their appearance usually frightened the persons accosted, so that in very few cases did their appeal meet with a favourable response.

Pentyrch residents of olden days were great believers in fairies, ghosts, corpse candles, phantom funerals and similar apparitions. Corpse candles (*canwyll corph*) and phantom funerals were said to be portents of imminent deaths in the locality. Phantom funerals were met usually at specified points; there were two or three such points at Pentyrch, and the Deri (Rhiwbina) was another place where such phenomena were stated to have been seen.

At Pentyrch *Y Brenin Llwyd* (King of the Mist) was believed to live in the old iron ore mine in the Lesser Garth, whilst on All Hallow's Eve the *Bendith y Mamau* (fairies) used to dance all night through in the woods in Cwm Llwydrew. A *Ladi Wen* also used to haunt the latter locality, and another at Castell Mynach, the old Mathew homestead at Creigiau, and were very much feared. This fear is expressed in the following rhyme which used to be sung in the locality:

>John Jones, cau dy ben,
>Paid a holi'r Ladi Wen,
>Neu daw barn ar dy ben

(John Jones, shut your mouth, never question a White Lady, or judgment will rest on your head).

A *Ladi Wen* was also said to appear by the old Whitchurch Tithe Barn, which formerly stood near to the present entrance gates of the Mental Hospital. A short distance away from this barn in the Tyclyd woods near the canal side, alongside the footpath leading from Melingriffith to Tongwynlais, there is a spring which has long been known as the White Lady's Well, which was also reputed to be a haunt of this unfortunate spirit. A stone placed in the water of this well was supposed to take on a reddish hue, due, it was said, to the blood of a maiden who had been stabbed in the locality by a jealous lover.

The red colour was, of course, probably due to the spring water being strongly impregnated with iron oxide. Nevertheless the spring bore until recently the reputation of being a haunt of the *Ladi Wen* and local youngsters always fought shy of the place after darkness fell. A *Ladi Wen* tale associated with the Radyr Ford differed from most others by reason of the fact that the White Lady rode a white horse.

The at one time lonely road from the Tithe Barn to Tongwynlais seems to have been haunted by other ghosts than those of the *Ladi Wen* type. One of the stories relates to the ghost of a man called Draper who is supposed to have committed suicide early in the 19th century by hanging himself to a rafter in the Tithe Barn. About 1866 considerable local commotion was caused by the presence of a reputed ghost in the same neighbourhood, which was seen by various people on the highway and in the local fields and woods over a period of a couple of months. A ghost hunt was at last organised, and the alleged ghost turned out to be a poor insane woman who went out at night even in the most inclement weather.

Spectral ladies used frequently to haunt wells and springs, especially those which were reputed to have medicinal properties or to be associated with the names of ancient saints. Throughout Wales there are scores of wells the waters of which were deemed to possess special properties for the cure of diseases or bodily defects, e.g., weak eyesight, rheumatism, scrofula, etc., whilst others possessed the magical power of realising the wishes of people drinking of them. The drinking of the water was in some cases preceded by the simple ceremony of dropping a pin—sometimes a straight one, sometimes a bent one—into the water, and in other instances by hanging a garment on a bush in the vicinity.

There were several reputed healing wells and at least one wishing well in the neighbourhood of Cardiff. Of the former type may be mentioned a formerly well-known well near Radyr Quarry, known as *Pistyll Goleu* (Sparkling Fountain), the water of which was supposed to be efficacious in cases of rheumatism, and *Ffynnon Bren*, a spring in a former cottage garden adjoining Albany Road, immediately opposite the entrance to Claude Road. The water of Ffynnon Bren was supposed to cure the sore eyes of persons bathing them therein. Not far away from Ffynnon Bren near Tygwyn Road was the very popular Penylan Wishing Well. There was also a reputed eye well within Fforest Goch, at a very short distance from Castell Coch entrance gates.

Several local wells had ghost stories associated with them, similar to that which attached to the Lady's Well at Melingriffith. There is, for example, that of the Grey Lady which is reputed to have frequented the medicinal spring at Taffs Well. This poor creature was, according to popular superstition, permitted to manifest herself at certain specified times for the purpose of enlisting the aid of some young man who would be bold enough to clasp her hand unflinchingly for a sufficient length of time to force away the evil spirit who held her soul in bondage. It is not recorded that anybody was courageous enough, or chivalrous enough, to attempt her rescue.

The Grey Lady of Llanishen was supposed to have frequented *Ffynnon Denis*, a holy well now enclosed in Roath Park, which was reputed to be efficacious as a specific for sore eyes, rheumatism and scorbutic complaints. There used also to be a Grey Lady of Crockherbtown which used to patrol the highway from the Spital Cottage (near the Capitol Cinema) to Canton Bridge, where she would stand and signal, and then disappear.

The Penylan wishing well stood on the Tygwyn Farm, and was much visited, especially at Easter, by young couples who desired the realisation of their aspirations. According to an old imhabitant's account the well took the form of

'A bowl about six inches in diameter with a lip that was supposed to be the impression of Jesus Christ's knee. The water emerged from the rock and was walled over. On Easter Monday, a large number of people wended their way thither to drop bent pins into the well.'*

It is stated that at times the bowl was nearly filled with bent pins, each pin representing the current wish of the person who deposited it in the well.

In the early part of the 19th century the well was believed to be haunted by the Black Lady of Penylan, whose pitiful moans and wails are reputed to have frightened away all but the most daring. It is recorded that one brave man held his ground when approached by the Black Lady and asked her why she was troubled. She replied that she was held in bondage by an evil spirit, and could be freed only if a man of courage gripped her waist firmly and in perfect silence.

The man is stated to have responded to the Black Lady's appeal, and attempted her rescue. He had not, however, sufficient endurance to break the spell, for immediately he clasped her body he was seized with intense pain in his arms that he cried aloud and was forced to release his grip. Whereupon the Black Lady gave vent to loud despairing shrieks, for the failure meant that she was condemned to a further 200 years of bondage, and then disappeared.

There used also to be a Black Lady at Boverton in the Vale of Glamorgan, whilst, in the early days of Cardiff's commercial development, a similar spectre was said to frequent the vicinity of the old Sea Lock. This Black Lady of the Taff used to manifest herself to sea-faring folk, usually wringing her hands and making imploring signs. The story goes that at last, after many efforts, she prevailed on a daring and kindly sailor to row her in a boat to the mouth of the Ely River.

As the voyage progressed the cargo appeared to grow heavier and heavier until the boat was in danger of sinking. At the Black Lady's entreaty the boatman hurriedly pulled towards the western bank of the river, and landed near the woods. The Black Lady beckoned the man to follow her to a large stone to which she pointed, and then vanished for ever. Beneath the stone the boatman is stated to have found a large crock filled to the brim with gold coins.

Such tales of treasure obtained as the result of ghostly directions are not uncommon. One such story had currency in Whitchurch less than half-a-century ago. At that time near Penylan Farm on Velindre Road stood a tree known as Llewelyn's Tree. A youth is stated one evening to have disappeared from his home. He was seen proceeding towards this tree with a dog-shaped spectral figure and then disappeared. On his return home some days later he would not utter a word as to his whereabouts and doings during his period of absence, but local rumour has it that he was from this period so well supplied with funds that it was unnecessary for him ever to work again.

Spirit ladies sometimes appeared in a garb of green, and several Green Ladies are locally recorded. The Green Lady of Marcross seems to have haunted a well-known eye well in that neighbourhood. Perhaps the best known local example was the Green Lady of Caerphilly Castle. She was reputed to have red, googly eyes set in a very large head,

* See *Cardiff Records*, vol. vi.

which glared wickedly at people. She wore a close, clinging green garment with a long flowing green veil over her shoulders, and is stated to have had the power of merging herself in the ivy which at that time covered the castle walls. She usually appeared alone, but at times was said to have been accompanied by a mailed warrior, a member of the family of the De Clare who built the Castle.

The Green Lady of the Garth was another distressed damsel who besought assistance from human beings to release her from an evil thraldom. She is stated to have approached many people, all of whom fled from her in terror. At last two men stopped in response to her entreaty, and she offered them large hoards of gold which she guarded if they would help to set her free. Failing their assistance there would not be a man born for another century who could help her. On their declining through fear to help her she vanished and was never afterwards seen.

There are other tales of female spirits not associated with colours. For example the Frog Woman of Llandaff was said to haunt the banks of the River Taff above and below the Weir. She moved by a series of jumps like a frog and croaked like the same animal. The legend ran that the Frog Woman was the ghost of a lady of good family who had, because of mental and bodily defects, been put out for adoption in the home of an agricultural labourer near Llandaff. One night she fell into the river and was drowned, and her ghost used to haunt the banks of the river on moonlit nights.

There were numerous myths associated with the Rivers Taff and Ely. Near the mouth of the Taff there used, it is said, to be a whirlpool which was deemed to be fathomless. This pool was reputed to be haunted by a lovely water lady who lured youths bathing in the river towards the vortex, into which they disappeared, their bodies never being recovered.

The lovely lady was in fact deemed to be a serpent who dwelt in the depths of the whirlpool and who lived on the bodies of unfortunate victims of drowning fatalities. It was sometimes believed that the whirlpool was one of the communications with the door of Hell. Similar beliefs were held concerning the Berw Pool at Pontypridd and of another pool near Cefn (Merthyr). There was also a belief that dead fish used to come up the Taff at full moon tides. A fisherman at Penarth Road is stated to have harpooned such a fish on one occasion. It emitted instead of blood a thick, black fluid which smelt of fire and brimstone.

Another interesting tale is that of the Devil of the Ely River. The story goes that a boatman was drowned in the river, and that his ghost frequented the Canton and Leckwith moors. On his appearance people fled in terror. One night, however, a man of greater courage than the ordinary allowed the ghost to approach and elicited the story of the disembodied boatman.

It appears that on the night of the drowning the man's head was in some way severed from the body and taken possession of by the river devils who used it as a football in their nightly games on the river banks, and refused to restore it to the owner. The ghost stated that until his head was recovered from the devils there was no hope of eternal rest for him. The kindly human, much touched by the ghost's story, accompanied him to the river bank, where, after a diligent search, they found the devils playing with the boatman's head.

The Good Samaritan immediately commenced to approach towards the devils, praying as he did so. Away they fled in terror. The rescuer then recovered the skull and buried it in the mud on the river bank, and said prayers for the soul of the dead boatman. On the conclusion of this simple ceremony the ghost disappeared and was never more seen.

According to another ancient tale, located near the river between Taffs Well and Cardiff, a young man returning from a visit from the former place to town late one night sat down near the river side for a rest. Suddenly he awoke and beheld near him the ghost of his departed grandfather. The ghost told him that under the roof thatch of his old home he would find hidden a pair of silver spurs, and that until these had been removed and thrown into the Taff his troubled soul would not find peace.

The young man went to the house, and in the presence of neighbours climbed the roof and found the spurs where the ghost had indicated. To the neighbours, however, the spurs were invisible. The young man dutifully carried out his grandfather's wish and threw the spurs into the river. Immediately a bright flame appeared on the water and then disappeared. From that time the ghost was seen no more.

Greenmeadow is reputed to have had several ghosts, of whom some members of the Lewis family were apparently quite proud. One of these ghosts haunted the Old Oak Room. Guests are reported to have been awakened at early dawn by three thuds on the room door, and to have seen the spirit of a tall red-haired man leaning on his sword and gazing out of the window. Suddenly he dropped his sword, crossed himself, fell on his knees as if in prayer and then vanished. There was also the Blue Room Ghost, the Hunch-Back Spectre who was seen only in an underground cellar, and the Green Man Ghost, who is supposed to have been a former liveried servant of the family.

I received from Miss Gwenllian Lewis, of Cookham Dene, a daughter of the second Squire Lewis of Greenmeadow, who seems to have no doubt that Greenmeadow was a haunted house, a copy of a letter written to her father from Greenhill, Rhiwbina, in 1878, by Miss Martha Moggridge.

Miss Moggridge describes how during a visit to Greenmeadow, she was sitting with her sick sister in the oak bedroom at 3 a.m., when the door opened and 'a face with a large prominent nose and a shock of rather white hair' peered in. Then entered 'a small old man clad in a green coat and white knee breeches,' with silver buttons on the coat and much lace hanging from the wrist. A silver rapier hung from a red sash at his side.

For a moment he stood still and passed his hands across his eyes in a perplexed manner. The figure ignored her challenge to identify himself and commenced tapping the walls of the room near the door, moving backward and forward as he did so. 'Suddenly he threw up his arm with a gesture of great despair,' and vanished.—In the letter

Miss Moggridge goes on to say that a Captain Mostyn on another occasion had a similar experience in the same bedroom.

Another house which was at one time deemed to be haunted was Cilynys, the old farmhouse on the right hand bank of the River Taff, adjoining the Iron Bridge at Tongwynlais. A legend attaches to this myth. Castell Coch is supposed to have been bombarded during the Civil Wars from the Tynant Mound, an operation suggested to Cromwell's soldiers by a local lady. She was captured by the Royalists, imprisoned in a bedroom at Cilynys and slain. Her blood is said to have bespattered the walls, and ever since that time, no matter what decorative treatment is applied, the bloodstains always show through. The Ghost of Cilynys was locally believed to be that of the Castell Coch traitress.

SHORT LIST OF SOURCES.

Some of the foregoing stories are drawn from books, others have been obtained from individuals. Amongst some of the books consulted have been:
Dr. T. Gwyn Jones. Welsh Folklore.
Sir John Rhys. Celtic Folklore.
Wirt Sikes. British Goblins (1880).
T. H. Thomas. Old Folks' Tales (1904).
Marie Trevelyan. Folk Lore and Folk Stories of Wales (1909).

CHAPTER XXVIII.

TALES OF THE TWMPATH AND CASTELL COCH.

The Twmpath at Rhiwbina has always been a source of wonderment both to local residents and to visitors, and it is perhaps not surprising that through the many centuries of its existence a number of legends relating to its origin came into being. Many of these have long since been forgotten, but until quite recent years a few still persisted. Here is an account embodying in a single story the supposed association of the Twmpath with the legendary account of the Norman Conquest of Glamorgan.

About 1089 Iestyn ap Gwrgan, Lord of Glamorgan, and his sons made war on Rhys, Lord of Deheubarth (i.e. South West Wales), with the object of winning back that territory and its throne for their family. A powerful chieftain, Einion ap Collwyn, who had quarrelled with Rhys threw in his lot with Iestyn and as a reward for his help he was promised the Lordship of Dinas Powis and marriage with Iestyn's daughter Nest.

Einion, so the story goes, had been in close touch with the Norman invaders of England, and at Iestyn's request he bargained with a powerful Norman baron, Robert Fitzhamon, to bring an army to Iestyn's aid. The Normans are stated to have landed at Porthkerry, linked up with the forces of Iestyn and Einion, and inflicted a crushing defeat on the army of Rhys at the Battle of Hirwain Wrgan, near Aberdare. Rhys fled over the mountains, but was caught and slain on the hill-top in the Rhondda Valleys at a spot where in later days a monastery called Penrhys was set up under Llantarnam Abbey.

After this victory the Normans marched into the Vale of Glamorgan and at a point near Colwinston (supposedly so named after Einion ap Collwyn) they received a large amount of gold as their reward. It is for this reason, says the legend, that the length of main highway in this locality has since been known as the Golden Mile. Having received their guerdon Fitzhamon and his men then made their way back to England overland.

Einion also put in his claim for his promised reward. Iestyn, his enemies having been disposed of, now broke faith with Einion, and refused to allow him to marry Nest. Thereupon, Einion in high dudgeon rode post haste after Fitzhamon and his men and overtook them at Pwll Meuryg near Chepstow. He laid his grievance before them and asked them to join him in avenging his wrong. In return for their help, he promised to aid them in winning Glamorgan for themselves.

The Normans agreed to his plea, and made their way back to Cardiff where Iestyn, who had been informed by his spies of the new development, had hastily gathered his forces to meet them. At that time a vast waste of heath land called Mynydd Bychan extended from near Cardiff as far as Llanishen Fach Farm, and Iestyn is said to have formed his men into battle array in the vicinity of the latter place.

At Einion's request he and his men were given the foremost place in the combined Norman-Welsh army, an arrangement which the Normans favoured, as the slaughter of Einion's men would make it impossible for him to betray them after they had won a victory. The rival armies met near the farmstead at Rhiwbina now called Tynycoed, adjoining the well-known modern landmark, the Butchers' Arms, and here a fierce battle was fought which lasted throughout a whole day, and in the course of which hundreds of men on both sides, including Iestyn himself, were wounded or killed. So much blood was shed in this battle that, according to report, the neighbouring brook ran red with gore. Thus it was, so many people still believe, that the stream got its present name Nant Waedlyd, which means, in English, Bloody Brook.

After this fearful fray some of Iestyn's followers took the body of their dead leader, together with that of his horse and all its trappings and other goods, from the field of battle to a hill a mile or so away. Here they set their dead lord on the back of his horse with all his possessions around him, and piled up a quantity of stones, which they afterwards covered with earth, thus forming the Twmpath (or mound) which has existed to the present day.

When the burial mound of their chief was finished, a wizard of Iestyn's tribe cast a spell on the mound to prevent the tomb from being desecrated. It was decreed that if any mortal tried to break into the mound all Nature's sternest forces would be let loose to protect the sacred grave. Right down through the centuries the sanctity of Iestyn's supposed resting-place was respected.

A hundred or so years ago, however, it was locally said, some strangers, believing there was treasure buried in the Twmpath, started digging into it. At once the sky clouded over and the mound was soon wrapped in darkness. Then broke out a terrific storm of thunder and lightning, accompanied by a deluge of rain. The men immediately gave up their unholy task, and fled away in terror. Since then, it is said, Iestyn's burial-place has not been disturbed.

In another version of the foregoing tale the army of Iestyn ap Gwrgan is stated to have encamped on a field at the junction of Pantmawr Road and Rhiwbina Hill on the corner of which once stood a smithy known as Efail Jervis. The ruins of this smithy existed until recent years. At this smithy, it was said, Iestyn's army had their armour rivetted on before they faced battle and death.

Another and even more picturesque account of the origin of the Twmpath ascribes it to the ill-temper of His Satanic Majesty. Here is the story told to me by a local resident over twenty-five years ago:*

Long, long ago, there were many good men in Glamorgan who used to set up monasteries and churches for the purpose of making people religious and good. They had opened such religious places at Llanfabon,

---

* This story is also given by Mr. Harry Lewis in *Archaeologia Cambrensis* (1919).

Llanwonno, Penrhys, Eglwysilan, Ystradyfodwg and at other localities, and the Devil's agents in those districts were afraid that unless some action was taken their master would have no following. One of them, therefore, went up to London to inform the Devil of what was happening.

His Satanic Majesty was much disturbed by the news and he called in his advisers to consult with the local agent as to the steps to be taken to deal with this serious threat to his might and influence. The agent described the geographical conditions of the district and suggested that if the Taff Valley could be blocked up at the Castell Coch Gorge, where the hills are only a short distance apart the river would be dammed back and the people of the area drowned. After much discussion it was decided, in the absence of a better plan, to act on the agent's suggestion.

Then came a discussion as to the material to be used. The agent thought that local soil would not be suitable for the purpose, and that it would be desirable to bring earth from London to form the dam. Accordingly, one summer's day the Devil made his way with his first shovel-ful of London earth into South Wales. By and by he got as far as Efail Jervis, by which time he felt very tired. He put down the load and sat down to rest on the stile, which gave access from Rhiwbina Hill to the path leading to Tongwynlais. While he was enjoying the "spell" and a smoke, he saw coming towards him along the path from Greenmeadow a man with a bag slung over his shoulder.

At length the man came up to the stile, and the old Devil had to get down in order to let him pass. As he was doing so the man caught a glimpse of his tail, and knew at once who the stranger was. He therefore resolved to act very warily, and not to do or say anything which would assist the Devil or endanger himself and his neighbours.

Having got over the stile he said 'Good Afternoon' to the Devil and was starting on his way when the Devil said, "How far is it from here to Castell Coch?" The man, who was a travelling cobbler and whose bag was filled with worn boots which he had collected at neighbouring farms and houses for repair, realizing that the Devil had some evil scheme afoot, was very careful as to what he would say, and feigned deafness. The Devil was deceived and repeated the question in a louder tone. Then the cobbler said, "Far, far away." "But how far?" came the Devil's further question. "Well," said the cobbler, "I can't tell you exactly, but I can show you." Whereupon he opened his bag, and laid out the worn-out boots in a row, saying as he did so, "All these boots I have worn out coming from Castell Coch."

The Devil looked aghast, and soon made up his mind that in his tired state, he would prefer to forego his vengeance rather than continue on his way. In disgust he picked up his shovel and threw his load of earth into the neighbouring field where it has since remained. This, according to my informant, was the true story of the origin of the Twmpath. As similar stories—with variations—are also told of mounds and hills in other parts of the country—at Ilbury in Wiltshire, Pencwrt (Carmarthenshire), Shobdon (Herefordshire), Wrekin (Shropshire) and so on, it is not surprising that few persons now give it credence.

Nearly every old castle in the country has associated with it legends relating to underground passages, ghostly visitations, hidden treasure and the like, and Castell Coch is no exception to this rule. The castle was, and still is, by some people, believed to be connected by subterranean channels with Cardiff and Caerphilly Castles, and also with caves in the Lesser Garth, and many persons are said to have embarked on the risky adventure of their exploration in the days before the castle's restoration to its present condition. The late Robert Drane wrote a racy account of his attempts in this direction. *

The main feature of the Castell Coch legend of buried treasure is that this treasure was guarded by two eagles, and in the many varying versions of the legend these fierce guardians of hidden property almost invariably occur. Here is the version contained in a popular local topographical work written eighty years ago. †

"Of course there is a legend connected with Castle Coch. It was communicated to us, and as we received it we give it. Many years ago a lady of good family, but small income, obtained permission to appropriate to her own use, and fit up according to her own taste, four or five rooms in Castle Coch; and there she resided, with two old servants, a man and his wife, who still followed her fortunes. She heard, and they heard, at different times, various noises, which, as they could not be accounted for in any other way, were set down to either rats or jackdaws.

"One night, however, the lady woke suddenly, and saw a venerable gentleman, in a full dress suit of the time of Charles I, looking fixedly on her: his face was deadly pale, and every feature impressed by sorrow. She started up, and he retreated, passing through a door that was in shadow. She had sufficient resolution to follow, when, to her amazement, she found the door securely locked and bolted as she had left it.

"She did not tell her servants, but a few mornings after her servant told her, he thought they had been too long living there, and that he really heard noises that could not be made by rats or jackdaws. She laughed away his fears, but her own were strengthened, for the same evening, coming from a turret garden she had made, along a corridor, which terminated in a dead wall, she saw the self-same venerable gentleman, who had disturbed her repose. She advanced to meet him, but he backed, and disappeared into the wall; the incident frequently occurred, and always with the same result.

"A tradition existed in the neighbourhood, that during the Civil Wars the then master of Coch Castle had deposited money and plate and jewels, to an immense amount, in an old iron chest, in the subterranean passage leading from his castle to that of Cardiff; and having been killed by the bursting of a petronel, he never returned to claim it. In process of time the lady found that her old servants were

---
* Castell Coch (1888).
† Mr. and Mrs. S. C. Hall. The Book of South Wales (1861).
Other versions of Castell Coch tales are told by Marie Trevelyan in *Folk Lore and Stories of Wales*.

too terrified to remain; she preferred giving up her apartments to parting with her humble friends, and so Coch Castle was deserted."

As Castell Coch was in ruins probably for at least a couple of centuries before the Civil Wars and so continued until its restoration by Lord Bute about 1870 the above story rests on very frail foundations, but that was no deterrent to the imagination or credulity of local residents, and other versions of the ghost story present the old Cavalier as haunting the ruins. The author of the above written version proceeds as follows:—

"Some years afterwards, a party of stout-hearted gentlemen resolved to explore the subterraneous passage—wherever it might lead to. So, provided with torches and pickaxes, they set out on their expedition. On and on they went, and at last, shining through the darkness, they saw four bright red lights—very bright and very red they were. Nothing daunted they advanced, and presently found that the four red lights were the eyes of two huge eagles, who were composedly perched on an Iron Chest.

"Now here was confirmation of the legend of Coch Castle! They walked bravely forward, when suddenly the eagles sprang upon them with claw and beak; and very glad they were to make good their retreat, while the royal birds flew screaming back to the chest. But the men were persevering fellows, and the following day returned armed with pistols and eight good bullets, and when they came within proper distance of the eagles they fired, but with no effect; their enemies flew screaming towards them, beat out their torches with their wings, and sent the intruders back crestfallen.

"They then cast some silver bullets, and got them duly blessed, and even persuaded a minister with his holy book to companion them. Again they saw the four red lights—an exorcism was read, which the eagles did not heed—the charmed bullets were fired with no better result than those of lead—a third assault was made by the eagles upon the disturbers of their watch and attackers of their ward, the enraged birds punishing them more severely than on either of their former visits. It is believed that the eagles are still there, though no one is bold enough to disturb them."

There are other versions of the legend recounted above. The treasure is usually represented as having belonged to Ifor Bach, and the two eagles are faithful henchmen of his who are charged to guard the treasure until the time of his return. They were given the form of eagles in order that they might conveniently feed themselves on the birds and animals in the adjoining Fforest Goch. They also uttered wild fiery cries which terrorized the neighbourhood and so kept would-be robbers away from the treasure, and which were interpreted by some as a clamour for transformation back to human form.

In spite of the provision thus made to deter people from taking the hidden treasure some persons are reputed to have taken the risk, and certain of them are believed to have died in the course of their attempts.

On one occasion two adventurous youths sought to explore the subterranean chambers of the castle ruins in the hope of speedily acquiring riches. They penetrated one of the passages, it is said, to a point where it dropped perpendicularly for a distance of twenty feet or more. The boys failed to see the danger and suddenly they fell into an unfathomable pool of black water, from which their bodies were never recovered. The mother of one of the lads, Dame Griffith, broke her heart over her son's disappearance and very soon died. For many years afterwards, it was said, her ghost haunted the castle ruins and the forest, searching for the body and soul of her missing son.

CHAPTER XXIX.

MISCELLANEOUS HISTORICAL NOTES.

Treoda.

In the so-called Aberpergwm version of *Brut y Tywysogion* (Chronicle of the Princes)—a document which is not today deemed authentic—appears the following:—

"A.D. 831, the Saxons came suddenly at night and burnt down the monastery of Senghenydd which stood on the site where the castle (*i.e.* Caerphilly Castle) now stands, and from there they come to Treoda Castle and burnt it. Afterwards they fled across the Severn Sea taking with them much plunder."

This statement may well be one of the many inventions of Iolo Morganwg and should not be accepted as historical fact.

The name Treoda, however, is compounded of the Welsh element *Tre*, meaning *homestead*, with a personal name Oda, which has a Danish or Saxon flavour, and the name seems to mean Oda's Homestead, but there is no evidence to show who Oda was.

Plas-Treoda.

Adjoining Whitchurch Common on the north-west formerly stood an ancient farmhouse known as *Gwaun* (or *Waun*) *Treoda* (*i.e.* Treoda Meadow or Common), and this is supposed to have been all that remained of an old residence, Tre-Oda, which was the patrimony of families of ancient lineage and social importance. The earliest of these was Yorath Mawr, who lived about the 13th century, and who, according to G. T. Clark, was a son of Cynfrig, Lord of Llantrithyd and Radyr, of the line of Iestyn ap Gwrgan, the territorial ruler who was defeated by Robert Fitzhamon, the Norman Conqueror and first Norman Lord of Glamorgan. On the female side Yorath Mawr was descended from Ifor Bach (the famous raider of Cardiff Castle in 1158) through his grandmother, a daughter of Griffith ap Ivor, from whom Melingriffith possibly dervived its name.

Rice Merrick's Account.

A very interesting account of Glamorgan was written in 1578 by one Rice Merrick, of Cottrell, the County Clerk of the Peace. In this book, *Glamorgan Antiquities*, reference is made to ancient Treoda and its occupying families. Thus:

"In Treoda standeth an old house sometime Yorath Mawr his House, whose Inheritance fell between his fower Daughters, and which David ap Richard Gwyn purchased of David Thomas of Jankyn Sonnes."

And again:—
"Within the precinct of this Hamlett standeth an ancient house called Troda, sometime the Mansion house of Yorath Mauer, whose lineall discent sprang from Justyn, Lord of Glamorgan, after whome the same house, with all his inheritance, discended to his 4 Daughters. This house and the Lands belonging to it, fell to the lot of Ma (? Madoc) Ychan, who marryed one of them, and continued in his Lyne, untill that the Sonnes of John ap Robert, ap Ma Ychan sould the same to Dafydd ap Jankin, ap Jem, app Dafydd; whose Sonnes sould it to Dafydd ap Richard Gwynn, whose Sonne Edward enjoyeth the same."

This Edward ap Richard Gwyn, who occupied Treoda in 1578, was possibly a cadet of the prominent and ancient family of Gwyn of Llanishen, later merged in the Lewis family.

A Local Stradling Family.

Treoda seems to have been occupied in the late 16th and early 17th century by a branch of the prolific family of Stradlings, one of whom married Joan Gamage, a daughter of another ancient Glamorgan family associated with Coity.

The foregoing information has been derived from old Welsh pedigrees which, owing to the absence of surnames before the Tudor period, are extremely complicated, and to a great extent the several connections are largely a matter of surmise. It seems, however, safe to conclude that Treoda was the residence of a family of ancient lineage connected with the royal family of the Welsh princes of Glamorgan. It is on account of the old associations of Welsh families with the Treoda locality, that the Cardiff Rural District Council adopted some of their names to describe new streets in the neighbourhood, *e.g.* Iestyn, Gwrgan, Yorath, Stradling, Madoc, Ifor and Nest.

Whitchurch Common.

Whitchurch Common was anciently known as Gwaun Treoda, *i.e.* Treoda Common. The greater part of it was within the ancient manor of *Album Monasterium*, which was later merged in the lordship of Senghenydd. This manor was renamed by the Lord of Cardiff and Glamorgan and was administered for him by a resident bailiff. Gwaun Treoda was part of the waste of the Manor of Album Monasterium, and the adjoining Manors of Roath Keynsham, Llystalybont and possibly Llandaff, and feudal tenants in its vicinity had grazing and other rights thereon.

In the reign of Edward VI the Lordship of Glamorgan was bestowed upon Sir William Herbert, afterwards Earl of Pembroke, and from the Herbert family it passed to the Bute family. The Lord of the Manor controlling the greater part of the Common is the Marquess of Bute. A small portion, on and adjoining which Ararat Chapel now stands, formed part of the Manor of Roath Keynsham, of which Lord Tredegar was Manorial Lord. Some years ago he transferred the manorial control in respect of his portion to the Whitchurch Parish Council.

The Great Heath.

Until the early part of the 19th century there extended from Roath to Llanishen, Rhiwbina and Whitchurch a large area of common land known as *Mynydd Bychan*, or the Great Heath. The portions of the Great Heath in or abutting the Parish of Whitchurch included stretches on both sides of Beulah Road and the area east of the Philog Brook. According to the *Roath Keynsham Surveys* of 1650 and 1702 tenants of the Manor had pasture rights on the Great Heath 'for all sorts of cattle.' Apparently these rights were disputed, for in 1662 a Cardiff manorial court complained:—

"That the adjacent parishes of Roath, Llanishen, Whitchurch and other parishes do daily intrude on the said liberty and common of pasture, for many years past, to the great wrong and detriment of the said Corporation."*

The burgesses evidently desired to claim a monopoly of common rights despite the fact that the Heath at that period was outside the Borough. Possibly the chief ground of the grievance, however, was that encroachments, some quite large, were made on the common by local residents. The largest encroachment near Tyglas was made by Thomas Lewis, of Llanishen. There were also smaller encroachments at Rhiwbina in the vicinity of the Butchers' Arms, and a number adjoining the Caerphilly Road between Tywern Road and the Philog. The Heaths were enclosed by Act of Parliament in 1801, and allotted to the Corporation and various individuals.

Ancient Mills.

The soil of the Whitchurch area is very fertile, and at one time corn was freely grown in the neighbourhood. This corn was ground in local mills of which there were several, viz. Melin Griffith, Little Mill, Deri Mill, Tongwynlais Mill, and later the Canal Lock Mill, also at Tongwynlais. In the vicinity also were other mills at Llanishen and Lisvane, Radyr, Llandaff and Llystalybont. All of them have now disappeared.

The Tongwynlais Mill, also known as the Castle Mill, was driven by water from two ponds formed by damming Nant Gwynlais. These ponds provided a sufficient head of water to operate a mill-wheel of 30 feet diameter. The names of the only proprietors I have been able to trace are Jacob Lewis, Robert Aeron Diamond, and 'Arthur the Grocer.' J. H. Williams, later R.D.C. building inspector, worked this mill for Mr. Arthur up to about thirty or so years ago, when corn from Llwyn Mallt was ground here. The mill fell into a ruinous condition and was demolished just prior to the outbreak of the World War.

The Ton Lock or New Mill was a small building, which still remains, near the canal bank below the Tongwynlais Lock. and was driven by water directed into a mill stream from the pond above the Lock. It was less ancient than the Castle Mill and probably dates from the early part of last century. The Mill was worked in the 1880's by William Jones (Llanmaes), who later worked the Llandaff Mill.

---

* *Cardiff Records.* Vol. II.

The Little Mill, which lies near the Taff Vale Railway, was driven by water diverted from the Whitchurch Brook in Merthyr Road into a mill stream. The remains of the building are still *in situ*. The mill has been closed for several generations. In 1837 it was worked by John Harding.

The Deri Mill stood in the meadow within a hundred or so yards of the Butchers' Arms, Rhiwbina. For a long time within living memory it was operated by Isaac Richards, who also had a butcher's business, and was also landlord of the public house mentioned. Edmunds, nicknamed 'The Old Duke,' worked for Isaac Richards. A man called Jesse Salathiel also was associated with the Deri Mill.

An old scrap book left by Eli Evans (1812-1875), a well-known local public man, contains a draft letter of a communication to be sent to the local justices by Isaac Richards, landlord of the Butchers' Arms, in support of his application in 1861 for a wine and spirit licence, and one of the grounds for the application was based on business at Deri Mill and the popularity of local chapels.

It was claimed that Deri Mill had become much busier by reason of the fact that steam power had been introduced to supplement water power. The locality had consequently become "a place of considerable traffic." The house was much used by farmers for selling cattle and receiving payment for their grain. Many of the farmers, it was said, travelled long distances, often through wet and cold, and the want of a spirit licence was a thing almost daily felt by them and expressed. The other reason advanced was the need for catering for the needs of persons coming to attend special services at Beulah Chapel.

Village Smithies.

Another indication of local intensive agricultural activity was the existence of blacksmiths' shops where horses were shod and agricultural implements made and repaired. Of those I have been able to trace not all were in operation at the same time. At Rhiwbina one stood on the site of the Beulah Schoolroom about 150 years ago. *Efail Jervis*, at the junction of Pantmawr Road and Rhiwbina Hill, existed within living memory, and the Penygroes Smithy in Beulah Road within the last twenty years. There were also two smithies at Birchgrove, one in the Caerphilly Road and another near Cross Inn. In Whitchurch Village there was one adjoining the Three Elms Inn, one near the Three Horse Shoes Inn, and one at the rear of the Plough Inn. There was also a smithy, now a garage, at Tongwynlais. Several of these smithies were popular gossip shops where the 'lads of the village' met to discuss current news.

Pigs and Potatoes.

Up to a century or so ago Whitchurch seems to have had a great reputation for pigs and potatoes. This was largely due to the fact that the proprietors of the Melingriffith Works took a great interest in their employees and encouraged them in the practice of gardening. Each year a very popular and well-attended Horticultural Show was held near the Whitchurch Common, which attracted exhibits by a large proportion of the cottagers of the locality. The production of fine potatoes seems to have been a speciality of Whitchurch gardeners. Many cottagers kept pigs in their back gardens, and fed them on the small potatoes and other surplus vegetables.

Locality Nicknames.

It was for this reason that the local community came to be known by the popular nickname of *Whitchurch Pigs*. Other villages in the neighbourhood also had soubriquets. Cottagers near Melingriffith were called *Melingriffith Quackers*, some say because of the noises made by rooks in the nearby trees, but more probably after the early Quaker proprietors of the works, whilst the Pentyrch folk were known as *Pentyrch Cuckoos*, and Llandaff folk as *Llandaff Wasps*. This practice of nicknaming communities used to be very common in Wales in olden times. Other examples which may be mentioned were *Morriston Monkeys, Cwmtwrch Donkeys, Blaen-y-cwm Colts, Neath Abbey Jacks, Glyn-Neath Foxes, Abergavenny Bulldogs, Carmarthen Whelps, Flint Mules, Merioneth Thieves, Caernarvon Whelps, Aberdare Snakes, Llantrisant Black Army, Wick Frolics, Llantwit Major One-a-wanting,* and *Cywion Bawddwr* (Bawddwr Chicks) for Llandovery folk, Cowbridge residents used to be known as "*Call Again Tomorrow.*"

Ploughing with Oxen.

In olden days oxen were extensively used for ploughing and other purposes throughout Glamorgan, and the farmers used to encourage the beasts by singing to a well-known Welsh refrain, four-line rhyming verses called *tribanau*. The practice of ploughing with oxen seems to have been dying out in the Cardiff district at the middle of the last century. Some local inhabitants, however, recall that as late as the 1870's two black oxen were regularly used in ploughing fields on the Village Farm, Whitchurch, which was then in the tenure of Mr. Barry Wride. This was probably one of the last survivals in Glamorgan of the ancient practice.

Ancient Trees.

Farm and street names at Rhiwbina bearing such names as *Deri* and *Derwen* (oak tree) derive their origin from the ancient lightning-blasted, and now somewhat decrepit oak, standing at the junction of Heol-y-Deri and Wenallt Road. This tree has been a well-known landmark for hundreds of years, and for this reason the Cardiff Rural District Council has from time to time taken steps to extend its life by treating it against fungoid growths and insect pests.

Another ancient oak tree until recent years stood in a garden near the old Foundry at Llandaff North upon which a petrol station now stands. This oak-tree was an ancient boundary mark between the parishes of Llandaff and Whitchurch and was supposed to have been planted in the 13th century.

Radyr Ford.

In olden times there were few bridges over the River Taff, but there existed a number of recognised fords by which vehicular traffic gained access from one bank to the other. Among them were Rhyd Llystalybont, near Gabalfa, Rhyd Llandav below Llandaff Weir, Rhyd Radyr connecting Llandaff North with Old Radyr, and Rhyd y Boithan and Rhyd y Tywod near Taffs Well. There was also a similar ford near Cilynys and another opposite Forest Farm and Radyr Station.

These fords usually formed parts of public highways repairable by the inhabitants of the parishes through which they passed. The Radyr Ford, which gave its name to Radyr Ford Road in Llandaff North (until 1923 a part of the Parish of Whitchurch) was evidently an important and much used crossing for centuries, and in 1733 a Glamorgan Grand Jury ordered Whitchurch residents to put the road approaches in a fit state of repair.

A Legend of St. Catwg.

An interesting legend mentioning Radyr Ford occurs in a Life of St. Cadoc (or Cattwg), the 6th Century Abbot of Llancarfan Monastery, which dates from the 12th Century. The following is a summarised version of the tale as told by the late Mr. Charles Morgan.* The Gwynllyw referred to was St. Gwynllyw, whose name survives in the Church of St. Woolos, Newport.

"When Gwynllyw was on his death-bed he sent his servant, Istan, to Llancarfan to bring his son, Cadoc, to see him before he died. Istan went on his way with haste until he came to the Taff, which was flooded. The breadth of the river extended from the ford of Penugual to the Hill of King Morgan, called in Welsh, Rhiw Morgan, and no one could cross without a boat. No boat was available, and Istan, calling on the hermit Tylyuguay, who lived on the other side of the river, besought him to go to Llancarfan. Cadoc came with Tylyuguay to his house, and here he and his train of twenty followers were entertained at *Villa Aradur*†, between Llandaff and the woods. The hermit, who depended on the Radyr fisheries for his sustenance, caught that evening in his net enough for Cadoc and his whole retinue.

"On the hermit's complaint that the spring was far off, Cadoc gave him his staff, saying, 'Strike the ground; the Lord will cause a fountain to flow.' This the hermit did, and a spring gushed forth. Next day Cadoc smote the river three times, so that it divided into two parts, and Cadoc and his companions passed through, dry shod. At the request of the hermit, Cadoc restored the river to its former course, at the same time diminishing its breadth. During the process a huge boulder was cast up on the hermit's land, which Cadoc ordered to be called the Carn of Tylyuguay."

The hermitage of Tylyuguay is supposed to have been on the site of Old Radyr Parish Church. Near the church was the ancient manor house of Radyr, where now stands the Radyr Court Small Holdings.

Tongwynlais Market and Fair.

Prior to the 1840's Tongwynlais was a very small village—almost a hamlet. In that and the succeeding decade a considerable number

---

* *Cardiff Naturalists' Society Transactions* 1924.

† Professor Ifor Williams has suggested that *Aradur* comes from the Latin *oratorium*, meaning an oratory or chapel, a place for private worship. (*Enwau Lleoedd*, p. 53).

of cottages were built, mainly to accommodate workers at Pentyrch and Melingriffith Works, and for a period Tongwynlais was almost as important a place as Whitchurch. It became quite a busy trading centre. There were four provision shops as well as a weekly market, whilst no fewer than eight public houses provided ample facilities for liquid refreshment for the workers in mine, forge, furnace, mill and transport, who lived there and in neighbouring villages. It was a particularly busy place on Friday and Saturday nights.

Once a year during the second week in August was held the annual Ton Fair, which drew crowds from a wide radius. The local works were closed for this event. In addition to a variety of sideshows, swings and other amusements, street stalls displayed a wide selection of wares, and particularly flannel and wool, which were essential elements in the clothing provision of those days. The pleasure fair extended over two days for the general populace, and on the third day was held the Boatmen's Fair, the canal barge workers having a special holiday for that event.

Fforest Goch Iron Ore Mines.

In connection with the old Pentyrch Furnaces there were subsidiary iron ore mines in the Little Garth and in Fforest Goch, the woodland adjoining Castell Coch. The ore was mined in open workings and shallow levels and slants, the remains of which may still be seen. One of these old mines, long since disused, was until recent years an attraction for ramblers who went there to inspect its "Blue Waters." There were no properly made cart roads leading from the mines and woods of Fforest Goch, and transport was by pack mules and donkeys. These were driven in lots of a dozen or so by hauliers, whose language in urging the beasts along was both loud and lurid. Here is a description of such a procession, written in 1888 by Robert Drane, the well-known Cardiff druggist*:—

"There were a number of asses following each others' tails, with sure steps and good-natured gravity, down the mountain pathway, which, by repeated journeys, they had trodden in a slough that nearly reached their knees at every step. They were loaded with mine (iron ore) obtained from parts of the hill, inaccessible to wheeled vehicles, and were conveying it in the most methodical and most business-like manner (almost without any direction from their biped superior), who only cursed them in Welsh, to the blast furnaces in the valley below."

Trains of as many as twenty donkeys were also employed to convey logwood from the forests to the Pentyrch collieries.

The Village Pound.

Tongwynlais also had a cattle *pound*, which still stands. During the Pentyrch Ironworks period it was in constant use for penning wandering horses and donkeys, as well as straying cattle, sheep and pigs. A regular tariff of charges for the return of the impounded beasts

---
* *Castell Coch*.

was in force, and the revenue to the pound-keeper at times was quite substantial.

The pound-keeper was the village blacksmith, who worked in the adjoining smithy. The smithy was very well patronised in those days, not only by the drivers of canal horses and pack mules and donkeys, but also by all the village gossips who met there to discuss village news and retail the tales then current.

Greenmeadow Hounds.

Fox-hunting was a popular sport of the period. The Bookers of Melingriffith maintained a pack of hounds at Greenhill (Rhiwbina) and later on the Fforest Farm near Radyr Weir. The Lewises of Greenmeadow, also, for a long time kept a pack of hounds in kennels near Tongwynlais Mill and at the rear of their mansion. Squire Lewis was Master of the Greenmeadow Hounds. These hounds were of a distinctive Welsh type, and the late Colonel Lewis used to claim that they were descendants of French boar-hounds which belonged to the ancient Monastery at Margam. Tongwynlais, in those days, was a very 'doggy' village. The Greenmeadow squires' were always keen sportsmen, and used to present spaniels to the villagers and pay the licence fees, on condition that the dogs were available for use during the numerous "shoots" which were organised in the adjoining forests.

Why Llandaff Yard!

Why is the locality adjacent to the Cow and Snuffers Inn, at Llandaff North, known as Llandaff Yard? Prior to the railway era, the canal was the principal means of transport between Cardiff and townships in the Taff Valley. The barges conveyed not only bulky materials, such as coal, iron and various other products of local manufacture, but also foodstuffs of all kinds, both for man and beast. This traffic continued into the present century. A wharf or yard was provided at each township, and a set-off or bay provided in the canal to facilitate loading and unloading. The yard served as a depot for assembling and distributing the various commodities, very much in the same way as do some railway sidings today. Local coal and corn merchants frequently had offices at the yards, at which they transacted both retail and wholesale business.

On the site of this depot was built in the 1870's the Eagle Iron and Brass Foundry. About three-quarters of a mile down the canal towards Cardiff, near Gabalfa House, stood a graving dock and yard, where canal boats were made and repaired. It seems clear that the name Llandaff Yard was derived from one or other of these depots, probably the former, but in the earlier Ordnance maps it is printed east of College Road and of the locality developed in the 1870's or earlier and commonly referred to as the Llandaff Freehold. Both the names of Llandaff Yard and Llandaff Freehold have now given way to the name Llandaff North.

Tongwynlais Lock.

Another busy centre on the canal was Tongwynlais Lock. Near the lock there existed a bay into which boats were shunted for the purpose of having their cargoes weighed. Much of the canal transport was undertaken by contractors, who supplied their own horses, for which stalls were provided at Tongwynlais and elsewhere, and were paid on the basis of tonnage carried. When a boat was properly in the bay, the water was let out and the boat rested on bearers which operated a scale erected on the canal bank. The tare of each barge was painted on its side, and the boatmen were paid on the basis of the net weight after deduction of tare.

The bargemen belonged to a somewhat colourful category of workers. They were a somewhat pugnacious, hard-drinking and loud-swearing body of men. Traffic on the canal was continuous by night and by day, and at times there was serious congestion near the Tongwynlais Lock. Often as many as a dozen barges would be waiting their turn to pass through. The delays frequently gave rise to disputes over questions of precedence, and these were often decided by resort to fisticuffs. At other times, when a better spirit prevailed, the boatmen used to while away the time in horse-dealing, gambling, drinking, or in performing a popular dance called "*The Boatmen's Jig.*"

Melingriffith Band.

Melingriffith Silver Band is one of the best known, and one of the oldest musical combinations in South Wales. A drum and fife band was established at Whitchurch in 1798 in connection with a company of volunteers formed to resist an anticipated French invasion of Britain. A brass band existed in the 1850's, if not earlier, in association with the 13th Glamorgan Rifle Volunteer Corps, of which T. W. Booker, of Melingriffith, was commandant. This band seemingly started as a drum and fife organisation, but at what period I do not know.

I have seen in an old Melingriffith account book the record of a payment, in 1856, a sum of £12 13s. 6d. to G. F. Davies "for a quarter's tuition, etc., for band." The band's headquarters were in one of the *New Houses* in the vicinity of the works. In the 1860's and 1870's the band used to play at club feasts and at other semi-public functions, and was frequently referred to as Booker's Band. In 1878 its leader was Mr. French Davis, but in April, 1880, Evan Owen seems to have been one in charge.

After the failure of the Booker undertaking in the late 1870's the connection of the Band with the Works was broken, but the organisation was apparently not disbanded. For a time there seem to have been three combinations—the Volunteer Band, a Temperance Band and a Drum and Fife Band. The first two combined to form a Village Band, and was under the direction of Mr. —. Chivers. In 1913, through the influence of Mr. Spence Thomas, the Managing Director of Melingriffith, the Village Band was incorporated with the Melingriffith Cadet Corps. In 1919 it was again reorganised as an independent unit by Mr. Frank Morgan, and in 1920 Mr. T. J. Powell was appointed conductor.

Local Friendly Societies.

I have shown in *Historic Melingriffith* that the Melingriffith Benefit Club was started in 1786 and was in existence until 1878, if not later, when it was merged in one of the national orders. In the 1850's there were two such clubs at Melingriffith, one for men and one for women, and the 1853 works accounts show that each of these had amounts of £1,000 on loan with the Melingriffith Company at 5 per cent. per annum. The works officials and the Booker family were subscribing members of these clubs, and in addition the Bookers made substantial contributions towards the costs of the annual club feasts. The headquarters of the clubs was at *New Houses.*

I do not know when the Melingriffith clubs were disbanded, but it must have been after 1878, for in that year the men's club rules were revised and reprinted. In addition to the Melingriffith Society there was started in 1839 at the Three Elms Inn (with George Lewis as secretary), the Treoda Lodge of Oddfellows. Lodges of the same Order were established at the Heathcock Inn, Llandaff, the Griffin Inn, Lisvane (1851), the Castell Pentyrch Lodge at the King's Arms (1838), and the Ivor Castle Lodge at Cardiff Castle Inn, Tongwynlais (1859). There was also a local lodge of Foresters in existence at Whitchurch in 1860, and in 1869 a Shepherds' Lodge was formed at the Three Elms Inn.

A Local School of Poets.

In 1834 T. W. Booker, of Melingriffith, and Taliesin Williams (ab Iolo) of Merthyr Tydfil, organised at Cardiff a notable gathering known as the Gwent and Dyfed Eisteddfod. This event seems to have aroused considerable interest amongst Melingriffith workmen and local residents, and poetic composition exercised the activities of many of them. A few of the productions of local bards were published in *Greal y Bedyddwyr* in October of that year, and some of these showed considerable merit. Unfortunately the identities of the several poets are not revealed, for they wrote under initials and *noms-de-plume,* viz., R.D. (Llandaff), J. ap J., Rhydderch, Eli Glan Camlas, and Ieuan ap Ieuan. The last-named showed great skill in the composition of *dehongliadau* (interpretations).

Mari Lwyd.

An old Welsh Christmastide custom was commonly called *Mari Lwyd.* The Mari consisted of a horse's skull decorated with coloured ribbons carried by a man, over whom was draped from the skull a flowing white sheet. Mari, accompanied by a band of choristers, used at Christmas time to pass from house to house, singing popular carols and indulging in impromptu rhyming repartee with the inmates. Ultimately the party would be admitted and given cakes and ale and other Christmas gifts. The practice was carried on in the Whitchurch neighbourhood up to the early 1880's, if not later. The last local expert *Mari* was Moses Llewelyn, of Tongwynlais.

Local Road Communications.

Until the commencement of the iron industry around Merthyr after the middle of the 18th century there was little valley-ward traffic, and the present main highway in the valley, except for certain sections, was non-existent. Iron was conveyed to Cardiff by pack-mule over ancient hill-top tracks via Eglwysilan or Nelson and Caerphilly and across Caerphilly Mountain along Thornhill or Rhiwbina Hill. The through valley road was not constructed until 1767, but the section between Tongwynlais and Cardiff, is shown on a Tredegar Estate plan to have been in existence in 1761. So also were practically all the main Whitchurch cross-communications, viz., College Road, Station Road (Llandaff) and Heoldon, Tymawr Road, Velindre Road, Tynypwll Road, Tynyparc (part of), Pantbach Road, Beulah Road, Heolyderi, Wenallt Road, Pantmawr Road and Rhiwbina Hill, as well as the Forest Road leading from Tongwynlais towards Caerphilly.

Some of these roads are doubtless very ancient. The routes from Cross Inn to Caerphilly, via Thornhill, Wenallt and Blaengwynlais, may well date back many centuries, possibly to the Romano-British period. College Road and Station Road (Llandaff) were also probably in being in medieval days, providing direct routes to Llandaff Cathedral by way of a ford immediately below Llandaff Weir, before Llandaff Bridge was constructed. Tynypwll and Velindre Road are also probably of medieval origin and gave direct connection between the manorial headquarters and the lord's demesne near Tynyparc and the ancient manorial mill at Melingriffith.

From Melingriffith there existed at least three centuries ago a highway alongside the River Taff to a point near the Forest Farm, where it joined up to a similar road from Tongwynlais, the continuation being then by way of a ford giving access to the parish of Radyr at a point near the modern Radyr Railway Station. Most of these highways were little better than dirt tracks. In addition there were numerous field footpaths connecting the northern portions of the parish with the Old Church, the Mill and Llandaff Cathedral.

Rhyd Nofydd Bridge.

The lane followed by ramblers leaving Rhiwbina Hill for the Twmpath and the Wenallt crosses the stream known as Nant Nofydd by a ford called *Rhyd Nofydd*. The footbridge here consists of a very large reddish-tinted slab of stone which seems to have come from the Radyr Quarry. At one period this stone served the same purpose at the brook crossing in Wenallt Road, but when a culvert was constructed at this point the stone was removed to its present position. This was in 1878, and a Llandaff Highway Board record states that three men and three horses were employed in removing the stone from Wenallt Road to its present site, an operation which, including the fixing of the stone at Rhyd Nofydd, cost in all thirty-five shillings.

The Glamorgan Canal.

With the advent of industry improved communications became essential, and in 1790 Parliament granted powers for the construction of the Glamorgan Canal between Merthyr and Cardiff. In 1794 the canal was opened for traffic, and the improved facilities contributed to the development of Melingriffith Works, and the stimulation of trade activity at Whitchurch and Tongwynlais. For forty years the canal was the main medium of transport, and it continued to render useful service for several more decades.

The Taff Vale Railway.

Canal transport was, however, too slow to meet the rapidly changing conditions, and in 1835 Parliament sanctioned the construction of the Taff Vale Railway. The first section was opened in October, 1840. A station for traffic and goods was provided in its present position to serve Llandaff and Whitchurch.

The Taff Vale Railway proved to be a most useful and profitable undertaking, and in time rendered the canal practically useless. During the past half century it has ceased to be of very real value as a means of communication, and during 1943 the Cardiff Corporation obtained Parliamentary powers to acquire and close the canal. Above Tongwynlais the Glamorgan County Council propose to utilise sections of it for road purposes.

The Cardiff Railway.

The Bute Dock authorities looked with longing eyes at the huge profits made by the Taff Vale Railway Company and conceived a plan to divert some of the traffic to a railway under their ownership and control. Forty years or so ago they got Parliamentary authority for the construction of a new line from Treforest to the Heath, with running powers over the Taff Vale and Rhymney Railways. The new line was constructed at enormous cost, but its proprietors were unable to secure a connection to the Taff Vale Railway at Treforest; and the new undertaking developed into a "white elephant."

A station was provided at Whitchurch, with halts at Rhiwbina, Coryton, and Tongwynlais,* and a passenger train service was commenced about 1910. As, however, the amount of traffic above Coryton was so small, part of the railway was taken up for War purposes in a few years' time, and the line above Coryton has since been practically derelict. The Coryton-Cardiff service, however, was continued, and has played an important part in the stimulation of building development, particularly at Rhiwbina.

Railways, however, do not now adequately meet the requirements of the travelling public, and since the European War there has been a considerable development of omnibus services by the Cardiff Corporation and other local authorities and public companies, and no suburb of Cardiff is today better served in this direction than the Whitchurch area, an advantage which must lead after the World War to increased building development.

Local Fisheries.

From the Middle Ages down to the period of intense colliery development in the valleys the River Taff was known to be a prolific haunt of salmon, sewin and trout, and the fisheries were a source of substantial

---

* At Tongwynlais it was necessary to demolish a number of cottages and an inn to enable the railway to be constructed.

income to the various manorial lords. At Radyr Weir the Melingriffith Company had an elaborate underground fishery (remains of which still exist), where salmon was trapped in considerable quantities, especially at week-ends, and collected and removed in trams on Monday mornings. River pollution with particles of coal and rock in suspension have destroyed the salmon, although coarse fish may still be caught.

The Whitchurch Brook was also prolific of trout until the past 40 or 50 years, and large catches of good sized fish were sometimes recorded. Fishing with rod and line was practised by people of sporting instincts; most of the fish was caught, however, by waders groping under stones. At times when the Deri mill-pond, after a process of cleansing, was being refilled, the brook from near the Deri into Whitchurch was so depleted of water for a short period that the various pools were flush with fish, and some gropers used to catch and carry home as much as twenty pounds weight of trout.

Public Rights of Way.

Whitchurch is intersected by a considerable number of footpaths through pleasant fields and woods which give access to different parts of the parish. Some of these have been obliterated as the result of building development, but the bulk of them still remain and are valuable amenities both for residents and visitors.

One such footpath leads from Castell Coch gates through the woods and along the summit of Fforest Goch to connect again with the highway near Blaengwynlais. To this path there was also a connecting link passing in the vicinity of the Castle.

About 1926 a member of the Bute family contested the validity of the alleged public rights over these footpaths. The Castle entrance gates were locked and wire fences erected to block access to the paths. This action aroused great indignation among the residents of Tongwynlais, and concerted action was taken to remove the obstructions. The Caerphilly Urban District Council, in whose area the locality was at that time included, also took action, and councillors and local residents walked the contested paths, removing all obstructions as they proceeded. Since that time, apparently, public rights over these paths have not been resisted.

Old Whitchurch Industries.

At the middle of last century Melingriffith Works was by far the most important local industry. There were also smaller works in the neighbourhood at which some local people were employed. One of these occupied the site of the present-day Fram Concrete Works. It belonged to a firm called De Bergue, and manufactured ironwork for bridges. Much of the material used in the ill-fated Tay Bridge was produced here. Hard by, on the other side of College Road, was the College Ironworks, which for a time had eight furnaces in full blast.

After the closing down of De Bergue's works in the eighties the South Wales Manure Company laid down plant thereon for steaming bones from slaughtered horses, and converting them into manure. Objection was taken to this somewhat obnoxious industry by local residents and by the Cardiff Rural Sanitary Authority, and legal action ensued. The Llandaff magistrates decided that the trade was offensive, and this decision was maintained on an appeal to Quarter Sessions. The South Wales Manure Co. then appealed to the Queen's Bench, when the judges declared that bone-steaming was not bone-boiling within the meaning of the Public Health Act of 1875.

In 1885 a works was established at Llandaff Yard for the manufacture of fiddle strings and similar articles from animal gut. The offensive odour from this industry also gave rise to objection by local inhabitants.

An Ancient Industrial Undertaking.

Until the middle of the 18th century, when the Melingriffith Works was started, Whitchurch was almost entirely agricultural in character. It would appear, however, that there was an industrial undertaking in the parish almost a century earlier. A *Plymouth Estate* deed, dated September 16, 1662, records a partnership agreement between John Greenuff of Vann, Richard Jones of Hautam (Glos.), gent, Alice Steevins of Ridgewrne (Glam.), widow, and Grigorie Iremonger of Edington (Wilts.), in respect of "forges or ironworks called Machen forge and appurtenances in Co. Glam., and *one iron furnace called Tave furnace in the parish of Whitchurch and Eglwyseland* Co. Glam., for a term of years at an annual rent of £79." The partnership was for a term of 16 years.

The only point at which a furnace near the River Taff could be in the parishes both of Whitchurch and Eglwysilan would be at Tongwynlais, and I have heard of a local tradition that there was formerly a furnace in this locality. A field adjoining the old tanyard in Market Street used to be called the *charcoal* field, and this may be associated with the old furnace.

An Ancient Taff Crossing.

For generations there has existed a footway linking up Whitchurch and Radyr, crossing the River Taff by a bridge near Melingriffith Works. References occur in Melingriffith Works accounts for 1786-7 to repairs carried out to this bridge, which was known as the 'Red Bridge,' a name which still applies to the present-day railway bridge. When the Taff Vale Railway was constructed (1835-1840—if not before) the old footbridge seems to have been demolished, but pedestrians continued to use the footpath and crossed the river by trespassing on the railway property. In the 1890's the Railway Company, following a fatal accident to a pedestrian, instituted court proceedings to prevent trespass. The Radyr and Whitchurch Parish Councils and the Llandaff and Dinas Powis Rural District Council took up the matter and claimed the existence of a public right of way over the railway bridge. This the railway company denied. Negotiations ensued between the various parties and ultimately in 1906 the Railway Company, without admitting the existence of a right of way, consented to the erection by the District Council of a footbridge alongside and attached to the railway bridge, on the Melingriffith side. This bridge was maintained by the Rural

District Council until its highway powers were transferred to the Glamorgan County Council under the Local Government Act, 1929. The latter authority seem indisposed to accept responsibility for the continued maintenance of the footbridge, and as the structure is fast deteriorating there exists a danger of the right of way being extinguished.

Castell Coch Vineyard.

About 1873 Lord Bute decided to undertake an experiment in wine-making from grapes grown locally in the open air. A site was selected in the fields below Castell Coch, now part of the Castle Farm. This faced due south and was protected behind and at the sides by hills. Lord Bute's gardener, Mr. A. Pettigrew, visited France to inspect vineyards and study methods of wine-making in the Medoc, Champagne and Bordeaux regions. The first plantings at Castell Coch were made in the spring of 1875 with two varieties of cane thought most suitable to the local climate. These were planted in rows, and kept down to a height of four feet. The crops during the first three or four years seemed promising, although the crops were not heavy. The first wine was made in 1877, when 40 gallons of the Castell Coch brand were bottled. Then in 1878 and 1879 bad weather conditions were encountered. In 1880 the crops failed, and the absence of sun, combined with the cold and wet weather of the succeeding seasons, led to the failure of the undertaking. A similar experiment near Lavernock also met with ill success and the venture was abandoned.

Disraeli and Greenmeadow.

There exists a popular legend that Disraeli visited Greenmeadow during the widowhood of Mrs. Wyndham Lewis, who later became his wife, and that during such visits he stayed at the Cow and Snuffers Inn, Llandaff North. This legend rests on very doubtful foundations, although it is possible that both parties may have visited Greenmeadow after their marriage. Disraeli himself denied that he had ever stayed at the Cow and Snuffers.

Wyndham Lewis, a son of the Rev. Wyndham Lewis, of New House, Llanishen, a director of the Dowlais Iron Company, in 1815 married Mary Ann Evans, of Bamford Speke, Devon. He probably built the recently demolished mansion of Greenmeadow on the site of an old farmhouse, and lived in it for some years. Bird's Cardiff Directory of 1829 refers to the house as "the gothicized residence of Wyndham Lewis." In 1820-6 he was M.P. for Cardiff, but on the withdrawal of Bute patronage in the latter year, he sought election for an English constituency. For a long period he represented Maidstone, with Disraeli as his junior colleague. He died in March, 1838, and within eighteen months, in August, 1839, his widow married Disraeli. It is very unlikely that during her widowhood Greenmeadow entertained Disraeli as a visitor, although he and his wife may have visited the mansion some years later whilst on a political mission to South Wales, at which time the property was in the occupation of Wyndham's brother, Henry Lewis.

Air Raids on Whitchurch.

Whitchurch like most localities near the sea-board of South Wales was frequently visited by German air-raiders during the recent War and high explosive or incendiary bomb attacks were made on the locality on about half a dozen occasions during the years 1941-3. The first direct raid which occurred on January 2, 1941, affected mainly the central portion of Whitchurch and caused damage to about 250 houses. None of them, however, were injured so badly as to necessitate total demolition. On the 26th day of the same month the Philog area was attacked and on this occasion 156 properties sustained damage. Four had to be demolished and others had to be temporarily evacuated. A few persons lost their lives.

On April 29, 1941, an incendiary bomb raid resulted in the burning of a house at Heoldon; 16 other premises were damaged. On May 14 bombs were again dropped in the Philog area and 44 buildings suffered broken windows and damaged ceilings. There were one or two slight raids in 1942, and on May 18, 1943, occurred the last and most serious raid which damaged 476 properties throughout the Rural District. The areas of Whitchurch mostly affected were Wenallt and Pantbach Roads, and the streets in the Velindre Ward lying between Park Road and the Cardiff Railway. One house in Wenallt Road was badly damaged by fire and six houses in Pantbach Road were completely destroyed, and there were a few casualties. The total number of houses classified in the "total loss" category at Whitchurch as the result of all the raids was fifteen.

CORRECTIONS AND ADDITIONAL NOTES

Page 1, *line* 8. During the War the Melingriffith Tinplate Works was used partly for Government stores and partly in connection with an adjoining factory built by the Ministry of Aircraft Production for the manufacture of aluminium forgings by the Northern Aluminium Company Ltd. At the time of writing negotiations are reported to be in progress for the acquisition by Richard Thomas & Co., Ltd., of the new factory, and it is thought that the manufacture of tinplate will shortly be resumed.

Page 43, *line* 22. For *poetry* read *pottery*.

Page 98, *line* 24. Mr. John Morgan retires from the headship of the Whitchurch Junior Boys' School in January, 1946.

Page 100, *line* 2. Under the provisions of the Education Act, 1944, the Whitchurch Senior School is to be graded as a Secondary School, probably of the Modern cum Technical type.

Page 232. Locality Nicknames.—In its early days by reason of the fact that some well-known Socialists lived there and were frequently visited by Socialist politicians, many of national fame, the Rhiwbina Garden Village was frequently referred to as Little Moscow, Bolshiville, and similar names. In later years following the European War when building by private enterprise attracted a large new population some of whom owed money to traders in Cardiff and elsewhere, Rhiwbina was often referred to as the Debtors' Retreat. The foregoing epithets are now rarely heard, but by reason of the fact that so many people of the professional classes live there the locality is sometimes referred to as the Home of the Intelligentsia.

INDEX.

A

Aberavon, 172.
Abercarn, 139.
Aberdare, 2, 222, 232.
Abergavenny, 10, 12, 232.
Abergwnleis, 183.
Aberpergwm, 194.
Abersychan, 147.
Abertillery, 167.
Aberystwyth, 147, 151.
Academy, 95.
Acts and Statutes :—
   Education, 1649-50, 85.
              1870, 71, 96.
              1883, 71.
              1889, 100.
              1900, 71.
   Highways, 1555-63, 66.
               1601, 66.
               1844, 69.
               1860, 69, 70.
               1862, 70.
   Local Govt., 1888, 65, 69, 71.
   Parish Councils, 1894, 65, 69, 71.
   Poor Law, 1601, 66, 67.
              1834, 67, 69.
              1929, 69, 71.
   Private Street Works, 73, 74.
   Public Health, 1872, 69.
                1875, 70, 241.
   Public Libraries, 80.
   Quarter Sessions, 69, 70.
Agriculture, Board of, 81.
Air Raids, 243.
Album Monasterium, 4, 9, 15, 18, 20, 21, 22, 23, 24, 26, 40, 65, 197, 229.
Allahabad, 187.
Allensbank Woods, 194.
Allt, 184.
Alltwen, 203.
Aluminium Manufacture, 243.
Angharad of Tre Deigr, 184, 191.
Annouid, Annovydd, 183, 184, 203.
Anthony, Evan, 121.
Anthony, Rev. T., 172.
Arawn, 213.
Arles, 204.
Armer, Jas., 176.
Ashe, J. C., 175.
Ashgrove, 207.
          -Farm, 108.
Assize, Rent of, 15, 21, 22, 26.
Austin, I. T., 176.
Avon, Afan, 6, 7, 28.

B

Badelsmere, Bartholomew de, 19, 20, 21, 32, 33, 34.
Balaclava, 191.
Bangor, 137, 152.
Bancroft, A., 86.
Bands, 236.
Bargoed, 153.
Bannockburn, 31.
Barnett, F., 176.
Baron, A., 192.
Barrington Park, Glos., 191.
Barry, 35, Hospital, 78, 100.
Barway, 56.
Bassaleg, 143.
Bassett, S, 24.
Beake, W., 149.
Beauchamp, Richard, Earl of Warwick, 26.
Beaupre, 214.
Bedford, Jasper, Duke of, 26.
Bedwas, 29, 105.
Beine, 201.
Bell, Dr., 89.
Bennett, Inspector, 79.
Berkerolles, Wm. de, 35.
Berw Pwll, 207, 219.
Beswarick, Rev. T. O., 130.
Bevan, Rev. Jas., 146, 163.
Bevan, Hopkin, 109.
Bidwal, 199.
Bine, 201.
Birchgrove, 41, 74, 175.
Bishopsgate, 60.
Black, E., 186.
Black Brook Colliery, 183.
Black Cock Inn, 183.
Black Lady, 218.
Blaenau, 6, 113, 139.
Blaengwynlais, 182, 204, 238, 240.
Blaenycwm, 232.
Blakemore, R., 102, 103.
Blancminster, Blancmoster, Blancmoustier, 4, 40, 197.
Bledri, Bp., 84.
Blue House, 164.
Blyton, A., 187.
Boards, County Road, 69, 70, 71.
      — Highway, 69, 71.
      — of Guardians, 67, 69, 71.
Bohun, Humphrey de, 36, 37, 38.
Boithan, 198.
Bolter, W. S., 176, 177.
Book of Llandav, 183, 184, 197, 198.
Book of Sports, 105.
Booker, C., 97, 119, 178.
      — Richard, 103.
      — T. W., 94, 98, 103, 128, 198, 237

Bord, borg, 5.
Boroughbridge, Battle of, 23.
Boverton, 218.
Bradney, Sir Joseph, 60, 185.
Brangham, E., 95.
Brecon, 13, 36, 172, Co. 191.
Breconshire, 7; Res., 75, 77.
Breos, Wm. de, 23.
Bridgend, 110.
Bristol Channel, 200.
Brithdir, 199.
British and Foreign Schools Socy., 89.
Briwnant, 2, 14, 55n, 56, 182, 202, 204; isaf, 204, 205.
Briwydd, 204.
Brown, Ann, 155, 156.
— Wm., 155.
Brownrigg, W., 192.
Brut y Tywysogion, 228.
Bryant, Thos., 144.
Bryn Derwen, 205.
Brynmawr, 177.
Buckinghamshire, 190.
Bugler, O. C., 170.
Bull, H., 186.
Bullock, A. H., 80.
Burgh, Hubert de, 10.
Burt, M., 193.
Butchers' Arms, 182, 230, 231.
Bute, Marquis of, 28, 30, 51, 80, 81, 113, 189, 190, 225.
Bwci Bo, 215.
Bwlch y Cwm, 204.
Byne, 201.

C

Cadifor ap Ceidrych, 50, 190.
Cae Bach, 204.
Cae Castell, 184.
Cae Cerrigog, 206.
Cae Coch, 206.
Cae Delyn, 210.
Cae draw'r heol, 206.
Cae Glanynant, 210.
Cae Glas, 205.
Cae Gwyn, 204, 208.
Cae Moat, 3.
Cae Nadda, 204.
Cae Noa, 205.
Cae Rhys, 206.
Cae Tinker, 204.
Cae wrth y ty, 204.
Cae Velyn, 102.
Caeau Cynrig, 55, 56.
Caeau Gerwon, 209.
Caeau Heoldon, 212.
Caerleon, 193.
Caerphilly, 100, 105, 109, 124, 131, 143, 147, 190, 192, 238.
Caerphilly Castle, 7, 12, 14, 18, 23, 25, 26, 28, 29, 35, 36, 46, 49, 214, 218, 225, 228.
Caerphilly Common, 1.
— U.D.C. 75, 240.
Cae'r Barra, 207, 208.
Cae'r Bont Garreg, 205.
Cae'r Celynen, 205, 206.
Cae'r Coed, 206, 207.
Cae'r Draenen, 205.
Cae'r Efail, 205, 207.
Cae'r Ffawydden, 212.
Cae'r Fforest, 205.
Cae'r Graig, 205.
Cae'r lloi, 206.
Cae'r Llwyn Bach, 205.
Cae'r Moat, 210.
Cae'r Pant, 205.
Cae'r Ty Mawr, 212.
Cae'r Wern, 204.
Cae'r Ynn, 207.
Caiach, 12.
Caireparke, 27.
Caithness, 194.
Calixtus II, Pope, 184.
Canton, 172, 219.
— Bridge, 217.
— Sanatorium, 78.
Capel Gwilym, 143.
Capel Ivor, 158.
Capitol Cinema, 217.
Cardiff, 3, 36, 38, 43, 50, 73, 74, 75, 82, 87, 106, 109, 110, 124, 127, 131, 138, 140, 143, 145, 149, 172, 190, 193, 206, 220, 230, 235, 238.
Cardiff Castle, 5, 6, 8, 9, 10, 12, 14, 20, 23, 25, 28, 32, 37, 225.
Cardiff Constable, 193.
Cardiff and District Baptist Board, 176, 177.
Cardiff Gas Co., 75, 78.
— Iron and Tinplate Co., 103.
— Lord of, 15.
— Railway, 182, 185, 188, 239.
— R.D.C., 65, 70, 72, 75, 77, 78, 82, 203, 204, 212, 229.
— Union Rural Sanitary Authority, 70, 75, 76, 78.
— Waterworks Co., 77.
— Workers' Co-operative Garden Village Socy., 100, 186.
Caredig of Powys and Ceredigion, 58.
Carlisle Nicholas, 73.
Carlyle, Thos., 58.
Carmarthen, 232.
Carnegie, A., 129.
Castan (Brook), 2, 55, 56.
Castell, 204.
Castell Coch, 1, 5, 12, 18, 25, 26, 28, 35, 36, 46, 47, 49, 50, 51, 61, 82, 97, 184, 185, 199, 204, 213, 214, 217, 221, 224, 225, 226, 234, 240.
Castell Coch Vineyard, 242.
Castell Ffrwd, 204.
Castell Nadda, 204.
Castell y Briwydd, 14, 204.
Castellan, 167.
Castleton, 143.
Castle Farm, 49, 204.
Ceffyl Dwr, 214.
Cefn, 184.
Cefn Carnau, 1, 18, 185, 194, 203.

Cefn Cibwr, 1, 61.
Cefn Garw, 14.
Cefn Onn, 1, 6, 43, 49, 61, 62.
Cefn y Vid—Fud, 199.
Chadderton, 140.
Chapels and Churches:
  Ainon (Tongwynlais), 121, 131-142, 171, 178, 179, 198.
  All Saints', Whitchurch, 178, 179, 182, 205.
  Ararat, 54, 88, 143-148, 176, 178, 179, 200, 208.
  Baptist (Rhiwbina), 176-7, 179.
  Bethel (Morganstown), 109, 110, 118, 120.
  Bethel (Whitchurch), 149-53, 178, 179.
  Bethesda (Gwaelodygarth), 154, 155.
  Bethesda (Tongwynlais), 121, 122, 171-3, 180.
  Bethesda'r Fro, 172.
  Bethesda Hall (Whitchurch), 176, 178, 180.
  Beulah, 154-170, 171, 178, 180, 181, 185, 231.
  Birchgrove, 175.
  Broadmead (Bristol), 113.
  Christchurch (Llandaff North), 165, 166
  Ebenezer (Whitchurch), 108-117, 118, 178, 179.
  Ebenezer (Cardiff), 154.
  Gilgal (Llandaff), 111 and n.
  Groeswen, 87, 113, 154, 158, 160, 172.
  Hermon (Tongwynlais), 111, 118-123, 178, 179.
  Hawthorne Road, 115.
  Llandaff, 84, 85.
  Lisvane, 88.
  Llanedeyrn, 88.
  Llaniltern, 88.
  Llanishen, 88, 175.
  Llantarnam Abbey, 222.
  Methodists, Calvinistic, 107, 108-123, 154, 178.
  Methodists, Wesleyan, 107, 124-130, 149, 175, 178, 180.
  Pentyrch, 88.
  Plasnewydd, 192.
  Plymouth Brethren, 176, 178.
  Radyr, 88, 233.
  Rehoboth (Tongwynlais), 177, 180.
  Rhiwbina Methodist, 175.
  Roath Road, 175.
  Salem (Tongwynlais), 131-142, 171, 178, 179.
  Seion (Cardiff), 111.
  Tabernacle, 108-117, 162, 178, 179.
  Trinity (Taff's Well), 123.
  St. John's (Cardiff), 193.
  St. Michael's, 178, 179.
  St. Teilo's (Whitchurch), 174, 179.
  St. Thomas', 41, 178, 179, 208.
  St. Mary's (Whitchurch), 40-42.
  Whitchurch, 88, 97, 177, 178, 179.
  Womanby Street, 105, 106, 184.
Chadderton, 140.

Chance, Prof. T. W., 176, 177.
Chappell, Rev. H., 130.
Chard, 138.
Charles I, 225.
Charles, Thos. (Bala), 87.
Charles, Thos. (Llandaff), 85.
Chepstow, 23, 124, 222.
Cheshire, 36.
Chester, 12.
Chivers, S., 100.
Chwech Erw, 209.
Cil, 198.
Cilfynydd, 139, 199.
Cilynis, Celynis }
Clun yr ynis, Clynis } 198, 199, 221.
Cylynnis }
Clais, 198.
Clare, Eleanor de, 31.
— Gilbert de (first), 10, 50.
— Gilbert de (the Red), 11, 12, 13, 16, 17, 31, 32, 33, 46.
— Gilbert (son of the Red), 21, 31, 37, 48.
— Joan de, 31.
— Richard de, 11.
Clark, G. L., 195.
— G. T., 185, 195, 228.
— Wyndham, 195.
Clarke, Rev. J. T., 41, 98.
Clatworthy, J. T., 186, 187.
Clavering, Alice, 189.
Clogg, Rev. W. H., 129.
Clwt-y-bont, 136.
Coed cefn garw, 204.
Coedwig, 204.
Coedwigdy, 182, 185, 204.
Coed y Wenallt, 203.
Coity, 21, 34, 35, 229.
— Castle, 46.
College Road Ironworks, 240.
Colley, A., 55.
Commorth, 27, 28.
Commotes, 7.
Cookham Dene, 220.
Corbett, J. S., 26, 30, 51.
Cornel y Waun, 145, 209.
Cory, J., 129.
— Richard, 129, 151.
— Sir Herbert J., 130, 160.
Coryton, 215, 239.
— House, 1.
Coslett, J., 134.
Cottars, 16.
Cottrell, 30, 191, 192, 228.
Court, Manorial, 15, 66.
County Council, 71.
Cow and Snuffers Inn, 214, 235, 242.
Cowbridge, 193, 232.
Cradock, W., 105.
Craig, 205.
Craig yr Allt, 105, 183.
Craig y Castell, 56.
Craig y Llyn, 2.
Craig Cibwr, 203.
Crea, Miss, 93.

Creigiau, 3.
Crickhowell, 137.
Crimean War, 191.
Crockherbtown, 217.
Crofft, 212.
Crofft Awst, 204.
Cromer, 193.
Cromwell, Katherine, 61, 63.
— Oliver, 58-64, 202, 221.
— Robert, 64.
— Sir Henry, 61, 64.
— Thomas, 60, 63, 64.
— Walter, 61, 63.
Crug, 184.
Crug Glas, 183.
Crug Ri, 184.
Customars, 15, 19, 22.
Cwmavon, 140.
Cwm Brynau, 183.
Cwm Castell, 59.
Cwm Glais, 204.
Cwm Gwynlais, 204.
Cwmllynfell, 172.
Cwm Nofydd, 14, 181, 184, 203, 204, 205.
Cwm Twrch, 232.
Cwn Annwn, 213, 214.
Cyfarthfa, 192.
Cynfrig, 228.

D

Dafis, Rev. (Llantrisant), 158, 159.
Dafydd ap Gwilym, 184.
— ap Jenkyn, 229.
— Richard Gwynn, 228, 229.
Danes, 202.
Dan-y-ddraenen, 56.
Daniel, Ed., 154, 155, 156, 157.
— Enoch, 158.
— Mary, 154, 155.
David ap Llewelyn, 26.
— son of Philip of Bedwellty, 185.
— Evan, 127.
— Martha, 155.
— Rev. J. J., 144.
— T. W., 167.
— Wm. (Methodist), 126.
— Wm. (Beulah), 157.
— Wm. (Peterston-s.-Ely), 155, 164.
— Amelia, 168.
— D., 128.
— D. H., 161.
— D. T., 41.
— Rev. D., 132, 133.
— Rev. (Ararat), 133, 145.
— Rev. Dd. (Pontrhydyfen), 110.
— Eben., 131n.
— G. F., 236.
— G. M. L., 187.
— H., 129.
— Rev. G., 131.
— J. (Tongwynlais), 134.
— J. (Glanynant), 161, 162, 163.
— Rev. J. (Taihirion), 134.
— Rev. J. (Newton), 139.
— Rev. J. S., 139.

David, Job, 111.
— Rev. Ll. Lloyd, 41.
— Lord, 187.
— Rev. Penry, 177.
— Robert, 129.
— W. M., 79, 168.
— W. R., 129.
Dawlish, 198.
Declaration of Indulgence, 105.
Deere, M., 85.
Derguist, Well of, 184.
Deheubarth, 222.
Deio, Mathew, 26.
Deri, 1, 2, 55, 154, 181, 182, 188, 205, 206.
— Duon, 205.
— Farm, 202.
— Mill, 182, 205.
Despenser, Earl of, 23, 25.
— Eleanor, 23.
— Hugh le, 24, 31, 32, 36, 38, 39.
Dew, J., 113.
Diamond, R. A., 230.
Dinas Powis, 71, 222.
Disraeli, B., 194, 242.
Ddwy Erw Annwyl, 205.
Dolau (Rads.), 146.
Dorset, 36.
— Marquis, 64.
Douglas, 198.
Dowlais, 147, 158, 190, 194, 195, 198.
Draenen Penygraig, 55, 56, 57, 203.
Drane, R., 225, 234.
Drew, Rev. S., 113.
Dulais, 197.
Duffryn Golych, 214.
Duncalfe, Rev. A. B., 130.
Duncan, J. D., 168.
Durham, 160.
Durston, Rev. F., 139, 140.
Dwy Erw, 209.
Dwy Erw Bwdwr, 208.
— Feinion, 211.
— Glanynant, 210.
— Gofion, 208.
— Grinion, 206.
— Heol y Forlan, 211.
— Isaf, 208.
— nesaf, 210.
— Uchaf, 205, 210.
Dwy Erw'r Felin, 209.
— -Ffawydden, 206.
— -Ysgubor Ddegwm, 207.
Dynevor, Lord, 94, 191.

E

Ealing Hampstead, 186.
Eagle Iron and Brass Foundry, 235.
Ebbw Vale, 102, 135, 177, 193.
Edeyrn, 4.
Edward I, 17, 53.
— II, 21, 23, 25, 31, 36, 37, 38.
— III, 24, 25.
— VI, 27, 28, 51, 189, 229.
Edward ap Richard Gwynn, 229.

Edmunds, Rev. J., 132.
Edwards, Rev. D., 132.
— Rev. J., 177.
— Dr. W. T., 162, 163.
Efail Jervis, 182, 206, 207, 224, 231.
Eglwysgwladys, 33.
Eglwysilan, 29, 32, 82, 86, 87, 97, 105, 138, 159, 161, 184, 198, 241.
Eglwysnewydd (Whitchurch), 196, 199.
— (Carm.), 59.
Eglwyswen, 196.
Einion ap Collwyn, 222, 223.
Eli Glan Gamlas, 237.
Eltham, 62.
Ely, 78, 82, 94, 124, 125.
— R., 20, 218.
Emmanuel, J. (Llanishen), 127, 158.
Enclosures, 81.
English Place Name Society, 196.
Energlyn, 6, 192.
Erbury, W., 105.
Enysvaiglon, 26.
Erw Bach, 210.
— Llefrith, 209.
Erw'r Fforest, 212.
— Ffynon, 204.
Erw Pant Rhydwalla, 205.
Erwi'r Delyn, 210.
Estates:
  Greenclose, 208.
  Lewis, the Van, 193-5.
  Homfray, Penlline, 193.
  Mackintosh, 192.
  Meredith, 184.
  Mountjoy, 189-90.
  Pentwyn, 186.
  Plymouth, 190, 203.
  Tredegar, 184, 190-1, 209, 238.
  Williams, Roath Court, 193.
  Wingfield, 191-2.
Evans, Annie, 98.
— Rev. Christmas, 131, 144.
— David, 94.
— David (The Brook), 113.
— David (Beulah), 168.
— Daniel, 113.
— Rev. Benjamin, 110.
— Rev. D., 113, 114, 163.
— Rev. D. (Cadoxton), 144.
— Eli, 96, 144, 231.
— John (Beulah), 162, 165, 166.
— Rev. J. (Maerdy), 155.
— Rev. J. W., 141.
— Rev. Morgan, 132.
— Richard, 132.
— Thomas, 162 (Traveller).
— Thomas (Smith), 134.
— Thomas, 112, 113.
— Rev. T. J., 21.
— Wm., 112.
— Wm. (Wesleyan), 124.
— Rev. Wm. (Tonyrefail), 109,110,119
— Rev. W. G., 147.
— W. Luke, 127.
Evesham, 11.

Ewbank, Rev. T., 130.
Ewenny, 209.
Eynon, T. J., 177.
Ezard, Rev. E., 172.

F

Fencley, Rev. Chas., 175.
Ffilog, Ffyliog ⎱ 200, 215.
Ffulawg, Ffyliog ⎰
Fforddlas, 109, 211.
Fforest Ganol, 2, 183, 204.
— Fawr, 183, 211, 213, 238.
— Goch, 12, 47, 48, 198, 199, 217, 225, 226, 234, 240.
— Isa, 68.
Ffynnon Bren, 217.
— Denis, 217.
— Hoba, 206.
— wen, 206, 207.
Fice, Rev. E., 127.
Fid Fedw, 199.
Fidgelyn, 199.
Fidlas, 199.
Findlay, Rev. J. A., 130.
Fire, Brigade, 79.
Fisher, S., 177.
Fisheries, 239.
Fitzhamon, 6, 8, 30, 222, 228.
Fleming, Sir Wm., 37, 38.
Flint, 232.
Follows, Rev. G., 128.
Fonmon, 46, 192, 204, 212.
Forlan, Foreland, 182, 209.
Forrester, Rev. K. C., 175.
Fox and Hounds Inn, 92, 174.
Fram Works, 14, 240.
Francis, R., 134.
French, Rev. J., 105.
Friendly Societies, 236-7.
— Oddfellows, 237.

G

Gabalfa, 3, 54, 106, 233, 235.
— House, 55.
Gadda Hir, 209.
Gage and Davies, 188.
Gamage, Joan, 229.
Garn, 184.
Garnant, 206.
Garn Lwyd, 184.
Garth, 3, 48, 210.
— Lesser, 1, 3, 225, 234.
Gascony, 17, 23.
Gelli Farm, 73, 204, 212.
— Quarry, 43, 182.
Gelligaer, 18, 35, 43, 105, 193.
Gelynis, 198, 199.
Geoffrey of Monmouth, 84.
Ghosts, 220.
Giffard, John, 22, 23, 37.
Giraldus Cambrensis, 8, 9, 50.
Glais, 198.
Glamorgan, 4, 11, 17, 25, 34, 35, 37, 49.
— Lord of, 15, 16, 18, 19, 20, 23, 24, 26, 28, 40.
— Canal, 238.
— Education Com., 75, 188, 191.

Glamorgan, Vale of, 1, 4, 6, 25.
Glancaiach, 191, 192.
Glanrhyd, 206.
Glanymor, 210.
Glanynant, 182, 205, 209.
Glascoed, 146.
Gloucester Abbey, 5.
— Wm. of, 8, 10, 48, 50, 53.
— Robert, 8, 40.
— Duke of, 15, 16, 17.
Gloucester, 36.
Glyndwr, Owain, 25.
Glynis, 198, 199.
Glynneath, 232.
Glynrhondda, 7, 10, 11, 18, 35, 189.
Goldsworthy, A. L., 175.
Gouge, Thos., 86.
Gough, A., 134.
Gould, Sir Chas., 191.
Gower, 23, 143.
Graig, 56, 182, 212; Farm, 204.
Granger, Dr. F. W., 75, 76, 77.
Greenclose, 9, 54.
Greenhill, 103, 181, 207, 235.
— Special School, 75.
Green Lady, 218, 219.
Greenmeadow, 39, 58, 62, 140, 189, 190, 197, 206, 214, 220, 238, 242.
Greenuff, J, of Van, 241.
Greenwich, 62.
Greyfriars, Cardiff, 37.
Griffith, Donne, 227.
Griffiths, G., 151.
— S. D., 162, 165, 166.
— Rev. D., 162, 163.
— Rev. D., 116, 122.
— Rev. Rees, 133, 149, 150.
Griffithsmoor, 15, 17, 19, 20, 22, 24, 26, 27, 28, 299.
Groes, Y, 74, 187, 207.
Gruffydd ap Ivor Bach, 9, 102, 203, 228.
— ap Rhys, 9, 11, 12, 14, 15, 31, 48.
Gruffydd, Prof. W. J., 187, 207.
Gummer, H., 130.
Guy, Rev. C. F., 175.
Gwaedle, 202.
Gwaelodygarth, 95, 154, 171.
Gwaethfoed, 32, 58, 60, 198.
Gwaun, 200.
Gwaungledyr, 105.
Gwaun y pentre, 56.
Gwaundu Rhoda, 200.
Gwaun Sir Edward, 204.
Gwauntreoda, 200, 214.
— Uchaf, 143, 208.
Gwern, 204.
Gwilym, son of David of Bedwellty, 185.
Gwinett, family, 193.
Gwrach y rhibyn, 214.
Gwyl Mabsant, 106.
Gwyn, J., 28.
Gwyn, family, 229.
Gwynlais, Gungleis, Gwynlas, 8, 12, 14, 48, 183, 197, 198, 230.
Gwynne, family, 57, 59.

H

Haddock, W. W., 98.
Hailey Park, 14.
Hamer, W., 167, 168.
Hamlin, Rev. G., 176.
Hammett, J., 150.
Hannon, Canon, 174.
Harding, J., 209.
Harding's Down, 44.
Hare, J. C., 60.
Harford, Messrs. 89, 90, 102.
Harford, Partridge & Co., 102.
Harper, Rev. W., 175.
Harris, Rev. E., 110.
— Howell, 108, 109.
— Rev. N., 150.
Harrison, F., 58.
Harvey, J. C., 176.
Hautam, 241.
Haverfordwest, 167.
Heap, Rev. D. N., 175.
Heath, 54, 55, 99.
— Enclosures, 95, 191, 193, 194, 230.
Hendre, 206.
Hendredenny, 18.
Hengoed, 131.
Henry III, 10.
— VI, 26.
— VII, 26, 60, 62.
— VIII, 53, 58.
Hensol, 191, 192.
Herbert (of Coldbrook), family, 185.
— Jane, 86.
— Lady Charlotte, 28, 189.
— Sir William, 28, 29, 30, 51, 189, 190, 229.
Hereford, 24, 36.
Heriot, 24, 57.
Herne family, 129.
— J., 98.
Herring, M., 193.
Hibbert, J. W., 129.
Hicks, A., 169.
— D. J., 169.
— J. H., 166.
— T., 166.
— W. T., 169.
Hill, Col., 78.
Hinton, W. J., 186.
Hirwaun, 2, 190.
Hirwaun Wrgan, 222.
Hobbis, J. W., 151, 153.
Hodges, A., 95.
Hokedaye, 27.
Hollier, H., 194.
Hollybush Inn, 2.
Homelands, 9, 208.
Homfray, J., 193.
— Sir J., 193.
— Col. R. R., 193.
— F., 102.
— family, 192, 193.
Honorius, II, Pope, 184.
Hopkins, Rev. M., 172.
Housebote, 34.

Housing Reform Co., 186, 187.
Howard, Lady Stepney, 187.
— Sir Stafford, 187.
Howards, 68.
Howell, Edmund. 161.
— Evan Thomas, 68.
— Llew., 158.
— William, 156.
Howells, H., 108, 109.
— L., 186.
Hywel ap Meredith, 11.
— Dda, 183.
Hubba, 200.
Hughes, Rev. D., 146.
— Rev. G., 124, 154.
— Rev. J., 124.
— Rev. J. D., 141.
— R. D., 169.
Humphries, S., 126.
Huzzy, E., 129.

I

Iestyn ap Gwrgan, 200, 222, 223, 228, 229.
Ieuan ap Ivor ap Ieuan, 26.
Ifor Bach, 8, 9, 10, 15, 17, 19, 30, 31, 47, 48, 49, 200, 228, 229.
Ifor Hael, v. Morgan, Ivor.
Ilbury, 224.
Ilston, 105, 143.
Ina, 201; forest, 183.
Industrial & Prov. Soc. Act, 186.
Iolo Morganwg, 88, 228.
Isan, 4.
Is-Caiach, v. Senghenydd.
Island Cottage, 174.
Israel, J., 134.
Istan, 233.
Istleidog, 183.
Ivorites, 161.

J

James, Chris., 125.
— C. H., 125.
— Rev. D. E., 167.
— John, 112, 113.
— Rev. J., 132.
— Rev. John (Pontrhydyfen), 144.
— Rev. J. Ll. (Beulah), 158, 159, 160.
— Rev. John (Bridgend), 110.
— Justice Melbourne, 125.
— Rev. R., 109.
— Rev. R. A., 137.
— Rev. T., 134.
Jeans, J. L., 177.
Jenkins, Mrs. A., 158.
Jenkins of Hensol, family, 191.
— of Hensol, D., 192.
Jenkins, John, 165, 166.
— Rev. D. E., 145.
— Rev. J. Onfel, 137, 139.
— Capt. R., 55.
Jevons, Prof. H. S., 166, 186, 187.
— Prof. (Junior), 186.
John ap Robert ap Madoc Ychan, 229.

John ap William ap Ieuan, 62.
— H. R., 80.
— T., 156, 157.
Johns, Rev. D. B., 140.
— Rev. R. O., 151.
Jordan, R., 102.
— Mrs., 93.
Joseph, Bishop, 84, 183, 184.
Jones, Catherine, 192.
— Chas., 129.
— Rev. C. E., 153, 177.
— Daniel, 162.
— Rev. Daniel (Beulah), 108, 109; Wes. Meth., 126.
— Rev. Daniel (Tabernacle, Cardiff), 132, 133.
— Edward, 126.
— Rev. Ed., 133.
— Rev. E. (Castleton), 144.
— Rev. Elfed, 169.
— Rev. E. Norman, 116.
— Rev. Griffith, 86.
— Rev. Gwilym, 173.
— Rev. Hy., 137, 138.
— Hewitt, 177.
— James, 126.
— John (Beulah), 161, 162.
— Rev. J. (Beulah), 156, 157.
— Rev.J. (Bethlehem), 158.
— Rev. J. (Gwaelodygarth), 154, 155.
— Rev. (Tongwynlais), 171, 172.
— Rev. (Llandyssul), 131.
— Rev. (Bridgend), 110.
— Rev. J. A., 151, 152.
— Rev. Dr. J. Cynddylan, 114, 116, 122.
— Rev. J. Meredith, 152.
— J. Rees, 108.
— Rev. Luther, 143, 147, 177.
— Miss Margaret A., 166.
— Price, 150.
— Rev. R. A., 139.
— Rev. Samuel (Beulah), 167, 168, 169.
— Rev. Samuel (Gabalfa), 177.
— Sidney, 150, 151, 152.
— Rev. T. Deri, 147.
— Rev. T. J., 120, 121.
— Thos. (Eos Glan Rhymni), 131.
— Rev. T. (Wes.), 128.
— Rev. Thos. Jones (Ang.), 85.
— William (Bethel), 150.
— William (Llanmaes), 230.
— Rev. W. (Bethany), 144.
— Rev. W. (Ainon), 132, 133, 135, 137.
— Rev. W. (Cwmavon), 110.
— Rev. W. D. O., 123.
— Rev. W. E., 147.
— W. M., 169.
— W. R., 140, 141.
— W. S., 98, 166, 169.
— Rev. W. T., 114, 115.
— W. W., 176, 177.

K

Kae John Kett, 212.
Kelpie, 214.
Kenewrek ap Howel, 18.
Kenfig, 23, 28, 35.
Kestrell, J. N., 129.
Keybote, 34.
Keynsham, Abbey, 8.
— Lordship, 53-57.
Kibour, Kibbor, Cibwr, 4, 5, 7, 8, 26, 28, 29, 30, 43, 44, 48, 55, 56, 61, 82, 203.
Kidwelly, 167.
Kilkenny, 12.
Kinsella, Father, 174.
Kip, 5.

L

Ladi Wen, 215, 217.
Lais, 198.
Lampeter, 113.
Lancaster, Joseph, 89, 90.
Langford, James, 162.
— Ll., 168, 185.
Laud Archbishop, 105.
Lavernock, 108.
Leckwith, 19, 20, 23, 28, 219.
Leland, 41, 47, 49, 59, 61, 197.
Lewis ap Guilim, 27.
— ap John Gwyn, 27.
— of St. Pierre, family, 185.
— of Newhouse, family, 194.
— of Van, family, 39, 53, 57, 58, 59, 60, 62, 190, 193, 194, 198, 206.
— A. M. P., 194, 195.
— Edmund, 80, 152.
— Edward, 53, 190.
— Charlotte E. Wyndham, 194, 195.
— Elizabeth of Van, 190.
— Gabriel, 59.
— George, 237.
— Jacob, 230.
— Gwenllian, 220.
— Capt. Harry, 194.
— Henry (Greenmeadow), 95, 97, 194, 242.
— John, 126, 129.
— J. M., 128, 129.
— Lewis, 56.
— Mary, 86.
— Morgan, 126.
— Rice, 30.
— Richard, 53, 55, 56, 191.
— Philip, 150.
— Solomon, 133, 134, 135.
— Thos. (Llanishen), 185, 194, 230.
— **Thos.** (Newhouse), 185.
— **Thos.** (Van), 29, 53, 190.
— T. J., 128, 129.
— T. W., 176.
— William (Tonyrywen), 154.
— Rev. William, 133.
— W. Price, 194.
— Wyndham, 194, 242.
— Rev. Wyndham, 131.

Leyrwyt, 24.
Lisvane, 1, 7, 26, 86, 87, 88, 92, 105, 106, 115, 124, 143, 144, 181.
— Craig, 1.
Lincoln, 35.
Lingen, Lord, 93.
Llanbradach, 138, 173.
Llancaiach, 7n, 191, 192.
Llancarfan, 4, 6, 105.
— Monastery, 233.
Llandaff, 3, 4, 5, 7, 9, 15, 20, 25, 40, 41, 53, 54, 65, 66, 67, 71, 73, 74, 77, 78, 81, 82, 86, 88, 93, 124, 125, 214, 219, 229, 232, 233, 241.
— Act Book, 84, 185.
— Cathedral, 183.
— Yard, 159, 161, 235, 241.
— North, 14, 15, 42, 80, 115, 160, 164, 211, 233, 235.
— Bridge, 67, 68.
— Highway Board, 238; Record, 208.
— Manor, 14.
Llandav, Book of, 40.
Llandaff and Dinas Powis R.D.C., 202.
Llandough, 4, 150.
Llandovery, 232.
Llanedarne, } 4, 7, 26, 29, 53, 88, 105.
Llanedeyrne, }
Llanelly, 124, 153.
Llanfabon, 29, 223.
Llanfedw, 3, 30, 35.
Llanforda, 4.
Llangollen, 139, 145.
Llanharan, 172.
Llanhilleth, 140, 141.
Llanilltern, 88, 154, 171, 194.
Llanishen, 4, 29, 39, 53, 55, 57, 59, 61, 76, 86, 87, 88, 106, 127, 175, 181, 185, 194, 205, 206, 217, 229, 230.
— Craig, 1.
— Fach, 54, 56, 61, 62, 164, 166, 168, 181, 190, 194, 223.
Llantarnam, 193.
Llanrumney Hall, 193.
Llantrisant, 11, 23, 36, 124, 132, 191, 232.
Llantrithyd, 228.
Llantwit Fardre, 132, 191.
Llantwit Major, 4, 6, 110, 232.
Llanwonno, 224.
Llewellyn, Moses, 237.
Llewelyn ap Ieuan Ithell, 26.
— ap Ivor, 184.
— Lord of St. Clears, 191.
— D., 149, 150.
— Rev. George, Beulah, 166, 169.
— Jos., 161.
— Thos., 134.
— William, 161.
Lloyd, T. Alwyn, 168, 177, 187.
Llwyd, Humphrey, 63.
Llwyn Bedw, 208.
Llwyncelyn, 207.

Llwyn Crwn, 56.
— Mallt, 212, 230.
Llyfr Baglan, 60, 61.
Llystalybont, Manor, 8, 9, 14, 29, 53, 54, 55, 65, 229.
— Ford, 233.
Llysworney, 6.
Llywelyn ap Iorwerth, 10, 11, 48.
— ap Gruffydd, 11, 12, 13, 31.
Llywelyn Bren, 19, 21, 22, 23, 27, 31, 39, 46, 49.
Long Wood, 206.
London Missionary Society, 110.
Lovegrove, Rev. T. H., 138.
Lumley, Rev. R., 111.
Lyon, Michael, 134.
Lyttelhaum, 26.

M
Machen, 29, 124, 157, 191.
Mackintosh of Mackintosh, 192.
— Mrs. (Cottrell), 191, 192.
— Institute, 192.
Madoc Ychan, 228, 229.
Maesteg, 123.
Maesyberllan, 137.
Maesyderi, 206.
Maesyfelin, 208.
Maindy, 77.
Mallt y nos, 213.
Marcross, 218.
Margam, Annals of, 6.
Mari Lwyd, 237.
Marsh, Bp., 108.
— E., 176.
Marshall, R., 10.
Martin, E. P., 104.
— Rev. S. J., 130.
— W., 139.
Marychurch, J. G., 162.
Mathew, Cradoc, 27.
— Family, 191, 198.
— John, 102.
— Sir David, 84.
— Sir George, 29.
Mathews, Family, 211.
— of Llandaff, 185.
— Rev. Ed. (Ewenny), 109, 110, 113, 119.
Mathews-Williams, Rev. W. E., 153.
Mavon Ely Forest, 28.
Maynard Bros., 188.
McCormack, Father, 174.
Meggitt, J. C., 167.
Melin, 203.
Melin Griffith, 12, 17, 18, 19, 20, 23, 24, 27, 33, 40, 41, 73, 88, 89, 90, 91, 92, 94, 96, 102-4, 108, 114, 118, 125, 136, 149, 171, 178, 189, 190, 199, 203, 211, 212, 214, 217, 228, 231, 232, 234, 236, 238, 240, 243.
— Cadet Corps, 236.
— Company, 104.
Mendus, Rev. L., 121.
Meredith of Tre Deigr, 184.

Meredith, J. Colston, 95.
Merricke, Rice, 17, 30, 32, 37, 199, 228.
Merthyr Tydfil, 2, 13, 18, 35, 49, 125, 190, 191, 209, 237.
Methodist Revival, 105, 111.
Metson, Rev. W., 138.
Meurig ap Hywel Dda, 183.
Michael, Rev. O., 132.
Michelston Wenllock, 29.
Michaelston-y-Fedw, 86.
Mid, 199.
Miles, D., 131.
Miles, J., 105.
Milford Haven, 60.
Mills, Thos., 127.
Mills:
 Canal Lock, 230.
 Castle, 230.
 Deri, 230, 231, 240.
 Lisvane, 230.
 Little, 230, 231.
 Llandaff, 230.
 Llanishen, 230.
 Llystalybont, 230.
 Melingriffith, 230.
 Radyr, 230.
 Tongwynlais, 230, 231, 240.
Miskin, 7, 10, 11, 18, 189.
Monasteries, Dissolution of, 53.
Monico, Cinema, 182, 208.
Monmouthshire, 10, 25, 191.
Montgomery, Treaty of, 12.
— Town, 113.
Montfort, Simon de, 11.
Monthermer, Ralph de, 31.
Mordaf, 4.
Mordecai, S. A., 98.
Moerr, 209.
Morfa Yvor, 9, 17.
— Riffydd, 9, 17, 18.
Morgan, ap John David, 27.
— ap John Gwyn, 27.
— Morgan ap William ap Ieuan, 62.
— of Afan, 17, 18.
— of Black Friars, 185.
— of Rhiwbina and Cefn Carnau, 185.
— of Llangattock Lingoed, 185.
— Morgan of Machen, 191.
— of Tredegar, family, 182, 184, 190, 206.
— Charles, 233.
— Sir Charles, 191.
— Sir Charles, M.R.M. (Baron Tredegar), 191.
— Charles, Evan Courtenay (2nd Viscount), 191.
— Rev. D. R., 172.
— Evan, 113.
— Rev. E., 169.
— Ed. of Castell Coch, 134.
— Eliz. of Rhiwbina and Cefn Carnau, 185.
— Col. F. C., 191.
— Frank, 236.

Morgan, Godfrey, Charles (2nd Baron Tredegar), 191.
— Henry of Rhiwbina, 185, 194.
— Sir Henry, 185.
— Ivor (Tredegar), 184.
— Jane of Rhiwperra, 191.
— Sir J. D., 186, 187.
— J. Hartman, 172.
— J., 98.
— John (Tredegar), 53, 54.
— Morgan, 133.
— Thomas, of Rhiwbina, 185.
— Sir Thomas, 185.
— Thomas, of Rhiwperra, 191.
— Thomas, 68.
— Thomas (Deri), 55.
— William (Tredegar), 53, 191.
— William (Schoolmaster), 85.
— W. T., 80.
Morganstown, 109.
Morganwg, 33.
— Lewis, 60.
Morgraig, Castell, 10, 36, 43, 56, 182, 184.
Morlais, 13, 18, 198.
Morland, 209, 210.
Morlangau, 209.
Morris, Rev. J. H., 172.
— William (Bethel), 150, 151, 152.
— Rev. W. D., 119.
— William (Roath Keynsham), 53.
Morriston, 232.
Mortimer Earl, 23, 36, 38.
Mortlake, 62.
Mostyn, Archbishop, 174.
— Rev. J., B.A., 175.
Mottram, A. H., 186.
Mount, The, 44.
Mountstuart, Lord John, 190.
Mountain Ash, 172.
Moxey, 3, 4, 129.
Murray-Threipland, Col. W., 194.
Mynachdy, 184, 214.
Mynydd Bychan, 54, 55, 56, 208, 209, 210, 222, 230; v. also Great Heath.

N.
Nant Castan, 15, 202.
Nantchurch, 59.
Nant ddu, 183.
Nantgarw, 32, 141.
Nantgwynlais, 230.
Nant Nofydd, 2, 8, 14, 48, 56, 181, 202
Nant Walla, 54, 56, 155, 156, 182, 196, 201, 202.
National Building Guild, 188.
National Society for Education of the Poor, 89.
Nant Waedlyd, 182, 223.
Nant y Gledyr, 214.
Neath, 7, 20, 34, 35, 36, 58, 213.
— Abbey, 232.
Nelson, 7n, 138.
Nest, daughter of Iestyn, 222, 229.
New Inn (Mon.), 153.

Newbridge, 153.
Newchurch (Whitchurch), 60.
— Carm., 59.
New House, 56, 58, 190, 194.
Newport, 23, 152.
Nicholas, D., 158, 159, 164, 168.
— Rev. E., 130.
Nicholson, Thos., 161.
— Rev. W. J., 160, 163.
Nicknames, 232, 243.
Noble, Rev. M., 59.
Noel, Rev. B., 175.
Nonsuch, 62.
Normans, 4, 5, 6, 7, 8, 10, 35, 222.
Nowell, G., 176.

O
Oda, Odda, 200, 228.
Ogmore, 6.
Osborne, E., 149.
Overseer, v. Local Government, 70.
Owain Glyndwr, 49.
Owen, F., 236.
— Rev. G., 151.
Owen, Rev. Wynne, 175.
Owens, Rev. G., 151.
Oxford Movement, 125.

P
Pantbach, 54, 55, 206, 208.
Pantgwynlais ⎫
Pantgwenlas ⎬ 194, 197, 198.
Pant-Gwaunlais ⎭
Pantmawr, 55, 206, 223.
Pantycelyn, 207.
Pantymarl, 206.
Pantyrywen, 182.
Pantysgawen, 205.
Parc, 205.
Parc yr Ustus, 194, 198.
Parish v. Local Government, 65 et seq.
Parry, W., 169.
Parsons, E. V., 166.
Paterson, Dr., 4, 5, 202.
Pedair Erw Mynydd, 208.
— Pwdr, 209.
Pedwar Erw'r Dderwen, 206.
Pembroke, 28, 29.
— Henry, Earl of, 29.
— Richard, Earl of, 10.
Penarth, 3, 48, 95, 100, 101, 108, 137, 172.
Pencwrt (Carm.), 224.
Pendarren, 146, 193.
Pendwyallt, 212.
Pengam, farm, 53.
Pengelly, E., 98.
Penlline, estate, 150, 192, 193.
Penmaen, 210.
Penmark, 110.
Penrhys, 190, 222.
Pentre (Rhondda), 152.
— Farm, 209.
— Gwilym, 56, 154, 205.
Pentwyn Ucha, 207.
— Isaf, 207, 212.

Pentwyn, 181, 186.
Pentyrch, 3, 11, 30, 35, 87, 92, 103, 106, 108, 109, 110, 118, 136, 149, 154, 171, 178, 191, 194, 215.
Penvbryn, 204.
Penygroes, 206.
Penylan, 212, 217, 218.
Peterston-super-Ely, 177, 209, 210.
Pettigrew, A., 242.
Phelps, T. W., 125.
Philip, Earl of Pembroke, 189.
Philip of Bedwellty, 185.
Phillips, A. E., 164.
— Blanche, 193.
— Ed., 109.
— G., 98.
— J., 96.
— John (Groeswen), 158, 159, 161, 162, 163, 164, 168.
— Rev. J. T., 177.
— Philip, 162.
— Rev. R. D., 139.
— Thos., 126.
— Thos. (Schoolmaster), 92, 93, 94.
— William, 156.
— Wm., 164, 165, 166, 167, 168, 169.
Philog, 2, 9, 14, 53, 80, 196, 199, 214.
Pike, G., 157.
Pines, T., 189.
Pistyll Goleu, 217.
Pitman, C. F., 164, 165.
Plas Treoda, 228.
Plymouth, Earl of, 39, 100, v. also Windsor.
Polydore, Virgil, 63.
Pontlottyn, 115.
Pontypool, 152, 219.
Pontypridd, 75, 115, 138, 140, 146, 152.
Poor Law, 67.
Poor Relief, 66.
Portal, Lord, 100.
Porth, 138.
Porthcawl, 151.
Porthkerry, 222.
Pound, 234.
Powell, J., 86, 105.
— Rev. L., 154, 158.
— Mary, 192.
— T. J., 236.
— R., 102.
— William, 102, 156.
Prestwich, Sir John, 60.
Price, A., 161.
— D., 170.
— D. Lyn, 170.
— E. J., 167.
— Mary, 194.
— Sir J., 63.
— S. H., 167.
— Rev. T., 150.
— William, 198.
Prichard, E., 192.
— J., 192.
— M., 192.
Prichard, Rev. R., 132.

Primrose Hill, 211.
Pritchard, Dr., 77.
Prosser, Ll., 89.
Public Assistance, 69.
Public Works Loan Commissioners, 186.
Pugsley, T., 99.
Pump Erw, 205, 211.
— Erw Grobos, 206.
— Erw'r Daure, 206.
Putney, 62, 53.
Pwll, 184.
Pwll of Ceicenn's Kiln, 183.
Pwll Helyg, 212.
— Meuryg, 222.
— Winci, 181, 207.
— Fach, 207.
— yr Julenn, 184.

Q

Quaker's Yard, 7n.
Quarrell, T., 86, 105.
Quarter Sessions, 69, 71.

R

Radyr, 3, 55, 68, 82, 87, 88, 108, 109, 138, 190, 198.
— Court Farm, 78.
— Ford, 211, 217, 228, 232, 233.
— Manor, 1, 11, 19, 21, 23, 26, 27, 28, 29.
— Weir, 102, 235, 240.
Raikes, Robert, 87.
Randell, A. S., 170.
Rebecca Riots, 69.
Red Bridge, 241.
Red Forest, 28.
Rees, A., 98.
— Sir Beddoe, 147.
— Rev. Charles, 139.
— D. M., 187.
— D. W., 162.
— Rev. D. G., 160, 161, 162, 163, 164, 165, 166, 167, 169, 172.
— Rev. Ebrard, 177.
— Emrys, 41.
— E. W., 187.
— Rev. H., 116.
— Dr. T., 150, 160.
— Rev. W. M., 159.
Reprise, 20.
Reynolds, Getley & Co., 102.
Rhayader, 137, 141.
Rhigos, 2, 172.
Rhiw, 184, 201.
Rhiwbina, 1, 2, 3, 8, 9, 14, 42, 50, 55, 56, 73, 74, 75, 77, 89, 95, 154, 161, 168, 175, 178, 181-8, 196, 201, 202, 210, 230, 231, 238, 239.
— Farm, 181, 192, 205.
— Hill, 181, 182, 184, 188, 206, 223.
— Reservoir, 205.
— Garden Village, 188, 207.
Rhiw Morgan, 232.

Rhiwperra, 1, 4, 61, 82.
Rhondda, 2, 73, 75, 213, 222.
Rhuddlan, Statute of, 38.
Rhyd, 198.
Rhydderch, 237.
Rhyd lydan, 183.
— Nofydd, 205, 238.
Rhydwaedlyd, 201, 202.
Rhyd Walla, 4, 54, 55, 155, 182, 185, 186, 201, 202, 208.
Rhydyboithan, 118, 184, 198.
Rhydygwern, 184.
Rhyd y maen goch, 56, 58.
Rhyl, 136.
Rhymney, 4, 7, 8, 9, 15, 17, 20, 61.
Rhys ap Griffith ap Ivor Bach, 9, 11.
Rhys ap Gruffydd (Dinefwr), 36, 184, 191, 222.
Rhys ap Morgan, 17.
Rice (Dynevor) Family, 191.
Richard, Miss, 95.
Richards, A. M., 193.
— David, 149, 150, 151.
— E. P., 94, 192.
— G., 151.
— I., 231.
— J. (Bethel), 151.
— J., 192, 193.
— J. M., 192.
— M. A., 193.
— Michael, 192.
— W., 192, 193.
— R., 134.
— Windsor (family), 192.
Ridgwerne, 241.
Rights of Way, 240.
Risca, 140.
Riu Brein, 183, 184.
Roads and Streets:
Beulah, 238.
College, 238.
Heoldon, 238.
Heol Derlwyn, 206.
Heol Las, 211.
Heol y Bont, 206.
Heol y Bryn, 207.
Heol y Coed, 207.
Heol y Deri, 206, 207.
Heol y Felin, 206.
Heol y Forlan, 209, 210.
Heol y Fforest, 211.
Heol y Nant, 208.
Heol yr Wyddfa, 208.
Heol Rhydwalla, 202.
Heol Tynycae, 207.
Heol Wen, 207.
Merthyr, 79, 80, 209, 231.
Mill (Tongwynlais), 131.
Parade, The, 74.
Pantbach, 238.
Pantmawr, 181, 182, 188, 231.
Penlline, 211.
Penydre, 188.
Providence Place, 108.
Richmond, 193.

Roath, 175.
Station, 238.
Tymawr, 238.
Tynyparc, 181, 188, 208, 238.
Tynypwll, 238.
Velindre, 73, 78, 80, 202, 211, 212, 218
Wenallt, 181, 182, 188, 232.
Roath, 9, 87, 192, 230.
— Park, 217.
— Power Station, 15.
— Court, 193.
— Keynsham, 7, 9, 14, 15, 19, 20, 23, 28, 30, 53, 57, 65, 81, 191, 229, 230.
Rock, Rev. P., 175.
Roman Remains, 4.
Roberts, Ed., 155.
— Mary, 155.
— Rev. Edward (Bethel), 153.
— Rev. Edward (Pontypridd), 133.
— Rev. D., 110.
— L., 95.
— William (Bethlehem), 155.
— William (Beulah), 167.
Roderick, Rev. W., 136, 137.
Rogers, J., 129.
Rogers & Davies, 188.
Rosser, J. E., 98.
— J., 150.
Rowland, R., 89, 90.
Rowland, D., 106.
Rowldon, 211.
Royal, Comm., 1842, 92; 1846, 93, 94.
Rudry, 18, 26, 28, 29, 30, 155, 171, 184.
Rumney, 3, 58.
— Bridge, 184.
— Manor, 19.
Russell, Miss, 163.
— Rev. W., 156, 157.
Rushton, Rev. J. R., 130.

S

Saith Erw, 209.
Saith Erw'r Ysgubor, 207.
Saulter & Sons, 129.
Salmon, J., 162.
— Rev. A. E., 167.
— T., 167.
Samuel, G. E., 167.
— T., 165, 166, 168.
Salop, 36.
Saunders, Rev. D., 144.
Scales, Lord, 62.
Schools: 84-101.
Barry, 100.
Caerphilly, 100.
Cardiff, 86; St. John's, 87.
Castell Coch, 97.
Dame, 95.
Eglwysilan, 87.
Ely, 94.
Griffith Jones, 86, 87.
Groeswen, 87.
Gwaelodygarth, 92, 95.
Hawthorn, 164.
Lisvane, 86, 87, 92.

Schools: 84-101 (contd.)
  Llandaff Cathedral, 84, 85, 91, 93, 94.
  — National, 85.
  — North, 99.
  Llanishen, 86, 87.
  Melingriffith, 88, 92.
  Michaelston-y-Fedw, 86.
  Penarth, 95, 100, 101.
  Pentyrch, 87, 92.
  Philog, 87.
  Radyr, 87, 92.
  Rhiwbina, 99, 177.
  Roath Parish, 87.
  St. Fagans, 86, 87.
  St. Nicholas, 86.
  Sunday, 88, 91, 92.
  Tongwynlais, 87, 95, 99.
  Wenvoe, 86.
  Whitchurch, 87, 91, 94, 95, 96, 97, 98, 99, 100, 243.
Seager, Sir William, 175.
Senghenydd, Lordship, 7, 8, 9, 10, 12, 13, 18, 25, 26, 29, 30, 31, 32, 34, 48, 53, 54, 55, 185, 189.
  — Lord of, 11, 15, 28, 38, 49, 102, 203.
  — Forest, 28.
  — Monastery, 228.
Seymour, M. T., 175.
Shail, W. C., 164, 165.
Sharpe, Peter, 98, 99.
Shea, I., 177.
Shenton, J. L., 169.
Shobdon, 224.
Small, R., 95.
  — Rev. W. J. T., 130.
Smeaton, Rev. A. J., 175.
Smith, J., 126, 128.
  — C. H., 97.
Smithies:
  Birchgrove, 231.
  Cross Inn, 231.
  Efail Jervis, 231.
  Penygroes, 231.
  Plough Inn, 231.
  Three Elms, 231.
  Three Horse Shoes, 231.
  Tongwynlais, 231.
Somerset, 36.
Southend, 167.
South Wales Manure Co., 240, 241.
South Wales Power Co., 75, 78.
Spence, J., 103, 104, 136.
Spencer, 55.
Spital Cottage, 217.
S.P.C.K., 86.
Splott, 102.
Stacey, Rev. C., 128.
  — Rev. T., 193.
Stanford, Semei, 126, 128.
Stephens, Rev. R., 132.
Stibbs, F., 186, 187.
Stonham, Rev. R. C., 175.
Stradling, Family, 229.
Strong, J. N., 175.
St. Athan, 35.

St. Brides, 157.
St. Catwg, 233.
St. David's, 6.
  — Parish, Cardiff, 174.
St. Dubricius, 183.
St. Dyfrig, 4.
St. Fagans, 3, 86, 108, 109, 190.
St. George, 35.
St. Gwynllyw, 233.
St. Lythans, 105.
St. Mellons, 3, 140.
St. Nicholas, 86, 108, 109, 214.
St. Oudoceus, 183.
St. Teilo, 4, 183.
St. Woollos, 233.
St. Donats Castle, 214.
Suffolk, 23.
Sully, 35.
Swansea, 2, 89, 124.
Symonds, J. E., 98.

T
Taff Railway, 14, 231, 239.
Taff, R., 2, 14, 20, 27, 32, 48, 55, 61, 68, 75, 102, 183, 184, 198, 213, 218, 219, 221, 224, 232, 241.
Taff's Well, 137, 183, 217, 220.
Taihirion (Llanillterne), 154, 159, 171.
Tai Mawr, 56.
Tair Erw, 209, 212.
  — Erw Bellaf, 212.
  — Erw Meinion, 208.
  — Erw'r Berllan, 206.
  — Erw'r Graig, 206.
  — Erw Nany Morse, 206.
Tan y Bwlch, 204.
Talbot of Hensol, family, 191, 192.
Talog, 199.
Talyfan, 28, 35.
Talygarn, 195.
Tanygelly, 212.
Tay Bridge, 240.
Taylor, E. V., 169.
Tenants, Socage, 15.
  — Customary, 15, 16.
Thomas ap Ieuan ap Llewellyn, 27.
Thomas, A. A., 98.
  — Ben, 169, 188.
  — Ben and Co., 168, 175, 188.
  — Rev. C. Tawelfryn, 163.
  — Rev. E. P., 41.
  — Edmund (Rhiwbina), 161.
  — Lewis Arms, 133.
  — E. M., 162.
  — Frank, 121.
  — Gwen, 121, 122.
  — Gwilym, 121.
  — John (Wesleyan), 126, 127.
  — John (Grocer), 137.
  — Rev. John (Ainon), 132.
  — Rev. Joshua, 135, 136, 138.
  — Sir Lleufer, 187.
  — Lewis, 68.
  — Rev. N., 133, 150.
  — Richard of Lydbrook, 104, 136.

Thomas, Rev. Richard, 109.
— Rosser, 193.
— Spence, 104, 236.
— Thos. (Melingriffith), 126, 128.
— Thomas (Pentyrch), 134.
— Thomas (Grocer), Tongwynlais, 96, 133.
— Rev. T. (Ararat), 145.
— Rev. T. (Croesyparc), 144.
— William (Thornhill), 113.
— William (Beulah), 161.
— William (Melingriffith), 126.,
— William (Contractor), 134.
— Wilfred, 121, 122.
— William (Tongwynlais), 120, 121.
— Sir W. J., 167.
— of Duffryn Ffrwd, family, 185.
Thompson, Charles, 186.
— William, 129.
Thornhill, 2, 10, 14, 43, 68, 92, 95, 154, 182, 184, 203, 205, 238.
Tipping, T. A., 187, 188.
Tir Bess, 207.
— Calan Mai, 27.
— Croft, 27.
— Hwnt (farm), 154.
— Iarll, 7, 18.
— Pwdr, 78, 182, 208.
— y Berllan, 27.
— y Beili, 27.
— y Cwningod, 27.
— y Whit, 56.
— y Winch, 208.
Toleration, Act, 105.
Tongwynlais, 2, 8, 12, 20, 32, 42, 47, 49, 68, 73, 80, 81, 82, 95, 97, 99, 111, 118-123, 131, 142, 158, 167, 171-3, 177, 183, 211, 215, 221, 224, 233, 234, 236, 238, 239, 240; St. Michael's,41, 42
Tonmawr, 56.
Ton yr Ywen (farm), 154.
Tonyfelin Ch., 131, 143, 147.
Ton Ysgubor Wen, 205.
Tovey, C., 98, 99.
Traveller's Rest Inn, 56.
Tredegar, 193.
— Estate, 78, 81.
— Family, 182.
Tref, 203.
Treforest, 2, 121, 239.
Treherbert, 153.
Trehill, 108, 109, 110.
Trelewis, 138.
Treoda, 4, 15, 24, 46, 55, 82, 200, 228.
— Gwaun, 53, 54, 200, 229.
— Court, 200, 209.
— Isa, 154, 200, 209.
Treorchy, 169.
Tribanau, 232.
Tristype, 27.
Tudor, Jasper, 28, 60, 62.
Turnpike Trusts, 68.
Turtle, Rev. A. C., 138, 141.
Turberville, Payn de, 21, 22, 34, 35, 36, 37.

Turberville, Gilbert de, 10.
— Gwenllian, 22.
Twmpath, The, 45, 222.
Twm Pwnch, 215.
Twynaugwynion, 1, 2, 41, 203, 204.
Tyclyd, 212.
Tyddyn, 211.
Tydu, 211.
Tyfry, 105.
Tyglas, 54, 56, 57, 230.
Tygwyn, 205, 217.
— Farm, 217.
Tymawr, 211, 212, 238.
Ty Isaf, 204.
Tynant, 3, 221.
Tylyuguay, 233.
Typoeth, 212.
Ty'n coed, 205, 210.
Tyler, D., 134.
— H. G., 192.
— Sir George, 192.
Tynte, Sir Charles Kemeys, 56.
Ty'n y caeau, 181, 207.
Ty'n y coed, 56, 182.
Ty'n y Parc, 14, 15, 24, 27, 160, 182, 209.
Tynvpwll, 14, 44, 211, 238.
Ty Pant yr Ywen, 78, 208.
Ty'r Efail, 206.
Tyr-y-mud, 56.
Tywern, 14, 181, 188, 191, 208, 230.

U
Underwood, Dr., 177.
Unwin, Sir R., 186.
Upward, W. C., 169.
Urban, Bishop, 40.
Uwch Caiach, 12.

V
Vale of Glamorgan, 218.
Velindre, 14, 68, 82, 103, 189, 203.
Vestry, 66.
Villa Aradur, 233.
Viner, Rev. J., 115, 116.
Vineyards, 242.
Volunteers, 236.
Voya, David, 26.

W
Waedlyd, 202.
Walker, 3, 95.
— Rev. J. H., 172.
Walla, 202.
Walls, C., 86.
Walter ap David, 27.
Wandsworth, 92.
Ward, J., 149.
Warwick, Co., 36.
— Earl of, 26.
— Isabella, Countess of, 26.
— Mrs. M., 98.
Watford, 105, 106, 107, 154, 155, 160, 166, 171.
Watkin, M., 164.
Watkins, Rev. C. H., 151.

Watts, Rev. J. G., 146.
Waunarlwyd, 138.
Waun Dyval, 54.
Waun Fawr, 208.
Waun Gwlyb, 205.
Waunwaelod, 105.
Waun Wenn, 183.
Waywardens, 70.
Welsh Town-Planning and Housing Trust 40, 177, 187.
Welshery, 7.
Wenallt, Y, 1, 4, 44, 45, 184, 203, 204, 238.
— Coed, 1.
— Camp, 182.
— Reservoir, 181.
Wenvoe, 86, 105, 193.
Werncleppa, 184.
Wesley, C., 106, 124.
— J., 106, 124.
West, J. O., 187.
Western Ground Rents Ltd., 189.
Whitchurch Boundaries, 14, 15, 81.
— Brook, 2, 181, 182, 231, 240.
— Castle, 8, 18, 20, 24, 26, 33, 35, 45n, 46, 47, 49.
— Manor, 14, 15, 16, 18, 22, 23, 26, 27, 28, 29, 32, 40, 46, 47, 208.
— School Board, 71, 98.
— Schools, 81, 101.
— Common, 80, 143, 150, 200, 209, 228, 229, 231.
— Library, 79.
— Tithe Barn, 79.
— Parish Council, 78, 79, 80, 81.
— Mental Hospital, 75, 79.
— Population, 73-83, 165.
White, T., 149, 150.
Whitfield, G., 106.
Wick, 232.
Wightwick, J., 192.
Wilcox, Rev. H., 128.
Wilkinson, Rev. H., 130.
William I, 6; William III, 105.
— William ap Ievan, 60, 61, 62.
Williams, Roath Court, Family, 193.
— Chas. (Caerleon), 193.
— Chas. Crofts, 131, 193.
— C. H., 118, 133, 135.
— D. (Beulah), 167.
— (Salem), 138.
— Rev. D. H., 116.
— Rev. D. (Merthyr), 109.
— Ed., 88, 131.
— Edwin, 112, 162.
— Rev. E., 110.
— Rev. E. Jones, 169.
— Frederick, 162.
— Rev. G. J., 137.
— Rev. H. D., 138.
— Rev. H., 41.
— Rev. Iona, 169.
— John, 122.
— Joan, 63.
— J. (Cromwell), 62, 63.
— J. H., 230.

Williams, Rev. J. (Saundersfoot), 167.
— L., 129.
— Lord of Thame, 63.
— Maud, 194.
— Morgan, 59, 60, 61, 62, 63.
— Police Sgt., 79.
— Messrs. R. & S., 80.
— Taliesin, 112.
— Rev. R., 117.
— Sir Richard, 58, 60, 61, 63.
— T. (Llanishen), 106, 185.
— T. (Tyclyd), 113.
— Taliesin ap Iolo, 237.
— T. (Cromwell), 60.
— W. (Panytcelyn), 106.
— Rev. W. (Caledfryn), 113, 133.
— Rev. W. (Ebbw Vale), 137.
— W. (Beulah), 158.
— W. (Tongwynlais), 134.
— W. (Wes), 129.
Williamson, Rev. J., 163.
Wills, F., 129.
Willis, Browne, 85.
Willsden, 185.
Wiltshire, 190.
Wimbledon, Manor of, 62.
Windsor, Albert Hickman, 2nd Viscount, 189.
— Charlotte J., 28, 190.
— E., 190.
— Herbert Hickman, 189.
— Other Archer, 3rd Earl Plymouth, 190.
— Other Lewis, 4th Earl, 190.
Windsor-Clive, family, 190.
Wingfield, Col., 191, 192.
Winks, Rev. W. E., 152.
Withers, Rev. W., 130.
Witton, Park Church, 146, 160.
Woodhill, 182, 185, 186.
Woodstock, Council of, 8, 40, 84.
Woolangus, 210.
Wootton Bassett, 172.
Worcester Co., 36.
Wrekin, 224.
Wride, B., 209, 232.
— T., 164, 168.
Wye, 35.
Wyth Erw, 209.

Y

Y Ddonen Las, 211.
Yates, Map, 208.
Yeban (Ieuan) ap Morgan, 60, 61.
Ynispeithan, 183, 184, 198.
Ynisyrysgallenfraith Farm, 45, 181, 182,
Ynis y Llewod Duon, 198.   [205.
— Bradwen, 183.
— Faelgwn, 26.
Ynys, 26, 32, 198.
Yorath Mawr, family, 143, 200, 228, 229.
Yorke, P., 59.
Ystradmynach, 110, 193.
Ystrad, Rhondda, 173, 177.
Ystrad Fellte, 36.
Ystumtaf, 4, 8, 40, 197.